HISTORY
OF RUSSIA

Sergei Mikhailovich Soloviev

The
Academic International Press
Edition
of
Sergei M. Soloviev

History of Russia From Earliest Times

G. EDWARD ORCHARD
General Editor

Contributing Editors

HUGH F. GRAHAM

JOHN D. WINDHAUSEN

ALEXANDER V. MULLER

K.A. PAPMEHL

RICHARD HANTULA

WALTER J. GLEASON, JR.

WILLIAM H. HILL

G. EDWARD ORCHARD

LINDSEY A.J. HUGHES

NICKOLAS LUPININ

GEORGE E. MUNRO

DANIEL L. SCHLAFLY, JR.

SERGEI M. SOLOVIEV

History of Russia

Volume 26

Peter the Great

A Reign Begins, 1689–1703

Edited, Translated and With an

Introduction by

Lindsey A.J. Hughes

Academic International Press

1994

The Academic International Press Edition of S.M. Soloviev's
History of Russia From Earliest Times in fifty volumes.

Volume 26. *Peter the Great. A Reign Begins, 1689–1703*
Unabridged translation of the text of Chapters II–IV of Volume 14
of S.M. Soloviev's *Istoriia Rossii s drevneishikh vremen* as found
in Volume VII of this work published in Moscow in 1965, with
added annotation by Lindsey A.J. Hughes.

ISBN: 0-87569-126-9

Composition by Peggy Pope

Printed in the United States of America

A list of Academic International Press publications is found at
the end of this volume.

ACADEMIC INTERNATIONAL PRESS
Box 1111 • Gulf Breeze FL 32562-1111 • USA

CONTENTS

the Dvina—Sheremetev's Victory at Erestfer—Grievances of the Little Russian Army—Troubles in Zaporozhie— Augustus Urges Sack of Livonia—Apraksin's Operations in Ingria—Founding of St. Petersburg

WEIGHTS AND MEASURES

Linear Measure

Verst: 500 sazhen, 1166 yards and 2 feet, .663 miles, 1.0668 km.
Sazhen: 3 arshins, 7 feet, 2.133 m
Arshin: 16 vershoks, 28in. (diuims) 72.12 cm
Chetvert: 1/4 arshin
Fut: 12 diuims, 1 foot, 30.48 cm
Vershok: 1.75 in., 4.445 cm, 1/16 arshin
Diuim: 1 inch, 2.54 cm
Desiatina: 2400 square sazhens, 2.7 acres, 1.0925 hectare
Chetvert (quarter): 1/2 desiatine, 1.35 acre (sometimes 1.5 desiatinas or ca. 4.1 acres)

Liquid Measure

Stof: Kruzhka (cup), 1/10 vedro, ca. 1.3 quarts, 1.23 liters
Kufa: 30 stofy
Vedro (paid): 3.25 gallons, 12.3 liters, 10 stofy
Bochka (barrel): 40 vedros, 121 gallons, 492 liters
Chetvert (quarter): 1.4 bochka, 32.5 gallons

Weights

Berkovets: 361 olbs., 10 puds
Pud: 40 funts, 36,113 lbs. (US), 40 lbs. (Russian), 16.38 kg
Funt: 96 zolotniks, .903 lb., 14.4 ozs., 408.24 grams
Grivenka: 205 grams
Korob (basket): 7 puds, 252 lbs.
Rad: 14 puds, 505.58 lbs
Chetvert (grain measure): 1/4 rad, 3.5 puds, 126.39 lbs., ca. 8 bushels
Chetverik (grain measure dating from 16th century): 1/8 chetvert, 15.8 lbs.
Zolotnik: 1/96 lb., 4.26 grams

Money

Chervonets (chervonny): A gold coin minted in the first half of the 18th century worth about 3 rubles
Muscovite Denga: 200 equals 1 ruble
Novgorod Denga: 100 equals 1 ruble
Ruble: 100 copecks, 200 dengas
Altyn: 6 Muscovite dengas, 3 copecks
Grivna: 20 Muscovite dengas, 100 grivnas equals 1 ruble, 10 copecks
Poltina (Poltinnik): 50 copecks, 100 dengas
Polupoltina (-nik): 25 copecks, 50 dengas
Poltora: 1 1/2 rubles
Peniaz: 10 equals one grosh (Lithuania)
Kopa grosh: 60 groshas, one Muscovite poltina
Chetvertak: silver coin equal to 25 copecks or 1/4 rubles (18-19th centuries)
Copeck: two Muscovite dengas
Foreign Denominations: 1 efimok or 1 thaler (Joachimsthaler)-about 1 ruble, 1 chervonets or chervonnyi—a ducat, about 3 rubles
Levok—Dutch silver lion dollar

Note: Weights and measures often changed values over time and sometimes held more than one value at the same time. For details consult Sergei G. Pushkarev, *Dictionary of Russian Historical Terms from the Eleventh Century to 1917* (Yale, 1970).

PREFACE

This book is an unabridged translation of Volume 14, Chapters 2-4, which are pp. 438-643 in Volume VII of the multi-volume edition of Soloviev's *Istoriia Rossii s drevneishikh vremen* (History of Russia from Earliest Times, 29 vols., St. Petersburg, 1851-1879) published from 1962 through 1966 in Moscow. Soloviev's original long chapters have been subdivided and in some cases given new titles and section headings, thus Chapters I-II of this volume coincide with his Chapter 2, Chapters III-V with his Chapter 3, and Chapter VI with his Chapter 4. This volume is a sequel to my translation of Volume 25 in the present series, *Rebellion and Reform. Fedor and Sophia, 1682-1689* (Academic International Press, 1989), to which I make a number of cross-references in the notes. Readers are referred also to my Introduction to that volume which analyses Soloviev's view of late seventeenth-century Russia and the place of these sections of his *History* in Russian historiography as a whole, which I do not repeat in my Introduction to the present volume.

The present translation endeavors to render the text and Soloviev's thought as accurately as possible. No attempt has been made to reproduce his style and text word for word for this would have yielded a bizarre Russianized text. The main consideration has been to make his history as readable as possible consistent with accuracy, while retaining at least something of the flavor of the language of the era. An effort has been made to find English-language equivalents for all technical terms Soloviev employs (ranks, offices, titles, legal, administrative and so forth) in the belief that English is no less rich in such terms than other languages. This is intended to smooth the flow of the narrative for the reader and to avoid marring the pages with annoying untranslated words. The exception involves Russian words which have become common in

English — boyar, tsar, cossack. In all of this the translator remains painfully aware of the inevitable shortcomings that may remain.

Soloviev's pages are featureless and interminable, one long and complex sentence marching after the last. To make the text easier to follow for today's readers, long paragraphs and sentences have been broken into shorter ones. Most of the subtitles are based on the descriptive topic headings clustered at the beginnings of the chapters in the Russian edition. These headings have been moved into the body of the text as subtitles to mark and ease for the reader the transition from one subject to another. In some cases, to even the frequency of breaks in the text or to show topics not listed by Soloviev at the beginning of chapters, new subtitles have been added. Soloviev's arrangement of the material has been followed strictly.

Brief explanatory or interpretive materials have been inserted into the text enclosed in brackets, or added as footnotes to each chapter at the end of the book. All material enclosed in brackets has been added by the present editor and all material in parentheses is the author's. Emphasized words or phrases in italics are the author's.

The general policy followed in annotating has been to identify prominent personalities at first mention, and to give explanation and elucidations of less common or obscure terms and passages, assuming the typical reader to have relatively little familiarity with Russian history. If brief, these have been included in the text in brackets; otherwise they appear as numbered footnotes at the back of the book by chapters. Most of the author's own notes are not included because their highly specialized archival, documentary and bibliographic nature is of value solely to specialists who, in any case, will prefer to consult the original Russian text. In addition, most of the notes added by the editors of the edition published in the Soviet Union which also are technical in nature—fuller bibliographic citations than those in Soloviev's notes—have not been included. When the author's notes and those of the Soviet editors are included, they are so designated. All other notes are those of the present editor.

Russian personal names are preserved in their Russian form except for Alexander, Alexis, Michael, Nicholas, Catherine and Peter, which English usage has made familiar with respect to Russian

historical figures, and for important ecclesiastics whose names have
been recast into Latin or Greek equivalents, especially for the earlier
period of Russian history. This applies to prominent individuals;
Russian forms usually are used for the less prominent. Certain other
names and terms have been anglicized for the sake of clarity and
because they are used widely—Casimir, Sophia, Danzig, boyar,
rubles, versts, Dnieper river, and others.

The editors of the edition published in the USSR frequently have
added patronymics and other names, and these have been retained
without brackets; patronymics appearing in the original edition also
have been included. Plural forms for names and terms which might
be confusing have been anglicized—Vologdians rather than
Vologzhane, Voguls and not Vogulichi, the Dolgorukys not
Dolgorukie, and so forth. Even so, in a few cases the Russian plural
form is used when this form is common. Most Slavic surnames show
gender, and this has been preserved. Since an "a" at the word end
usually signifies a female, Golovkin would have a wife or daughter
Golovkina. The final "iia" in feminine personal names has been
shortened to "ia"—"Maria" and "Evdokia" instead of "Mariia" and
"Evdokiia."

Non-Russian names, locations, terms, ranks and so on are spelled
according to the language native to the person or particular to the
city, region or culture when this can be determined. Confusion arises
at times because the text is not clear about nationalities. An
excruciating example is Lithuania where at least three languages
intermingle. In such cases the context is the guide used and as a
last resort the Russian spelling in the text is accepted. Individuals
whose names were once non-Russian but had been in Russian
service for generations are named by the original spelling of the
family name. Turkish, Tatar, Persian and other names and terms are
spelled in the original according to accepted forms in scholarly
books. In some instances, if not otherwise ascertainable they are
transliterated from the Russian as given by Soloviev. The names
of geographical locations conform to commonly accepted English
usage—Podolia, Moscow, Copenhagen, Saxony and so forth.

Finally, with respect to transliteration, this translation follows
a modified Library of Congress system omitting diacritical marks
and ligatures, and rendering the initial "ia" and "iu" as Ya and Yu

("Yasnaia" and "Yury"), and occasionally the initial E as Ye ("Yermak," "Yevlev," etc.), the suffixes, "ii", "skii", "skaia" and "skoe" as "Dmitry Poliansky", "Polianskaia", "Polianskoe", and the form "oi" has been replaced by "oy" ("Donskoy" not "Donskoi") for certain family names familiar in this form in English. In some cases "i" has been inserted in place of hard and soft signs, or apostrophes indicating these signs. Hence Soloviev, not Solov'ev. The soft sign is not indicated by an apostrophe, as in some transliteration systems, but is dropped completely.

All dates, as in the original, except where otherwise specified are according to the Julian calendar ("Old Style"); that is, for the seventeenth century ten days, and for the eighteenth century eleven days, behind the Gregorian used in the West. A table of weights and measures is included at the front of this volume for the convenience of the reader, as is a table of Muscovite court and service ranks.

In preparing the present volume I wish to thank Jim Cutshall, who subjected the text to an "intelligent layman's" scrutiny and helped compile the index, and Professor G.E. Orchard, the General Editor of Soloviev's History, who applied not only the expert eye of the historian and a discreet editorial red pen, but also the sympathetic ear of a fellow contributor. Errors which remain are, of course, my own. Libraries in the School of Slavonic and East European Studies in London, University of Illinois at Champaign-Urbana, and State Public Library in St. Petersburg furnished reference materials for the later stages of the work, which was carried out in parallel with a comprehensive study of the reign of Peter I, which I am writing for Yale University Press. Close contact with Soloviev's magisterial study has provided both stimulation and inspiration for my own investigation of the Petrine era.

Lindsey A. J. Hughes

INTRODUCTION

"Only a great nation is capable of producing a great man; in recognizing the importance of a great man's work, we recognize the importance of the nation." *Public Readings on Peter the Great*

The reign of Peter the Great (1682-1725) is a crucial era for all historians of Russia, but Sergei Mikhailovich Soloviev, writing in the decade of Tsar Alexander II's reforms and on the eve of the bicentenary of Peter's birth in 1872, had more reason that most to focus on Russia's first and probably greatest reformer. Five of the twenty-nine volumes of his *History of Russia* were devoted in full or in part to Peter's reign, and he wrote on Peter elsewhere, notably in his 1872 anniversary series of *Public Readings*. Many historians had investigated the Petrine era before Soloviev, and many more have done so since his death in 1879, but Soloviev's writings remain major landmarks in Petrine studies.

The period covered by the present volume begins in 1688-1689 with Peter's first experiments in sailing and boat-building and the overthrow of the regent Sophia, whose rise to power is charted in Volume 25, and ends with the founding of St. Petersburg in May 1703 in the early stages of the Great Northern War against Sweden. These thirteen years contain some momentous events, including the campaigns against the Turks at Azov in 1695 and 1696 and Peter's grand embassy to the West in 1697-1698, but much remains unfamiliar. In English-language scholarship in particular the 1690s have been treated by and large as an interlude between Peter's unorthodox childhood and the real business of reform. This is reckoned to begin symbolically with the shearing of the boyars' beards after the tsar's return from the grand embassy (Soloviev is illuminating on the motivation for this act) and for real with the outbreak of the war against Sweden, which was the lever for most of the subsequent military, economic and social reforms. A few Russian and Soviet scholars such as M. Pogodin, E. Shmurlo, and M. Bogoslovsky specialized in the pre-1700 period, but mostly their work is out-of-print and untranslated. Even the revisionist works of the best modern Russian scholars such as E.V. Anisimov and N.I. Pavlenko tend to treat the 1690s in fairly cursory fashion. The problem for them and others may be that although Peter became to all intents and purposes sole ruler in 1689 he elected to pursue personal interests—training his "play" troops, building boats and drinking with his motley company of friends—rather than affairs of state. The course of reform is less easily analyzed through decrees and institutions than it later became.

In fact, the decade of the Azov campaigns is vital for understanding both the man and his Russia, for elucidating the problems which Peter faced, the shaping of his priorities and the options open to him, both at home and abroad. Peter finally saw real action in the first, unsuccessful campaign against Azov in 1695, regarded by some as a mere continuation of his adolescent military games, which involved assaults upon toy fortresses. But for Soloviev it was a crucial landmark: "The Azov disaster marks the beginning of the reign of Peter the Great." The emphasis here is on the last word. Soloviev's detailed examination of this neglected period, based as always on primary sources, as discussed below, is thus especially useful to scholars and of interest to the general reader, even if certain aspects have been illuminated further by later researchers and some of Soloviev's conclusions superseded.

If the adolescent Peter of Volume 25 was a shadowy figure, relegated to the background by those who ruled during his minority, in Volume 26 he enters center stage, still immature, but armed with all the prerequisites of future greatness. Soloviev's view of Peter owes much to his predecessors (N. Riasanovsky, *The Image of Peter the Great in Russian History and Thought* offers an excellent introduction to this topic), for many of whom Peter was like a hero of antiquity, who grew from a "young Hercules" who strangled snakes in his cradle to a Russian Caesar. The opening lines of this volume compare him to Romulus, the founder of Rome. But for Soloviev, with a dozen volumes of his *History* completed and an unrivalled grasp of the whole flow of Russian history, writing in an age of growing national awareness, Peter became a more specifically Russian brand of hero, a *bogatyr* or warrior adventurer. Soloviev depicted him as a direct descendant of the warrior princes of ninth to eleventh-century Kievan Rus, whose swashbuckling exploits are recounted in Volume I of the *History*. Peter's all-jesting "synod" of fools and drunkards becomes a latter-day version of the warrior retinue or *druzhina* of the princes of old. His visit to the West is compared with that of Princess Olga to Byzantium in 957. Like the warriors of the epic tales Peter was weighed down by his own strength in a palace built for lesser, more compliant mortals, oppressed and restricted by stuffy protocol until he escaped onto the "street", by which we may understand any place outside the Kremlin where Peter could indulge in his favorite pastimes: training "play" regiments at Preobrazhenskoe, drinking in the Foreign Quarter, sailing on Lake Pereiaslav and the White Sea and, the ultimate escape, building ships in Amsterdam and London. These and other locations form the background to Soloviev's narration.

Not only does Soloviev depict Peter as a specifically Russian national type rather than a hero of antiquity. He also regards him essentially as a representative of a people (a "historical" but "uncivilized" nation) which sensed the obsolescence of the old ways and the need for reform, but lacked the knowledge and authority to implement changes. In this Soloviev represents a school of historians who believed that "the activity of a great man is always the result of all of a nation's previous history." He also believed that the key to reform was education in the broadest sense, hence the potency of Peter's claim that he was "a student seeking teachers." Any scholar writing in the 1860s, even a patriotically-inclined one like Soloviev, was also heir to dualistic interpretations of Peter, the most brilliant example of which is Pushkin's *Bronze Horseman* (1833), which suggests both the splendor and the gloom of Peter's reign, weighing national glory against the cost to the "little man." Historians like Nicholas Karamzin had accused Peter of making Russians citizens of the world whilst depriving them of their national identity, an accusation taken up with greater vigor by Slavophiles such as Constantine Aksakov writing in the 1840s-1850s, who believed that Peter had forced Russia from its natural path of development, destroying "every aspect of Russian life." Soloviev stands somewhere between Peter's Slavophile critics and his adulators. His Peter is "divested of his divine attributes." He is subject to doubts, he sometimes behaves badly. As Electress Sophia of Hanover observed in 1697, "This sovereign is very good and very bad at the same time. With regard to manners, he is a true representative of his people."

Next to Peter himself, focus is on the first members of his "jolly company," foreigners such as Franz Lefort and Patrick Gordon, who performed the dual role of mentors and drinking companions, Russians like the early favorite Boris Golitsyn, who provided the nucleus of Russia's new class of officers and civil servants, and Russified foreigners such as Andrei Vinius and James Bruce. All relied ultimately on "personal chemistry" for their advancement. All were expected to serve for life, go where they were ordered, often cut off for years from their homes and families. Their origins, foreign or Russian, humble or high-born (Peter did not shun the latter, as recent studies by Brenda Meehan-Waters and John LeDonne have underlined), were immaterial as long as Peter liked and trusted them. Alexander Menshikov was the most successful, although in the period in question his power was determined by closeness to the tsar rather than by titles and offices, which came later. Soloviev inclines to the popular view that Menshikov once may have sold pies. Recent research confirms that his father served in the Guards, which did not preclude selling a few pies on the side. Menshikov had many admirable qualities, including energy and loyalty, but he was "frighteningly" ambitious, unscrupulous and illiterate. The fact that he remained powerful until Peter's death can be explained only by the power of the tsar's patronage.

A remarkable feature of Peter's interaction with his associates, of which Soloviev gives many examples without entering into detailed analysis, is his pretence that he was not the tsar at all but a simple bombardier, skipper, or ship's carpenter, plain Mr. Peter Alekseev or Peter Mikhailov rather than Great Sovereign Tsar Peter Alekseevich of All Russia. This fiction required a substitute tsar, a role fulfilled willingly by Fedor Romodanovsky, king of Pressburg in the mock battles, then "prince-caesar", reigning at home while Mr. Mikhailov went to Europe. The fiction was kept up in their letters, Peter responding to the "king's" reproach about not getting a personal letter with the excuse that "the likes of us shipbuilders are inexperienced in matters of etiquette." Readers should be aware of this, for Soloviev often assumes familiarity with this subterfuge when referring to Peter in his "commoner's" guise. These and related phenomena of pretendership and masquerade have been illuminated in the work of semioticians Yury Lotman and Boris Uspensky.

Foreign policy occupies a significant proportion of this volume, which covers a vital transitional stage in Russia's relations with the outside world. The old enmity and rivalry with Poland, which dominated the middle of the seventeenth century, had been set aside temporarily by the 1686 Treaty of Moscow, which reopened Russian hostilities against Turkey and the Crimea (cancelling a 1681 truce) on behalf of the Holy League coalition of Poland, Austria and Venice. But suspicion of Catholic Poland remained intense, both over Polish claims to Muscovite Left Bank Ukraine, exemplified by the account of the Solomon affair in Chapter II, and the persecution of the Orthodox in Poland, of which Soloviev gives numerous examples. Focus on the Crimea, with the aim of ending Tatar raids and securing borders, continued to 1695, when Russia changed tactics away from the Tatars to Turkish territory proper by attacking Azov. A second campaign in 1696, a landmark in Russian military history, captured Azov with the help of foreign engineers, newly-recruited troops and newly-built ships, but the Holy League was falling apart and the embassy which left Moscow in March 1697 with the aim of propping up the coalition returned in 1698 with eyes directed to Swedish territory in the north. Soloviev's description of the grand embassy concentrates on selected highlights, notably Peter's visits to Prussia and Holland, but is disappointingly cursory on Peter's three months in England.

The last chapter of this volume recounts the prolonged negotiations which ended the war with Turkey and the opening phase of the war against Sweden, introducing the main protagonists: Peter's enemy Charles XII of Sweden and his friend Augustus II of Poland, although without mention of the latter's fame as the reputed father of over three hundred illegitimate children. In his analysis of the reasons for hostilities Soloviev dwells on the halt to ambitions in the south caused by the truce with Turkey and the possibilities offered by a coalition in the north, for which the intervention of ill-fated Livonian noble Johann von Patkul acted as a catalyst.

Here as in previous volumes Soloviev devotes much space to Ukrainian (Little Russian) affairs, which were a vital aspect of Russia's relations with Poland. The generosity of the coverage is determined also by the overall conception of the *History*, which begins with the pre-history and foundation of Kievan Rus and considers the different characters of the north (Novgorod) and south (Kiev) and their inevitable (in Soloviev's view) reintegration into a single state under the leadership of Moscow. Soloviev was a man of his time in regarding Ukrainian history in the context of the history of Russia, although he was not obliged to resort to the bogus claims of "brotherly friendship" which were required of Soviet scholars. For him Russian-Ukrainian unity was more a pragmatic question of solidarity against the threat from both Muslims and Catholics, based on ethnic, religious and territorial proximity, which was disturbed temporarily by the loss of most of the southern portion of Kievan Rus after the Mongol invasion of 1240.

But Soloviev's own evidence indicates that strong local loyalties developed during this period of separation. The integration of Ukraine with Russia was far from peaceful and was regarded as temporary by many local leaders, including the apparently loyal Hetman Mazepa who seems to have maintained a "lesser of two evils" approach. "Like savage lions they open up their jaws and try to devour us, and make us their slaves.... Which is better—to be a peasant serf to some Muscovite or Pole, or to be a free cossack?" asks the rebel Petrik. But the advantage was Moscow's, for both Poland and Turkey were in decline. With hindsight, it is clear that the famous cossack liberties were doomed because the Moscow government and its successor in St. Petersburg could not tolerate categories of citizens without fixed duties, not to mention those without fixed loyalties, be they the "itinerant persons" in the towns of Russia proper, Old Believers or the fractious cossacks in the south. Soloviev also seems to have had a penchant for some of the colorful, troublesome warrior leaders. In Volume 25 it was Peter Doroshenko, Ivan Serko and Ivan Samoilovich, in this Volume Semyon Palcy and Petrik who give Moscow a headache by wavering precariously between Russia, Poland and Turkey.

As in Volume 25 the study of domestic politics centers on rebellion and revolt, with the musketeers again to the fore. In the crisis of August-September 1689, in which, according to Soloviev, Sophia and her supporters made an abortive attempt to prevent Peter's coming to power, the musketeers remained indifferent. But the 1698 musketeer mutiny, famous for the brutality of the subsequent executions, shattered the corps and hastened the formation of new military units. As in the previous volume, Soloviev shows little sympathy for the musketeers, who represented the "outmoded ways of the past." He meticulously charts their muddled attempts to combine their own ends, an understandable desire to return home to their wives and children after years of campaigning, with claims to "save" Russia from the grip of foreign heretics. Nor did Soloviev, a liberal intellectual, have much sympathy for the "guardians of antiquity", clerics and laymen, who denounced shaving, tobacco and other foreign "abominations" and with whom some of the musketeers threw in their lot. What he fails to point out is that Sophia, the musketeers' alleged choice to replace Peter in 1698, had no record of xenophobia or sympathy for the Old Belief. The case against her remains unproven. Even more than in 1682, the musketeers' revolt had a momentum of its own, fuelled by genuine hardships, and required no leadership from a royal figurehead.

Other plots were nipped in the bud, for example the curious Tsykler and Sokovnin affair of 1697, which was barely known before Soloviev extracted documents from the archives. Apart from the plotters' gruesome execution, which was carried out over the coffin of Ivan Miloslavsky, this affair is remarkable for the glimpse it offers of both popular and aristocratic anxieties about Peter's "impious" behavior, his consorting with foreigners, sending Russians abroad to study and his own imminent foreign travels. Here and elsewhere Soloviev brings to life the tensions between the old and the new, the battle over Russia's future as "some argued that it was better overseas and that they should look there [for aid]. Others repeated that the first task was to expel the Germans who were the source of all evil." Some dissenters attempted to opt out, notably the Old Believers, whose story is continued in the aftermath of the repressive measures introduced during Sophia's regency. After a brief reassertion of its authority in late 1689, the official

Church, headed by the conservative Patriarch Joachim, then by his like-minded successor Adrian, seemed to be fighting a losing battle both against these dissenters on the fringes of society and the new rulers at its center. Further evidence of the decline of Old Russian religious culture in this decade may be found in the art, architecture and literature of the period, which are omitted from Soloviev's analysis.

In general, Soloviev does little to mask the violent, primitive nature of the society of which Peter was an integral part. The strong terrorized the weak at all levels: the tsar loses his temper and beats up his companions, Fedor Romodanovsky burns a colleague, thieves (some of them nobles) rob with impunity, provincial governors deprive local residents of their money and their wives. Siberia in particular is portrayed as virtually ungovernable, despite reports of "improvements." Such evidence puts into perspective the first substantial reform of domestic government, the introduction in 1699 of the Chamber of Magistrates, which was intended to protect merchants and townsmen from abuse at the hands of governors and crown officials by giving them more control over their own affairs and at the same time to get more taxes into government coffers. It turned out to be the first of many abortive attempts to bring social and financial order to the provinces. As Soloviev points out, these were "early days" and principles of communal action and effort took time to take root. Alexander II was still grappling with the same problems when Soloviev was writing these words.

In the eyes of Soviet scholars, Soloviev's greatest shortcoming was his disparagement of the role of the "people." He paid them too little attention and the few glimpses which he did concede painted a dismal picture of national morals and customs. There are peasants in Soloviev's narrative, but they are usually either victims, easily duped, ignorant and superstitious, or rogues. At the other end of the scale, not only did Soloviev omit to attack the nobility on class grounds, although he was scathing about the shortcomings of individuals and quick to point out bribery and corruption, but also failed to detect the "bourgeois elements" which, in the Marxist scheme of things, were destined to effect the transition from feudalism to capitalism. Post-Soviet revisionist scholars would be kinder to Soloviev on both counts. It is no longer compulsory to praise the masses. In particular it has been conceded, for example, by E.V. Anisimov in his 1989 *The Time of the Petrine Reforms* that far from laying the foundations of capitalism Peter's reign actually may have delayed it by extending forced labor in industry and tying the merchantry more firmly to the state. For his part, Soloviev charts Peter's early efforts to encourage the formation of companies for ship-building and trade.

As always, one of the strengths of Soloviev's approach is his utilization of primary sources, many of which were unpublished at the time of writing. Soloviev had at his disposal the *Complete Collection of Laws of the Russian Empire*, published in the 1830s, and other compendia, but many more papers were consulted in the archives of the old government departments, including the Preobrazhensky Chancellery. Some, like the *Letters and Papers of Peter I*, which today have progressed only as far as the volumes for the year 1713, and the records of the trial of Fedor Shaklovity began to appear in print shortly after Soloviev's death. Others have appeared comparatively recently, for example documents on the musketeer revolt of 1698 published by V.I. Buganov, others not at all, for example papers on Little Russian, Polish, Turkish and Crimean affairs. Some of the events examined by Soloviev, such as the Tsykler affair, were hitherto unknown. A few items, for example a letter to Peter from Boris Golitsyn and a memorandum on Silvester Medvedev, have disappeared completely. It should be added that only a few of the more important Petrine documents, and just a handful from the 1690s, are available in English translation. Volume II of G. Vernadsky, *A Source Book for Russian History from the Earliest Times to 1917* (New Haven, 1972) and B. Dmytryshyn, *Imperial Russia. A Source Book* (2nd ed., New York, 1974) contain a selection.

Even the most assiduous work in archives will not unearth materials which never existed. Apart from Peter's own writings, confined in this period mainly to letters about practical matters, and the letters of his circle, which Soloviev quotes to vivid effect, there is a dearth of first-person narratives—memoirs, diaries, autobiography—written by Russians until well into the eighteenth century. A rare example of a contemporary Russian memoir for this period, albeit in terse annalistic style, is Ivan Zheliabuzhsky's *Notes*, which cover the years 1682 to 1709. Prince Boris Kurakin's memoir, with its caustic portraits of Peter's circle, evidently was not available. Thus Soloviev, like scholars after him, had to rely heavily on foreign sources for insights into personalities. The most important quoted in this volume are Foy de la Neuville, a Frenchman who visited Moscow in 1689, the Austrian envoy Johannes Korb, witness to the musketeer executions in 1698-1699, and General Patrick Gordon, a Scottish mercenary who became close to Peter during the 1690s. The English original of the latter's diary until very recently has laid inaccessible in a Moscow archive. There are plans for its publication. Amongst the secondary sources used by Soloviev, German writings are to the fore, for example A. Fryxell's life of Charles XII (1861). Soloviev's also makes use of the work of his nearest competitor, Nicholas Ustrialov, whose richly documented but over-adulatory *History of the Reign of Peter the Great* was published in 1858 and draws on the eighteenth-century compiler Ivan Golikov, whose multi-volumed *Acts of Peter the Great*, although outdated in concept and eulogistic in tone, was based on sources, many of which long since have disappeared.

Soloviev's work on Peter was continued by his successors, notably V.O. Kliuchevsky, whose influential *Peter the Great* (Volume IV of his *Course of Russian History*) is available in L. Archibald's English translation. In the Soviet period Stalin's admiration for Peter ensured that Petrine studies (based on the "bipolar" view of Peter as brutal representative of ruling class interests but praiseworthy promoter of Russian imperial power flourished. English-language treatments of Peter's reign have tended towards the sensational and anecdotal rather than the scholarly and, as mentioned earlier, few writers have lingered over the 1690s. Among reliable general surveys, B.H. Sumner, *Peter the Great and the Emergence of Russia,* (London, 1951) and M.S. Anderson, *Peter the Great,* (London, 1978) provide compact life and times, while L. Jay Oliva (ed.) *Peter the Great. Great Lives Observed,* (New Jersey, 1970) and J. Cracraft (ed.) *Peter the Great Transforms Russia,* (Lexington, 1991) offer a good selection of sources and commentaries. R.K. Massie's lengthy popular study *Peter the Great. His Life and his World,* (London, 1981) may be recommended for liveliness and local color if not for its scholarly reliability. My own

Sophia, Regent of Russia, (New Haven, 1990) deals with Peter's reign before 1700, although the spotlight is not on Peter himself. On the Swedish background readers with confidence may consult R. Hatton, *Charles XII of Sweden,* London, 1978, and D. Kirby, *Northern Europe in the Early Modern Period. The Baltic World, 1492-1772,* (London, 1990).

Soloviev's Volume 14 and our Volume 26 end with one of the symbolic landmarks of Russian history—the founding of St. Petersburg on May 16, 1703 on land newly conquered from the Swedes. For Soloviev this event marked the beginning of the restoration of the ancient road from the Varangians to the Greeks, the river trade route from the Baltic to the Black Sea. It was the beginning of a new era of Russian history. Whether the restoration of the city's name in 1991 after almost seventy years as Leningrad will prove to be a similar landmark remains to be seen. Whatever the future holds, Soloviev's characterization of the mood of late seventeenth-century Russia sounds uncannily familiar in the context of the "revolution" of the late twentieth. Here was a society "subjected to powerful moral vacillation, insecurity and upheaval until the moral restraints are made fast again or replaced by new ones. There is some truth in the saying that a period of transition is the worst time of all from the point of view of social morality."

History of Russia

Volume 26

Peter the Great

A Reign Begins, 1689–1703

I

THE FALL OF SOPHIA
1689

PETER AND HIS REVOLUTION

"In a certain land a royal child was in great peril as a result of internecine strife and persecution by his relatives, but by a miracle he was saved and was brought up in isolation in the midst of common folk from whose ranks he assembled a new and valiant band of followers. He eliminated his enemies and became the founder of a new society, a new and mighty state, spending his whole life in battle and leaving behind him a dual legacy, for there were some that blessed his name, others that cursed him." Who is the subject of this tale? It brings to mind the old legend of Kira and Romulus[1], but who still believes in that old tale?

As it happens, this is no legend about some mythical Kira or Romulus, but a summary of the incontrovertible facts about the life of Peter Alekseevich, tsar of Russia, who lived from the late seventeenth century to the third decade of the eighteenth.[2] Now is the time to set aside disputes about myths and legends and to focus on the general laws to which the historical process is subject.

In the second half of the seventeenth century the Russian people had set off decisively upon a new path.[3] After centuries of moving eastward they had begun to turn towards the west, a change of direction which was bound to cause a virtual revolution and deal a painful jolt to the nation's life and essential character, for it was to bring them into closer contact with civilized nations from whom they must learn and whom they must imitate. In order to decide whether it was possible for Russia to achieve this closer contact with European nations and assimilate their cultures peacefully, gradually and without arousing passions, we need to make a close study of the general laws of the historical process. When we speak of enlightenment and civilization we are speaking of mighty forces which place those nations which possess them on an infinitely higher level than those who do not; how can the concept of weakness be combined with the concept of strength? Who would expect an uncivilized nation to possess breadth and clarity of vision, restraint, and independence, the fruits of ancient and stable civilization? On the other hand, certain phases can be observed in the lives of nations, periods when they adopt a certain set of principles by which to live, adhering to them unswervingly. Then another age ensues, and a new set of principles to which the people devote themselves appears. The new principles begin to predominate over the old and usually one may observe a strong antipathy to the old ways, a rejection of everything that existed under the sway of the old way of life and a negative reaction to the period that went before. In this respect nations cannot love or serve two masters; if they adore one, they are sure to loathe the other. A bitter struggle between the two tendencies, the old and the new, is bound to follow, a struggle which inevitably exasperates, arousing passions and leading to excesses.

Try to imagine a young people, bursting with life but made painfully aware of their own shortcomings by contact with other, superior nations. How could they resist seizing upon everything which seemed best in the others? How were they to slow the pace of change when their general insolvency, both material and moral, was so blatantly obvious?

It was impossible to embark on any one project without embarking simultaneously upon many others in order to expedite the first and bring it to completion. At the time in question the nations of Western Europe were far in advance of Russia in terms of their civilization. Russia had to learn from them. But those same European nations had yet to progress beyond the stage of being enslaved by things foreign, neglecting and disparaging their own culture. Blinded by the glitter of antiquity, they had an irresistible urge to grasp it, sometimes at first with wild enthusiasm; they gave themselves up to studying the Greeks and Romans, even the Italians, who had been the first to become acquainted with the Greeks and the Romans. Indigenous culture fell into disfavor; it was regarded as barbaric. They were unable to appreciate the significance and stature of their own history in relation to the history of the Greeks and the Romans.

Russia's turn to prostrate itself before alien civilization came too, but for various reasons it came later than for others, which was a great disadvantage, but a disadvantage which was conditioned by the whole course of Russian history and by the circumstances in which the nation appeared and our country was founded. Russia's long separation from Western Europe and its civilization, the extreme and exclusive nature of the direction it had adopted, were bound to make its new course correspondingly extreme. Russia's so-called "transformation" acquired a revolutionary aspect because so many requirements had to be satisfied simultaneously.

Russia's early eighteenth-century revolution may better be understood by comparing it with the political revolution which occurred in France at the end of the century. In both cases ailments had accumulated as a result of the stagnant, monolithic and exclusive nature of the course which had been adopted. But the people had no chance to work out the new principles in a practical way. Everyone sensed the need, but the principles were elaborated in a theoretical way in the minds of leaders and there was a sudden rush to reform. No wonder the resulting shock was so terrifying. In France the weak government collapsed and there followed those sad events which reverberate in that country to this very day. In Russia the course of the revolutionary movement was steered by one man, a man endowed with unprecedented strength, a man born to lead his country. French historians feel justified in bewailing the turn of events in their country and look with envy at their island neighbor [England] where the foundations of the edifice were laid from time immemorial, gradually and soundly. In fact they should bewail the whole preceding course of French history, of which the Revolution was the inevitable outcome. There something which elsewhere was accomplished by degrees over a period of time and therefore easily and peacefully had to be carried out suddenly, accompanied by those abnormal stresses which we refer to as a revolution. We would be justified in bewailing our own revolution, but again we would have to bewail in addition the whole of the history which leads up to it, for healthy conditions do not breed diseases.

If such is the common law and if our early eighteenth-century revolution was the inevitable outcome of all that had gone before, this explains the significance of Peter the Great, the chief agent of that revolution. He was indeed the leader, but not the creator of the deed itself; for that the nation was responsible, it was not the personal achievement of Peter alone. At all times and in all places a great man is the representative of his people. His activities satisfy certain national requirements at a given time. The form which a great man's activities takes is conditioned by history, by the way of life of the nation in which he acts. Ghengis Khan and Alexander the Great were both conquerors, but they were very different, the difference stemming from the differences between the nations of which they were the representatives. The activities of a great man are always a result of his people's previous history. A great man does not force his people, does not create anything which is unnecessary or impossible for them. The current achievements of historical science mean that great men have been divested of their divine attributes, ceasing to be creatures who destroy or create at whim. Instead, they have acquired the significance of representatives of a given nation at a given time, as products and yardsticks of national life and national history. In this way great men retain their importance while the people are not reduced to the level of the common herd, charging blindly wherever an alien will drives them.

The revolution was accompanied by a fierce struggle. The reformer met with strong opposition from amongst the people and therefore the work of reform had to be carried out by force on the part of the supreme authority. Foreigners always loved and still love to repeat, and not without an understandable measure of satisfaction, that Peter civilized the Russians prematurely and by force, and that this was bound to end badly. In general, they are opposed to reform from above. We cannot know what the future holds and therefore shall not speak of it, neither shall we say in advance what we intend to say later after we have traced the legacy of Peter's work after his death. But in order to have done with fruitless debates let us again turn to comparisons from the past. Nowadays no European writer, be he believer or non-believer, would deny the civilizing role of Christianity. Every European is proud of the fact that Christianity put down its deepest roots primarily in Europe, which was a tribute to the higher stage of development and the greater maturity of the tribes inhabiting that part of the globe.

But they should recall the history of the acceptance of Christianity by the peoples of Europe, the fact that generally the process was carried out from above. First the prince and his retinue were converted, then the courtiers, and only then did the new faith spread among the masses, but rarely without a ferocious struggle and fearful resistance on the part of the people, who clung doggedly to their old ways and to the faith of their forefathers. Even after they accepted baptism for centuries the masses maintained a dual belief and refused to abandon their ancient deities. What should we conclude from this? That the nations of Europe were converted forcibly to Christianity by their governments! Take another, more recent example. In England King Henry VIII decided to secede from the Roman Catholic church,[4] but we know how fiercely his plan was resisted. He had to contend with violent revolts by magnates and ordinary people alike. In other words, the English people had to be wrested from the Pope by force, and the reform of which the English are so proud was carried out by Henry VIII personally. Such a view would certainly be very welcome in Rome.

Peter was the leader and representative of his people in an affair which was of national concern. The historian is obliged therefore when describing that great turn of events not to detach the leading player from the people and society. From the outset he must trace the formation of the leader's character against a background of conditions formed by the nation's history, for clearly even the most chance phenomena which influence the character of a historical figure are colored by the hues predominating in society at a given time. In this way society exerts its influence on a historical figure.

We have seen already how by the end of the seventeenth century, as a result of a certain set of conditions, Russian society had developed few forces of its own which might have restricted the strength of individuals for which there was so much scope. This is why that virgin land offered such a broad arena of activity for strong men of all kinds, for the sort of men who, in the words of the song, were bowed down by their own strength, straining to flex their powerful shoulder muscles, so that once they managed to break free they knew no bounds.[5] Generally a country's heroic age of epic warriors comes to an end with the coming of civilization and the development of social forces. A civilized, developed society knows how to restrain the strength of individuals, keeping it within limits by the specialization of occupations, which explains why in civilized societies strong men are not built on such epic proportions as in young countries. We are well aware of how exercise develops strength of all kinds and therefore it should come as no surprise that the strong men of old were stronger than those of our own day, for they had more opportunities for trying out their strength. Because of Russia's history Russian society gave wider scope for the exercise of power from above than any other country in Christian Europe. It comes as no surprise that two of Russia's eighteenth-century sovereigns, Peter I and Catherine II,[6] acted on an incredibly vast scale. A young and underdeveloped society does not care for the division of labor, therefore the strong individual can and must try his hand at everything and exercise his strength in a wide variety of occupations. This explains the multifarious activity of Peter. Later we shall see how similar social conditions influenced the varied career and many-sided activity of Lomonosov.[7]

In fact, with Peter and his supporters the ancient epic period of Russian history draws to a close. Peter was the last and the greatest of the epic warriors. Only Christianity and the closeness of the events to our own time have diminished (and then not entirely) the cult of that demigod and our mythical notions of the heroic feats of that Hercules.

A young society seething with unruly forces produced a giant in much the same way as the young earth in the antediluvian age produced gigantic creatures whose vast skeletons fill us puny mortals with amazement. But it is frightening to think where such power might be directed in the absence of principles of moderation and discipline. What sort of moral swaddling clothes did society have ready for Peter? How was it going to raise and educate such a giant?

The moral condition of Old Russian society was highly unsatisfactory, as we have seen. Yet the movement which began in the latter half of the seventeenth century and the struggle which ensued could only make matters worse. However feeble the moral condition of a given society, if it is alive and does not collapse altogether it means that at least some moral restraints and ties survive in order to prevent it from disintegrating completely. But if that society is set in motion and is convulsed by a violent revolution, the old ties are bound to slacken and sometimes may snap completely. Society is then subjected to powerful moral vacillation, insecurity and upheaval until the moral restraints are made fast again or replaced by new ones. There is some truth in the saying that a period of transition is the worst time of all from the point of view of social morality. Until the latter half of the seventeenth century the authority of the spiritual fathers had been beyond dispute. Now on the one hand the Old Believers,[8] on the other new teachers, both Orthodox and non-Orthodox, were undermining their authority. Priests and archpriests proved to be useless as teachers. The younger generation and its leaders were being raised in the conviction that there was no point in listening to such teachers, who talked a lot of rubbish because they were ignorant and needed to be educated themselves.

Old Russian society found its moral restraints in the life of the family. A member of a clan respected his elders, was subject to their supervision and authority which, as we know, was very extensive and when necessary was brought to bear heavily upon anyone who disobeyed. A clan member respected the opinion of the clan and feared to bring it into disrepute by bad behavior. Now patrimonial ties were slackening, but as yet society had failed to produce any replacements.

Old Russian society supplemented moral restraints with material ones. For example, well bred men of substance kept their wives and daughters locked up in the women's quarters or terem.[9] Now that form of incarceration was about to come to an end. But just as a prison is incapable of educating and training a person to exercise freedom, and does not develop or consolidate strength, the terem too failed to educate Russian women for their new situation or to consolidate their moral forces. At the same time society was not yet ready to accept the change and was unable to offer women any purely moral restraints, just as it had none to offer men, either. The Amazon tsarevna Sophia Alekseevna[10] was just such an example of a woman who escaped from the terem but failed to emerge from it with any moral restraints or to find any in society, either.

PETER'S EDUCATION

How then was the young Hercules Tsarevich Peter brought up in that crumbling society?

Peter was three when his father [Tsar Alexis][11] died. When his elder brother [Fedor][12] came to the throne he was removed and persecuted along with his mother and her relatives. A calm, orderly environment during infancy is conducive to an orderly rate of growth in a child, and does not force the tempo. On the other hand, a disturbed early childhood, persecution and upheavals, lead to premature development in able children. Peter was constantly confronted with his sad mother,[13] who complained to a small circle of friends about her misfortunes, the banishment of her brothers and her benefactor Artamon Matveev.[14] The child was excitable and impressionable, he took it all in, was upset by all the talk of family feuds. What other children learn of only though their nanny's stories, tales of wicked relations harassing innocent children who either perish or triumph, Peter experienced in real life. He was the hero of the drama, one of the actors; he hated the villains with a real loathing, and his sympathy for the heroes was stronger than that which other children felt for their fairy-tale heroes, for these heroes were himself, his mother and his uncle. They began to teach him to read and write, summoning, as was the custom, a secretary who could read and write well. This secretary was Nikita Moiseevich Zotov, subsequently renowned as the patriarch of Pressburg.[15]

Peter was almost ten when Tsar Fedor died. He was elected tsar, but the choice led to the musketeer rebellion.[16] Up until then the child was merely irritated by being edged out and persecuted. Now frightful scenes of bloodshed occurred before his very eyes; he witnessed the agonizing death of relatives, the despair of his mother as power was snatched and passed into the hands of their former persecutors. Later, people close to Peter told foreigners how at the time of the musketeer rebellion the young Peter maintained a remarkable calm. They interpreted the fact this his demeanor did not change as a sign of future greatness. But regardless of Peter's behavior at the time of the musketeer revolt, these bloody scenes must have affected him. The feelings aroused by them must have had a damaging effect, even if they were repressed at the time.

Again he had to face banishment and persecution, the sight of his constantly grieving mother, her never-ending complaints and moans that power had been usurped and that mischief was being done in the realm. It must have been sad and wearisome, terribly wearisome for a child already beginning to feel "oppressed by his own strength as though by a heavy burden". With the departure of Zotov his education ended. Peter's elder brothers, after learning basic literacy from a secretary, were passed on to another teacher, Simeon Polotsky,[17] but there was no such teacher for Peter. What was to be done with an excitable boy who when he grew did not know how to walk, only how to run? One occupation was open to him, "to wander along the wide street and amuse himself with the lads," in the words of the old song. So Peter ran out of the palace onto the street, never again to return to the palace in the same sense in which his ancestors had ruled there. In his amusements with the lads on the street and in his martial games the new Romulus issued a summons to a new warrior band and the warrior band gathered, the bold *stableboy playmates*,[18] model regiments of the future. The young warrior was testing his strength. At a time when Russia had turned onto a new path, as if on purpose grief and tedium drove the young tsar from the palace onto the street and into a new environment where he was surrounded by new people, where he was the chief of a new band of warriors who had broken with the old ways and relationships. Without a backward glance he escaped from the boring palace, clean and fresh, a new man, capable of surrounding himself with new people. Fleeing the courtiers he sought new friends, accepting anyone who appeared suitable for the work that had to be done. A new society was being formed, a new state, and as always the retinue appeared with its leader, going into action to destroy the old and create the new. The tsar by birth (*rex ex nobilitate*) became the leader of his band by merit (*dux ex virtute*) and that is what he remained by and large. There was nothing about him which Russian people of old customarily associated with the title of tsar. This was a hero of antiquity. The modern age has seen only one such gigantic figure, of which there were so many examples in the murky past when human society was in the process of formation and organization. When charting Peter's career we

career we should not forget for one moment that we are dealing not
just with a sovereign ruler but with the leader of a new society, the
chief of a retinue founding a new state, a man imbued with a single
idea serving a single purpose. New relationships were bound to be
expressed in new terms. Hence the change in the manner in which
Peter addressed his men, the simple, comradely tone of his
correspondence with these new men, regardless of their status or
their origins, as long as they belonged to the new society and were
the tsar's associates in the cause of reform. Contemporary society
understood these relationships very well. When Russians split into
factions and the struggle began, those who supported the old ways
directed their hostility against this retinue and against the new men
who surrounded Peter.

   That, then, is the significance of the circumstances whereby the
young Peter was driven from the palace by sadness and tedium, and
fled onto the street, where he flexed his muscles in amusements
which were so in keeping with his nature and fell into that
comradely way of life so much in keeping with his career and
historical role. This comradely way of life, of course, involved not
only hard work and heroic achievements. It also involved
merrymaking and dissipation, which appealed equally to the natures
of those who were fitted to be members of the warrior band. Thus
it was in ancient Rus, where the prince first and foremost was the
leader of his retinue. A bit of work then a drink with the warriors:
that was the typical day for the Old Russian prince who rejected
Islam because "it is Rus's pleasure to drink."[19] It comes as no
surprise that the new warrior band of Peter's era did not differ from
the bands of old in this respect. At the same time we must not lose
sight of another set of circumstances which help to explain the
matter in greater detail, namely that for Peter's grandfather, father
and brother, regardless of their differing characters, the palace,
inaccessible and surrounded by holy majesty and awe, performed
the same function as the terem did for the women of medieval
Russia by preserving moral purity, even though we know that Tsar
Alexis, more lively by nature, enjoyed giving banquets for his boyars
and his chaplain and getting them drunk. His youngest son, with his
excitable, passionate nature, abandoned the palace for the street but,
as we know, the Russian street at the end of the seventeenth century

was a grubby sort of place. By inquiring into the vices which prevailed in that society we may better comprehend those habits of Peter's which we find so unappealing.

But was the young Peter really left entirely to his own devices? Was there not a single individual in his circle with the strength of character and status to restrain him from the excesses into which his passionate, excitable nature inevitably led him? In this respect the most influential figure was probably the royal carver[20] Prince Boris Alekseevich Golitsyn, cousin of the famous Prince Vasily.[21] Prince Boris was intelligent, energetic and capable. He was just as well educated as Prince Vasily. He knew Latin and enjoyed speaking it and performed his duties to Peter conscientiously insofar as he remained unwaveringly loyal and protected his master's interests, rendering valuable services in the fight against Sophia and later against the musketeers. He treated his pupil honorably when the latter was on the threshold of his glorious career. This was his reply to a letter he received [from Peter] informing him of a victory: "I received your kind and sincere letter about the victory with thanks, and give great praise to God. I do not intend to fawn or flatter, but may God ever grant you such favor and glory." But this same Prince Boris was also described by foreigners and Russians alike as a drunkard. One foreign writer recounts how Prince Boris and the young Andrei Artamonovich Matveev[22] invited themselves to dinner at his place and brought with them their friends, the Danish commercial agent and several foreign merchants. They enjoyed the food so much that they sent several dishes to their wives and without a by your leave carried off various desserts.[23]

This is an important piece of information for the light it throws on the society of the time. Here we have some leading figures, among the first to embark upon the new road and conscious of the need for education and reform, but what a short distance they as yet had traveled! Men of dual faith, two-faced Januses with one face turned towards the future, the other looking back, speaking Latin and getting drunk, carrying off the desserts from someone else's table. Here is another curious story about Prince Boris. This expert on Latin invited foreigners to his house and astounded them by his crude treatment of some Polish musicians and horrified them by his outburst against his children's unfortunate tutor, also a Pole.

Evidently Prince Boris was not fond of self-restraint. He was also very frank in his letters to Peter. Usually he began them with phrases in Latin, but one he ends "drunkenly yours, Boriska."[24]

In foreigners' accounts a young man who was very close to Peter is often associated with Boris Golitsyn. This was Andrei Matveev, son of the famous Artamon. It was said of the twenty-two-year-old Matveev that he was very clever, spoke good Latin, liked reading and listened eagerly to accounts of events in Europe and had a special liking for foreigners. His wife was the only Russian woman who did not paint her face.

The people closest to Peter were very attracted to the West and sought the company of foreigners, and Peter, consumed with an unquenchable thirst for knowledge and activity, could not long remain isolated from people who had something to teach him or tell him.

Once Empress Elizabeth entered the room of her nephew Peter Fedorovich, who was sketching, kissed him and said with tears in her eyes. "I can't tell you how happy it makes me to see you usefully occupied. It brings to mind an occasion when my dear father found my sister and me at our lessons and said with a sigh 'If only I had been properly educated as a young man!'"[25]

On his own admission, Peter was not properly educated, but he still knew a great deal. Where did he acquire his knowledge? Let him tell us himself.[26]

FOREIGN TEACHERS

Prince Yakov Dolgoruky talked with fourteen-year-old Peter before his departure on a mission to France and said, amongst other things, that he had had an important scientific instrument which unfortunately had been stolen.[27] With it you could measure distance without actually going to the point. The spark hit the powder. "Buy one for me in France." Dolgoruky bought the astrolabe and placed it in Peter's hands, but he could do nothing with it as he did not know how it worked or whom to ask. He asked a German doctor whether he knew. He did not, but he promised to get a man who did, the Dutchman Franz Timmerman.[28] A teacher was found, and the pupil "set about studying geometry and fortification with great enthusiasm." "Through this incident," writes Peter, "this Franz visited the palace and was in our company all the time."

A knowledgeable man was found, but things were not confined to lessons within four walls, for this pupil could not walk but only run. The excitable boy dragged Timmerman all over the place and each time they saw some new object he pestered him with questions about what it was and what it was for. But there were few new objects and the restless boy poked his nose into everything, made them get out everything and show it to him in the hope of finding something useful. In Izmailovo he got into some outhouses where some old things which once belonged to the tsar's great uncle Nikita Ivanovich Romanov had been discarded. There he unearthed a special type of boat, a foreign one! He asked Timmerman what it was. "An English dinghy," he replied. "Where is it used?" "For embarking and disembarking on ships." "In what way is it better than our boats?" " It can sail not only with the wind but also against the wind." "Against the wind? That can't be possible. Still, find out if there is someone who can repair the dingy and show me how it works." Someone was found, a Dutchman by the name of Carsten Brandt,[29] who was invited to build ships at Dedinovo during the reign of Tsar Alexis. Brandt repaired the dingy, made a mast and sail and began to tack on the river Yauza. "I found this quite amazing and really enjoyed it," said Peter. "But after we had been doing it for some time and the dingy didn't always turn properly but got stuck against the bank, I asked him why, and he said it was because the channel was too narrow. So I took the boat to Prosiany pond (at Izmailovo), but it didn't really improve matters much and my enthusiasm grew greater by the hour."

SHIPBUILDING

Peter relates how this impatience was aroused. "Our grandfather[30] purged and pacified the Russian realm, leaving the exacting of revenge on his enemies and the expansion of his realm to his son, who invested much effort in it, especially in warfare, as everyone knows. He made inroads not only upon land but also upon sea (a thing so strange in our country that it was unheard of), as evidenced by the siege of Riga and the construction at Dedinovo of two ships for the Caspian Sea. But why he was unable to complete the task and why this burden was placed on our shoulders by the will of the supreme ruler, we must attribute to inscrutable fate."

Posterity is no longer puzzled by what mystified Peter. Russia's need for the sea and a fleet was recognized before his time. Tsar Alexis built ships at Dedinovo and even proposed to the duke of Courland that Russian ships be built in his ports. But as we saw, the ships at Dedinovo were built incredibly slowly and were subject to all sorts of delays. Some gave orders and others carried them out, ineptly and reluctantly, and the work never got off the ground. To set it in motion it was insufficient to sit in the Kremlin palace and issue orders. The tsar himself needed to be consumed with a passion for seafaring, he needed to grab hold of the axe and start building, he needed to regard the wretched marshy terrain on the Neva estuary as heaven on earth, *paradise*, simply because it was close to the sea and ships could be built there. The need for change, for new institutions was acknowledged before Peter's time but only Peter was capable of bringing to fruition what previously others only attempted.

"His enthusiasm grew greater by the hour." He began to make enquiries about where he might find more water. He was told that the nearest sizeable lake was at Pereiaslav, 120 versts away. But how was he to get there? If he were to tell his mother that he was going to a big lake to sail and build boats she would forbid it, so he would have to get away by deception. He said that he had promised to make a pilgrimage to the Trinity monastery,[31] but from Trinity he made his way to Pereiaslav. Needless to say, the sight of a lovely spacious lake where his dinghy would not forever be hitting against the bank was too great a temptation to resist. He asked his mother's permission to amuse himself on the lake and she agreed. Brandt and Master Kordt [another Dutch ship's carpenter] set off for Pereislav to build boats.

PETER'S MARRIAGE

The young warrior had escaped from home and mother, to flex his powerful muscles and try out his young man's strength, not in the open field but on a broad expanse of water. His mother tried a powerful means of keeping him at home. When Peter was not quite

Tsaritsa Evdokia Fedorovna Lopukhina in later life.
First wife of Peter I.
Artist Unknown.

seventeen he was married to Evdokia,[32] the daughter of lord-in-waiting Lopukhin. The bride's father, as was the custom, changed his name, from Ilarion to Fedor [to signify his new status]. The Russian proverb "a married man is a changed man" did not apply in Peter's case. He continued to escape from home, from his mother and his young wife. In April 1689 he was back on Lake Pereiaslav, where he wrote to his mother, "My dearly beloved mother, dearer to me than life itself, sovereign lady, tsaritsa and great princess Natalia Kirillovna, your son, Petrushka, who is working here, asks your blessing and enquires after your health. We are all well, thanks to your prayers. The lake has been clear of ice since the 20th and the boats, all except the big ship, are ready. But we cannot get going for lack of ropes. So I beg you to send 700 sazhen of cables from the Artillery Chancellery without delay. Without them we'll be held up and have to stay here longer. I ask your blessing." It is interesting to note Peter's cunning approach: the sooner they had the ropes, he warned his mother, the sooner they would be home. "Without them we'll be held up and have to stay here longer."

Peter had plenty to occupy him—lessons with Timmerman, games on land and water, drilling the infantry regiments which had been formed from the old play troops and new bands of volunteers who arrived from every quarter, drawn from the nobility and commoners alike but primarily from grooms from the royal stables, building a fort which bore the foreign name of Pressburg (on the banks of the Yauza), building boats on Lake Pereiaslav. He had no time for leisure. When his mother summoned him back to Moscow to attend a requiem mass for his brother Fedor he replied: "I'm willing, but, oh dear, there is so much to do." One thing in particular occupied his thoughts, as he confirmed to his mother. "I tell you again that the boats are all excellent."

SOPHIA PLANS TO BE CROWNED

Stupid boats were the last thing on Tsaritsa Natalia's mind. The unspoken struggle between herself and the stepdaughter [Tsarevna Sophia] who had robbed her of the government continued. The usurper was in an unenviable position. An instinct for self-preservation had made her resort to desperate measures, inciting the

Tsarevna Sophia

From an engraving of the "Coronation" portrait

musketeers to rebellion, wresting the government from the hands of her stepmother and placing her elder, handicapped brother Ivan[33] on the throne. But how long could it last? The Naryshkin heir was still tsar. Soon he would be a man, and then the regent would be dispensed with. The nunnery had been postponed for a while, but it was always there in the background.

Sophia's position was similar to that of those characters in legends who make a pact with an evil spirit to enjoy all the delights life has to offer for a given period, but when the appointed time is up consign themselves to hell. Naturally Sophia was forced to find a way of consolidating her power, and in this she was aided by the men she had raised to favor and who had everything to lose in the event of her fall. Sophia was regent thanks to the incapacity of one brother and the minority of the other. Once the latter became a man Sophia's rule would come to an end, so it was essential to ensure that it did not.

The first step had been taken by establishing a dual monarchy, with two brothers crowned as tsar. Why not a triple monarchy? Why should not Sophia be crowned too? No one would try to overthrow God's anointed. In state papers Sophia added her name to those of her two brothers, calling herself *autocrat* of All Russia along with them.[34] The secretary Volkov, sent on a mission to Venice, proclaimed that their sister the great sovereign lady Tsarevna Sophia Alekseevna ruled with the great sovereign tsars. One of the senators remarked: "The doge and the senate wonder how their royal majesties' subjects manage to serve three such lofty and glorious royal personages." Volkov replied that the subjects carried out the orders of all three persons jointly. But all these proclamations lacked authority. It was not the same as if they had come from someone who had been anointed.

Meanwhile the dreaded hour approached; Peter was growing up, and with him the hopes of the stepmother were raised too, and her words became bolder and sharper. When Sophia added her name to those of her brothers the tsaritsa said outright to the other tsarevnas, daughters of Michael and Alexis,[35] "Why has she started writing her name with the great sovereigns? We have people who won't let this matter rest." Two of Tsaritsa Natalia's chambermaids passed on to Sophia all the negative and hostile things that were being said about her in her stepmother's apartments, and let it be known that the most outspoken in their criticism of Sophia were the tsaritsa's brother Lev Kirillovich Naryshkin[36] and Prince Boris Alekseevich Golitsyn.

VASILY GOLITSYN AND FEDOR SHAKLOVITY

Lev Naryshkin and Prince Boris Golitsyn were the men closest to Tsaritsa Natalia, and Prince Vasily Golitsyn and Fedor Shaklovity[37] were the closest to Tsarevna Sophia. Prince Vasily was averse to measures involving crime and bloodshed, but we have seen in what a difficult position his relationship with Sophia placed him. In this situation his mind was flooded with all sorts of frightening ideas from which he drew the conclusion that it would be good if something were done as long as it were done by others and not by him. Once he said "It's a shame that Tsaritsa Natalia was not banished along with her brothers after the musketeer rebellion [of 1682], then there would have been no problem." Shaklovity's character was quite different. He would stop at nothing. He was not one to content himself with fruitless regrets about the past. Obliged to Sophia for everything, he would perish with her downfall. Why should the highborn aristocrats and their highborn relatives lift a finger to save a lowly clerk who was raised to the rank of lord-in-waiting by Sophia's favor? The obligation to be loyal to his benefactress colored his view of where his self-interest lay. With Sophia or Natalia? Shaklovity expressed his choice with terrible naivety: "Rather the tsaritsa should perish than you should go, my lady."

ATTEMPTS TO INCITE THE MUSKETEERS TO REBEL

So Shaklovity hastened to lay hands upon anyone who declared his attachment to Peter. He tortured and banished from Moscow the table attendant Yazykov who had said that Peter Alekseevich was tsar in name only and that no one dared to petition him. But apprehending and banishing some person or other who expressed himself carelessly meant nothing. Tsaritsa Natalia had said "We have the people", and Peter indeed had people who would not stop at words if the need arose. Peter had his troops, the hated *playmate* stable lads,[38] the *naughty boys* as Sophia and her supporters disparagingly referred to them. Their only refuge was the musketeers.[39]

They would have to turn to them again, just as they had in 1682. But perhaps that particular weapon was blunted since 1682, aided to no small extent by Sophia and Shaklovity themselves when they wrested it from the hands of Khovansky?[40] The most insolent of the musketeers had been removed from Moscow at Shaklovity's suggestion and mostly the placid ones remained, those who were happy with their lot and hard to rouse to rebellion. Indeed, what could induce them to rebel? In August 1687 Shaklovity suddenly proposed to the musketeers' officers that they write a petition for Sophia to be crowned with the royal crown."We don't know how to write a petition," the musketeers replied. "It will be written for you," Shaklovity assured them. A petition would be written, but to whom would it be presented? To the tsars? Nobody took any notice of the elder; everything rested with the younger. "Will Tsar Peter listen to us?" asked the musketeers. "If he won't listen, go to the palace and arrest the boyar Lev Kirillovich Naryshkin and the royal attendant Boris Alekseevich; then they will accept the petition." "But what about the patriarch and the boyars?" again the musketeers asked. "The patriarch can be replaced; as for the boyars, they're no more than a fallen, rotten tree. Only Prince Vasily Vasilievich Golitsyn will remain standing."

So this was what it came down to. In order to carry out the wishes of the tsarevna and Shaklovity they had to riot in the palace, arrest two of the tsar's closest advisers and replace the patriarch! On the previous occasion the musketeers were prepared for the rebellion in gradual stages by irritation and taunts, then the people were raised by the news that the Naryshkins had strangled the tsarevich. But now they were being told to revolt for an unprecedented, curious cause even after all measures had been used to cool the musketeers' desire to revolt and make them fear it.

The officers were given five rubles apiece and ordered to talk to their comrades in the garrisons. But in the garrisons the proposal was given a cool reception, and Sophia hastened to reject it herself.

They at least had to stimulate the loyalty of the musketeers and ensure they would provide protection in an emergency by representing to them the danger which threatened Sophia. The regent summoned a group of musketeers at night and began telling them that Tsaritsa Natalia and her brothers and Boris Golitsyn were planning a revolt and that the patriarch was against her, Sophia, causing trouble instead of reconciling. Shaklovity made as though to advise Sophia, making known to the musketeers what measures needed to be taken in order to calm Sophia's fears. "Why not kill Prince Boris and Lev Naryshkin? And why not kill the tsaritsa? You know, my lady, what her origins are and how in Smolensk she went around in bast shoes."[41] Sophia replied: "I feel sorry for them; even so God has doomed them." The musketeers answered vaguely: "As you wish, sovereign lady, do as you think fit."

The musketeers responded to vague demands and vague complaints with vague replies. What rebellion was the tsaritsa supposed to be raising? It is understandable why out of all the musketeers Shaklovity could find only five who were willing to act. These five were Petrov, Strizhov, Kondratiev, Chermny and Gladky, men whose interests were closely linked with those of Sophia. Shaklovity told Chermny "They want to destroy us, and the tsaritsa is making trouble for everyone. They want to remove me from my office and to disperse those of you who visit me in my house to other towns." Chermny, in order to avert this misfortune, began talking to his fellow musketeers. "What's to be done? You can exterminate the lot of them and still not get to the root of the trouble. The old tsaritsa, the *she-bear*, has to be removed." They objected that Tsar Peter would try to protect his mother, but Chermny kept on: "Why should he be let off?" Gladky said: "They have blocked off Tsar Ivan's doors with heaps of firewood and logs, and the royal crown has been broken. Why let their side do all the smashing?"

The musketeers reacted coolly to all this talk of heaps of firewood and crowns being broken. Last time they said that he had been strangled, and look what happened then. More powerful inducements were tried. One night in two separate locations an armed mob went up to the musketeers' sentries and grabbed a corporal whom the ringleader ordered be beaten to death. As they began to pummel the unfortunate victim a voice was heard from the crowd: "Lev Kirillovich! Why beat him to death. He's a Christian soul." Later it transpired that the man alleged to be Lev Naryshkin in fact had been a clerk from the Treasury called Shoshin, an adherent of Sophia's.

But even this incident failed to arouse the musketeers. Nor did they succumb to promises of looting when Gladky tempted them with the prospect of robbing the homes of the boyars and merchants and sharing out the rich booty. Gladky, who was Shaklovity's man and therefore also Medvedev's,[42] brought in religious affairs, accusing the patriarch of introducing a new practice whereby the congregation no longer was told to prostrate themselves when saying the amen (after "take and eat").[43] But the musketeers reacted coolly to the accusation against the patriarch. They remembered July 5, 1682.[44] Nor were they moved by Gladky's attempts to compare the behavior of Peter and Sophia: "Our sovereign lady prays constantly to God, but in his place all they do is play on organs and viols."

PETER'S DISPLEASURE

The musketeers were unmoved, but by 1689 acts of provocation by Peter against Sophia were in evidence. There was nothing particularly significant or systematic about these incidents. Peter was still young and occupied with his boats. Even so, Sophia was bound to be annoyed and perturbed as she detected the beginning of a process which surely must end in the nunnery. On July 8 in the cathedral of Our Lady of Kazan, Peter told his sister not to join the procession of the cross. Sophia disobeyed, picked up an icon and set off.[45] Peter lost his temper, did not parade with the crosses and left Moscow. As far as he was concerned, the incident was over and done with after this outburst. But Sophia's position was such that she deemed it vital to prepare to defend herself against the play regiments who could come and divest her of her power.

On July 25, when Peter was expected to come to Moscow to celebrate the nameday of Tsarevna Anna Mikhailovna, fifty musketeers were posted secretly by the Red Porch [in the Kremlin] with orders to listen for an alarm bell which would signal that "plots were being hatched" against the tsarevna.[46] No "plots" were being hatched, but now there was a new act of provocation on Peter's part which annoyed Sophia intensely since it involved the reputation of her regime and of Prince Vasily Golitsyn. Peter refused to sanction the distribution of rewards to Golitsyn and his fellow officers for the second Crimean campaign.[47] He allowed himself to be talked round but vented his irritation by not admitting Golitsyn and his generals to thank him for their awards. That was July 27. That same evening Sophia attended a vigil service at the New convent,[48] accompanied by musketeers, brigadiers and sergeants. After the service she began to complain to them about Tsaritsa Natalia, ending with the same old threat, "If we are of any use to you, stand by us. If not, we shall leave the country." The musketeers' response was that they were ready to do as she wished. Sophia told them to await further instructions. But the majority of the musketeers were against the idea of using a bell to raise the alarm. If some member of the royal family were really in danger they should follow the proper legal procedure with a conciliar secretary reading a royal rescript. This they would accept, but without official orders they refused to act, no matter how loudly the alarm sounded. There should be an appeal for a full investigation. Shaklovity's supporters tried in vain to counter this proposal from the majority of the musketeers. In vain did Strizhov argue that nothing would come of an investigation. The identity of the tsarevna's ill-wishers was well known to all, so why not just kill them? Without Sophia the musketeers would be in a difficult position. Peter sent for Strizhov, but Shaklovity refused to hand him over. Peter had Shaklovity himself arrested at Izmailovo, but he was quickly released. One side was acting, timidly and indecisively, but acting nonetheless, and this was enough to make the other side extremely nervous and agitated.

MUSKETEERS GATHER IN THE KREMLIN

On August 7 there was talk in the palace of the discovery of an anonymous letter claiming that the play regiments were coming from Preobrazhenskoe that very night to kill Tsar Ivan and all his sisters. That evening Shaklovity made his preparations. He ordered four hundred musketeers to assemble in the Kremlin with loaded weapons and another three hundred to muster at the Lubianka. Three orderlies were to be dispatched to Preobrazhenskoe to keep an eye on Peter's movements. But the orders were poorly executed. The orderlies did not go to Preobrazhenskoe as instructed and no troops gathered on the Lubianka. In the Kremlin Gladky and Chermny were in a state of high agitation but their nerves were not communicated to the others. No one was quite sure why they had been summoned—

to defend or attack. In either case there would be a bloody struggle, and one in which they had no wish to participate. At this moment of tense anticipation and universal alarm Tsar Peter's chamberlain Pleshcheev[49] rode into the Kremlin from Preobrazhenskoe. Gladky, who had long awaited a pretext to set things in motion, rushed at Pleshcheev, dragged him from his horse, grabbed his saber, beat him and took him into the palace to Shaklovity. The action had begun, with Gladky as its initiator.

The mass of the musketeers were impervious to the goading of Shaklovity and his supporters and reluctant to start a revolt on behalf of Sophia, but neither did they make a move in the opposite direction. As we have seen, only five men stood out from this mass as willing, as on May 15, 1682, to impale people on their spears in support of Sophia. In opposition to them there formed a small group of eight men who regarded the activities of Shaklovity, Chermny and Gladky as criminal and foolish and decided to act in opposition in support of Tsar Peter who had right on his side. These eight were from the mounted bodyguard of musketeers: Brigadier Elizarev, Sergeants Melnov and Ulfov and Corporals Ladogin, Feoktistov, Turka, Troitsky and Kapranov. On the night of August 7-8 while the mass of musketeers remained immobile all the action was to be expected from these two extreme groups, for here were the most decisive people, men with well defined goals who neither hesitated nor wavered. Elizarev and his friends were stationed at the Lubianka that night. One of them, Melnov, was sent to observe what was going on in the Kremlin and upon his return he reported Gladky's assault on Pleshcheev. They interpreted this assault as the beginning of the mutiny and decided that their side must act, too. Melnov and Ladogin were sent to Preobrazhenskoe to inform the tsar that there was a plot to murder him and his mother.

PETER FLEES TO THE TRINITY MONASTERY

But Melnov and Ladogin were not the only ones to hasten to Preobrazhenskoe with their news. That evening the magnates learned that only people very well known to and trusted by the regent were being admitted to the Kremlin. This so alarmed Peter's supporters that they set off at once for Preobrazhenskoe. A little after midnight, when Peter was sound asleep, he was awoken and told that musketeers and others had arrived from Moscow with the news that a large number of musketeers had assembled in the Kremlin and were preparing to march to Preobrazhenskoe in revolt. The terrified tsar leapt from his bed just as he was and ran out into the stables, got on a horse and rode to a nearby wood where his clothes were brought to him. He got dressed and galloped to the Trinity monastery accompanied by his chamberlain Gavrila Golovkin,[50] a dwarf and one of the musketeer informers, arriving at about six in the morning, utterly exhausted. As soon as he entered the room he flung himself on a bed and in floods of tears told Archimandrite Vincent, who had run in, of his plight and begged him for protection. On August 8 Tsaritsa Natalia with her daughter and daughter-in-law arrived with members of the nobility loyal to Peter, the play regiments and the Sukharev Regiment of musketeers. The man in charge was Prince Boris Golitsyn.

Moscow was horrified when on August 8 it learned the news of the tsar's flight from Preobrazhenskoe. The contest had begun, but how would it end? The people in the palace tried to give the impression that they attached little importance to these events. When Shaklovity heard about it he said "Let him run off if he has got himself into such a rage." Sophia told the musketeers that if they did not watch out the play regiments would crush them. Peter was told a quite different story when on August 9 he sent a message to Ivan and Sophia to ask why the musketeers had been assembled at such an unusual time. The reply was that the musketeers were there to escort Sophia to a convent for a pilgrimage. Another missive from Tsar Peter soon followed in which he demanded the dispatch of Colonel Tsykler and fifty musketeers. Later it transpired that this was Tsykler's own idea. As we saw, he was an ardent supporter of Sophia and a participant in the [1682] musketeer rebellion.[51] Now he realized that Peter was very likely to gain the upper hand and he let it be known that if he was summoned to the Trinity monastery he would reveal much useful information. Tsykler was released after long discussion and excuses. He was followed there by Elizarev, Feoktistov, Ulfov, Turka, Troitsky and Kapranov, all ready to inform.

SOPHIA'S ATTEMPTS TO MAKE PEACE WITH PETER

Sophia could not rest in calm anticipation of something happening at Trinity. She must have realized what an advantage Peter had in the contest. After all, in her own duel with Khovansky she had found the road to the Trinity monastery the most convenient battleground. On August 13 Prince Ivan Borisovich Troekurov[52] was sent to see Peter. On the 15th he returned with a less than gracious reply, and the day after a letter from Peter to the regiments of musketeers and infantry was received in Moscow, in which he ordered the officers and rank and file soldiers from each regiment to report to Trinity by the 18th. After consultations with advisers Sophia summoned the officers of each regiment and delivered a powerful speech strictly forbidding them to go the the monastery or to meddle in the quarrel between herself and her brother. When the colonels expressed their bewilderment she warned that anyone who went would be arrested and beheaded.

A speedy resolution was needed and the same day Tsar Ivan's tutor Prince Peter Ivanovich Prozorovsky[53] and Peter's chaplain were sent to the Trinity monastery to say that, regrettably, it was impossible to comply with the tsar's demand and send the troops he required. At the same time Prozorovsky and the priest were told to use all means at their disposal to bring about a reconciliation between Peter and his sister. To calm the musketeers and infantry in Moscow it was rumored that the royal letter was sent without Peter's knowledge on the initiative of Prince Boris Golitsyn. On August 18 Prozorovsky and the priest returned having accomplished nothing. Clutching at straws they decided to send the patriarch, a man of whom Sophia had once said "He has it in for me. Whatever he says to the contrary, I know he has it in for me."[54] Joachim was glad of the chance to escape from Moscow and the clutches of his enemies. He left for Trinity and remained there, providing Peter with an important ally. Several days passed in anticipation. On August 27 a new royal rescript was sent out from Trinity addressed to the regiments of musketeers, the guild of chief merchants, the palace free settlements and the urban tax-paying communities, ordering the officers and ten men from each regiment and the elders and ten members of each tax-paying community to go at once to Trinity. Anyone failing to appear would be put to death. Crowds of musketeers obeyed the order and set off from Moscow. At the monastery the tsar himself came out to the front of the palace with his mother and the patriarch and revealed Shaklovity's plot. A secretary read extracts from responses to questions and the musketeers' denunciations, then the patriarch began to admonish the new arrivals to tell the whole truth about what they knew, threatening to withhold his blessing if they made false statements.

The musketeers wailed that they knew nothing about Fedka Shaklovity's wicked schemes. They had served the great sovereigns and toiled for them, just as their forefathers had served and toiled. They were willing to apprehend criminals and traitors and to do the sovereigns' will in all things. And a few had something else to tell.

Sophia decided to go to the monastery. In the same village of Vozdvizhensk where seven years previously she had ordered the execution of Khovansky, she was met by Table Attendant Buturlin[55] who announced in the name of the great sovereign that she must not proceed to the monastery. "I will go," Sophia protested, but after Buturlin Prince Troekurov appeared with a declaration that if she went any farther she would be subjected to humiliation. A detachment of armed men had already arrived at Vozdvizhenskoe.

Sophia hurried back to Moscow and summoned the musketeers, *senior* men in whom she thought she could place her trust, and complained that she almost had been shot at in Vozdvizhensk and had been forced to turn back. The Naryshkins and Lopukhins were planning to murder Tsar Ivan and then her. "Can I rely on you?" she asked. "Do you need us? If not, my brother and I will search out a cell in some convent." She complained bitterly that Boris Golitsyn and Lev Naryshkin gave her no peace. They had sent her younger brother out of his mind with too much drink, and had no respect whatsoever for the elder. They had filled his room with firewood. They had called her, Sophia, a whore. Had they forgotten that she was the daughter of Tsar Alexis Mikhailovich? They wanted to cut off the head of Prince Vasily Golitsyn, who had done so much good and made a treaty of permanent peace with Poland. Previously no fugitives were ever returned from the Don, but now they handed them over freely. Her life was being made a misery. She had taken care of everything and they were taking everything away from her. "Don't go to the Trinity monastery," she said. "Swear you won't run off, and kiss the cross to prove it. " And she made the musketeers swear not to go.

Then the first day of September arrived, New Year's Day.[56] Sophia and her supporters celebrated in dismal mood. Colonel Nechaev arrived from Trinity with a letter for Tsar Ivan and Sophia in which Peter informed them of the plot against his life and demanded that Fedka Shaklovity and the monk Silvester Medvedev and their accomplices be handed over to a tribunal. This created consternation at court. The people were thunderstruck but most, in the words of an eyewitness,[57] resolved to keep calm and see how things turned out. Nechaev was summoned to the palace and asked how he dared to bring such a letter. He replied that he dared not disobey the tsar's command. Sophia ordered that he be beheaded but he was saved by the fact that no executioner could be found, or perhaps no one made the effort to look for one.

In the meantime Sophia's anger abated. Some musketeers had accompanied Nechaev from the monastery. Sophia had them brought to the Red Porch. She descended the steps and asked "What are you doing here? What are your orders? Did you believe what they told you at Trinity? Those letters were the work of criminals. You must not leave Moscow for the Trinity without authorization because my brother Peter did not admit me to the monastery to see him. I refuse to give you the men you were sent to arrest. You may take nine but there they will slander nine hundred. Who are you going to believe? Those doing the slandering should be sent to Moscow to be interrogated, but I won't let you have anyone. Nor shall I hand over the people who have been arrested and are locked up in detention. I'll send a boyar to Trinity. See how they distort everything. They want to destroy me. Wicked men have engineered a quarrel between Peter and me and started rumors of a conspiracy against Tsar Peter and others. Because they are envious of the loyal service and enthusiasm of Fedor Shaklovity they accuse him of being the initiator of a wicked plot. To find out just what was going on I went to the monastery but Tsar Peter stopped me on the advice of wicked counsellors and I had to suffer the humiliation of turning back. You are all aware that these past seven years I have been your ruler. I took over the government during a troubled time, made a glorious eternal peace with a neighboring Christian ruler,[58] and the enemies

Tsar Ivan V Alekseevich
Artist unknown

of Christ's cross are in fear of my weaponry. For your services you have been rewarded generously, and you always have been aware of my favor towards you. How after all that can you be so disloyal as to believe the inventions of wicked men who wish Christian folk no good and stir up trouble? It's not the head of Fedor Shaklovity that they are seeking, but mine and my brother Ivan's."

In the midst of her agitation Sophia was tireless. She summoned leading members of the merchant and town's communities and delivered them a similar speech. Finally she asked for everyone in the Kremlin to be summoned and, according to a witness [Gordon], delivered a long, eloquent speech.

Meanwhile in the Kremlin preparations had been made for celebrating the New Year. But the patriarch was absent, Tsar Ivan was unwell and the regent was in no mood for celebrating, so the preparations were cancelled. The musketeers were treated to vodka. The aristocracy and foreign officers received a cup of vodka from the hands of Tsar Ivan himself. At that time Shaklovity was performing his last duty to the tsarevna, writing a statement to be issued to all ranks of men of the Muscovite realm in order to present matters so as to exonerate Sophia and incriminate her opponents. He wrote that the tsarevna had accepted the government after an appeal from the whole nation and with the patriarch's blessing, but now the Naryshkins were treating her and her brother Tsar Ivan disrespectfully and did not kiss their hand; they had called in the play regiments, at whose hands many people had suffered insults and injuries. There was no reply to a complaint on that count to Tsar Peter. Tsar Ivan's room was strewn with logs, they had broken his crown.

Whilst Shaklovity was rendering his final service Vasily Golitsyn was taking no part whatsoever in the events in Moscow. There was an exchange of letters between relatives. Prince Boris wrote to Prince Vasily advising him to go to the Trinity monastery in order to secure Peter's favor. Prince Vasily sent a clerk to the monastery to try to persuade Prince Boris to reconcile the parties. Prince Boris sent the reply that it would be best for Prince Vasily to get to the monastery with all speed and the tsar would give him an excellent reception. New demands for handing over Shaklovity came from Trinity. The musketeers grumbled that things had dragged on for too long. Sophia made it known that she herself intended to go to the monastery with her elder brother. The musketeers in Moscow whispered that the affair was taking a long time to resolve. Their comrades at the Trinity monastery also were losing patience. Their wives, children and businesses were in Moscow. They brought a petition asking permission to go to Moscow and arrest Fedka Shaklovity and his accomplices. But the young tsar and his advisers would not allow it for fear of bloodshed. At Trinity there was disagreement about what to do next: some wanted the tsar to resolve things quickly by moving closer to Moscow and staying either at Alekseevsk or Preobrazhenskoe. But more sensible people opposed this idea, saying that it could result in bloodshed, whereas the matter probably would resolve itself. Prince Vasily Golitsyn thought that they should try to win over a dozen or so musketeers from Trinity in the hope that the others would follow their example and flee; when the musketeers ran off the sovereign would have to come to Moscow, and the parties would meet and negotiate.

On September 2 several people from the Foreign Quarter[59] set off for the monastery and Gordon asked them to send apologies that he had not gone with them but he was not sure how his arrival would be greeted. On September 4 a royal letter dated August 31 arrived in the Quarter summoning all foreign officers to the Trinity monastery. The foreigners decided that they ought to show this letter to Prince Vasily Golitsyn, who was their commanding officer. Gordon and several other officers went to see the guardian of the royal seal,[60] who was very embarrassed when they handed him the letter but quickly regained his composure and said that he would show the document to the elder tsar and tsarevna and then tell them what they should do. Gordon said that they feared for their lives if they failed to obey. Golitsyn promised them an answer by evening. But the foreigners decided not to wait for an answer. That evening they set off and at eleven the next morning reached the monastery. They kissed the hand of the tsar who gave them each a cup of vodka. At a time of nervous tension and indecision every movement in one direction or the other was extraordinarily important and produced a strong impression. People began to speak out in favor of Tsar Peter when they heard that the Germans[61] had gone over to his side.

THE MUSKETEERS FORCE SOPHIA TO GIVE UP SHAKLOVITY

Sophia still had the musketeers, but when it became known that Sophia did not intend to go to Trinity because she would not be admitted the musketeers lost patience and on the evening of September 6 a big crowd of them went to the Kremlin with a petition urging the tsarevna to hand over Fedka Shaklovity, whom they would take to the monastery. At first Sophia refused to give him up, told them to live peaceably and stop meddling in the quarrel between her and her brother. The crowd was in uproar. Voices were heard saying that there was nothing to wait for and that it was time to sound the alarm. Sophia was shaken. The scenes of 1682 were being repeated, only with a change of cast. Then the musketeers had pressed Tsaritsa Natalia to hand over her brother Ivan Naryshkin,[62] and the cowardly boyars had urged the tsaritsa to sacrifice her brother lest they all perish for the sake of one man. Now it was the musketeers ordering Sophia to give up Shaklovity, and those surrounding the tsarevna were urging her to comply with the demands otherwise many would pay for it with their lives. Sophia gave up Shaklovity. But Medvedev managed to escape. That day the boyars who remained in Moscow responded to Peter's summons and set off for Trinity. Golitsyn was the only one to remain. He and his family went off to his estate at Medvedkovo just outside Moscow. He was upset by the news of Shaklovity's arrest.

SHAKLOVITY'S INTERROGATION

On September 7 Shaklovity was delivered to the monastery. Questioned about his criminal intentions, he replied that during Lent 1687 in the cathedral of Our Lady of Kazan behind the icon of the Mother of God a letter was found containing words of abuse about Tsarevna Sophia. At this time Tsar Peter was forming the play regiments and this gave rise to anxiety. Tsarevna Sophia told Shaklovity to select zealous musketeers loyal to her and Tsar Ivan and he summoned the brigadiers and told them that at any sign of trouble they should guard the sovereigns. The musketeers often came and told him about insults and beatings they received from the play regiments. "They'll get you too. If we don't deal with them now it will be the worse for everyone." But he dissuaded them. At the first torture session after fifteen blows he made a full confession of all charges against him. After the second he promised to reveal everything without concealment and wrote that he had never plotted against the life of Tsar Peter. There had been conversations about murdering the tsaritsa with Kuzma Chermny who had started it. Prince Vasily Golitsyn expressed regret that they had not got rid of the tsaritsa in 1682. They had planned to start a fire at Preobrazhenskoe; they had assembled the musketeers for their own protection and not to raise rebellion. Who had given the tsarevna the idea of being crowned he did not know, except that neither he nor Golitsyn advised her on it, and Golitsyn had even written about it in a horrified tone while on campaign. Finally, he, Shaklovity, had written a last declaration for the people about the affronts to the tsarevna. Shaklovity did not confess to a plot to murder Peter even though Filipp Sapogov declared that Shaklovity had tried to persuade him to throw grenades onto the road as Tsar Peter passed by, or to place them secretly in his sledge, or to kill the sovereign during the fire at Preobrazhenskoe. Later, in 1699, the musketeer Petrushka Krivoy testified: "After 1682 I was often in the home of Fedka Shaklovity and with Fedka at Prince Ivan Zasekin's house, and on one occasion Fedka and Prince Ivan said in my presence 'The tsar goes to fires accompanied by only a small number of men. The musketeers could kill him.'"

THE GOLITSYNS ARE EXILED

Shaklovity was closely linked with Golitsyn. The fate of both had to be decided simultaneously. On the same day they brought Shaklovity, September 7, at about five o'clock in the afternoon Prince Vasily also arrived at Trinity with close colleagues who held important military and state service posts: Lord-in-waiting Leonty Nepliuev, Venedikt Zmeev, the state servitor Grigory Kosogov and Conciliar Secretary Emelian Ukraintsev.[63] They were not admitted through the monastery gates, but were ordered to stay outside in the artisans' quarter and not to leave without permission.

In the evening Gordon visited Golitsyn and found him in pensive mood. On the evening of the 9th Golitsyn and his son Alexis were summoned to the palace. When they climbed the stairs a conciliar secretary came out to meet them and read them an order to the effect that they had been stripped of the rank of boyar and banished with their wives and children to Kargopol, and their property was to be sequestered by the sovereign because (i) they had reported to the great sovereigns' sister on affairs of state, bypassing the sovereigns themselves, and had written her name jointly with those of the great sovereigns and ordered it to be printed in books and on coins together with those of the great sovereigns; (ii) when he was sent to attack the Crimean encampments in 1689 Prince Golitsyn had gone to Perekop but failed to engage the enemy and retreated and as a result of this lack of zeal great losses were inflicted on the treasury, the realm was ruined and the people overburdened.

DISPUTE OVER THE GOLITSYNS' FATE

There was a fierce struggle over Golitsyn's fate amongst some of Peter's closest advisers. The abolition of the Code of Precedence[64] had dealt a hefty blow to patrimonial politics, but the results of that blow could not become consolidated in such a short time. Everyone was still deeply imbued with the principles of clan unity, as a result of which the honor of one member of the clan was upheld by the clan as a whole, whilst one member's shame fell upon all others. That is why Prince Boris Golitsyn went to such great lengths to ensure that Prince Vasily was not convicted of treason, which would have been a blot on the entire Golitsyn clan. The following testimony by Gordon is reliable: after the first session of torture and when a second was threatened, Shaklovity promised to present the tsar an accurate written statement of the whole affair. Prince Boris went to see him and brought him pen and ink. Shaklovity covered about nine sheets of paper with writing. By the time he had finished it was past midnight. The tsar had gone to bed and Prince Boris took the paper back home with him intending to present it to the tsar the following day. But those who were angry with Boris for his wish to save Prince Vasily from a charge of treason (that is, the Naryshkins and their friends) kept a sharp eye on every move Prince Boris made and reported to the tsar that he probably had taken the statement in order to read it and tear out anything which might be harmful to Prince Vasily. The tsar sent to Shaklovity and asked if he had written a confession, and he replied that he had and that he had given it to Prince Boris. But a friend managed to warn the prince of the danger and he hurried with the papers to the tsar, who confronted him with the stern question of why he had not handed it over immediately. Golitsyn replied that the hour was already very late. Peter was satisfied with this answer and continued to keep Prince Boris close to him as previously. But Tsaritsa Natalia and her friends did not make peace with him.

After sentence was passed on Prince Vasily Golitsyn they pronounced sentence on his assistant Nepliuev. He also was stripped of the rank of lord-in-waiting and sentenced to exile in Pustozersk[65] (later Kola). The charges were his cruel treatment of soldiers under his command, whose complaints Nepliuev's friends so far had managed to stop from reaching Moscow. Zmeev was ordered to go and live on his estate in Kostroma. Kosogov and Ukraintsev remained in their former posts.

EXECUTION OF SHAKLOVITY AND HIS ACCOMPLICES

Shaklovity and his chief accomplices were sentenced to death. A curious story survives that Peter did not consent to their sentence and was persuaded only by the patriarch, and that when the news leaked out that Shaklovity was going to be executed without a second round of torture, many servitors assembled in the monastery, "in service of the great sovereign," as they put it, and appealed for Shaklovity to be tortured again so that he might reveal the identity of his accomplices. The tsar let it be known that he was satisfied with Shaklovity's deposition and that they had no business to meddle in the affair.

On September 11 Shaklovity, Petrov and Chermny were executed. The brigadier Muromtsev, Colonel Riazantsev and the musketeer Lavrentev were flogged with the knout and banished to Siberia with their tongues cut out. But the fight over Vasily Golitsyn continued. His enemies insisted that exile to Kargopol was far too light a sentence and that he should be sent to Pustozersk. But evidently Prince Boris prevailed, and Yarensk was selected as the place of exile. It was insisted that at the very least the Golitsyns should be questioned about the reliability of Shaklovity's deposition. They were interviewed on the road, in Yaroslavl. Father and son swore that they had no part in Shaklovity's plots. After questioning they sent a petition to the tsars: "We swear to you, great sovereigns, as to God in highest heaven, before his redemptive throne, that Fedka Shaklovity was never a close friend of mine, but I was simply acquainted with him, as I was with many others." The Golitsyns were taken further. When they stopped in Vologda the palace table attendant Prince Kropotkin arrived unexpectedly to see Prince Vasily, bearing not a new interrogation but a consoling letter and money from Tsarevna Sophia. Upon arrival in Yarensk the Golitsyns wrote another petition to the tsars: "We are suffering, poor wretches, close to our life's end, but we have been discredited unfairly in your eyes, great sovereigns. When they were transporting us, your slaves, to Totma before we had reached the town on the river Sukhona, the wagons carrying our wives and children and domestic servants toppled into the water and our wives and small children had to be dragged from the river and lay senseless for a long time." The Golitsyns' warder, who was supposed also to administer the town, wrote to Streshnev to complain that there was nothing to eat. "The settlement is most wretched, a total of thirty households including crown officials, clerks and the guard. The local people rarely visit the town. They administer justice themselves and allocate the sovereigns' taxes amongst themselves. Only we are in need."

NEW DEPOSITIONS AGAINST GOLITSYN

The Golitsyns did not stay long in Yarensk, either. The case of Shaklovity's accomplices dragged on, there were new depositions and Golitsyn was accused of consorting with magicians. His correspondence with Shaklovity from the time of the first Crimean campaign was discovered and from this correspondence it transpired that he was indeed a *close friend* of Shaklovity and not simply an acquaintance. It was alleged that Golitsyn had taken money from the khan and then retreated from Perekop. Kropotkin was also implicated. Then the most dangerous allegation of all was made. A monk called Joseph alleged that when he was in Yarensk Prince Golitsyn asked him to send a message to Prince Boris that he should take good care of him in case he was needed, because Tsar Peter had only a year to live. This denunciation was pure slander. The monk had never even been to Yarensk but took it into his head to libel Prince Vasily in the hope of winning the favor of Prince Boris!

Golitsyn repudiated the remaining charges. Nonetheless he was transferred to Pustozersk. On the way he wrote a letter to the tsars: "Every step of the way is torment and we have become wanderers in the name of Christ, reduced to penury and forced to sell the shirts off our backs to buy food. The price of grain and other provisions in Pustozersk is very high and we may die of exhaustion and hunger. Merciful great sovereigns! Order that your poor innocent subjects be spared such a wretched plight." The Golitsyns were transferred to the Pinega district and promptly forgotten.[66] Prince Boris, as we shall see shortly, lost his dominant position to the Naryshkins.

INTERROGATION AND EXECUTION OF MEDVEDEV

The fate of a third of Sophia's close associates also was decided, his name inextricably linked with those of Golitsyn and Shaklovity. We saw that the "forest bear,"[67] as Silvester Medvedev was called by his enemies, had managed to escape westwards to the Polish border, but the governor of Dorogobuzh arrested him in the Biziukov monastery together with the notorious Sergeant Gladky and sent them both to the Trinity monastery. Silvester said at his inquisition: "Shaklovity said nothing to me about the tsar's health or about killing him. It was the brigadier Larion Elizarev who told me. He came to see me in tears and said 'A great misfortune has overtaken us and we don't know what to do. Shaklovity summoned me, Andriushka Kondratiev, Aleshka Strizhov and Obroska Petrov, and said that secretly at night we were to kill the boyar Lev Kirillovich Naryshkin and the tsar's carver Prince Boris Golitsyn and others.' I replied that if they obeyed they and Fedka together would perish now and incur eternal damnation. I said to tell Fedka that they could not carry out the deed alone, and did not dare tell anyone else. He himself should tell them. So Larion and his companions told Fedka that they refused to do the deed. Fedka twice told me, Silvester, in confidence. I did not cause dissension in the holy church, and as for the treatises on transubstantiation,[68] which were written by Deacon Afanasy from the Savior cathedral near the palace, the deacon brought a leaflet for me to look at and made two copies of the leaflet. There was nothing against the patriarch in the booklet, it was all against the Greeks. The booklet entitled *Manna* I wrote on the orders of Tsarevna Sophia, and that book was sent to Hetman Ivan Mazepa[69] and to the leading clergy of Ukraine as evidence and with it another Greek book. In Kiev a denunciation of the Greek book was written and sent back by Prince Vasily Golitsyn, as in 1689 he was there on military service. The denunciation made by Filipp Sapogov, to the effect that Shaklovity and I were plotting to murder the patriarch, was a lie. I kept a bodyguard in attendance from Holy Week to prevent the patriarch from banishing me secretly. I also wrote a book of chronicles, beginning from 1682 about the great sovereign lady's government and what happened from that year;[70] this book was copied from the text written by Karion [Istomin]. I made a draft and it was copied out by the deacon Ivashka."

At his confrontation with Sapogov, Medvedev refused to speak. He was defrocked and tortured, given fifteen blows, but still he refused to confess. He confessed to one thing only, that he had said to the musketeers "Never fear, Tsar Peter's side may be in luck for ten days or so, but then the tsarevna's side will gain the upper hand." Shaklovity told him this, having heard it from some holy fool.[71] He admitted to describing the patriarch as poorly educated and ignorant of theology. He also admitted that under the tsarevna's portrait were inscribed the full titles, "all powerful autocrat," seven virtues and a set of verses.[72]

Defrocked and now known as Senka, Medvedev was given over to the church authorities who appointed two admonishers, Archimandrite Ignatius of the New Savior monastery and Sofrony Likhud. Senka repented of heresy and declared his *Manna* to be a fraud. The church council instructed that all copies of *Manna* be burnt and that Medvedev be released from his vows to the church and banished to a monastery under custody. But matters did not end there. After remaining at liberty for some time one of Shaklovity's chief associates, Strizhov, was arrested and testified against Medvedev who he said was associated with some Pole by the name of Silin who practised black magic and had been summoned to Moscow to treat the eyes of Tsar Ivan. Silin for a long time lived at Medvedev's house, where he said he was told that Sophia wanted to marry Golitsyn and to appoint Medvedev to the patriarchate in place of Joachim. Medvedev was subjected to another terrible ordeal by fire and iron, then executed on February 11, 1691.

SOPHIA IS OVERTHROWN AND SENT TO A CONVENT

What was Sophia doing all this time that her supporters' blood was being shed in torture sessions and executions? After Shaklovity, the tsarevna's only hope, had been given up, as insisted upon by the musketeers, her fate was decided. Peter wrote to his elder brother from the Trinity monastery that "by the grace of God the scepter of government was entrusted to us two, as is known to our neighboring fellow sovereigns, but there was never any mention that a third person should rule equally with us. And you know very well how our sister Tsarevna Sophia Alekseevna chose to rule our state by her own will, and how in her rule there was much that was disagreeable to us and burdensome to the people, and how we suffered. And now those miscreants Fedka Shaklovity and his accomplices, unheedful of our favor and in violation of their oath, plotted with other rogues to kill us and our mother, and admitted as much under interrogation and torture. Now, sovereign brother, the time has come for us to rule the realm entrusted to us by God, since we are of age and we must not allow a third party, that shameful person, our sister, to share the title and government with us two males; may you consent, for she chose to interfere in affairs of state and to include herself in titles without our leave and even, as a final insult to us, wished to be crowned with the royal crown. It is disgraceful that in our majority this shameful person should rule the state in our stead. So I declare and beg you, sovereign brother, to give me your paternal permission for our own good and for the pacification of the nation to appoint without consulting with you worthy judges in the chancelleries and to dismiss the unworthy in order to bring tranquillity and joy to our state. And when we are together again all shall be put in order and I am ready, sovereign brother, to respect you like a father."[73]

In this rescript nothing was said about the fate of the deposed regent. But some time later Prince Ivan Borisovich Troekurov arrived in Moscow from the Trinity monastery with orders that Sophia go to a nunnery. After lengthy protests she was forced to comply and went to live in the New convent.

THE DENUNCIATIONS CONTINUE

Sophia was in a nunnery, Golitsyn in exile and Shaklovity in his grave, but still the executioners worked on. Denunciations, torture and execution continued over this same affair. It is not known why the senior table attendant Bezobrazov was forced against his will to become military governor on the Terek. When he was on his way there information turned up from a bondslave about his relations with Shaklovity and various sorcerers, who used their art to bewitch Tsar Peter and Tsaritsa Natalia to show him favor and return him to Moscow. Under torture Bezobrazov and the sorcerers all confessed. Bezobrazov was beheaded and the two sorcerers burned at the stake.

Four year later letters of denunciation were discovered at Beloozero, in which monks of the St. Cyril monastery[74] confessed to terribly immoral conduct, relations with Prince Vasily Golitsyn and wishing to ruin Tsar Peter and his household. At the beginning of 1694 it was revealed that the author of the letters was the monk Ioanniky, in the world Ilarion Semenovich Lopukhin. He admitted that he had written them in the hope of being released from the monastery and defrocked. He was flogged with the knout and banished to Solovki.[75]

THE NEW GOVERNMENT

Sophia was in the convent and Tsar Ivan was, as previously, tsar only in name, occupying the royal throne in ceremonies. Power now passed to Peter alone. But seventeen-year-old Peter was still incapable of governing the realm. He was still completing his education, training himself by means which he himself found and which were in keeping with his character. The young tsar's mind was occupied with thoughts of amusement; the great man came later, and only then were the seeds of great enterprises detected in those adolescent games.

BORIS GOLITSYN'S FEUD WITH THE NARYSHKINS

Who ruled the realm, or who, at least, wielded most influence in the government? At the Trinity monastery, as we have seen, Prince Boris Golitsyn assumed overall command because he was cleverer, bolder, and more energetic than all the rest. Patrick Gordon wrote: "Prince Boris Golitsyn was in charge of everything at Trinity because no one else dared to meddle in what at first appeared to be a ticklish affair." But, as we have seen also, Prince Boris earned the strong disapproval of Tsaritsa Natalia and her relatives by shielding Prince Vasily Golitsyn from the charge of treason. This quarrel with the Naryshkins meant that once the danger was past and with it the need for a man who was capable of governing in a dangerous situation, Prince Boris found upon his return to court in Moscow that the prominence he enjoyed at Trinity had waned and that Lev Kirillovich Naryshkin and his relatives had assumed the leading positions in the administration. Lev Kirillovich took over as director of the Chancellery of Foreign Affairs, the most crucial of the government departments, but he did not assume [Golitsyn's] title of guardian of the royal seal. Prince Boris Golitsyn had to be content with the Chancellery of Kazan.[76] The relatives of the younger tsaritsa [Evdokia] got their share of power in the person of the boyar Peter Abraamovich Lopukhin, who was given the Chancellery of the Royal Household and the Palace Chamber of Justice. The Chancellery of Musketeers went to Prince Ivan Borisovich Troekurov, the Crown Appointments Chancellery to Tikhon Nikitich Streshnev.[77]

In addition to being deprived of his former prominence, Prince Boris Golitsyn also was subjected to major humiliations at court, where he was savagely attacked by the Dolgorukys. In 1691, for example, after they had quarrelled in the palace, Prince Yakov Fedorovich Dolgoruky called him the "great-grandson of a traitor," because during the reign of Dmitry the Pretender[78] his great-grandfather was a preacher at the Yauza gates. The hostility remained undiminished. The following year in Tsar Peter's apartments the Dolgorukys—Prince Yakov Fedorovich and his brother Prince Grigory—attacked Prince Boris, accusing him of ordering his henchman to beat up their brother Prince Boris Dolgoruky. "You drunkard!" shouted the Dolgorukys. "You get together a mob of tipplers like yourself and go off with them, then you fill your henchmen with drink and order them to beat up our brother. You take this inebriated crew to places where they have no business going. You should keep off other people's property; you deserve a knife in you. Why don't you go to see our brother Prince Boris who is waiting for you at the church of the Savior in the palace? If you grab him by the hair he'll cut your insides out, and if you come near us we'll slit your guts and pull them out. We'll knock the booze out of you, you wine-bag. Instead of grabbing our brother by the hair when you got drunk on raw homebrew, you should have knocked your own block off. Why, you'd grab your own father by the beard. Don't set too much store by this affair. Times have changed, you can't order people about with swords." The Dolgorukys were made to pay a fine of over three thousand rubles to compensate the Golitsyns, father and son, for the dishonor suffered. But Prince Boris Golitsyn petitioned that on his deathbed his father had refuted claims for compensation for acts of dishonor and therefore he, Prince Boris, was not pressing a complaint against the Dolgorukys on these grounds.[79]

FRANZ LEFORT

Gordon referred to Lev Naryshkin as the new favorite or new chief minister, contrasting him with the former incumbent, that is, Prince Boris Golitsyn. As it happens, only the second of these designations is correct, for neither Golitsyn nor Naryshkin was Peter's favorite: that honor went to the foreign mercenary, the renowned Franz Lefort.[80]

Opinions about Lefort and his significance are quite varied. Some say that he made himself known to Peter at a very early date and influenced him from an early stage.[81] Others claim that Peter became friendly with Lefort no earlier than August 1689 when Lefort was one of the first foreigners to report to the Trinity monastery, where he declared his support for Peter. Some who are in sympathy with the cause of reform credit Lefort with exerting a beneficial influence on Peter by awakening the genius in him, whilst others regard Peter's meeting with Lefort and his attachment to him as a misfortune, for Lefort contemptuously dismissed Russian customs whilst praising to the skies all things foreign. Others deny that Lefort had any influence on Peter at all.

Establishing exactly when Lefort became friendly with Peter is not important. Whenever it occurred, what is important are its consequences.

Franz Lefort
Contemporary Engraving

All agree on one thing: that Peter's affection for Lefort was stronger than for anyone else, and that is enough. The important question is: what sort of a man was Lefort? We saw earlier how Russians had turned towards the West and in so doing had encountered the West on their own doorstep, in the Foreign Quarter. The young tsar, aflame with unquenched thirst for knowledge, was already beginning to create something new and to make the acquaintance of men who had been summoned precisely in order to teach Russians essential skills and to initiate what the Russians were incapable of setting up by themselves. Naturally the tsar had to turn to men such as these. But it was not enough that one taught him various aspects of mathematics, or another built small boats for him. Among the foreigners he found a man for whom he formed a strong attachment and from whom he became inseparable. That man was Lefort.

Lefort was a characteristic and shining example of the people who inhabited the Foreign Quarter. He had no solid education and was incapable of instructing Peter in any skill or trade, for he himself was master of none, but he was a man of the world, unusually lively, agile, cheerful, open and likeable, the life and soul of the party, brilliant at organizing parties. A foreigner might teach Peter geometry or demonstrate the use of the astrolabe but if he did no more than that he was unlikely to influence his famous pupil. Only a man with the character of Lefort who knew how to make himself an indispensable companion and friend to the young tsar could really exert powerful influence. This influence did not make itself felt in the sphere of domestic politics, for Lefort by reason of his character did not interfere in this area. It was felt elsewhere. It was Lefort, for example, who encouraged Peter to undertake the campaign to Azov [in 1695] and who persuaded him to travel abroad. It was on his prompting that the tsar allowed free entry and exit to foreigners. It is evident that the bent of Peter's reforming activities was determined ultimately in the period of his close acquaintance with Lefort, namely from 1690 to his return from abroad [in 1698]. In that period he left Moscow for the Foreign Quarter and the Foreign Quarter for Western Europe. And in the absence of irrefutable evidence, it is impossible to subscribe to the theory that Peter regarded Lefort merely as a convivial companion for comradely chats, indispensable as a peerless master of ceremonies.

The fact that Peter had a high regard for Lefort is demonstrated by Lefort's appointment as one of the commanders in the Azov campaign, as an admiral and as head of the embassy to Western Europe. If Peter had regarded Lefort merely as a convivial companion at parties he would have made him not an admiral or an ambassador but a patriarch of Kokui,[82] like Zotov. It may be argued that Peter was mistaken about the abilities of Lefort, who was a mediocre commander on both land and sea. But the mistake is itself instructive, for it shows what an exaggerated opinion Peter had of Lefort and how easily he fell under his sway, hardly surprising when we recall Peter's age at the time. The Peter of 1690 was not the Peter the Great of 1709 or 1721. The young Peter attached himself to the foreigner Lefort and accorded him an important position in the realm, whereas the mature Peter had a rule not to raise foreigners to leading offices of state.

II

MOCK BATTLES AND UKRAINIAN AFFAIRS
1690-1694

PETER'S MOCK BATTLES

Lefort did not interfere in internal government affairs, nor did the tsar himself, leaving all that to Lev Naryshkin and his assistants. Young Peter was engaged in his mock battles as before, and sometimes they cost him dear. On July 2, 1690, for example, during the storming of Semenovskoe court, his face was singed. On September 4 a mock battle was staged near Preobrazhenskoe. The best musketeer regiment, the bodyguard composed of cavalry and foot, was to fight the play regiments, the Semenovskoe foot and the mounted grooms. Simultaneously two regiments of musketeers were to fight each other. They fought until dusk, and many were wounded or received powder burns. In October 1691 there was "a great and fearful battle with Generalissimus Friedrich Romodanovsky,[1] who held the capital city of Pressburg. The cavalry of Captain *Peter Alekseev*[2] distinguished themselves, as did the captain himself, by taking the enemy generalissimus prisoner." The battle was like the day of judgement. The privy table attendant Ivan Dmitrievich Dolgoruky "as a result of his severe wounds and by the will of God went to his eternal rest, to the bosom of Adam, where in time we shall all go," Peter wrote.

In the fall of 1694 battles were staged on a lavish scale, including the famous Kozhukhovo manoeuvres[3] near the village of Kozhukhovo not far from the Simonov monastery. The Russian army was led by the old generalissimus Prince Fedor Yurievich Romodanovsky, who had command of the play regiments—the Preobrazhenskoe and Semenovskoe, the Lefort and Butyrki select infantry regiments, three companies of grenadiers, eight select companies of cavalry, two companies of auxiliaries under the command of Nakhalov and Naletov and twenty companies of table attendants. The opposing side was commanded by the mock "king of Poland," Ivan Ivanovich Buturlin, with regiments of musketeers, and companies of secretaries and clerks, 7,500 men in all. The king defended an unnamed fortress, but Romodanovsky besieged and, naturally, captured it. Bombardier Peter Alekseev distinguished himself in this battle too, taking prisoner a musketeer colonel. After losing the fortress the Polish king ensconced himself in a fortified camp and stubbornly beat off the attack, but in the end had to surrender. This mock battle, too, had its casualties and even deaths.

Mock battles on land were accompanied by the same on water. The tsar built a yacht with his own hands and launched it on the Moscow river in the fall of 1691. Work continued in the wharfs at Pereiaslav, and the tsar was so engrossed in it that in February 1692 Lev Naryshkin and Boris Golitsyn went to Pereiaslav to try to persuade him to come to Moscow to receive a Persian delegation. On May 1 the first ship was launched on the lake. In July the whole court went to Pereiaslav and stayed there until September. Tsaritsa Natalia, unable to keep her son in Moscow, had herself to travel to the site of his favorite pastimes.

But it was still difficult for the mother to keep track of her warrior son, who sought ever broader expanses of water "commensurate with his desire." Pereiaslav soon began to seem cramped. He looked at Lake Kubensk, but that was too small also. An irresistible force drew him to the sea. He asked his mother's blessing to go but was refused. Finally "in view of his great wish and importunate desire" she had to let him go, exacting a promise that he would not go to sea, only look at the ships. In July 1693 the tsar set off northwards for Archangel with a large retinue. One glimpse of the sea, and his promise to his mother was forgotten. He went to sea to escort foreign ships. His mother sent one letter after another begging him to return. "My light, my joy, I am so sad that I can't see you. I have written to you, my hope, asking when I might expect you back and you, my light, have caused me grief by not writing anything on the subject. I beg you, be merciful to her who bore you and come back without delay. It makes me unbearably sad that you are such a long way off. May God's mercy keep you, my light, and I entrust you, our common hope, to the immaculate Mother of God—may she preserve you."

"At the moment I can't write anything definite (about my return) as I am waiting for some ships to arrive," Peter replied. "No one is sure when they are coming but it should be soon. As soon as they do, to make amends I shall travel day and night to get back. I ask one thing—why are you so worried about me? You wrote that you had entrusted me to the care of the Mother of God. With such a protectress why be worried? By your prayers and representations the Lord preserves not me alone but the whole world. I ask your blessing. Your unworthy Petrushka."

Peter writes that he had been to sea: his promise had been broken and there was a new reason for his mother to worry and to urge her son to come home. "As a favor to me, my light, come home without delay. I'm so very sad that I can't see you, my light and joy. You wrote that you intend to await the arrival of all the ships, but you have seen the ones that have arrived already, so why do you have to wait for the rest to come in? Don't scorn my request. You write in your letter that you have been to sea even though you promised me that you wouldn't."

But her son's main concern was how to travel even further afield the following year. He built a wharf at Archangel, laid the keel of a ship and ordered another from Holland. On religious festivals he went to church; he read the Acts of the Apostles and sang with the

choristers in the choir stalls. He had dinner with Archbishop
Afanasius of Kholmogory with whom he had conversations about
navigating the seas and rivers with ships and other craft. He also
dined with foreign merchants and ships' captains who were able to
pass on much interesting information.

After staging a firework display, on September 19, 1693 Peter
left Archangel for Moscow. Here he worked all fall on preparations
for a new naval campaign and adopted the title of skipper to go with
that of bombardier. This time there were to be no obstacles to the
voyage. On January 25, 1694 Tsaritsa Natalia died in her forty-
second year after a five-day illness. Peter mourned his mother's
death deeply, wrote an eyewitness. On the evening after the funeral,
which took place on January 26, the brothers and relations of the
deceased came to visit the tsar, which was cause for further deep
grieving. But two days later, on the 28th, Peter attended a banquet
at Lefort's, and was there again the next day. Lefort's feasts were
not the only thing to provide consolation in his grief. "Fedor
Matveevich," he wrote to Apraksin,[4] governor of the Dvina, "It is
hard for me to tell you how bereft and sad I feel; my hand is
incapable of describing it fully or my heart of expressing it. So, like
Noah, a little rested from my misfortune and leaving behind what
cannot be restored, I write of what is alive." This consisted of
making all necessary preparations for building a new ship at
Archangel.

On May 1 Peter embarked upon his second campaign at sea,
which bore the same "play" character as his land campaigns. The
famous generalissimus Fedor Romodanovsky, "a man bold in
warfare, and even more so on the ocean wide," as Peter joked, was
appointed admiral. The vice-admiral was the former "King of
Poland" Ivan Buturlin, and Gordon was made rear-admiral. The first
thing that Peter did on reaching Archangel was to launch the ship
he had commissioned the previous year. Then the tsar set sail on
the yacht St. Peter for the Solovki islands. On the way a terrible
storm blew up and shipwreck seemed inevitable. Peter even received
the sacraments from Archbishop Afanasius, who was in attendance.
Fortunately a skilled pilot was found, one Anton Timofeev, who
managed to bring the ship into the Bay of Unsk. They rested at
anchor near the Pertomin monastery. With his own hands Peter made

a cross three and a half feet in height and planted it on the spot
where he had come ashore. It bore the Dutch inscription "This cross
was made by skipper Peter in the summer of 1694."

After visiting the Solovetsk monastery Peter returned to
Archangel where the ship which in the meantime had been launched
was fitted, armed and named St. Paul. They eagerly awaited the
arrival of the ship ordered in Holland, which finally docked—the
forty-four-gun frigate Santa Profeetie. The joy of receiving this
treasure was marked by great feasting. "What we long desired has
been accomplished," wrote Peter to his relatives in Moscow. "I'll
write more by the next post, but now I'm enjoying myself so much
that it's inconvenient to write more, and anyway I can't. On
occasions like these you have to contend with Bacchus, who covers
the eyes of those who would like to write with his foliage." When
the feasting was over the tsar and his fleet, consisting of three
vessels, set sail to escort some foreign ships. They sailed as far as
Sviatoi Nos, the furthermost point on the White sea. At the
beginning of September Peter was back in Moscow.

THE JOLLY COMPANY

As well as these amusements, another of the young Peter's favorite
pastimes was making and detonating fireworks. In all these
amusements his company of friends took part, that renowned warrior
band assembled from people of various social classes and different
origins, comrades in the name of their commander, bombardier and
skipper. Peter, notwithstanding his youth and the playful character
of his occupations, succeeded in attracting the best elements in the
society around him, the best people distinguished by a variety of
talents. With regard to these talents we should not be put off by
various foreign accounts which claimed that some of Peter's
associates had little knowledge of the business with which they were
entrusted. It would be odd to imagine that Peter had at his disposal
a great number of men of genius who by some miracle were fully
equipped for the tasks in hand. If Peter had wished to surround
himself only with people who were fully trained he would have had
to surround himself exclusively with foreigners, setting all Russians
aside. But this was precisely what he wished to avoid, and so he
delegated all the most important tasks to Russians who, even if they

were not fully trained, were capable men. He was loth to entrust these new tasks to foreign hands: it would have made life easy for him, but was not in Russia's best interests. He needed to train Russian hands to tackle vital new tasks. But of course at the outset foreigners, who were to apply their knowledge in the service of the new cause, were essential and in Peter's company we find them alongside Russians, Russified and non-Russified; alongside Romodanovsky, Pleshcheev, Streshnev, Apraksin, Golovkin, Trubetskoy, Kurakin, Repnin, Buturlin, Matveev and Golovin[5] we find Vinius, Weide, Crevet and Bruce."[6]

Men who knew foreign languages, a powerful means for acquiring knowledge, came to prominence, and those of them who were versatile and energetic and capable of applying their knowledge, were called up by Peter. One of the men who became closest to him was Conciliar Secretary Andrei Andreevich Vinius. The son of the well-known Dutch émigré Andrew Denisov Vinius, Andrei was born in Russia; he was Russified, an Orthodox Christian, and distinguished from Russians only by his education. In Tsar Alexis's reign he was famed as the translator of books and the compiler of a short geography. Now in his old age Vinius responded to the summons of the young reformer with a wide range of activities remarkable for a man of his years. Crevet, a translator of English in the Chancellery of Foreign Affairs, was equally active. In the chancellery there was another translator by the name of Shafirov, the future vice-chancellor.[7] There was much to be done but too few hands to do it, and the members of the warrior band were obliged to tackle many different tasks, following the example of their leader—bombardier, skipper and ship's carpenter.

After the mock battles of Mars and Neptune the warriors relaxed in merry feasting, in a fierce battle between the foreign Bacchus and their own homespun John Barleycorn.[8] In the land and naval campaigns Fedor Romodanovsky was general and admiral, with Peter as captain, bombardier or skipper, but at feasts the company was headed by Nikita Zotov, "all-jesting father Ioannikity, the patriarch of Pressburg, Kokui and All the Yauza." Here too Peter was just a deacon. In the Yuletide season the company went out to praise Christ.[9] The tsar went round visiting the boyars and courtiers, and Zotov visited the merchants. In January 1694 there was a big celebration: the jester Yakov Turgenev was married to a secretary's widow; he was followed in procession by boyars, lords-in-waiting, gentlemen of the council and all ranks of courtiers, mounted on bulls, goats, pigs and dogs, and they wore comic costumes of bast[10] sacks and bast hats, coarse linen kaftans, hung with cats' paws, and kaftans of various colors, hung with squirrels' tails, straw boots, mouse-fur gauntlets and hats made of bast strips. Turgenev and his wife rode in the best royal velvet-upholstered carriage, followed on foot by members of the Trubetskoy, Sheremetev, Golitsyn and Gagin clans in velvet kaftans. Yakov was married in a tent in a field between Preobrazhenskoe and Semenovskoe, and the great banquet lasted for three days.

THE STATE OF SOCIETY

While the young tsar was amusing himself with his jolly band, elsewhere in society events were taking place which on the one hand help to explain the band's behavior, and on the other indicate how vitally that society was in need of a reform which could not be achieved with its own internal resources. The following chronicle of events makes sorry reading.

In 1693 Tatiana, the wardrobe mistress of Tsarevich Alexis,[11] widow of the table attendant Vsevolozhsky, submitted a complaint that in the home of the boyar Kondraty Fomich Naryshkin in the presence of the boyar and other witnesses the table attendant Afanasy Korovaev had called her a thief. The witnesses testified: Korovaev said that Vsevolozhskaia was a thief, and if she came to his house as she had to Stepan Fefilatiev's he would cut her down. "Now even the womenfolk are going out committing robberies!" said Korovaev. When Naryshkin asked him which women he meant, he replied that the princess of Macedonia[12] had been led out to the block for robbery, and that the widow Tatiana had gone to Fefilatiev's house with the purpose of setting fire to it. Korovaev testified that he had been at Naryshkin's to appeal on behalf of his relative Stepan Fefilatiev over the dispute with Vsevolozhskaia. Tatiana was compensated for dishonor under the 1649 Code of Laws.[13]

Prince Alexander Krupsky was flogged with the knout for murdering his wife. In 1694 the table attendants Vladimir and his brother Vasily Sheremetev appeared on a charge of robbery on the testimony of informers. At the trial Prince Ivan Ukhtomsky, Lev and Grigory Polzikov and Leonty Shenshin were interrogated under torture; under torture the informers accused them of coming to Moscow in broad daylight to attack some peasants in the artisans' quarter and loot their homes; they committed acts of murder and called themselves lords. The Sheremetevs were released on bail and placed in the custody of the boyar Peter Vasilievich Sheremetev and after that the informers were executed. The same year Fedor Dashkov committed treason by attempting to enter the service of the king of Poland. He was arrested at the border, interrogated and accused of unlawful flight. He was brought in irons from Smolensk to the Chancellery of Foreign Affairs in Moscow, but there he was released because he gave Conciliar Secretary Emelian Ukraintsev two hundred gold pieces.

In 1693 a royal rescript was sent to the governor of Alatyr ordering him to send musketeers to the Pechersk hermitage for the protection of pilgrims against robbers. "Each year just before the feast of the miracle-working icon of Our Lady of Kazan on July 8 there is a pilgrimage to that monastery, and at that time both the monks and the pilgrims are subject to assault and robbery by thieves and highwaymen, and in previous years the robbers smashed up the Pechersk hermitage on more than one occasion." That same year in Solvychegodsk on the orders of the great sovereigns the former elder of Pachezersk district, the peasant Stepan Pustynnikov, was sentenced to be beaten without mercy with rods on the square in front of the local government office with his shirt removed. This was because when he was district elder for just a short time on the recommendation of men of inferior rank, without the authority of the salt miners[14] in the town and rural communities, he petitioned the great sovereigns, claiming to speak with the authority of the whole community, to ask for Maksimka and Fedka Pivovarov to be restored to the posts of clerk in the local government office. He, Stepan, signed the petition twice: above he signed himself as the elder Stenka Pustynnikov and a second time instead of the delegate Kozyrev he signed himself as Stenka Fedorov, peasant of Pachezersk district. In addition he had sent a petition which purported to be from the whole community to the distinguished personage Grigory Dmitrievich Stroganov; he wrote a petition in which he called the archimandrite of the Presentation monastery a liar, schemer and self-willed man, and said that this was causing discord in the community. He had the delegates, artisans and district people put their signatures to his election and to the petitions, but the artisans and the peasants of the community failed to elect him elder at the commune council and the artisans' delegate and the delegates of the community did not have him elected.

PATRIARCHS JOACHIM AND ADRIAN

People realized that things were going badly and had to change, but how were the ills to be cured? Opinions were divided. Some argued that it was better in foreign lands and that they should look there. Others repeated that the first task was to expel the Germans who were the source of all evil. This latter view was shared, as we have seen, by Patriarch Joachim. He was triumphant about the overthrow of Sophia. His enemy Medvedev was defrocked, charged with heresy and executed as a traitor, and the clergy of Little Russia hastened to give assurances that they were in complete accord with his holiness. To Lazar Baranovich,[15] who pleaded Little Russian practice as an excuse for not replying, the patriarch sent the following missive: "We wrote to you hoping to be notified of your agreement and accord with the holy eastern church and with us, your father and archpastor; but you, treating us with contempt and belittling us, your father and archpastor, have hardly written a word for some time, which is not what one would expect of one so wise. We asked you about one thing and you replied about another. We asked you to respond about the East and you, jumping to the opposite side, speak of the West; even a simple man would be ashamed to speak thus. Instead of opposing us with practices handed down by the holy Church fathers you go on about your outdated practice and about novelties lurking undetected in your newly compiled books. Give us an honest reply as soon as possible and don't show your contempt and obstinacy. Or perhaps you alone stand outside the authority invested in us? Metropolitan Gedeon [of Kiev] and Archimandrite Varlaam send us their agreement and accord on all points. Do not dare to officiate until you report to us and until the investigation into the case is completed. Acknowledge your leader and father, learn to be less disdainful and disobedient to your archpastor and the holy eastern church. If you are in agreement with the holy eastern church and declare your agreement and accord at once, you may officiate without restriction."

Now that Prince Vasily Golitsyn, the protector of Jesuits,[16] was in exile, the patriarch and all the consecrated assembly made the following appeal: "The Jesuits have lived in Moscow for a long time with nothing to do, but previously in the time of your royal ancestors the Roman Jesuits never visited the Muscovite realm and never lived here. But now that they reside here those Jesuits have done much that is offensive to the holy apostolic church and its doctrine by distributing printed sheets and images on canvas and carved of bone, and other artful devices. The holy apostolic eastern church is in serious disagreement with the western Roman Catholic church. On account of the aforementioned abuses the great sovereigns ought not to allow the Jesuits to reside in the Muscovite realm." The great sovereigns decreed: "The Jesuits (David and Tobias)[17] are to be granted permission to leave Moscow and given money and transport to the Lithuanian border."

The Jesuits begged to be allowed to report the circumstances of their expulsion to the Austrian emperor and to be given time to sell their home in the Foreign Quarter which had been bought with funds from the emperor's treasury. They would then make arrangements for their departure. They were not allowed to communicate with the emperor and were given only two days to prepare for their journey. In order to prevent Jesuits gaining access to Russia in the future an order was issued: "The great sovereigns agree that one or two priests may come to Moscow because of their brotherly friendship for his imperial majesty but only on the understanding that while resident in Moscow those priests do not meddle in affairs which do not concern them or in other people's business, and do nothing which might be contrary to the Russo-Greek faith, neither converting Russians or visiting Russian homes. They are allowed to conduct services in the homes of officers of the Catholic faith. They are not allowed to write or send by post any messages or subversive letters to other countries. No Jesuits shall reside in Moscow posing as priests and assuming their garb, as they were supposed to be secular clergy and not Jesuits. But if the supposed clergymen residing in Moscow turn out to be Jesuits, they are to be expelled forthwith, along with any other clergy, and not be allowed to reside in Moscow in the future."

In his triumph over Medvedev and the Jesuits Joachim was not likely to become more lenient to foreign servicemen, to whom he was always strongly opposed. On February 28, 1690, to mark the occasion of the birth of Tsarevich Alexis, the most distinguished foreigners were to have dined at the royal table, but the patriarch insisted that they not be present, and this at a time when the young tsar and his magnates could not manage without foreigners and constantly visited them and invited them to their own homes. Before his death, in March 1690, Joachim composed a testament in which he exhorted the sovereigns not to allow Orthodox Christians to become friendly with foreign heretics, Latins, Lutherans, Calvinists and godless Tatars and not to allow men of other faiths to build their prayer houses in Russia and to demolish those which had been built. The damned heretics should be banned from becoming officers in the army and throughout the realm. "What aid can they give to the Orthodox troops? Rather they arouse the wrath of God. When Orthodox Christians pray, heretics sleep; when Christians ask for the help of the Mother of God and all the saints, heretics laugh at them; Christians fast, but heretics never. Wolves are commanding lambs. By the grace of God the Russian realm has ample pious men, skilled in the arts of war. Again I repeat that foreign heretics not be allowed to build their Roman churches, Lutheran chapels and Tatar mosques,[18] nor should Latin and foreign customs be introduced, or changes in dress after the foreign fashion. I am surprised at courtiers and officials of the tsar's council who have been on embassies to other lands and seen that all countries have their own manners and customs in dress and behavior and maintain their own ways and do not accept alien ones. Give no merit to men of other faiths and do not allow them to build their places of worship. Where in any of the German states can there be found a church of the true piety?"

Only three months after Joachim's death, in July 1690, did the church council begin to deliberate on the election of his successor. The higher clergy indicated their preference for Markell, metropolitan of Pskov, a learned and educated man, but the lower clergy opposed Markell and supported Adrian, metropolitan of

Kazan. Peter joined the higher clergy in their support of Markell but Tsaritsa Natalia with archimandrites and abbots of monasteries and the parish clergy were in favor of Adrian.[19] Markell's enemies disliked his erudition and said that a learned patriarch would show favor towards the non-Orthodox. One archimandrite presented the tsaritsa with an essay in which he accused Markell of heresy. Markell's enemies won the day and Adrian was made patriarch.

The new patriarch had to contend with a terrible evil in the shape of disorders in family life created by bad relations between the sexes, which stemmed from the method of arranging marriages. In November 1693 he issued an edict: "Priests officiating at weddings are failing to inquire about the agreement of bride and groom and neglect this matter with the result that a great many people who do not wish to wed and do not love each other are being married. From the start husband and wife get on badly and hate each other and children are not born; this is highly sinful and unlawful. The great lord has indicated that henceforth priests are to make a point of questioning grooms and brides coming to be married and asking firmly whether they are marrying for love and whether they have both agreed to be married, and are not being forced to do so against their will. If a female, a virgin, is too bashful to speak then her parents should be questioned, preferably her mother, and if there is no mother, her sister. And if someone, especially a virgin, refuses to speak or makes some other sign such as turning away her face from her fiancé, spitting or pushing him away, they should not be married unless they both declare themselves to be in complete agreement." Naturally the methods proposed in the edict could not eradicate or attenuate this evil; it seemed strange to question the father and mother when they were the very ones who arranged the marriages; but this edict is very important in that it serves as an introduction to Peter's subsequent measures on marriages.

The secular administration was obliged to turn its attention to irregularities being indulged in by monks and nuns, priests and deacons of no *fixed abode*. In March 1694 a personal edict was issued: "Itinerant monks and nuns in the Kremlin, Kitay Quarter, Earthwork Quarter and also itinerant priests and deacons are behaving in a scandalous and insincere manner, as are vagrants who bind up their arms or legs, or veil or clutch their eyes and pretend

to be blind or lame and by means of dissimulation and cunning beg
for alms, but when examined are found to be quite healthy. Such
monks and nuns and priests and deacons shall be arrested and taken
to the Chancellery of Musketeers, and from there to the Patriarchal
Chancellery to prevent homeless monks and nuns, priests and
deacons henceforth from wandering round the streets and going
round the taverns." Before this Metropolitan Cornelius of Novgorod
ordered his clerks and hired men to apprehend persons of clerical
rank at ale houses and also anyone found inebriated on the streets
and to bring them to the metropolitan's office and not to allow them
to be bailed out, neither to accept bribes from them, and not to let
them go.

OLD BELIEVERS

The struggle with the Old Believers continued as fiercely as ever.
We saw how schismatic cossacks left the Don for the Agrakhan river
in the territories of the shevkal of Tarkov.[20] At the beginning of
1691 the servitor Basov was sent there with a summons. When in
the middle of March he arrived on the Don and demanded that the
local cossacks supply him with an escort and let him go on to
Agrakhan, they replied: "We can't allow you to go because we have
already sent messengers to the dissenters with the tsar's letter and
they killed one envoy and sent two others back to the Don with
orders that we shouldn't send any more messengers with letters from
the tsar or from the cossack host. If we did, they would kill them."
They sent to Moscow for the sovereigns' instructions. Instructions
came: Basov was to go to the Terek to see the widow of Prince
Aleguk Sungenevich Cherkassky, Princess Tauka Saltanobekovna,
and to do as she told him. Basov took with him three cossacks from
the Don and went to see Princess Tauka by way of Tsaritsyn,
Astrakhan and the Terek and from the Terek reached the camps of
Princess Tauka. Having heard what was going on the princess sent
word to the camps to the shevkal's brother Alibek to come to see
her. Alibek came and Tauka told him to take Basov and the cossacks
to his brother Shevkal and try to persuade him to hand back to the
tsars the fugitive dissident cossacks from the Don. They went to
see Shevkal. When he had listened to what Basov had to say he
replied "The cossacks came to me from the Don of their own free

will, and live in my domains of their own free will. I did not send for them and I cannot send them back against their will, because that is not how we do things. I honor them as my guests. I shall tell them that they ought to expiate their guilt to the great sovereigns and return to their former abodes on the Don, and assure them of their sovereign's favor as best I can, but I'm not sure whether they will pay any attention or return to the Don. If they agree to return I shall not detain them, I'll release them immediately; but don't you go to see them or they'll kill you. Let me deal with them."

First the shevkal sent a cossack lieutenant to the dissenters. The lieutenant returned with the reply that the cossacks refused to see Basov. If he went, he would be killed. The second time the shevkal sent his brother Alibek, who brought back a more detailed reply from the dissenters. "From now on there's no point in sending messengers to us from Moscow and the Don and losing men for nothing. We are happy here and free. Shevkal does not persecute our faith; we live as we like; we keep our faith each as best he can; we want for nothing so what's the good of returning to our former homes? We know what will be waiting for us there!"

Some time later the dissenters sent three men to see the shevkal. They had a long session with him, then had a meeting with Basov. The latter did his utmost to reassure them, assured them of the tsar's favor and gave them the royal rescript. But the dissenters refused to accept the rescript and said, "Your tsars lied to Shevkal about the allowance, they didn't send what was promised. They're even more likely to lie to us. Even if they sent troops to attack us we shall immediately be notified by the foreigners in Astrakhan, and when we get word we shall go to join the khan in Great Kabarda; no one will do anything to us there." Basov learned that the reason Shevkal was unwilling to hand over the dissenters was because he was carrying out raids with them, sending his men with them to engage in piracy and taking half the booty for himself.

At the beginning of 1693 Semyon Saratovets, the ataman of the cossack Old Believers, appeared before the khan of the Crimea with seven men to make a complaint against the Kumyks, the khan's subjects, who that fall had attacked the cossacks and taken two hundred and fifty women and children prisoner. In addition they had stolen all the booty the dissenters had taken after sinking two Persian ships. The cossacks asked the khan for compensation and also to indicate a place where they might settle on the river Kuma as they no longer wished to live among the Kumyks and the Cherkassians. At the khan's council it was ordered that all the cossacks' requests be met, and the khan promised also to give them two cannon with ammunition. At that time the Russian messenger Aitemirov was living in the Crimea. At his meeting with Saratovets his interpreter asked him: "Why have you forgotten the sovereigns' favor to you and abandoned Christianity, what good do you seek for yourself amongst Muslims?" Saratovets replied "How are we supposed to live on the Don? The old faith is being destroyed and the new one maintained, and they no longer make the sign of the cross[21] like they used to, and for the sake of this new faith they removed some of our best service men from the Don to Moscow, Kirey Matveev and his comrades, and executed them for some unknown crime, and for that reason we cannot live on the Don. We'll see how the Tatar law works here and what they give us. If the Tatars do us no good we know the way back to the Don and hope that the great sovereigns will give orders that we be allowed back."

Evidently the dissenters were satisfied, for in June 1693 the governor of Krasnoiarsk notified the governor of Astrakhan that on June 6 armed bandits had ridden down unannounced from the camp, a hundred or more, and attacked the town, and the battle with these bandits went on a long time. There were Old Believer cossacks amongst the bandits. The governor of Astrakhan replied to the governor of Krasnoiarsk that Ataman Frol Minaev had written from the Don that two prisoners had come to their camp from beyond the Kuban and told them that dissenter cossack bandits who lived beyond the Kuban were preparing to link up with the murzas [chieftains] of the Crimea and Edisan in a great mob and make bandit raids on the Tsaritsyn defense line in the direction of the Volga, on the fishing crews and on Cherny Yar.

There was discomforting news from the north, too. In March 1690 in Ustiug district in the Cherevkov rural district more that a hundred Old Believers, men, women and babes, burned themselves to death. On July 21, 1693 dissenters, unknown to people and residents, forced their way into the Pudozh churchyard, entered the church, rang the bells, took the church from the priests and ensconced themselves. They attacked the priests, looted their homes and destroyed them. The dissenters numbered about two hundred or more, and included a monk and many deacons. One was called Vasily Emelianov, whom the others called their teacher. The dissenters climbed the domes of the church, and washed the crosses on top and the icons inside the church with water. While all this was happening three women seemed to have a fit, and when they came round said that Vasily Emelianov ought to officiate in the church with his helpers and the priests be rejected. On the tsars' orders the military governors of Olonets sent a musketeer captain and a secretary to deal with the dissenters. The envoys, learning that the dissenters had ensconced themselves in four huts in the village of Strokinaia set off with witnesses to try to persuade them to repent. But the dissenters responded with a stream of abuse and blasphemed greatly against the church and the four-pointed cross.[22] The musketeers surrounded the huts and tried to take the dissenters alive, but they fired back. The musketeers started to cut down the outer walls, then the dissenters set fire to the huts and were all burnt to a cinder.

In the Olonets district the famous Vyg monastery was founded, the beginnings of which are recounted by the peasant Terenty Artemev from the Shuia churchyard in Munozero rural district. "The peasant Mitroshka Terentev from our district came to visit his sister in our village of Ek-navolok and recognising me he tried to talk me into joining the Old Believers in the forests beyond Lake Olonets. I agreed and went with him to join the dissenters. And some of his friends also came with us. Five of us arrived at the Shuia churchyard on the estates of the Tikhvin monastery for the feast of the Annunciation, and lived in the village at Khoshozero for two weeks during the time when roads were impassable. We stayed with Mitroshka's confederates, and the peasants of the Shuia parish came to consult Mitroshka about the schism and decided to go into the forest to form an Old Believer community. After we lived there two weeks we made our way over the ice across Lake Onega on skis and reached the bank where the quay was and headed for the forests to the east, but the road was passable only on foot. Only with great difficulty could one pass on horseback because of the bogs, marshes and forests. On White Lake [Beloozero] Mitroshka had built a cell where he lived with about a dozen schismatics from various places. From Mitroshka's cell to Upper Vyg it was fifteen versts on foot through wild forests, bogs and marshes, but impassable on horseback. Along that river about ten cells were built where the dissenter leader Kornily, a fugitive monk from Solovetsk, lived with his friends and confederates. This monk was short in stature, graying and elderly. He had been joined by about a hundred dissenters, men, women, girls and elderly nuns. The cells were built along the Vyg river on individual sites with about half a verst or more separating them. On the river opposite the cells a mill had been constructed. There were no weapons or ammunition in the cells. They have small outhouses built on stilts attached for storing grain. They plow without horses, loosening the soil with iron staves."

"When I was there people from the other cells used to visit the monk to make confession, and he heard their confession and administered the sacraments. I saw how he conducted communion: he took red whortleberries and white rye or wheat flour, mixed them together and used them as sacraments. When I was staying at that refuge in the forest I learned that there is an Old Believer settlement further upstream on the river Vyg. The leader is the former church sexton Danila Nikulin. A great many people have joined him and the numbers continue to increase. Danila has a large cell fitted with windows behind which they can defend themselves from posses. Three small cannon were brought from the sea, arquebuses, pikes and powder. They travel round the markets buying up weapons. They plow the fields using horses and catch fish on the wild lakes."

DECLINE OF MORALS

The Old Believers were not the church's only enemies. It had others who did not flee to the forests or the steppe but declared their views quite openly in the capital without fear of being imprisoned or burnt at the stake. A curious sermon had come down to us from the time in question delivered by the patriarch on the feast of St. Alexis the Metropolitan[23] before one of the campaigns against the Turks. Taking up arms against the old vice of drunkenness the preacher also spoke out against new sins. "There are those who deride not only the other legitimate fasts but even hold in contempt the major forty-day Easter fast. Men, women, youths, even members of the priesthood keep on drinking. They are drunk with wine, tobacco and all sorts of beverages without ever being replete, and not only do they devour forbidden foods but they devour each other with rage and envy, kill and rob, inflict injustices and insults. The old saying—that one drunk causes everybody grief—holds true. Measure in everything prompts a man to do good deeds, intemperate use not only of harmful and vile tobacco but also of Rhine wine leads to ruin. Now both the well-born and common folk, even youths boast about drunkenness, shamelessly telling each other how on such and such an occasion I was drunk and overslept so I missed the church service on the Lord's feastday. It's not only in their drunken and nocturnal revelries that people show their ignorance. Being unaware of the goodly devout rites of the holy church and not asking others about them, they consider themselves to be wise, but in fact they have been made simple-minded by the tobacco pipes and wicked words of the Lutherans, Calvinists and other heretics. Turning aside from the path of their fathers, they ask why does the Church do things this way when there is no point in it? It was thought up by a man and we can live without it. These people scarcely know the names of the holy books or the alphabet, but already they are telling bishops and priests what to do, running monasteries, trying to order everyone about and organizing offices in church and state. Heretics and dissenters ask: what's the use of these consecrations, memorials for departed souls, prayers to God, the Mother of God and the Holy Saints?"

At the Zaikonospassk monastery the learned monks Ioanniky and Sofrony Likhud,[24] summoned to defend the church, were teaching rhetoric in Greek and Latin and logic according to the system of Aristotle. But these activities were interrupted by an embarrassing incident. Ioanniky had a son, Nikolay, who in Moscow bore the title of prince although he was more commonly known as the "teacher's son." This Nikolay struck up a relationship with Maria Selifontova, the daughter of one of the grooms from outside the palace. He abducted her, dressed her in male attire, took her to the school and locked her in a store-room. Then he rented quarters for her where she was held under the custody of his slave and his wife. He told her that he was going to dress her in men's clothes and fit her with false hair then take her to the school and have her taught Greek while posing as his nephew. Maria Selifontova didn't think much of this proposal. She was particularly displeased when Nikolay announced his intention of taking her to Venice or marrying her off to one of his relatives and threatened to kill her if she resisted. Maria managed to win the slave who was guarding her over to her side and through him got a message to her father. Her father hastened to her aid and "extricated her with the help of musketeers," although he earlier looked favorably upon his daughter's behavior.

When Maria told her story in the Chancellery of Crown Appointments they sent men to the school to arrest Nikolay Likhud and bring him in for questioning. Clerks and musketeers from the chancellery set off for Nikolsky Street. The clerks posted musketeers at the gates and then went in to issue the summons to the teachers. They had arrested Nikolay and were escorting him along the upper passageway when suddenly monks and students ran out of the school, grabbed the clerk and began to hit him and pull his hair. The clerk shouted to the musketeers to hold their ground, but even the musketeers could do nothing this time. A monk and pupils ran after them, threw a bench at them and shouted "Why do you come here like thieves?" Such behavior on the part of the elder Likhuds was hardly likely to incline the government favorably towards Prince Nikolay, even though he swore that he had never had any intention of going to Venice as he was obligated to the tsars, and that the maiden Manka was renowned for her immoral behavior and was not to be believed. Evidently after this incident the Likhuds began to dislike it in Moscow and in August 1694 instructions were sent out to military governors on the borders to apprehend the Greek monks the brothers Ioanniky and Sofrony and the children of the latter, Nikolay and Anastasia, who had run away from Moscow. The fugitives were caught. Naturally they could not remain in their previous important position and were banished from the academy to the Typography[25] where they taught Italian.

EDUCATION AND INNOVATION

A document survives from 1694 listing sons of boyars and other ranks studying Italian with the Greek teachers Ioanniky and Sofrony Likhud. Boyars' sons numbered two sons of Prince Peter Ivanovich Khovansky, two of Fedor Petrovich Saltykov, two sons of Alexis

Petrovich Saltykov, two of Ivan Fedorovich Volynsky. Sons of table attendants were two sons of Prince Fedor Andreevich Khilkov, six sons of Prince Ivan Mikhailovich Cherkassky, one of Semyon Alekseevich Yazykov. Sons of secretaries included one Volkov, one Kondratov, one Stepanov, two Ivanovs, two Vereshchagins, one Poliansky, one son of the cossack general secretary Inekhov. Servitors were one Palitsyn and one son of an administrator. Twenty-three from the chief merchants and the senior Moscow merchants.

The innovations which began to be introduced in this period, ships and fireworks, stimulated mental activity in some and fired the imagination of others, as in the following incident. In April 1694 a peasant shouted for help and asked for sanctuary. He was taken to the Chancellery of Musketeers and said under interrogation that he made himself a pair of wings in order to fly like a crane. On the orders of the great sovereigns he made the wings from mica, at a cost of eighteen rubles to the treasury. On the appointed day the boyar Prince Ivan Borisovich Troekurov came out to watch the crane flying. The peasant put on the wings, crossed himself and began to lift the sails but he could not lift himself off the ground. "You have made the wings too heavy," he said, and appealed for other wings to be made at a cost of only five rubles. But the boyar was exasperated and instead of new wings ordered the peasant beaten with sticks on his bare back as a punishment and to pay a fine of eighteen rubles, the sum to be raised by selling all his property.

UKRAINIAN AFFAIRS. MAZEPA

The administration's activities abroad in the four years following the overthrow of Sophia contain little of note. After Vasily Golitsyn's demise Lev Kirillovich Naryshkin took over the direction of foreign affairs. His quality of calm impartiality was an important asset in this particular post, but overall he was not an enterprising man. Additionally, the failure of the Crimean campaigns and the cold, even hostile attitude of Russia's Polish allies offered little prospect of an active continuation of the war. In the meantime curious events were taking place in Little Russia and in the Russian territories which lay under Polish rule.[26]

On August 10, 1689, when Moscow was in a state of fear and bewilderment as a result of Tsar Peter's flight, Ivan Stepanovich Mazepa, hetman of both sides of the Dnieper, rode up to the Kaluga gates leading into the city. By order of the great sovereigns and the great sovereign lady the secretary Bobinin was sent out to meet him with a carriage from the royal stables. Mazepa got into the carriage and said "Praise be to the Lord God that thanks to the great sovereigns' generosity he has allowed me to be sitting here in their royal majesties' carriage. What sort of carriage is it? It seems to be of ancient German handiwork." The secretary replied that this was the carriage that was always used for the entry into the city of great and plenipotentiary foreign ambassadors. The hetman delivered a speech about the Crimean campaigns and the victory of the Russian and Ukrainian troops over the Tatars. "Never before has there been such a victory over the Crimeans, never before have they been as terrified as they were by the operations of the boyar Prince Vasily Vasilievich Golitsyn. But on account of the difficulties posed by the waterless and fodderless terrain and other obstacles the ramparts and towers of Perekop were not destroyed."[27] The hetman read an extract from a chronicle. In ancient times King Darius of Persia came to the Crimea with a huge army and tried to take it and lay it waste. At that time the Crimea was not as heavily fortified as it is now, but because of shortages of water and fodder and other difficulties he was unable to capture Perekop and lay waste the Crimea. He lost some eighty thousand of his men outside Perekop and had to make a forced withdrawal with great humiliation from Perekop and he vowed that never again would he wage war against the Crimea. Now their royal majesties' men-at-arms have fought bravely with the Tatars outside Perekop and deposited a great number of pagan corpses and have withdrawn in safety."

In the palace a long speech of greeting was delivered in Mazepa's honor to the effect that thanks to the courageous and bold service of Prince Vasily Vasilievich Golitsyn and the hetman, the Muslims in unexpected and unprecedented fashion had been defeated in their own abodes and had laid waste their own lands in their terror.

Things had gone badly for Sophia and Golitsyn. Shaklovity was surrendered and everyone hastened to join the victors in the Trinity monastery, including Hetman Mazepa who was in great terror on account of his relations with the fallen regime. Indeed, in the monastery there were those who counselled getting rid of Golitsyn's former client.[28] But others thought differently, for hitherto hetmans were replaced only as a result of blatant treason or by the will of the Ukrainians. If the hetman was not replaced then he must be won over to their side by favors. So at the Trinity monastery Mazepa was greeted with another speech praising his faithful and zealous service and his ardent devotion to the business of warfare. The hetman, who complained of being ill, replied with a short speech in which he promised to serve the great sovereign to the last drop of his blood. In view of this gracious reception Mazepa hastened to dispel any suspicion that the new government might harbor by making a complete break with the old regime. He testified that he had been forced by threats made by Leonty Nepliuev to present Golitsyn with lavish gifts of money and goods, and appealed for compensation from Golitsyn's estate.

This appeal was taken as a sign of complete loyalty to the new regime and all of Mazepa's requests were granted. He had come to Moscow to receive a charter confirming all the previous rights and freedoms of the Ukrainians, which charter now was issued. Mazepa also appealed for reinforcements of Russian troops in the Ukrainian garrisons; for an accurate register of cossacks so that it would no longer be possible for anyone to claim to be either a cossack or a peasant as it suited him; the reinforcement of the volunteer regiments; and that Russian envoys not dare demand transport without producing the tsars' authorization. All were granted.

The hetman brought up the question of limiting distilling, which was causing such terrible damage to the forests, as a result of which the majority of the inhabitants were suffering and were likely to suffer even more damage whilst a small minority were getting rich. The sovereigns ordered the hetman to act at his discretion, taking great care that none of the people suffer oppression and ruin because the Little Russian people had been granted their former rights and freedoms. Mazepa promised to consult with the cossack high command. Some personal matters were then discussed. The hetman made a complaint against Dmitry Raicha,[29] former colonel of Pereiaslavl, who was continually insulting him behind his back and humiliating him in front of the cossack officers and the colonels. Mazepa announced that he intended to make a complaint about Raicha at the Christmas assembly of the cossack officers and colonels. Finally Mazepa succeeded in obtaining a royal decree ordering the table attendant Prince Yury Chetvertinsky[30] to leave Moscow and return to Ukraine. Upon his return Chetvertinsky married the daughter of Samoilovich[31] and lived, on Mazepa's instructions, in Glukhov district on Dunaev farm together with his mother-in-law.

RELATIONS WITH POLAND. THE SOLOMON AFFAIR
The fall of Sophia and Golitsyn thus failed to disturb the hetman's good relations with the Russian government. Mazepa's enemies were severely disappointed, but still did not abandon the hope of discrediting the hetman with Moscow. Poland was a ready means to this end. On December 16, 1689 Table Attendant Volkov, the Russian resident in Poland, had a private visit from the Polish noble Podolski, an Orthodox Christian who held the office of gentleman of the chamber in the household of King Jan Sobieski.[32] Podolski brought important news. About three weeks earlier a monk by the name of Solomon, who had carried the icon of the Savior to the Crimean campaign, arrived from Russia via Smolensk to see the king. He bore a letter from Hetman Mazepa for the king, written at the time when the hetman had just left Perekop to return to Baturin. Podolski could not say what the letter contained but he did mention that it was not signed in the hetman's hand, only with the hetman's great seal. The king ordered the monk to stay in a monastery near Zolkwa and did not know how to reply to the letter for he knew that the tsars were favorably inclined towards the hetman and the whole of the cossack high leaders. Volkov replied that Mazepa was the tsars' loyal servant and that the letter must be a fake or a forgery, not the hetman's, forged in order to bring the hetman into disfavor with the tsars. It was obviously a forgery because the signature was not in the hetman's handwriting and a copy could have been made of the seal. The king should give no credence to such letters and should send the monk back to Russia. The noble remarked that they could not surrender the monk because he and the authors of the letter could be in danger.

At the same time Volkov learned that colonels Lazuka and Zabiaka had come from Zaporozhie[33] to see the king bearing letters from Ataman Husak. The Zaporozhians were complaining that they were being persecuted by the tsars' side. Supplies were not being allowed through to the Camp, and they were unable to make booty raids along the lower Dnieper; they were in danger from the Tatars. Therefore they had made a truce with the Crimean khan and were appealing to the king to take them under his protection, send instructions about how to defend themselves from the Russians and advise them whether to maintain the truce with the khan or go to war with him. The same Podolski told Volkov that the king did not intend to accept the Zaporozhians as his subjects, but he might issue some secret order. He had it on reliable authority that the king was on friendly terms with the Crimea and would welcome dissension between the town-registered cossacks[34] and the Zaporozhians because the current permanent peace was unprofitable and unnecessary for the king, who begrudged the towns and lands which had been ceded to the tsars. Podolski announced that the king had sent the nobleman Iskritsky to Ukraine on an unknown mission, and Iskritsky's daughter had been married to Apostolenko, the colonel of Mirgorod.

At his first meeting with the crown hetman,[35] Jablonowski, Volkov asked the meaning of the Zaporozhians' visit to the king. Jablonowski replied that the king would never violate the peace treaty and had no intention of taking Zaporozhie into his domains. The Zaporozhians had applied to enter the king's service on the pretext that Zaporozhie was experiencing severe hunger as a result of supplies not being let through from Russia. But the enlistment of a few Zaporozhians did not constitute a breach of the treaty.

On December 24 Podolski again brought news to Volkov: on the 22nd the king had allowed Solomon to return to Ukraine. He had not given him a letter but had told him to win the hetman over with words and to assure him of his favor and promise rewards. Podolski reaffirmed that the Zaporozhians were indeed seeking the king's protection. The king had summoned Lazuka and Zabiaka, after which rumors had spread at court to the effect that the king wanted to take all the Zaporozhians under his wing by subterfuge. The king was doing everything within his power to stir up the town-registered cossacks and to win them over to his side.

At the beginning of 1690 there was more news of Polish hostilities. Mozyra, a cossack from Lubensk, had been to Poland on business and on his return to Baturin recounted a conversation he had with Jablonowski. After questioning him on the situation in Ukraine the hetman pronounced: "We know for a fact that Hetman Mazepa has been arrested in Moscow with his officers and has been banished to Siberia where old Samoilenko is.[36] You've seen how crafty and mendacious the Muscovites are. They don't want the freedoms of the Zaporozhian host to spread, they want to reduce them to nothing, God preserve us. Moscow has deceived us, too, but we intend to pay them back in kind."

In March the monk Solomon returned to Poland from Ukraine and, stopping about half a mile outside Warsaw, in the village of Solka, he hired a student to write letters in the name of Hetman Mazepa: one to the king, the other to Hetman Jablonowski. In both letters it said that he, Mazepa, with the whole of the Zaporozhian host, wished to become subjects of his majesty the king. The monk paid the student two efimoks[37] for his work, signed the hetman's name himself and sealed the letters with a forged seal. The monk stayed in Solka and the student set off for Warsaw where he got drunk with some friends in a tavern and boasted about how he had earned the efimoks; to prove it he read out the drafts of the letters, which he still had. The king was informed and summoned the student who recounted what had happened. Some time later Solomon himself arrived in Warsaw, went straight to the king and handed him the letter from Hetman Mazepa. Immediately a confrontation was arranged with the student, who offered the draft letters in final evidence. Solomon was forced to confess his guilt, and also confessed that on his previous visit he also had traveled with forged letters and had never met Hetman Mazepa. The king had him detained in the dungeons of Jan Casimir's[38] palace under a strong guard. The student was given two lengths of cloth and a few efimoks. Volkov learned all this from trustworthy men, Orthodox priests, who were acquainted with people close to the king.

The matter could not end there, however, because the king, when he first received the hetman's letter from Solomon and sent back the latter with an oral reply for Mazepa, also instructed Bishop Joseph Shumliansky of Lvov[39] to make contact with the hetman. Shumliansky was glad to take on the task because he regarded Mazepa's alienation from Moscow as a means of obtaining the metropolitanate of Kiev which was his cherished goal. He speedily dispatched a trusted man to Mazepa, the nobleman Domoradzki, also with a letter. "I beg your honor quickly to inform us on what basis he wishes to enter into relations with the king and the Commonwealth. Now while the Sejm [parliament's diet] is in session is a convenient time to respond with your wishes to his majesty through me, who is well disposed to you, the Commonwealth's and the king's servant. We ask one thing, that you dismiss as speedily as possible the bearer of this letter informing him of what you wish to do for the king and the Commonwealth. Work and devise a way in God's time of casting off that yoke from the free neck of your people. As soon as we are assured of your honor's friendship towards us, we shall begin to work to obtain the guarantees which the king and the Commonwealth will have to give you." Domoradzki informed him orally that the hetman should make his willingness known directly to the Sejm, which would deliberately drag out its business until it received his response. He, Domoradzki, had been ordered to make haste and be back without fail by Easter Sunday of the new calendar.[40] Two colonels stationed close to the Ukrainian border were ordered to stand at the ready and at the first call from the hetman to make haste without delay into Ukraine. If the hetman were to respond rapidly that he was favorably inclined towards accepting Polish rule then Bishop Shumliansky would don his secular merchant's attire and visit Baturin in secret in order to conduct negotiations face to face on the king's behalf. Discussion of the liberties and rights of the cossack host and the hetman's status would take place later.

Mazepa was stationed with his army at Lubna when he received this terrible embassy. He ordered Domoradzki placed under arrest and subjected to torture, and immediately sent Shumliansky's letter to Moscow, closely followed by Domoradzki, who was brought before the Polish resident Dominic d'Aumont and made to repeat by whom and for what reason he had been sent to Mazepa. The resident was made to understand that this action of the king's was regarded as blatantly hostile. How were they to act, what should they believe, what about the reliability and obligations of an ally and the demands of truth?

In March 1690, in the meantime, an anonymous letter addressed to the tsars turned up in Kiev containing the following message. "All of us living on Polish territory who profess the true Orthodox faith give notice and warning to the pious monarchs lest our refuge and defence be destroyed by the wicked and artful Ivan Mazepa, who previously sold us out—Podolians, Galicians and Volhynians[41]— to the Muslims and sold off the church silver and icons to the Turks. Then, having defamed his master utterly, he seized his estate and bought his sister estates in our territory and continues to buy them. Lastly, in collusion with Golitsyn he traveled to Moscow with the intention of banishing you, pious Tsar Peter Alekseevich, not only from your throne but also from this world and to consign your brother Ivan Alekseevich to oblivion. Others have been condemned, but Mazepa, the source and instigator of your downfall, is allowed to remain in a position in which even if he fails in his first aim he can hand over Ukraine to the Poles. Some people have been ruined, others exiled, but he was given a free pardon. He is awaiting the time when he can accomplish his foul scheme in secret. Moreover, our Bishop Shumliansky is a Uniate[42] but in reality a Catholic, and is deliberately subordinating himself to the patriarch of Moscow in order, together with Mazepa, to achieve the destruction of your royal throne all the easier."

The governor of Kiev, Prince Mikhail Romodanovsky, sent this letter to Moscow, from where it was dispatched immediately to Baturin with the clerk Mikhailov, who was told to hand it to the hetman, reassure him of the tsars' favor and ask whether he thought the letter might have been written in Poland and whether he had any suspicions about Poland. Or maybe he suspected a Russian or a Ukrainian, perhaps someone from Zaporozhie. The letter referred to matters which probably were not known about in Poland and Lithuania. What did the hetman think would be the best way of investigating the matter?

Mazepa took the letter from the envoy then bowed to the ground five times, thanking the tsars for their kindness. Then he read the letter, looked round about him, glanced at the icon of the Virgin, burst into tears and raising his hands towards the icon, declared "Immaculate Mother of God, my hope, look upon my wretched and sinful soul and vouch that I labor day and night in order to serve God's anointed monarchs, ready to serve them to the end of my life and to shed my blood for their well-being. But my enemies never sleep. They are forever seeking some means of destroying me."

With regard to the question of the author of the letter, the hetman wrote to the tsars: "I cannot, given my small intelligence, wholly comprehend where this crafty, poisonous and ill-intentioned letter could have come from. I suspect Mikhail Gadiatsky, who recently showed his hostility towards me and tried to turn the tsars against me. Under the former hetman he spread slander against me, accusing me of poisoning the hetman's son Semyon [Samoilovich] and his daughter, wife of the boyar Sheremetev, and of giving the hetman an eye disease. When he was living in Moscow he wrote a libel against me. He has an incurable passion for sending letters to all and sundry—to Zaporozhie, the Don, Belaia Tserkov, the Crimea. He has retired from the office of colonel of Gadiach but his longing for fame and honor will never diminish. I humbly beseech you to transfer him from the village where he is living in Lebedinsk district near to Ukraine to somewhere else. I also dare humbly to suggest that whoever wrote this letter must know about the monk Solomon who was sent into Poland with forged letters by one of my enemies, because in the letter it says that Shumliansky is in collusion with me on everything. Solomon took refuge with this same Shumliansky when he was in Poland. If this enemy did not hope that Shumliansky would write to me at Solomon's instigation, why mention Shumliansky in this libel?"

In conversation with Mikhailov, Mazepa also said that he suspected Raicha and Polubotok as well as Gadiatsky. The letter contained the expression "for God's mercy," which Raicha always used in his letters, and Polubotok was a friend of both Raicha and Gadiatsky. "I have also had to suffer much unpleasantness from Yury Chetvertinsky, the metropolitan's son and Samoilovich's son-in-law, who is now living in Ukraine and forever spreading evil gossip amongst the people that Samoilovich should be hetman again. He recently said to Vasily the priest at Baturin that where water once flowed it would spring up again. He said that the tsars are favorably inclined towards his father-in-law. He will be restored to his former position and then see what becomes of his persecutors!" Mazepa asked for Chetvertinsky and his wife to be transferred to Moscow and the mother-in-law to be reunited with her husband. Prince Yury was a table attendant and with that rank he ought not to live so far from Moscow.[43] When Mikhailov took his leave of Mazepa and asked him to return the forged letter for safe keeping in the Chancellery of Foreign Affairs, the hetman's expression changed. He drove everyone out of the reception chamber and said "At first I was encouraged by the tsars' kindness but now I am saddened a hundredfold. It seems that the tsars have decided to believe the letter and are thinking about punishing me." Mikhailov hastened to assure the hetman to the contrary. The letter was needed in Moscow in order to try the criminal who had written it. But Mazepa refused adamantly to surrender the letter, saying to the secretary Kochubey "Another splinter has entered my heart: they want the letter back."

Mazepa's request was granted. Mikhail Gadiatsky was taken from Lebedinsk district to Moscow, where Prince Yury Chetvertinsky, his wife and mother-in-law were sent also. Leonty Polubotok was dismissed as colonel of Pereiaslavl. But Mazepa was not satisfied with respect to Gadiatsky and Polubotok. He wrote to the tsars that after Polubotok was replaced the new colonel of Poltava, Lysenko, and more than a hundred Poltava residents made a complaint against Polubotok, accusing him of insulting, ruining and abusing them and insisting that if he was not executed the people of Little Russia would become extremely indignant against the hetman, cossack officers and colonels on account of their tormenter being treated with such leniency. When he heard of the misfortune that awaited him Polubotok fled to Moscow, but was sent back to Ukraine to be tried under the law of the cossack host. Mazepa reported to Moscow that when Polubotok was in Kiev he had slandered him to the governor, Mikhail Romodanovsky, saying that he, Mazepa, was plotting treason, intended to flee to Poland, where he was sending money from the cossack treasury and buying up estates and corresponding with the crown hetman.

The governor was asked at once to confirm whether this was true. Romodanovsky replied that Polubotok told him nothing of the kind. He had complained only that Mazepa treated him badly, and tried to ruin him at every turn, and that the hetman was the author of his current troubles. And the hetman himself was no paragon of virtue: he was sending large sums of money to his sister in Poland via a nun called Liplitskaia who lived with his mother in the Maidens' convent in Kiev, and was buying estates for his sister. Polubotok cursed Mazepa roundly. When Romodanovsky's statement was sent to Mazepa the latter replied that "in his simplehearted lack of vindictiveness" he had already released Polubotok and allowed him to return to his home in Chernigov, after which Polubotok sent him a letter full of terrible oaths swearing that he had never said any of the things about which Romodanovsky had written.

MAZEPA AND PALEY

Having sent Gadiatsky and Chetvertinsky packing from Ukraine, Mazepa was concerned also to transfer another of his deadly enemies to Russian citizenship, a man whose name is closely associated with his own in popular legend. The cossack Semyon Paley,[44] a native of Borzna, went first to Zaporozhie, then entered the service of the king of Poland with several of his comrades, assembled some emigrants from Moldavia and the Dniester region and ensconced himself in the town of Khvastov. In 1688-1689 he sent Mazepa requests that the great sovereigns take him and the cossacks and ordinary residents of Khvastov under their rule because the Poles were trying to kill him. Moscow's response to the hetman's report was that the treaty with Poland prevented them from accepting Paley's application, but he might go to Zaporozhie with his men, stay there for a time and then move to Ukraine.

The Poles may have learned about Paley's wish to transfer his allegiance to Russia, or there may have been some other reason, but they arrested him and threw him into prison in Nemirov, then transferred him to the citadel and held him there all winter. Two Uniate priests took advantage of Paley's arrest and went to Khvastov, where they announced their intention of converting the Orthodox church, which Paley had built, into a Uniate one.[45] But the cossacks managed to defend their church despite the absence of their leader. In the spring Paley managed to escape from prison. When he returned to Khvastov the first thing he did was send the priests packing. But they refused to leave and insisted that the church become Uniate. They started to argue with Paley who became so enraged that with the agreement of his cossacks he ordered that the priests be beheaded. After this incident Paley naturally begged Mazepa even more fervently to accept him as a subject of the tsars, indicating that he and his men would like to move into the abandoned town of Tripolie on the Russian border. They could not move to Zaporozhie because his men had wives, children and livestock. The Poles had no right to complain because the Wallachians, who formed his band, were free men. On this basis Mazepa asked the tsars to give Paley permission to move to Tripolie, where he would provide useful reinforcements to defend Kiev and Ukraine.

Moscow twice responded, in April 1690, that accepting Paley's change of allegiance would be a violation of the treaty [of 1686] with Poland and he should go first to Zaporozhie. In 1691 he made a raid on the Turks outside Belgorod (Akkerman). As he returned to the Povolochie district he encountered a detachment of Poles sent by Jan Druskewicz, the castellan of Kholm, to capture him. Paley attacked the enemy, but these enemies were Russians and were unwilling to fight their own kind on behalf of a Pole. They killed Apostolets, the officer in command, and surrendered to Paley. The colonel of Khvastov kissed the icon and announced to Moscow that he had no intention of remaining any longer under Polish sovereignty now that the Poles had made their intentions clear. Three times the Tatars had invited him to come over to their side, but he would serve only their majesties the tsars. Mazepa wrote to Lev Naryshkin that Paley ought to be assured of the tsars' favor and appeased with an allowance. He was a highly warlike man and had about three thousand armed troops under his command. Moscow again rejected Paley's application but to keep him from aiding the Tatars it was decided secretly to send him ten lengths of fine velvet and two forties of sables worth 80 rubles a forty.[46]

RELATIONS WITH CRIMEA

The Russians were anxious not to violate the treaty with Poland but the Poles were more than happy to foment unrest in Ukraine and to negotiate openly with the Crimea for a separate peace. In Vienna they were equally dismissive of their Russian ally, but the Austrian minister in Vienna did not miss an opportunity to impress upon the Russian resident that the tsars could expect little good from the Poles. The Russian government thus was forced to enter into negotiations with the Crimea, initially through the mediation of Mazepa who told Khan Saadat Girey on his own account that if he wanted peace he should sent envoys to Moscow. Saadat sent a messenger to announce that he was prepared for peace on the old terms.[47] But Moscow's main reason for going to war in the first place was to rid itself of these old terms, of the dispatch of petty gifts of money or, to put it bluntly, tribute. At the beginning of 1692 the clerk Aitemirov was sent to the Crimea with a demand for the renunciation of these terms on the Crimea's part and the return to the Greeks of the Holy Places on the part of Turkey. The privy councillors of the new khan, Safat Girey, who had replaced Saadat, asked Aitemirov: "When was the sepulchre of the Lord handed over and to whom? Was it when Turkey was at peace with Moscow or after the rift?" Aitemirov replied that the sepulchre of the Lord had been given over to French monks about two years ago.[48] The Tatars objected. "Do you mean that it should be taken away from the French because the French king gave aid to the sultan against the emperor? If we take it away from the French and give it to the Greeks and the French declare war on the Turks, will Moscow help the Turkish sultan? There has never been any agreement with Moscow about the sepulchre, so we do not understand why it is being brought up now." Aitemirov replied that it was not included previously because the Holy Places of old always had been administered by the Greeks.

The Tatars were much more interested in other clauses, for example the article on the return of prisoners of war from both sides without a ransom payment and the article on abolishing the dispatch of cash payments. The Tatars said "In the Crimea we are holding more than a hundred thousand Muscovites and cossacks, whereas in Moscow you have two or three thousand of our men, so how can we release them without ransom?" But they were most adamantly opposed to the article on cash payments. "Why have the great sovereigns decided to end the cash payments? Who put this idea into their heads? They are great sovereigns and have many clever boyars who have long experience of Crimean affairs. They would be wrong to abandon the annual cash payment because the great sovereigns are not ruined by it and previous khans, and our grandfathers and fathers were satisfied with the tsars' allowance; in what way is the present khan inferior to his predecessors, or we, his privy councillors, to our predecessors? We know that previously hostility between us and Moscow stemmed from the money tribute; when it wasn't sent the Tatars would invade Rus.The present khan and all the Tatar hordes are not afraid of Moscow and are prepared for peace or war, for if Moscow's troops invade the Crimea there is nothing for them to take because a Tatar's worldly belongings consist of three things: two horses and his soul. The hordes rise up to defend the tribute; there will never be friendship if you try to abandon payment altogether." Aitemirov poured oil on the flames by remarking that maybe both sides could exchange gifts. "Previous khans never sent any gifts to the tsars of Moscow and the present one will not send anything either," the Tatars retorted. The negotiations were terminated because the Tatars were encouraged by a fierce revolt in Ukraine, whence they were invited to attack Moscow in alliance with the cossacks.

After the hetman the next most important man in Ukraine was the cossack chief secretary Vasily Kochubey. Kochubey at first was a member of Doroshenko's chancellery. In 1675 he was sent to Turkey by the hetman but on the return journey not far from Umani his slave stole the vizier's letters and other documents and disappeared with them. Kochubey was afraid to return to Chigirin empty-handed so went direct from Umani to join Samoilovich and there was raised to the office of chief secretary.[49]

ZAPOROZHIE AND PETRIK

At the time in question the chancellery official Petrik, who was married to Kochubey's niece, ran away to Zaporozhie having stolen some documents from the chancellery. The first thing he did upon arriving in the Camp was to publicize Mazepa's negotiations with the Crimea on Moscow's behalf. Then he spread the rumor that Mazepa was in agreement with Moscow about destroying the Camp and exterminating the cossacks. As a result, when in the spring of 1691 the table attendant Chubarov visited Zaporozhie to deliver the tsars' allowance consisting of five hundred gold pieces, sables and cloth, one of the unit commanders shouted "This allowance doesn't deserve the name. We have served for a long time, but we have earned more than this measly amount for our service. We have seen sables like this before!" He grabbed the sables and flung them to the ground, saying "These Muscovite scum come and order us to fight the Turks while they themselves are making peace with them." Other cossacks yelled "If this is the case we ought to kill the Muscovite commanders or imprison them in Chertomlyn and put the others in the cells. They have sent sables only for every fourth man but they should send enough for everyone, like they do to the Don Cossacks. And look at the amount of allowance—they sent five hundred whereas they ought to send five thousand."

In Perevolochna Mazepa had a very vigilant and loyal supporter in Rutkovsky, who reported to him on everything that was taking place. On February 22, 1692 Rutkovsky wrote to the hetman: "Zakhar, son of Archpriest Luke of Poltava, with an inhabitant of Poltava called Ivan Gerasimenko have returned from Perekop where they were buying horses and repeated word for word a conversation they had with the secretary of Kazykermen, Shaban. 'Do you realize, gentlemen of Poltava,' said Shaban, 'what sort of man that Kochubey of yours is?' They replied that they did not know him but had heard only that he was chief secretary. 'I'll tell you what sort of secretary he is,' Shaban continued, 'he's a secretary who wants to be hetman. He has already written twice to the Crimea to summon the Horde to install him as hetman. It would have been done only the khan was away. He, Kochubey, and the chancellery clerk Petrik have sent a message to the Camp.'" Thereupon Zakhar avowed and swore to Rutkovsky that Petrik had said in secret "I know that the hetman will not escape with his life if my master the chief secretary gets his way and finds an opportune moment to stab him. I expect news of it any day." Mazepa reported this information to Moscow and added that he was keeping a sharp eye on Kochubey and if he was really up to no good he would inform the sovereigns immediately.

In May 1692 Petrik's plot was uncovered. He suddenly disappeared from Zaporozhie and turned up amongst the Turks in Kazykermen, from where he sent a letter to the Camp which was read out at the assembly. Petrik thanked the Zaporozhians for their

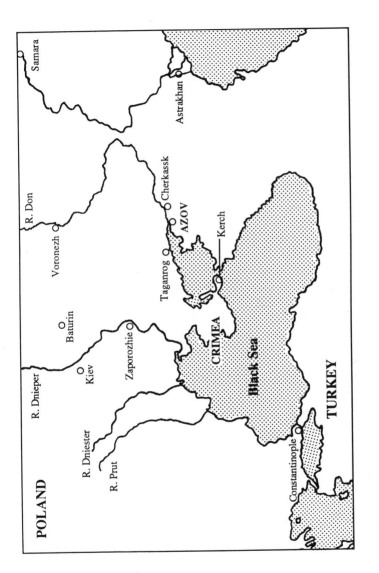

Ukranian and Turkish Affairs

hospitality and for the secretarial post which he had occupied; he begged forgiveness for leaving the Camp without the Host's permission. "I told you many times," he wrote," about the danger our Little Russian region faces from its enemies and what a decline it has suffered, thanks to its hateful rulers, and I told you that you must take energetic action. But no one wanted to take it on, so I have decided to act on behalf of the Zaporozhian Host and all the people of Little Russia which is why I have journeyed to the Crimea. When our ancestors lived in alliance with that realm no one laughed at us, and now all you brave lads will be pleased with the pact which I shall sign with the Crimea." Having listened to this document, the commanding officers declared that they were against uniting with the Crimean Tatars and against a campaign to attack the tsars' towns in Ukraine. But a good half of the troops shouted "We are ready to join the Crimeans and Petrik to make war on the Ukrainian towns." Rumors circulated in Ukraine that Petrik was raising up the Tatar horde and intended to wipe out the landlords, nobles and all the rich. *Reckless* persons began joining up with him. Rutkovsky let it be known that Petrik was saying in Kazykermen "Once I go into action I shall do better than Khmelnitsky.[50] The hetman sent a letter ordering them to give me up, but now I shall go to him myself."

On May 6 Petrik sent a letter to Zaporozhie in which he announced that he had signed a treaty with the khan: the Zaporozhian Host freely and without any taxes might catch fish and game and collect salt on the Dnieper and all the tributaries along both banks of the Dnieper; the Chigirin side since it was won by Khmelnitsky from the Poles was to be under the authority of the Zaporozhian Host. "Anyone who wants to take fish, salt and game, let him do so, but he who wants to capture Muscovite booty let him go with us because we shall soon be taking away the whole Ukraine from Moscow with the Zaporozhian Host and the Tatar hordes." Rutkovsky informed Mazepa that "You must at all costs contain the recklessness of the registered cossacks to stop them going off there because they are beginning to set off not only by land but also along the river, five or six men in a boat."

They made it known in Zaporozhie that the decent cossacks were deeply distressed at Petrik's criminal activities, but drunkards and riff-raff were saying amongst themselves "Let's join Petrik and get rid of the landlords." Luckily the opinion of the better sort prevailed. They were dissatisfied with their commander Fedka and shouted at him at the assembly to give up an office in which he was incapable of mending his ways. At first Fedka refused to relinquish his command, but when they rushed to fetch cudgels he stepped down and by popular acclaim Husak was elected to replace him. He said: "Now the world has been set on fire and you are driving me into the flames to put them out. Let the man who started it all put an end to it." But he had no alternative but to accept.

The new commander received an exhortatory letter from Mazepa to which he replied: "The Zaporozhian Host has no wicked intentions and doesn't wish to hear about such things. Only someone who was ignorant of the one true God in the holy Trinity could contemplate such folly. It's true that Khmelnitsky was in alliance with the Tatars, but later he subordinated himself to the illustrious monarchs.[51] At that time in the general assembly they reached this verdict in order to relieve Ukraine of vexations. But now we see that poor folk in the regiments are suffering great deprivations. Your honor writes the truth when you say that under the Poles cossack freedoms were greatly restricted, and Bogdan Khmelnitsky even declared war on them to liberate us from their authority. Then we thought that the Christian people would never again for all eternity be subjected to foreign rule. But now we can see that the poor are worse off than they were under Polish rule, because even if a man has no right to subordinate people to him, he does so by making them bring him hay or firewood, stoke his stoves and clean his stables. Of course, if a man is raised to the officer class by the favor of the Host then he has that right, no one is vexed. This is how it was in the late Khmelnitsky's time. But we hear of people whose fathers did not keep servants but they keep them and have no idea what to do with the poor creatures. Such men should not be allowed to keep servants. Let them work for their bread as their fathers did."[52]

Mazepa sent the cossack Gorbachenko to the Camp with gifts for the commander, the chief justice, military secretary and chief lieutenant. Husak drew Gorbachenko aside to a storehouse and said "My benefactor the lord hetman should not worry, because I am ready to do his bidding in everything. Tell the hetman from me that if he does not cut off the heads of those three men, the first being Polubotok, the second Mikhail (Gadiatsky?) and the third, the one who is always with him (Kochubey?),[53]—he'll know the one I mean—he will never have any peace as hetman and Ukraine will never prosper. The hetman shouldn't imagine that all revolts start here in our host on the lower Dnieper, or with those men who come from the towns to get booty. They revolted in the Lubna Regiment because they don't want to pay rents; they want to join Petrik. The cossacks of Gadiach and Poltava are saying that the hetman posted many officers in the towns and in the villages and they are also rising in revolt in anticipation of Petrik's arrival." The commander asked the hetman to prepare a force of about 15,000 men to deal with Petrik. He promised to lure him to the Camp and arrest him there. In conclusion he asked the hetman to see that Moscow dealt more kindly with the Ukrainians because visitors from the Ukrainian towns were complaining about the resident "Muscovite scum", who were said to be injuring, robbing and abducting people, stealing small children and taking them off to Moscow."

Gorbachenko brought with him a copy of the treaty signed between Peter Ivanovich (Petrik) and the khan: the principality of Kiev and Chernigov with all the Zaporozhian Host and the Little Russian people was to remain an autonomous region with its liberties intact. The Crimea was obliged to protect it from the Poles, from Moscow and from all its enemies. The Chigirin side would come under the authority of the Little Russian principality; the regimental districts of Kharkov and Rybinsk would be transferred to the Chigirin side. The routes through the grassland of Ukraine should be open to the Crimeans for campaigns against Moscow; the Crimeans should have the right of plunder in Muscovy in return for the aid they were now giving to the Little Russian people. When God granted the Little Russian principality full dominion it would establish order freely according to its own wishes; there would be a Little Russian envoy resident in the Crimea and a Crimean in Little Russia.

Petrik sent another long letter to Zaporozhie urging the fine young warriors to unite with the khan. "When I have visited you in the Camp again and again I have told you of the danger in which our Little Russian region now finds itself and the ruin that is being brought upon our native land by the despised monarchs [i.e., Russian, Polish and Crimean] between whom we live. Like savage lions they open their jaws and try to devour us, and make us their slaves. It is no surprise that the king of Poland acts in this way as we were his subjects for a long time but with God's help escaped his domination and inflicted a loss upon him from which he has not recovered even to this day. The Crimean khan is hostile to us because we inflict damage on him on land and on water. But it's a wonder that the tsars of Moscow, who did not capture us with the sword, should transfer our Chigirin region to the other side of the Dnieper,[54] and should surround themselves with our people on all sides, with the result that no matter what direction the enemy comes from, it is our towns and villages which burn and our people who are taken into captivity; thanks to us Moscow remains safe as though protected by a wall. Not content with this now Moscow is trying to make us all its slaves and captives. To this end our former hetmans Mnogogreshny and Popovich,[55] who stood up for us, were taken prisoner and after that they tried to subjugate us all forever, but God did not grant it. They failed to lay waste the Crimea and besiege the towns of Kazykermen with their troops and then drive us from the Camp and appoint their own military commanders. Failing to achieve their goal, they allowed the present hetman to hand out estates to the cossack officers, and the officers shared out our brethren amongst themselves and registered them for themselves and their children forever, and the next thing they will be doing is harnessing them to the plow. They treat them just like their slaves. Moscow allowed our officers to do this so that our people should be so harshly subjugated that they could not plot to oppose them; when our people try to cast off these burdens Moscow will besiege the Dnieper and Samara from its forts.

"The Polish king, who was very annoyed with the tsars of Moscow for failing to capture the Crimea, wanted to attack Moscow with the hordes but first to take over our Ukraine. If this had happened, would we have been any better off? You yourselves are well aware of what occurred in the time of Czarniecki[56] and other Polish landlords who came to Ukraine with their troops, how they tormented us. Don't your recall how our comrades were impaled on stakes and drowned in ice-holes and how cossack women were forced to boil their own children in boiling water? Or how the Poles poured water over our people in the frost and filled their boots with hot coals, and how the soldiers confiscated our property? The Poles haven't forgotten it and are ready even now to do the same again. And if the Muscovite tsars make peace with the Crimean khan they will take us back into eternal servitude, like a plucked fowl. If the Polish king or the Muscovite tsars were to make peace with the Crimean khan, which side would we favor, who would offer us help in such a plight? I have talked with you a lot on this subject but as none of you was willing to stand up for your men, I undertook this task. You're sensible men, so tell me. Which is better—to live in freedom or in servitude? Is it better to serve a foreign master or to be your own boss? Which is better—to be a peasant serf to some Muscovite or Pole, or to be a free cossack? Was it not a good thing for Ukraine when Bogdan Khmelnitsky broke away from Polish domination with the Zaporozhian Host and the hordes? Then the cossacks had gold and silver, fine cloth and horses and herds of livestock, but when we became the bondslaves of the Muscovite tsars our lands around Chigirin were laid waste and we were driven across to this side of the Dnieper. Not only did we lose our landed estates, we even lost our bast sandals. Most of our comrades settled in the Muscovite towns under duress, and every year some are captured by the Tatars. I also beg to inform your honors that the hetman, in consultation with all his officers, secretly sent a messenger to tell me that as soon as we approach Samara they will break with Moscow, unite with us and make war against Moscow. This is the hetman's man. He is with me now and I shall show him to you. Therefore be of good hope and feel secure, come with us."

At the beginning of July Tatars under the command of Kalga-Sultan appeared at Kamenny Zaton.[57] Petrik was with them. As soon as they heard about this in the Zaporozhian Camp several unit commanders and the former commander Grigory Sahaidachny set off to meet Kalga-Sultan. Petrik told him that he had letters from the hetman, only he refused to show them unless the cossack commander himself came. The commander with the unit commanders and men numbering about six hundred set off for a meeting. The commander demanded to see the hetman's letters, to which Petrik responded "There's no use demanding the letters. You have to take my word for it." But the commander persisted. "Show me the letters, or swear on your oath that you have them." Then Petrik admitted that he had no letters and nobody had talked him into carrying out this enterprise. He himself had devised the treaties with the khan to be concluded on behalf of the whole Zaporozhian Host out of pity for the abuse suffered by the ordinary people of Little Russia. Kalga demanded that the commanders take an oath of their friendship for the Crimea and the commanders agreed, but when they had sworn it, Kalga began insisting that the Zaporozhians join the Tatars in an attack on the Muscovite towns. The commander replied that the Zaporozhians had dispersed in various directions and that the troops who remained in the camp were unreliable; it was impossible to use them where you wanted. "If any of them wishes to join you we shall not hold them back, but neither shall we force any who are unwilling to go." The commander returned to his detachment and asked whether anyone wished to comply with Kalga's request. Some replied that it wasn't right to cooperate with Muslims to make war on Christians, but others said "Seeing that you have sworn allegiance to Kalga we may as well go to war with him."

Returning to the Camp early in the morning of July 28, the commander summoned the cossack assembly and resigned his office. The chief justice, secretary and chief lieutenant did likewise. They complained that there were a number of loudmouths among the troops who were trying to force them with their shouting to join Muslims in making war on Orthodox Christians, "but we refuse to see such evil perpetrated in the Camp while we are in charge." For a whole day the ataman's mace lay in the assembly chamber and various voices were raised among the troops, some urging good, others mischief. Early the next day there was another meeting which ended with the leading members by common consent going to see the commander in his quarters and appealing to him to remain in office, and all the other commanding officers, too. The commander came to the assembly and said "If any of you wants to join that rogue Petrik I won't stop you. Any of you who wishes to remain in camp will not be forced to go." About three thousand cossacks joined Petrik.

When Mazepa heard of these developments he sent an urgent request to Moscow for troops, reporting that he was stationed outside Gadiach but was reluctant to proceed further not so much for fear of the Tatar hordes as of the trouble that was brewing inside Ukraine. Moscow responded by ordering the boyar Prince Boris Petrovich Sheremetev[58] and Lord-in-waiting Prince Fedor Boriatinsky to march against the enemy, the first from Belgorod, the second from Sevsk. On August 5 the brigadier of the musketeer regiment attached to Mazepa arrived in Moscow and reported that the ordinary people in Ukraine were grumbling on the slightest pretext and declaring openly that when Petrik arrived with the Zaporozhian Host they would join him, kill the cossack officers and landlords and restore the old system whereby everyone was just a cossack and there were no lords.[59] Only a few of the cossacks to whom the hetman sent call-up papers turned up in the camp, whereas all sorts of reckless types and riff-raff arrived without being summoned and spread wild and negative tales amongst the troops. Mazepa complained bitterly that Sheremetev and Boriatinsky were making very slow progress. A conflagration could break out at any minute, and the hetman himself was prevented from marching against the enemy with the Little Russian Host because he had to keep an eye on the situation at home. In the meantime the residents of the Orel townships of Tsarichenko and Kitay-Gorodok had surrendered to the enemy already. The hetman did not wait for the Muscovite commanders to arrive but was forced to set out from Gadiach towards Poltava.

The Tatars and Petrik did not wait for the hetman either. Mazepa reported to Moscow that at the beginning of August the Tatars had laid siege to the township of Moiachka, but on hearing that several Ukrainian officers were on their way to relieve the town on the hetman's orders, they lifted the siege and departed. In Moscow there was rejoicing at the outcome of an affair which had threatened to unleash a major rebellion in Ukraine. The tsars sent Mazepa a sable coat worth eight hundred rubles. Then the boyar Boris Sheremetev sent a letter to Moscow explaining why they had failed to join forces with the hetman. Mazepa had written instructing him to go to Rublevka to meet him and to be there by August 5 without fail. In response to this letter Sheremetev arrived at Rublevka before noon on August 6 to find that Mazepa, instead of going to Rublevka, had headed for the provinces around Poltava by way of the fortified places beyond the Vorskla. He sent the boyar a report on his manoeuvres in the Poltava region and told him to join up with him, but he did not indicate precisely where. Sheremetev went on towards Poltava but on August 8 while underway he received news from the colonels of Sumy and Akhtyrka, who had been sent on in advance, that the Tatars, alarmed by the news that the boyar was going to join forces with the hetman and by the approach of the vanguard from Sumy and Akhtyrka, had taken to their heels.

END OF THE SOLOMON AFFAIR

Be that as it may, Mazepa received a valuable fur coat. Shortly afterwards the Solomon affair reached its conclusion. From 1690 onwards the Russian resident Volkov continually urged the Poles that the king must send the criminal Solomon to Moscow for trial and punish Shumliansky. In October 1690 Solomon was taken to see the king in Zolkwa and told of the claims of the Russian government. The monk appealed to be tried in Poland rather than being handed over to the Russians. Mazepa too made overtures for the release of Solomon to Moscow. When Volkov was in Lvov his clerk Gerasimov met a cossack at the market who told him that his name was Alexander Ivanovsky and he had served under Hetman Mazepa and came from him to Crown Hetman Jablonowski with a request that Solomon be sent to Smolensk. Ivanovsky had been in Zholkov also and seen Solomon there unfettered. At the same time as they were there the bishops of Lvov and Premysl had arrived to see Solomon and told him that it was high time he confessed and told the truth. The monk responded with his previous speeches but the cossack did not say which ones. Volkov applied to Hetman Jablonowski with a demand for Solomon's handover. Jablonowski replied: "The king orders that the monk be handed over. And I can say for certain that the letters which Solomon brought were forged copies and not the real thing. I know Hetman Ivan Mazepa's handwriting, and his signature and the way he writes, but in Solomon's letters one discerns neither the hetman's writing nor his manner of thinking."

After that Volkov learned that another monk by the name of Irakly Rusinovich was visiting Poland from Ukraine and bringing news to the king. This information was being passed to him by two of the hetman's servants who had emigrated from Poland and married Russian girls, but had remained Catholics. Both knew of Solomon's crime and had helped him forge the seal. Mazepa himself knew nothing of this as he had no one to find out from.

In August 1691 the Polish envoy Jan Okrasa arrived in Moscow for an explanation of the Solomon affair. He announced to the lord-in-waiting Chaadaev, who was in correspondence with him, "His majesty the king has a constant desire to be on terms of brotherly friendship and love with their majesties the tsars and does not believe any quarrels; but last year the monk Solomon turned up in Poland bearing forged letters and counterfeit seals and gave the king a letter in the name of the hetman of Russian Ukraine (of the other side of the Dnieper). When the king saw that the letters were forged and the seals counterfeit, he ordered the monk placed under strong guard and now that monk has been sent to Mogilev and handed over to the border judges. And for the sake of brotherly friendship and love the king has given me the false letters and the two counterfeit seals to pass on to you." With that Okrasa handed over three letters and two seals.

The following is an example of one of the letters, in which Mazepa writes to the king: "Most illustrious king and gracious sovereign, invincible monarch! For a third time we write to you, gracious sovereign, as our father and great monarch. It is odd, gracious sovereign, that you refuse to take us, your servants, under your wing; you give us no comfort through our monk but send your own people, especially Iskritsky with whose son-in-law I have fallen out. I could trust Domoradzki, but Moscow keeps a sharp eye on what is going on in the towns and along the Dnieper from Kiev down to Chernobyl, and would spot a newcomer. But Solomon knows the best place to cross the Dnieper and will keep away from the towns. I ask my gracious lord for reliable information because I can do nothing. The colonel of Poltava writes urging me not to admit the Muscovites to the towns but to send without fail for the horde. We can hold off Shelenbey-murza from attacking your majesty until Solomon's arrival, but another Tatar came from the Crimea not long ago, in the third week of Lent, and told us that a Tatar ambassador had been sent to your majesty. I must also inform your majesty that I was afraid to write to the crown hetman on account of the fact that I heard that your majesty is angry with him and I didn't write to the lord crown treasurer, either, as I am well aware that he doesn't know any secrets because your majesty does not wish him to. Just send us a reliable message by the hand of our man Solomon and we shall fight Moscow with the horde. We shall begin it, and your majesty can give us help by sending several thousand of your men-at-arms to the appointed place, across the Dnieper to Kanev. If your majesty wishes to send a trusted servant with Solomon we shall trust him, too, but he can't travel though the towns or cross the Dnieper alone. God grant that nothing goes wrong—we could perish at Muscovite hands at any moment. Judge for yourself, your majesty, that we have begun a dreadful business and shall bring it to a conclusion as best we can. We trust in God's grace and in your royal grace. We have made preparations in total secrecy. We await your majesty's instructions, and in the meantime bow to your majesty."

After inspecting the letters Chaadaev had another conversation with Okrasa. "You said that the king sent the letters and the seals out of brotherly friendship for their majesties the tsars, but that brotherly friendship is in some doubt. The king chose to send the last of Solomon's letters, the ones he composed outside Warsaw on the third occasion. They are brief, and don't divulge the real business. There is a mention of the first and second letters which Solomon gave to the king and Shumliansky, in which he wrote in some detail about the reception of Hetman Ivan Stepanovich under the king's protection. These first letters were believed at the king's court and were sent to Hetman Domoradzki. The crown hetman Jablonowski on the king's orders sent copies of these first letters to Hetman Mazepa which were nothing like the real letters that you handed over." Thereupon Chaadaev showed Okrasa Jablonowski's letter to Mazepa and copies of Solomon's earlier letters, all of which Mazepa had sent to Moscow. "Tell his majesty the king," Chaadev continued, "that if he genuinely wishes to treat their majesties the tsars like brothers he should send the originals of Solomon's first and second letters."

"Solomon did indeed give the king the first and second letters," replied Okrasa, "only at the time the king gave them no credence and they were thrown away without being properly looked at, were mislaid and before my departure efforts to find them were unsuccessful; only the later letters, which I brought, were found. There were never any missives from the king inviting Mazepa to become a Polish subject. Let the great sovereigns agree to receive Solomon at the border and let Domoradzki with Shumliansky's letter be handed back to the king."

"The great sovereigns have not ordered Domoradzki's release," said Chaadev, "because he still has to have a confrontation with Solomon and only after that is over can he be released. You say that the king did not believe the first letters and sent no word to Mazepa, but on whose instructions did Shumliansky write?" Okrasa was shown the original of the letter from Shumliansky to Mazepa, and also read out Domoradzki's testimony in which he declared that he had been sent to Mazepa by Shumliansky, who was acting on the king's orders. Okrasa attempted to defend Shumliansky, arguing that the letters contained no more than a call to wage war on the heathen Muslim. "But what is this 'yoke' that Shumliansky refers to and says has to be cast off?" asked Chaadaev. "The people of Ukraine are not living under any Tatar or Turkish yoke." Okrasa was silent.

Solomon was handed over. He was brought to Moscow, defrocked and under his former secular name of Semyon Grodsky was subjected to trial by torture. What he testified is not known, but what is known is that the tsars' messengers brought the news to Baturin that Mikhail Gadiatsky had been banished to Siberia and at the same time delivered Semyon Grodsky to the hetman. Mazepa had been making persistent demands that he be sent and also had complained that Conciliar Secretary Emelian Ukraintsev had ordered Kochubey to observe his movements without the authorization of the tsars or of Lev Naryshkin and that Kochubey was getting up to mischief in the process. The hetman knew nothing of all this because he was held to be of no account, and Kochubey was a friend of Polubotok. Polubotok had been spreading abuse about the hetman in Kiev and denouncing him in Moscow, but he could furnish no proof and was sent to the hetman's custody, but a rescript from the tsars ordered that he live on his estate until further notice. The hetman found this most humiliating. Petrik, Kochubey's nephew, was sent to the Crimea on the same criminal mission on which Solomon was sent to the king of Poland. The hetman prayed tearfully to God to deliver up his enemy Solomon in order that other enemies might be unmasked.

But when Grodsky was brought to Baturin to be executed the hetman thanked the tsars for their kindness and announced that he could not execute Grodsky in the absence of the Russian colonels and in fact did not wish him dead at all but would prefer to take him on a tour of the towns of Ukraine and show him to the people in order completely to clear the name of the hetman, cossack high command and all the Zaporozhian Host. But Moscow took a different view. Mazepa was sent an order to execute the monk Solomon, traitor and troubler of the realm, at the assembly of the cossack officers in Baturin. He should not take him on a tour of the towns as his criminal deeds were known to all. When the officers had assembled, Mazepa ordered the chief secretary Kochubey to read out the account of Solomon's trial in Moscow and to display his forged letters and counterfeit seals.

When they had inspected the letters the cossack officers and colonels declared that Solomon could not have done this wicked deed alone. It was obvious that he had been hired and told what to do by other villains. The hetman had the miscreant summoned and asked whether he had had a accomplice in this wicked business. Solomon was brought before the officers and repeated his former testimony on oath, that apart from Misha Vasiliev he had no other accomplice and if he had he would have said so in Moscow and thus avoided the cruel trial by torture and fire. On October 7 Grodsky was executed, still sticking to his former testimony at the execution. Mazepa was unhappy that Solomon had been executed, while Mikhail Gadiatsky merely was sent to Siberia. "Misha should be executed too, without mercy," he wrote to the tsars. "Just before he was executed Solomon identified Misha as the man who incited him to commit this crime. Let it be as the monarchs will, but we humbly beseech you not to send Misha's son back to Ukraine because a rotten tree produces bad fruit." It was impossible to comply with the hetman's request concerning Gadiatsky for, in the words of a contemporary account, "The Cherkassian colonel Mikhail Gadiatsky was tortured in a state trial, but he confessed to nothing under torture, cleared his name with his blood and was sent into exile."

THE LIQUOR FRANCHISE

In his inflammatory proclamations Petrik indicated two particularly onerous burdens in Ukraine for which he blamed the Muscovite government—the arenda or liquor franchise, and the practice of granting inhabited lands to officials, who were persecuting their serfs. Moscow took note of this and asked the hetman whether he could think of some way of eliminating both these problems. Mazepa replied that the liquor franchise in the towns of Little Russia was regarded as burdensome not so much because of the duties which were levied as the fact that the very words had been hated since time immemorial, probably because in the days of Polish rule the system was run by Jews who had thought up many ways of exploiting people.

"In consultation with the cossack high command and the colonels," wrote Mazepa, "we have sent out universal proclamations to regimental headquarters and towns, in which we exhort the cossack officers to ensure that people are not being harmed by the franchise; for example, people should be allowed to distill liquor at home or to buy it for weddings and baptisms in places other than the franchise stores. We also have sent edicts to assure the people that the hetman and his general staff are seeking ways of abolishing the franchise system and replacing it with some other method of obtaining funds for military expenses. Let the whole people, old and young, consult together and let us know whether they would prefer to pay a new tax in place of the franchise or impose a duty on all taverns. On the subject of landed estates my councillors and I have come to the following decision: any person deemed unworthy by the Host or the people in respect of their service record but who owns estates on the basis of grants from us shall be deprived of those estates. But we dare not confiscate estates granted by the tsars, for this would be a violation of the monarchs' will. We ask for the tsars' gracious instructions on this matter and report that the Zaporozhians have informed us again and again, and most recently via a messenger, that estates should be confiscated from persons of inferior status. They are more offended by the ownership of estates than by the liquor franchise, and if we fail to confiscate them there may be a popular uprising. For a long time now we have been sending out general proclamations forbidding estate owners to burden the inhabitants of the villages granted to them with excessive work and requisitions, or to cause them any offence whatsoever, and inviting the peasants of oppressive landlords to submit complaints which will be acted upon promptly." The new policy of confiscating estates was entrusted first to Leonty Polubotok. Then the colonel of Mirgorod, Danila Apostol, reported that when Mazepa was in Moscow Polubotok's son had told him, Apostol, about Mikhail Gadiatsky's hostile intentions. "If young Polubotok knew of Gadiatsky's schemes he must have known about Solomon's schemes, too, and so also must his father, the more so since Polubotok senior, when he was colonel of Pereiaslavl, had designs on the hetmanship." As a result the Polubotoks, father and son, were placed under arrest and their estates confiscated.

PALEY

While Mazepa was pursuing his enemies at home, on the west bank Paley was earning even more notoriety in his tireless struggle against the Tatars. He was a nuisance to the Crimea, where people compared him with Serko,[60] and he continually received assurances that the khan would treat him better than Khmelnitsky if he came over to the Tatar side. Paley's situation was indeed becoming more and more like that of Bogdan Khmelnitsky. He did not wish to live on the Polish side because a cossack found it impossible to live in harmony with the Polish lords. He had appealed to the great sovereigns, but they had rejected his offer for fear of violating the peace with Poland, the same fear which prevented their father from accepting Khmelnitsky as his subject.[61] But Khmelnitsky had scared Moscow by threatening to swear allegiance to the Muslim khan if the Orthodox tsar refused to accept him. Now as a result of the missives from the Crimea Paley too had the opportunity to use the same threat. At a private meeting with Mazepa in Baryshevka he told the hetman that the great sovereigns should accept his offer right away, but if they had no need of his services, they should say so outright and he would seek a position elsewhere—the Tatars would accept his allegiance. The great sovereigns were wrong to fear a breach of the peace with Poland. The Poles were anxious to find any pretext to start a war.

Mazepa reported this conversation to Moscow, adding that if Paley went over to the Tatars the Zaporozhians would join him, which would be very harmful to Russia. Therefore it would be best to accept Paley's allegiance and explain it to the Poles by telling them that he had been born in Borzna [in Muscovite Ukraine]. If the sovereigns accepted Paley, he, Mazepa, would make him colonel of Pereiaslavl. But Moscow's reply remained the same: they could not accept Paley. The hetman must try to persuade him not to go over to the Muslims out of desperation. If he was badly ill-treated he would leave his regiment secretly for the Pereiaslavl side. Mazepa was not satisfied. In December 1692 he wrote again to the tsars about Paley asking them to impress upon the Polish government the damage that would be caused to Christianity if Paley were driven to desperation by Polish persecution and defected to the Tatars. At the same time the hetman repeated his earlier advice: "It would be best to take Paley with all his men and the township of Khvastov under the tsars' protection. Given his Little Russian origins and the notoriety he had won, if he were to defect to the enemy it would cause trouble in Little Russia. Many people would be enticed at the prospect of lawlessness and booty to go across to him." The tsars replied that in an emergency Paley with those of his men who came from Zaporozhie and the left bank of the Dnieper could return to Zaporozhie, spend some time there and then disperse to the Ukrainian towns, as they wished, to where they had relatives. A transfer of this kind would not earn rebukes or sermons from the Poles and it would be no disgrace for Paley to go to Zaporozhie. He could return to Zaporozhie from Poland by the same route that he had gone from Zaporozhie to Poland.

SHUMLIANSKY

On the Polish side of the Dnieper there were many besides Paley who looked to Moscow for help. Bishop Shumliansky hastened to vindicate himself with the tsars. In the spring of 1692 the Russian resident in Poland, the table attendant Mikhailov, was in Lvov. On April 30 the bishop sent an archdeacon to invite him to visit him the next day to attend mass in the cathedral and to see a play which was to be performed in honor of St. George the Martyr, and after the performance to dine with him. The resident excused himself on grounds of ill-health. The next day, May 1, another messenger arrived from Shumliansky, the monk Krasinsky, a priest from the cathedral to whom the resident had made his confession during Lent. The monk spoke of the bishop's great disappointment at not being able to see the resident. Solomon was to blame for all this, but the bishop was not guilty; Solomon had undertaken this business on his own initiative. Mikhailov replied that he knew nothing of any business, and it had been ill-health and lack of time which prevented him from meeting the bishop. If Shumliansky really must see him he should come to the out-of-town hermitage of St. John the Theologian on May 4 with some people to escort him. The resident would be attending mass there.

Shumliansky arrived as agreed, sent away his companions and began to speak to the resident. "I find myself in this unexpected trouble and the object of the tsars' anger quite unintentionally." He thereupon took a cross, kissed it, burst into tears and continued: "Let me tell you the whole truth: when the monk Solomon arrived to see the king with the forged letters the king at once sent for me and said 'Father, the time has come for you to help us. You are the only one who can do this deed.' So on the king's orders I wrote a letter in my own hand to the hetman Mazepa inviting him to return to his hereditary sovereign if such was his wish. Apart from that I wrote nothing bad. The former resident Volkov piled up accusations against me quite cruelly, calling me a lawbreaker and a criminal, saying that I had written fake letters to Ukraine and sent some letter or other in the king's hand with my archdeacon. This is slander and it is getting to the stage where I shall be forced to act as the bishop of Premysl did.[62] Tell me, what is this letter from the king and how did it get to Moscow?"

"I have heard nothing of this and don't know what you are talking about," replied Volkov, "but from what you say I gather that the letter you wrote to Hetman Mazepa was a very wicked letter, and I think that you acted on your own initiative, without the king's authority, and you are casting aspersions on the king in order to justify yourself."

Shumliansky bowed and swore that he had acted on the king's instructions. "I have two letters from the king on this matter, with his signature and seal. Anyone can see that I couldn't have done it of my own accord, because Mazepa and Ukraine would never subordinate themselves to me and I could not invite them on my own behalf. Their majesties the tsars demanded that the king send me to Moscow to be tried and the king said nothing. If I had written to Mazepa on my own initiative the king would have been angry with me and would not have defended me. But praise God that nothing has come of it. Everything is as it was before and will be a lesson to us in the future. The king to this day regrets what happened and is anxious that the affair be concluded forthwith and Solomon handed over."

"Since you are the only person from whom I have heard about all this I can't really judge or reach a conclusion," said the resident, " but from the little you have told me I realize that this was a matter of some importance and you need to make every effort to put matters right and rid your soul of a grave sin." At this Shumliansky sighed and said "I was tempted by Satan. And even the king, who, you'll agree, is a clever man, and other clever people who got involved in this affair were fooled by that monk and acted incautiously. I tell you truly that the Poles are hoping to reclaim Ukraine. In the middle of Lent the king suddenly sent for me. I went and was greeted with the words 'Father, an old piece of business had been concluded. Mazepa is already ours. He has come to Belaia Tserkov.' All that day the king was cheerful and treated me to the sort of good wine to which no one has been treated for some time. Then a few days later he sent for me again and said that the business had been postponed and was not yet concluded. You can see what hopes they cherish."

"I am amazed at what you are telling me," said the resident. "I did not expect that a man of your calling and rank would fall into such grave sin so recklessly. But tell me how you intend to put matters right and atone for your guilt."

"What's done is done," replied Shumliansky. "I angered the great sovereigns with my letter to Mazepa, and I am very sorry, but I cannot turn back the clock. But to atone for my guilt I wish to serve the great sovereigns in the following way. Their majesties the tsars have concluded a treaty of permanent peace with the Poles, but that peace is very insecure. The Poles are ill-disposed towards the great sovereigns and are awaiting their chance to take back the Little

Russian towns, therefore the peace treaty is not printed in their constitution but is sealed only by the king's oath and not confirmed by the Commonwealth. But it's common knowledge that the king's decisions can be challenged by the lowest little provincial squire.[63] As soon as the Poles recoup their strength and see a convenient opportunity they will break the truce. It's impossible to have an alliance with them because they are deceivers and always seeking ways of making mischief. In return for the permanent peace they forcibly transferred almost all the Orthodox parishes into the Uniate church. I and my bishopric are the only ones that remain.

"There is only one way of putting a stop to this wickedness and consolidating the permanent peace and that is by demanding at the Sejm that the treaty be printed in the constitution, and saying that if they refuse the great sovereigns will not ratify this peace. It would be a good thing to threaten them by asking why the bishopric of Premysl was converted to the Union. They will try to say that the bishop converted of his own free will, to which you can reply that in that case he alone should belong to you, the Poles, but the Orthodox people of his bishopric should choose another bishop. Many Orthodox will attend the Sejm to submit an appeal for such an election and I can draw up the petition. The Poles will not be able to refuse, the bishopric will be restored and the true faith strengthened for a long time to come. Then let the tsars' ambassadors raise the case against me at the Sejm and demand that I be punished for my letter to Mazepa. I, being protected by the constitution, will speak out boldly against the king and show everyone the king's letter. I think at this point the king will withdraw. At the Sejm you must deal with people after the French fashion. Some senators will have to be bought off. You'll not defeat the Poles in warfare, but bribes will do it. With gifts the tsars can achieve whatever they want at the Sejm. But if the great sovereigns bring up the case against me before the treaty is ratified I shall join the Union or go abroad. God sees my conscience and that I wrote that letter under extreme duress, against my pious judgement. I am forced to act suspiciously, sometimes wearing red boots, sometimes yellow, a cap instead of my bishop's cowl, anything to keep the Polish politicians happy and to protect my bishopric from persecution."

On May 15, Holy Trinity Day, Shumliansky officiated in the cathedral and prayed solemnly and fervently for the tsars, the ecumenical patriarchs and the patriarch of Moscow, for the royal house and for the proliferation of the pious faith of the Greek rite. The resident was in church and the Lvov Orthodox brethren[64] "with great devotion and sermons expressed their goodwill towards the great sovereigns and their desire to serve them."

POLISH PERSECUTION OF ORTHODOXY

Thus the religious struggle between Russians and Poles continued and as previously the Poles kept on restricting their Orthodox subjects. The Russian resident Volkov sent the following report. On May 14, 1690 in Warsaw the crown chancellor Ernst Dengof passed judgement on the dispute of the burghers of Vladimir-in-Volhynia with the bishop of Vladimir, a Uniate and apostate from Orthodoxy. The bishop wished to convert two Orthodox churches built by the Vladimir brethren to the Union. He made out that all Russian churches now belonged to the Uniate church and came under its pastorate. Only these two churches remained outside and their priests did things their own way, disobeying the bishop's orders. The parishioners testified that the churches had been Orthodox since time immemorial and it would be wrong to make them Uniate. At his election the king had sworn that the faith would not be subjected to persecution. The chancellor's ruling was as follows: "Although these churches were not formerly Uniate, from now on they shall be." No sooner had he uttered these words than everyone felt the ceiling vaults of the chamber begin to creak and the walls begin to tremble. Everyone made a dash for the exit. The chancellor was caught in the doorway by something catching his wide sleeves and he fell over and the people running behind him fell on top of him, almost suffocating him. He was carried out half alive. The chancellor recovered in the porch and sent trustworthy men to investigate whether there was someone on the roof and what was threatening to make the ceiling collapse. But no one was found on the roof and the vaults stood completely undamaged. In spite of this the chancellor did not give a final verdict and he never again entered that particular chamber. The decision was left to the king, who judged in favor of the Uniates.

A report written by Volkov shows how many Orthodox there were in Warsaw at this time. Volkov's residence contained an Orthodox church, served by a priest from Premysl. A large number of Orthodox Christians attended this church—chamberlains, royal courtiers and nobles, and the priest celebrated various rites, heard confession, administered communion, baptized infants and celebrated weddings. The Polish clergy disliked this intensely. On May 20 Bishop Witwicki of Poznan had the priest arrested on the street and brought to him. Letting out a stream of abuse about the Orthodox faith, the bishop had him placed under arrest in his own residence. The next day the royal falconer, a Russian Orthodox Christian, died unexpectedly. His fellow falconers requested that the king give permission for the deceased to be buried in the Orthodox rite. The king agreed and on his instructions the priest was released from the bishop's custody. In the fall of that year Malakhovsky, the Uniate bishop of Premysl, seized five Orthodox churches and the Uniates also took the Orthodox priests' homes and looted their property. The king ordered the priests' homes and arable land restored, but the Uniates paid no heed. Ursula, the widow of the former crown treasurer Andrzej Modzrewski, on whose land the confiscated churches stood, ordered that one priest be arrested and flogged with a cudgel. The wretch received three hundred blows, after which he was taken by some other priests to Zolkwa to be examined by the king, but received no compensation. At first Russian Orthodox believers had free access to education in the Jesuit schools in Lvov, but in the 1690s the Jesuits began to attempt to force them to accept the Union and swear allegiance to the king. Any Russian Orthodox student who completed the course in grammar and rhetoric in their schools would be admitted to the philosophy faculty for only a year. Anyone wishing to stay longer must convert.

In 1691 Volkov was replaced as resident in Poland by the table attendant Boris Mikhailov. In Minsk Mikhailov was visited by the Orthodox burgher Demian Shishka and his friends who complained that they were being subjected to fierce persecution by the Lithuanian magnates, Hetman Sapieha[65] and others, and being forced in various ways to become Uniates. In May the Uniate priest Salgan Yurievich accompanied by a great mob of Catholics and Uniates went to the monastery of Saints Peter and Paul in Minsk with the intention of turning it into a Uniate monastery. The archimandrite of the monastery, Peter Pashkovich, and the brothers were warned and sent the Orthodox parishioners word in advance. The latter assembled and ensconced themselves in the monastery with weapons and stones for three days and nights, vowing to defend the monastery to the death. They fought off the Catholics and Uniates spiritedly and in the end said that they would perish in the monastery and anyone who survived would flee to Moscow with their wives and children and find a way of avenging them. The besiegers withdrew from the monastery. The Uniate metropolitan Kiprian Zhukovsky, Bishop Konstantin Brestovsky of Wilno and priest Yurievich continued to persecute the Orthodox and impose all sorts of taxes and expropriations throughout Lithuania. The burghers claimed that Tatars and Jews were treated with more respect by the Polish magnates than were pious Orthodox Christians. The Tatars were allowed to build new mosques and the Jews synagogues, but the Orthodox were not allowed to roof or repair their old churches. Soon the faith would be eradicated entirely.

In the summer of 1692 when the resident was in Lvov he was walking one day in an outlying district and behind the Jesuit church met an elderly man of respectable appearance who came up to him and announced that he was a noble of Orthodox faith by the name of Popara and asked to speak to him without witnesses present. Popara began his speech with a deep sigh. He had been in Moscow when Tsar Michael was still alive and had kissed his hand on many occasions. In Tsar Alexis's reign for a number of years he had conferred with the boyar Matveev[66] on secret matters. He even said that as a result of his services Kiev had remained in the tsar's domains. These years had been a time of great tranquillity for all Orthodox Christians, there had been no forced conversions to the Union, the Poles treated Russians with respect and dared offend no one for fear of incurring the tsar's wrath. But when the eternal peace treaty [of 1686] was signed and the Jesuits were given permission to propagate their faith in Moscow, the Poles had begun to persecute God's church strongly; more than seven hundred churches had been made Uniate and now the last bishopric, in Lvov, was being put under pressure to convert. The Poles boasted that even in Moscow people preferred the Polish faith to their own Russian one. "The Poles pay no heed whatsoever to us Orthodox," Popara continued. "They treat us like cattle. Recently Bishop Joseph Shumliansky called me to see him and told me that a royal edict had been sent ordering him to join the Uniate church. I alone and without the Orthodox brethren told the bishop that he should announce to the king our Russian decision. We shall never accept Union voluntarily, by God's grace we have a good faith of our own, and never have we harassed your royal belief. The king should protect us from the Tatars; he shouldn't have to defend us from religious persecution. I am an old man and already I see death awaiting me on the threshold, so for the sake of the Christian faith I declare what I know to be the truth: the bishop of Lvov won't stick by his faith. If not this year, then in the near future he will join the Uniates, because Shumliansky was raised by force to the bishopric, by the patronage and wish of the present king, when the latter was still hetman.[67] When he was appointed he promised to become a Uniate without fail. Shumliansky made the bishop of Premysl make the same promise and he accepted the Union last year. Shumliansky is a Uniate in secret but he will not take the vow openly because the brethren are standing firm. This weakness stems from the fact that the Catholics were given permission to reside in Moscow. The Jesuits became familiar with the whole realm, made descriptions of all the towns and customs, and recently three Frenchmen[68] went to Moscow for the same purpose. The Pope, the emperor of Austria and the kings of France and Poland have all agreed that if the war with the Turks and the emperor's war with France come to an end then together by war and other means they will introduce the Catholic faith into the Muscovite realm. Many Jesuits who were in Moscow have proposed schemes to this end and many enthusiasts are gathering to put the plan into operation and swear that it will be possible to achieve this in the Muscovite realm in a short period of time. We Orthodox are extremely apprehensive."

The resident consoled the old man, arguing that none of this was confirmed; he was speaking of things unprecedented of which he knew too little. But Popara insisted. "I know for certain that the Poles through the Jesuits, Pope, emperor of Austria and king of France have agreed to introduce Catholicism into Russia."

It was difficult to calm the fears of Russian Orthodox inhabitants of Western Russia with respect to the Jesuits, who in their eyes always had been the chief instigators of persecution and would stop at nothing. The clergy of Mogilev informed the resident that commissioners Lord Werbiecki, Lord Szpielowski, Zembocki and Ilinic had come to Mogilev from Wilno and at the insistence of the Jesuits in a very violent fashion destroyed the church of Saints Peter and Paul in the village of Ezera, three miles from Mogilev, by allowing some Tatars who lived nearby to demolish it. They killed the parishioners defending the church, climbed onto the roof and kicked down the cross, then dismantled the building down to the last plank of wood and smashed up the icons violently. The place remained deserted and the Orthodox Christians, left without a church, began to waver and many went over to the Jesuit doctrine. When the men of Lvov appeared before the king on an official visit bearing greetings and gifts the procession was headed by Poles, followed by Armenians with Orthodox Russians bringing up the rear, whereas previously the Orthodox had precedence over the Armenians. After the bishop of Premysl, Innocenty Winnicki, accepted the Union he became a cruel persecutor of Orthodoxy. On his initiative, nobles attacked the Orthodox church of the Holy Trinity in the village of Komorna four miles from Lvov. In the church the priest Ivan Revenets was conducting mass and the nobles tried to drag him out and kill him, but the congregation locked themselves in the church and defended themselves for three hours or more. When they saw that they could not hold out much longer, they dressed the priest in women's clothing and smuggled him out, then opened the doors. The nobles, not finding the priest, beat the parishioners to death and sealed up the church to transfer it to the Uniates.

Moscow could not remain indifferent to reports such as these. The resident was instructed to demand that the Polish government send official circulars to all the Russian districts strictly forbidding conversions to the Union and making arrangements in those places where bishops had apostatized to Orthodoxy to elect new ones, who would go to Kiev to be installed by the metropolitan. This was the reply: "The monarchs should not poke their noses into the internal organization of each other's realms, neither the king into Muscovy nor the tsars into Poland. The nobles of Smolensk[69] were forced to become Orthodox, but we shall not speak of this matter because in both realms there is one Christian faith and any sovereign is free in his own realm." The resident objected. "It's not a matter of poking noses into other people's countries. The nobles of Smolensk were not converted under duress and are still not forced to comply. It is a question of the violation of treaties, the violation of the oath sworn by the king and the whole Commonwealth. Compulsion in matters of faith, violations of oaths—these are fundamental matters." "Two wrongs don't make a right, therefore things cannot be different from what they are," replied the Poles.

Violence did not cease. In 1693 Krasinsky, the governor of Polotsk, gave the church of the Intercession on his estate at Sokolov to the Uniates after intimidating the parishioners into submission with armed men. "Russian people groan and weep but can find no relief and are plunged into eternal darkness." In Kamieniec the vice-chancellor of Lithuania Prince Radziwill converted the Orthodox church of the Nativity of the Virgin to the Union. The Russian resident's protests were countered with the response that in Kamieniec there were only about thirty Orthodox Christians, who themselves applied to join the Uniate church. As for the governor of Polotsk, he was master in his own patrimony and it was difficult to restrain him. The resident was told to speak to him personally. "You go on about the permanent peace," said the magnates, "but on the basis of this treaty the great sovereigns are trying to order us about in our own patrimonial lands, as though this treaty had made us their slaves. According to our own law each nobleman is at complete liberty on this own estates; he can punish his peasants as he wishes without the king's authorization, so why should he not be allowed to replace some worthless little cleric? The treaty with their majesties the tsars is applicable only to the king's estates but has no force on the estates of the great magnates or the gentry because a magnate cannot be ordered about on his own property. Moscow expelled the Jesuits [in 1689], which was a restriction on the Roman faith, but the king said nothing because the tsars are at liberty within their own domains."

PETRIK RETURNS

Nothing more could be done because a major war was about to break out, this time not a Russian campaign against the Crimea but a Tatar attack on Ukraine.

At the beginning of 1693 forty thousand Tatars accompanied by Petrik appeared in Ukraine but failed to lure Zaporozhie over to their side or to take a single town and returned with a negligible amount of booty. "They barely touched your royal majesties' God-protected domains with their heathen hooves," Mazepa informed the tsars. Petrik, who, as contemporaries expressed it, continued to "dangle his soul over the infernal abyss," resorted to writing letters to Zaporozhie in which he tried to turn the cossacks against Moscow. "Be sensible, realize that the Muscovite tsars will not always send you your allowance as they often do now in gold pieces. Moscow acts in this way because they can hear the wolf in the forest but when the danger is past not only will Moscow not send you any allowance but they will make peace with the Crimea, drive you from the Camp and take away your military liberties. Part of our Ukraine they will surrender into the captivity of the horde and the rest they will take for themselves into eternal servitude. To whom then will you turn, who will help you and release you from captivity? You're familiar with the saying: he who is supported by the Crimean khan, that man will be a lord. It's amazing. Once you used to complain about unjust treatment from Moscow and from your masters, you complained that there wasn't a man capable of taking action. And now that such people have been found you seem to be reluctant to allow yourselves to be liberated. A volunteer force has been unleashed on Russia but you, the elders, remain in the Camp. I advise your honors, my fine lads, take advantage of this opportunity. If you let it slip by you won't get another chance like it and when you lose your liberties you will have to take upon your conscience the sins of the whole Ukraine which is defended by you and relies on you." The Zaporozhians responded to the "enemy incarnate" that a curse would fall upon him for coming with the Muslims to lay waste the heartland of the Orthodox faith, Moscow and especially Little Russia.

Petrik was cruelly mistaken to put his trust in the words of a disaffected minority in Zaporozhie and to attempt to play the part of Bogdan Khmelnitsky. The vast majority in Ukraine stood firmly by the unity of the Russian land, in other words for union with Moscow in the name of Orthodoxy. The following report was made by the tsars' envoy, the secretary Andrei Vinius, who visited Little Russia at the beginning of 1693 and attentively observed the current mood. "In the towns, villages and hamlets I observed in the people a staunch adherence to the Orthodox Church, great devoutness and an absolute and constant loyalty to the great sovereigns. They say: where else could we find the protection, defense and happy life which we have under the tsars' rule? We live under the Orthodox faith, peacefully in our own homes with our rights and liberties intact, which we never had under the Poles under whom we lived in slavery, like Israel under Egypt. Which of us could even think of uniting again with the Poles who, if they could, would hand us all over to the Muslims or put us to the sword, or force us to convert to the soul-destroying Union. As for what that work of the Devil Petrik is doing, it's clear that a Christian should never be in alliance with a Muslim. Just look at how Moldavia and Wallachia were devastated by the Muslims."

The retreat of the enemy gave an opportunity to deal with internal matters. The problem of the arenda or liquor franchise had to be resolved. The hetman ordered the colonels to assemble in Baturin and to bring with them the regimental high command, the garrison commanders, leading members of the Host and townsmen with whom they could consult and resolve the matter of the franchise. Many people of differing status gathered and talked and debated for a long time about whether to leave the franchise system intact or to abolish it. Many insisted that the system be retained because it harmed no one except the innkeepers, and in the towns it produced a big profit. They were able to satisfy all their needs thanks to the franchise and in some towns they were even able to put aside a thousand or more crowns. But the majority opposed the liquor franchise: it had long been detested. They said it gave restless people cause for reproof, a constant pretext for harming the common good, and now the Zaporozhians were shouting and clamoring because of it. It was decided to abolish the franchise and to collect the funds essential for paying the volunteer troops and for regimental expenses of various kinds from the people who kept the taverns and from the distillers who traded their liquor in the markets. But it was agreed that the new system would be introduced for a year in the first instance to see how it worked.

Petrik did not come to Ukraine with the Tatars, but the hetman continued to be harassed by him. Cossacks fleeing from Petrik testified that he had letters from Mazepa. This testimony was such that in Moscow it was given no credence but Mazepa was extremely aggrieved. At dinner in Glukhov with Miklashevsky, the colonel of Starodub, Mazepa flung himself on Kochubey, boxed his ears, kicked him and shouted "You and Petrik wrote those letters in my name, which is why I am so distressed because I am innocent and I am giving you this reprimand." "I'm not to blame. I know nothing about it," replied Kochubey. "If Petrik got hold of some old letters from my office it's nothing to do with me." After this scene Mazepa immediately left Glukhov to go to the camp of Table Attendant Colonel Baturin and asked "What am I to do now?" Baturin replied: "You have aggrieved one and insulted the other. Go back to Glukhov to Miklashevsky's." Mazepa returned at once to Miklashevsky's, sent for Kochubey and made peace with him.

The continual arrival of reports about Petrik's latest schemes also gave Mazepa no rest. Petrik assured the khan that in Little Russia there certainly would be an uprising of the common people against the landlords and tax-farmers, especially if the khan were to march on Little Russia and the hetman were to concentrate all the regiments in one unit. There the rank and file would attack the officers, then the common people in the towns would slaughter the landlords and tax-farmers, then all the people of Little Russia would unite with the Crimeans and wage war on the Muscovite realm. The first priority of Petrik and the khan was to win over Zaporozhie, where there were always men willing to join them and murmurs of discontent were constantly heard in in the cossack units. "If the khan gives the Host money and horses we're ready to serve the khan and the lords of the Crimea. With support from the khan, a man's a lord." On his return from the Camp the hetman's envoy Gorbachenko related the following: "There are many unreliable people there, poor sorts, without food, without weapons. The Camp commander Husak told me: 'You can see how many poor people have arrived from the towns but we cannot raise our voices against them at the assembly. If war broke out against the Muslims on the hetman's initiative all these types would join up and the wranglers would perish in battle.'"

PALEY

Mazepa tried to get Moscow to give permission to launch an offensive against the Turks. The hetman was greatly troubled by a report that the cossacks had switched their allegiance to Paley. Petrik had tried to play the part of Bogdan Khmelnitsky, promised much but done nothing, but the cossacks could see the renowned field warrior, who made no promises but did much, fighting constantly and successfully against the Tatars. To many cossacks Paley seemed the ideal leader for the whole of cossackdom, bold and successful. When Paley was advancing on the Turkish settlements, in Zaporozhie they were saying "Let's make Paley hetman, bestow all the insignia of office upon him. Paley won't go the way of Petrik. He knows how to take the Ukrainian landlords in hand."

An occasion soon arose to draw Paley into a more distant and dangerous venture, of which Mazepa was very eager to take advantage. The hospodar of Moldavia was quarreling with the hospodar of Wallachia and sent Mazepa an appeal for help in capturing his enemy, saying that if the hetman didn't wish to use his own cossacks for the purpose perhaps the job could be entrusted to Paley. Mazepa immediately wrote to Lev Kirillovich Naryshkin. "Paley abhors the Poles, but our great sovereigns refuse to accept his allegiance on account of their treaties with the Poles. He doesn't wish to come across to us with just his family because in Khvastov he enjoys complete dominion over many people. It would be good to involve him in some business in which his Christian Orthodoxy were not put at risk, for he is in communication with the leaders of the Belgorod horde and we must take care that the Muslims don't entice him. If he undertakes a military campaign useful to the Christian cause, then the enemy's enticement loses its appeal." But the great sovereigns replied that this enterprise must be postponed because reports were coming in of large Turkish forces about to enter Wallachia, which could be dangerous for Paley.

At the end of June the poorer elements in Zaporozhie gained the upper hand and peace was made with the khan. Ataman Husak, who did not want peace with the Muslims, resigned his command and Ruban was elected in his place.

In Moscow a rescript was written to appease the Zaporozhians in which it was said that there would be no military campaign against the Turkish settlements that summer and that they should not blame the hetman for this fact. Mazepa sent the cossack Knysh to Zaporozhie with the letter. When the letter was read out in the Camp a cry went up. "It's obvious that the campaign was cancelled on the hetman's orders. He obtained this letter from the great sovereigns to stop us complaining about him. When we heard that there was to be no campaign against the Turkish settlements we made a truce with them, but when the hetman heard of it he sent our old Ataman Fedka to Ochakov. Fedka seized some Turks and Tatars who were collecting salt and killed many of them, and then the Tatars retaliated by capturing about fifty of our innocent Zaporozhians who were foraging for salt. The hetman ought to send us all the prisoners taken by Fedka and Fedka himself. If he refuses, tell him to expect a visit from us and the Tatars this winter. He'll see what's coming to him and his tax-farming landlords and overseers. The former hetman Ivan Samoilovich didn't play such dirty tricks on us. Once he tried to play a trick but when Serko wrote to warn him that he was preparing a hundred thousand sabres he took fright and immediately sent us wine, ham and other provisions. But this hetman calls us herdsmen, his overseer Rutkovsky doesn't allow the teams with the supplies through to Zaporozhie. But we are soon going to deal with Rutkovsky and stop him doing us any more harm. As long as Mazepa is hetman we can expect no good from him because he wishes Moscow well and looks only to Moscow's interests, but does not wish us well. The only hetman who will suit us is one whom we elect in the general cossack assembly."

The Zaporozhian chief secretary told Knysh in private: "As soon as the khan returns from the Hungarian war the Zaporozhians immediately will ratify their truce with him and stage an attack on the towns of Great Russia, but there is no point in their waging war in Little Russia because people there will make war on their own domestic enemies—the distillers, herdsmen, shepherds and poor folk will kill their bosses and lords. The Zaporozhians wish to attack the Great Russian towns because Moscow sends them a smaller allowance than it does to the Don Cossacks. The Zaporozhians are also angry because forts have been built on the Samara river and settled with people, their ancient forest has been chopped down and a military commander is stationed with troops in Orel whereas in Khmelnitsky's articles[70] it was written that Muscovite troops be stationed in only three towns in Ukraine. And the Zaporozhians are worried by the fact that hetmans, officers and colonels are taken to Moscow without their knowledge and banished to Siberia."

There was also unpleasant news from Paley. He had sent one of his cossacks to the king and the crown hetman with Tatar informers. The crown hetman summoned the cossack to him at night and asked: "Why doesn't Semyon Paley trust me? I have never yet deceived him with my word as hetman. It would be better for Paley if he obeyed my orders and went where I told him to go rather than independently going round the Tatar camps, which brings him no benefit whatsoever. Because he disobeys my commands, you receive no money from the king's treasury. If Paley transfers his service to the other side, he will be lost, falling between two stools. Let him know that if I so wish I can have him delivered to me this minute. The commanders across the Dnieper write and tell me that they all hate him and will do nothing to defend him. If you, my fine fellows, abiding by your loyalty to his majesty the king were to elect another commander it would be a good thing; it's not unusual for you cossacks to change your officers and if you were to do so, you would immediately be given a substantial payment from the king's treasury."

Moscow deemed it expedient to send a hundred additional bales of cloth to Zaporozhie. When the cloth was brought to Baturin it was inspected and three bales were found to be soiled with tar. Mazepa was much aggrieved, but nothing could be done. He sent the cloth with his cossack Sidor Gorbachenko. When he was within four miles of the Camp Gorbachenko sent a messenger ahead to warn the commander of his arrival. The latter called an assembly and ordered the liquor to be sealed up in all the cossack barracks to make sure that no one got drunk. When Gorbachenko arrived the ataman asked him to come to the assembly which was convened by the chapel, as was the custom. Gorbachenko entered the assembly, spent some time in prayer before the chapel, bowed to the earth in

four directions and handed the commander the hetman's letter. The
secretary read it out and all began to bow down and give thanks for
the great sovereigns' gift. They looked at the cloth and admired it,
saying that they had never been sent cloth like this before. They did
not get round to inspecting the soiled bales because the secretary
and the chief justice spotted them and hid them, ordering everyone
to disperse to their quarters and saying they would accept the cloth
on their behalf.

On the night of December 27 Captain Yaryshkin galloped into
the Little Russian Chancellery [in Moscow] on important business.
Mazepa had ordered him to make the following announcement to
Lev Kirillovich Naryshkin and Conciliar Secretary Ukraintsev: "If
the great sovereigns decide to accept Semyon Paley's allegiance they
should send him instructions without delay. If Paley's offer is
accepted then fresh troops should be sent to Ukraine to defend Paley
and Ukraine from the Poles who will not accept Paley's defection
without a price. Paley writes and informs the hetman by word of
mouth that if he receives no protection and assistance from the
hetman he will turn to the other side which has long been inviting
him because the Poles wish him nothing but ill and seek a way of
seizing and executing him. If they cannot find a convenient
opportunity they intend to have him killed secretly by evil and crafty
people. If Paley joins the Muslims the whole Ukraine would be
destroyed because the cossacks would all go over to Paley and there
would be no way of preventing it. Paley is a military man, lucky
in war, which is why the cossacks love him so much. There is no
other man like him in Ukraine. And now, even though they have
been given a stern warning not to do so, a large number of cossacks
have joined him from the Kiev Regiment."

In his letter to Mazepa Paley reported that the crown hetman had
sent out circulars to the cossacks and townsmen urging them to keep
away from Paley. After that Polish ensigns and cossack troops made
a surprise attack on the companies of Paley's regiment, killing many
people. Paley wrote that he must retaliate and asked Mazepa to send
instructions, advice and troops. Without awaiting advice or
instructions, on December 29 Paley sent another letter to Mazepa.
"I request an immediate reply. If I cannot rely on your honor's
military aid then allow me and my men to resettle in Trepolie or

Vasilkov, because the tormenting assaults of the Poles are intolerable. We are surrounded by their strongholds and Belaia Tserkov is close at hand, from which Khvastov has suffered damage on more than one occasion. Falling at your feet a thousand times I implore you to let me know: will you assist or must I flee from my enemies?"

Moscow sent the usual reply. They could not accept Paley directly and settle him in Trepolie because this would constitute a blatant violation of the treaty. First he must go to Zaporozhie and from there cross over into the territory of their majesties the tsars.

Mazepa did not change his tune. He continued to insist that Paley must be accepted and stated outright that if he was not he, Mazepa, feared that he would make a dangerous rival of Paley, another Khmelnitsky. Mazepa wrote to Moscow: "Now Paley cannot end his feud with the Poles because both sides have suffered about two hundred casualties. Paley wants to leave Khvastov and move to Umani. If he moves there he might summon the Tatars to aid him against the Poles. He will enlist their aid and wage war against the Poles and destroy them, but he may well destroy this side as well because he wants to have the title of hetman and entice cossacks from our side of the Dnieper. He could become another Khmelnitsky. You must work out quickly how to deal with him. It's easier to extinguish a small spark than a conflagration, especially as he could easily spark off an uprising in Little Russia and depopulate it by transferring the inhabitants. It will be impossible to hold them back because the people of Little Russia have beehives and other economic resources on the other side of the Dnieper."

Paley beat off the Poles, but in view of the fact that the tsars were not willing to accept him on the terms he desired he wrote to Crown Hetman Jablonowski to say that he was ready to make his peace with the king. Jablonowski replied: "Be sensible, your honor. Why, any one of the terms that you list here would invite condemnation, punishment and the sword! You disobeyed my orders on the most vital matters. You distributed lands from the patrimonial estates of various persons to unruly types from your own regiment. You beat, killed and tormented members of the nobility, their stewards and comrades and various people. You took money from the nobles; you drove peasants from their villages by force. You took over control of the whole Polish border region. You seized my beehives, you settled people on my estates. On the roads you intercepted letters addressed to me containing vital information and reports; you commandeered people coming to collect letters from me and gave them your own letters. There is simply no end to your assaults, crimes, murders, acts of lawlessness and disobedience and wicked words.

"All this forced his majesty the king and me to send troops into Polesie to make you come to your senses, but you have added insult to injury by having Dragomir, who was sent to you, savagely beaten and put in the stocks, which contravenes the customs observed by even the most uncivilized nations. You had the cossacks Iskritsky and Yarema beaten and robbed, and chased before you like slaves. I have always treated your envoys with respect. They were always at liberty, wanted for nothing, went away rewarded and well fed. Now you are making your peace, appealing for mercy and promising to mend your ways, whilst at the same time you arrest and rob Captain Blandovsky, who was on his way to Belaia Tserkov on my orders. How can I believe you after that? Despite all this, even now I am interceding with the king on your behalf and ready to forgive you all your wrongdoings if you will only keep your promises. As proof that you have reformed, release Blandovsky and his men and in return we shall release cossack prisoners from your regiment. I have sent my stepchildren and daughter as hostages. Take the oath to the king and Commonwealth and then you will be left in complete peace. If you refuse, I shall give orders for this affair to be brought to an end, concluded with fire and sword. If you opt for loyalty and obedience you have nothing to fear, you may rely on my good faith and conscience and come in person to receive the king's charter of privileges and to bow before his majesty the king and beg indulgence. Have no fear, you will be safe and secure."

On receiving this missive Paley went not to the king but to Baturin to see Mazepa and to make the same appeal. "May I move to Trepolie?" "You may not," was the hetman's reply. Paley then said: "I don't want to go to Zaporozhie. Even though the cossack Host has invited me to go there twice and offered me the post of commander and even a higher office, I'm used to living in town and don't want to go to the Camp. If I go to the Host of the lower Dnieper I'll have to do what the Host wants. I'm better off staying in Khvastov for the time being rather than going off somewhere unfamiliar. I know that the Polish troops won't attack in full strength because they have plenty else besides me to occupy them in this interminable war with the Turks and Tatars, and I can always defend myself against small forces. Also I'll show humility to the Poles and release Captain Blandovsky and all the Polish prisoners. I won't offer my own men as hostages but I'll swear an oath not to raise my hand against the king in person, though this won't apply to those who attack me. I'll gladly send part of my infantry to serve the king because that infantry won't desert me. They'll clothe themselves at the Poles' expense then return. In this way I can remain in Khvastov for a little longer. I would be sorry to leave this place, not just because I have my home here and a wide area sown with grain, but because I found the place deserted and populated it, not with Polish subjects but partly with members of the Zaporozhian Host from the Dnieper river and partly with Wallachians. I have built and decorated churches, which it would be wrong to abandon."

We saw earlier that in order to remove some of the causes for disaffection constantly voiced in Zaporozhie the liquor franchise was abolished, but only for a trial period in order to determine whether it was possible to do without it. The experiment proved unsuccessful. The hetman began receiving reports from all sides of disputes and quarrels caused by the collection of money from stores and taverns. There was a considerable shortfall in revenue compared with the old franchise system. At the Christmas assembly of the officers and colonels in Baturin the hetman announced that the experiment had failed and asked what should be done. The officers and colonels replied that the hetman should appeal to the great sovereigns to send money to pay the volunteer troops and for other military expenses, just as Tsar Fedor had sent ten thousand gold crowns in response to a petition from Hetman Samoilovich. Mazepa wrote to the boyar Lev Naryshkin and to Conciliar Secretary Ukraintsev. He received no written reply, only a message delivered by an envoy. "In response to Hetman Samoilovich's constant badgering thirty thousand gold crowns were sent from the estate of the boyar Matveev. The hetman should not appeal on this basis because the need now is not as great as it was at the time of the Chigirin campaigns [in 1677-1678], and especially because there are various sources of income for the hetman, commanding officers and colonels. It is shameful to beg for money."

When the commanding officers and colonels gathered in Baturin after Easter Sunday in 1694 Mazepa announced Moscow's reply. The officers and colonels said that in that case the liquor franchise must be reinstated. The franchise was more profitable, whereas requisitions from the ordinary people were more burdensome, seeing that they were taken even from someone who made do with bread alone without any trade, as a result of which the poor man was ruined. The hetman objected that there would be an outcry from Zaporozhie, but they replied that the Zaporozhians had not been overburdened by the franchise. The people were more burdened by their own Zaporozhian franchise which had been set up in the Camp. A third part of every barrel of liquor was taken by the commanding officers and unit commanders, and the rest sold at a fixed price, not freely. Then the hetman told the colonels and cossack elders to go home and collect people from all the towns and villages and ask whether there should be requisitions or the franchise system. This was done in all the towns, townships and villages and the verdict was everywhere unanimous: the franchise should be restored. On receiving these reports, the hetman sent them to Moscow with a request that a royal edict be issued.

III

THE AZOV CAMPAIGNS
1695-1696

PETER PLANS TO BUILD A FLEET
Even the White Sea, as we have seen, seemed restricted, gloomy
and pointless to Peter. He was growing up, and games satisfied him
no longer. He dreamed of discovering a passage to China or India
across the northern ocean, but lack of resources and time were soon
to dispel this youthful dream. He felt the lure of the Baltic, he
wanted to go there, but how was he to do so? The key to that sea
was held by the Swedes. There was also the Caspian, as foreigners
demanding free passage there to trade with rich Asia had been
pointing out for a long time. Why could Russia not acquire this
source of wealth for itself by establishing a fleet on the Caspian Sea
and gaining control of trade with the countries on its shores? As
long ago as Tsar Alexis's time a ship had been built for the Caspian.
That ship was burned by Razin,[1] but building a powerful fleet on
the Caspian would eliminate the possibility of another Razin. On
July 4, 1694 Franz Lefort wrote from Archangel to Geneva: "There
is talk of a journey to Kazan and Astrakhan in two years' time, but
maybe in two years it will have passed. I am always ready to carry
out orders. There is a plan to build several galliots and sail to the
Baltic (next bit deleted in the original). I am to be raised to the rank
of admiral of all his majesty's ships. This is Tsar Peter Alekseevich's
most fervent personal wish." On September 13 Lefort wrote:
"Next summer five big ships are to be built and two galleys, which,
God willing, will be sent to Astrakhan in two years' time for the
conclusion of important treaties with Persia."

LEFORT
Much could change in two years, thought Lefort, and much did
change. Lefort was singled out as the architect of these changes,

as the man who persuaded Peter to undertake the campaigns against Azov. It was time to put a stop to the tsar's military games. People were grumbling that the tsar was involved with Germans, and what good could come of that? Only games, in which people perished and suffered for nothing. In his own interests Lefort had to insist that the games stop and that some major enterprise be embarked upon in order to show the tsar and his companions in a favorable light. Otherwise, unfavorable comparisons might be made between this and the deposed regime. In Sophia's time the Crimean campaigns may have ended in failure, but at least Russian men-at-arms had pursued the foe into his own abode. Now it was the Tatars who were attacking the Ukraine. The allies were reproaching Russia for inaction.[2] Hetman Mazepa wrote that it was essential to launch an offensive. This was what the people wanted. It was vital as an exercise for the restless forces gathered at Zaporozhie.[3] Lefort wanted Peter to make a journey abroad to Western Europe, but how could he show his face in Europe before he had achieved anything or taken an active part in the holy war against the Turks? It should not be forgotten that the journey abroad was undertaken straight after the capture of Azov. The two events were closely linked.

GREEK CLERGY REQUEST ASSISTANCE AGAINST THE TURKS

Appeals for the active continuation of the war also came from a quarter whence, given previous experience, they were least expected. In September 1691 a letter dated March 18 arrived from Patriarch Dositheus of Jerusalem.[4] "The French ambassador has arrived in Adrianople," he wrote, "and has visited the patriarchs. He brought a letter from his king concerning the holy places and the Crimean khan himself happened to be there at the same time. The French presented the vizier with seventy thousand gold crowns and the khan with ten thousand and urged the Turks to hand over the holy places to the French because the Muscovites were planning to invade the Crimea. The khan talked about the same matter. They took the Holy Sepulchre away from us and allowed the French to officiate in it. We were given just twenty-four icon lamps. The French took half of the Mount of Golgotha from us, the whole of the church [of the Nativity] at Bethlehem and the Holy Cavern. They destroyed the icons, excavated the whole of the refectory where we dispense the holy light and did worse things to Jerusalem than the Persians and the Arabs ever did. The harm done to our monks there is impossible to recount. There were also monks from Mount Sinai who asked the vizier for an improvement of their status. The French intervened on their behalf in order to do us down, but the vizier paid no attention. Only he is stubborn and refuses to give us back the holy places.

"The Turkish people are shouting that the Muscovites were at peace but will now declare war over Jerusalem, but the vizier takes no notice. Now the French are asking permission to renew the church statutes in Jerusalem, which will make it appear as though they were the original owners. If you, God's sovereign rulers, desert the holy church what praise will you earn? If you send an ambassador here, his first priority must be to sort out our affairs and to have the holy places restored to us. Otherwise he should refuse to make peace. For if you make peace without this condition then don't bother to make any proposals about Jerusalem, because the Turks will assume that you don't care about it. Then the French will take possession of the holy places forever and we shall be unable to appeal against them. If you want to make proposals about Jerusalem, in the event of refusal don't make peace but declare war. Now is a convenient moment. First take the Ukraine, then demand Moldavia and Wallachia, take Jerusalem, then make peace. We would rather live with the Turks than with the French, but it is no use to you if the Turks continue to live to the north of the Danube or in Podolia or in Ukraine. If you leave Jerusalem in their hands it will be a bad peace, because the Turks are more hostile towards you than towards any other nation. Eighteen years ago, when I wrote a letter from Adrianople to your father Tsar Alexis of blessed memory, I advised him to leave the Poles alone and first pacify the Turks, because they longed to get to the Dnieper. He took no notice, he refused to believe me, but everything turned out just as I had predicted. Now I advise you: if you want to make peace, make peace on condition that Ukraine is liberated and Jerusalem restored and the Turks retreat beyond the Danube. If not, it would be better to fight together with your neighbors, and drive out and subjugate the impious ones, but there is no need to worry about the Poles. You can subjugate them whenever you are ready. The present vizier is a worthy man. He took Nissa and Belgrade, but that is your fault, because he had the Tatars with him. If you had constrained the Tatars the Turks could have done nothing.[5] They are not in the least bit grateful to you, of course, very likely because your generosity was born of folly.

"Now the vizier intends to deceive you with the help of the khan. He will defeat the Germans, but he won't take any account of you because he is profound and artful. Having defeated the Germans they will fight with great fury for many goals. Therefore I repeat: if Ukraine and Jerusalem are not liberated and if the Turks are not driven out of Podolia, don't make peace with them but stand your ground. You will enter peace negotiations and first demand Jerusalem and if they refuse to give it, don't conclude peace. The Turks will kill the vizier for waging a useless war. If they give you Jerusalem but refuse to relinquish Ukraine or withdraw from Podolia, don't make peace because if they sit firm in Podolia they will wait till the time is right. They won't stay silent for long. Help the Poles and the others while the people here perish. If the Tatars perish the Turks will perish with them, and your power will extend to the Danube, but if the Tatars remain safe they will deceive you. You won't get such an ideal opportunity again. We wanted to take Jerusalem from the French through you and not just for Jerusalem's sake. We don't want you to allow the Turks to live on the other side of the Danube and beyond the Danube. Destroy the Tatars, and Jerusalem will be yours. Alexander the Great went to the war with the Persians not for God's sake but for the sake of his fellow tribesmen. All the more reason that you should be vigilant and make every effort to drive off your wicked neighbors for the sake of the holy places and our Orthodox faith. Your prayed to God for the Turks to be at war with the Germans. Now the time is right but you do nothing. The Turks gave Jerusalem to the French to spite you. They hold you in low regard. Just look how they laugh at you. They sent letters to all sovereigns announcing the accession of a new sultan, but they didn't write to you at all. The Tatars are a mere handful of men, but they boast that they take tribute from you, and since the Tatars are Turkish subjects it follows that you also are Turkish subjects. Many times you boasted that you intended to do this and that, but it was mere words, nothing came of it." The patriarch felt constrained to add: "Take care that the Greeks living in Moscow don't get to hear about this letter, with the exception of Nicholas Spafarius." [6]

On September 2, 1691 Dositheus wrote another letter to the tsars, which did not reach Moscow until the beginning of 1693. The patriarch was extremely concerned that the French had obtained permission to renew the church statute in Jerusalem. He asked the tsars to enter peace negotiations with the Turks and to demand that the holy places be restored to the Greeks, for the English and Dutch were trying to bring about peace between Austria and Turkey, and with the Pope's encouragement the Austrians might include a clause in the treaty for the holy places to remain under Catholic protection. "We hope that the Turks will grant your request," Dositheus wrote, "because you will not be asking for anything new. Do not ask to control the holy places yourselves; just say that they be under the authority of the Greeks, as previously. As the Greeks are Turkish subjects, the sultan will not lose face."

THE FIRST AZOV CAMPAIGN (1695)

The Kozhukhovo campaign[7] was the last of the mock battles. "In the fall we were engaged in martial games at Kozhukhovo" wrote Peter. "They weren't intended to be anything more than games. But that game was the herald of real activity."[8] Golitsyn's experience demonstrated that campaigns in the steppe were doomed to failure and therefore it was decided to wage a campaign against Azov, access to which would be facilitated by the Don river and Don Cossack settlements close to the town. The capture of an important Turkish stronghold might have a stronger impact in Europe than war with the Tatars. The "skipper" must have been tempted by the thought that Azov was the key to the sea of Azov. They intended to catch the Turks out with a surprise attack on Azov so at the beginning of 1695 a campaign was announced, only against the Crimea. Indeed, a huge army, the old noble cavalry[9] under the command of the boyar Boris Petrovich Sheremetev, set off for the lower reaches of the Dnieper, taking with it the Little Russian cossacks. But an army of the new type consisting of the Preobrazhensky, Semenovsky, Butyrki and Lefort regiments, with the Moscow musketeers, town infantrymen and courtiers,[10] thirty-one thousand strong, appeared outside Azov under the command of the three generals Avtamon Golovin, Franz Lefort and Patrick Gordon. The company of bombardiers was led by *bombardier Peter Alekseev.* In April the lead division of Gordon's regiment gathered in Tambov and was sent overland towards Azov by way of Cherkassk. Golovin's and Lefort's troops embarked on ships in Moscow and sailed down the Moscow, Oka and Volga rivers. "We jested at Kozhukhovo, and now we are going to Azov to play," wrote the bombardier to Apraksin in Archangel. Deacon Peter[11] added "We are drinking your health in vodka and wine, and especially beer." The campaign met with a number of setbacks. From Nizhny Novgorod the bombardier wrote to his mock generalissimo King Romodanovsky: "Min Her Kenich![12] your excellency's most gracious royal letter written in the capital city of Pressburg has reached me, and in return for your majesty's gracious kindness we must spill our blood to the last drop. This is why we have now been sent, and we expect to accomplish it for your many and warm prayers to God, by your letter and our labor and blood. On matters here I can report that your slaves, generals Avtamon Mikhailovich [Golovin] and Franz Yakovlevich [Lefort] and all the troops are well thanks to God and intend to set off tomorrow, but have been delayed because it took the other boats three days to get here, and many of them are in a sorry state because of the carelessness of stupid helmsmen, as are the ships made by the chief merchants, and the others hardly arrived." To Vinius Bombardier *Piter* wrote: "Min Her! The winds kept us stuck in Dedinovo for three days, and another three in Murom; but the main reason for delays were the stupid helmsmen and workers who call themselves masters but whose work is as far from mastery as the earth from heaven."[13]

The troops sailed along the Volga until they reached Tsaritsyn and thence they made their way overland to the cossack settlement of Panshin on the Don. It was hard work because the troops, who were already exhausted from rowing, now must haul the guns and artillery supplies because there were not enough horses. In Panshin a new problem arose: the contractors had failed to provide sufficient food supplies. From Panshin the army set sail on the Don, rested in Cherkassk for three days and on June 29 [Peter's nameday] approached Azov, outside which Gordon was already camped. "Min

Her!" wrote Peter to Vinius, "On the day of the holy apostles Peter and Paul we arrived at the river Koisa, about ten versts from Azov, and we trust completely in the prayers of the holy apostles, as in a firm rock: the sons of hell will not overcome us." In the meantime in Moscow there was great anxiety about the fate of the tsar and the army, and various sinister rumors began to circulate. For this reason the letter delivered to Vinius caused great joy. Vinius replied: "The post brought us all such joy that many people at once offered up prayers of thanks in the churches and in their homes for the receipt of this mail, which has dispersed false rumors like the sun driving away the darkness; everywhere it brought great joy, *even in the musketeers' quarters.*" On July 8 the Russian batteries went into action. At one battery for a period of two weeks Bombardier Peter Alekseev loaded grenades and bombs and fired them off in person. Later he wrote in his service record: "My service as a bombardier began on the first Azov campaign."

On July 6 the Turks received reinforcements by sea, but it was impossible to keep the Russians supplied with food by water. They were hampered by two Turkish watchtowers, built on both sides of the Don. Between the watchtowers hung iron chains, and piles had been driven in. A challenge was issued to volunteers from the Don Cossacks to storm the watchtowers. They were each promised ten rubles. The cossacks captured one tower. Then the besieged were offered a chance for revenge. Jacob Jansen, a Dutch sailor who had entered Russian service and converted to Orthodoxy, deserted and showed the Turks a weak spot in the Russian defenses. He recounted that the Russians slept at midday when the heat was at its most intense. The Turks came out of Azov at that hour, sending on ahead one of the Kuban or Agrakhan Old Believers,[14] who when challenged by the sentries replied in Russian that he was a cossack and when he had ascertained that the Russians were asleep gave the signal to the Turks. The Turks rushed into the camp, attacked the sleeping men and although they were driven off with heavy losses they succeeded in carrying off nine field guns and wrecking the siege artillery. Even so, that night the Turks ensconced in the second watchtower abandoned it and their guns, and in the morning the cossacks occupied the watchtower.

This was greeted with joy in the Russian army. "Now we have been liberated," Peter wrote, "and supplies can be brought into our camps. Barges have arrived from the Koisa river with food for the troops, which previously had to be brought into camp overland at great risk from Tatar attacks. God be praised, now that the towers are captured it is as though the gates of success have opened into Azov." These hopes were dashed, however. Peter saw that it was impossible to "play" outside Azov. "We walk with our heads lowered," he wrote to Crevet, "because we have got too close to the nest and annoyed the hornets which sting hard in their fury; still, their nest is gradually falling apart." Concerted efforts were needed to break up the nest, but skill and unity were lacking.

In Moscow people became anxious because letters from Azov were being delayed. Peter was obliged to cheer them. "You write," he replied to Romodanovsky, "that there was no post on the usual days; this omission must be blamed on lack of time, because all these men skilled in military affairs did not manage to get their letters written; also your sovereign father and man of God (Zotov) was constantly occupied with making records of the questioning of numerous captives and other matters. Here, sovereign, thanks to God's grace and your prayers and good fortune we are all, thank God, well. For God's sake, don't fret about the mail being delayed. The reason truly is lack of time and not, God preserve us, some catastrophe. If some disaster were to happen, do you really think it could it be concealed? Pass on all this to anyone who needs to be told." To Vinius Peter wrote: "We are permanently harnessed to Mars's yoke. Here, praise be to God, all is well and in the town all has been tilled and sown with Mars's plow, in the ravine as well as the town. Now we are awaiting a good harvest, with the help of the Lord for the glory of his holy name."

That year the seed bore no fruit. Two attempts to storm the fortress failed. On September 27 it was decided to withdraw from Azov, having captured only the watchtowers. The troops sent to attack the small Turkish settlements on the lower Dnieper had better luck. Sheremetev and Mazepa took two, Kazykermen and Tagan, by storm; two others were left in Turkish hands.

On November 22 the tsar entered Moscow in triumph, but it was difficult to conceal the failure. An arduous and long campaign led by the tsar in person and heavy losses were not compensated by the capture of a couple of watchtowers, whose significance was scarcely enhanced by christening them with the impressive-sounding title of New St. Sergius Town, following the example of Tsar Alexis, who renamed towns captured in Livonia after Russian saints.[15] What a disaster! The young tsar's first venture was not exactly crowned with success. Evidently there was more to it than building dinghies, staging mock battles at Kozhukhovo and feasting with Germans! But of this failure a great man was born. Peter did not lose heart. Instead the catastrophe made him grow up and discover astonishing reserves of energy to make amends for the disaster and assure the success of a second campaign. The Azov disaster marks the beginning of the reign of Peter the Great.

THE VORONEZH FLEET

People were grumbling about the young tsar's close friendship with foreigners. No doubt in the wake of the Azov defeat many recalled the late Patriarch Joachim's[16] warning that success and God's blessing would elude them if Russian armies were commanded by heretical foreigners. And what did the tsar do? Why, as soon as he returned from the campaign he made arrangements for even more foreigners to be sent! He hired engineers and mining experts from Austria and Prussia. Until now the tsar built boats with foreign masters for his own amusement. Now he was summoning new master craftsmen from abroad, summoning foreign ship's carpenters from Archangel with the intention of building ships which would sail to Azov and prevent Turkish craft from bringing aid to the besieged fortress. The ships were to be ready by the spring of 1696, but was this feasible? We know what a long time it took to build a ship in Tsar Alexis's time, but Tsar Alexis's son was a shipwright himself. With him in charge things would be different.

The galley built in Holland and earmarked for the Volga and Caspian Sea was brought to Moscow, to the saw mill in Preobrazhenskoe. There they began to build ships on the same model and by the end of February 1696 the components of twenty-two galleys and four fire-ships had been cut from green, frozen wood. The work was done by soldiers of the Preobrazhensky and Semenovsky regiments, by carpenters hired from all over the

country, just like in the old days when workers were rounded up
and brought to Moscow to do the sovereign's business, and by
foreigners. In the forests close to the Don, in Voronezh, Kozlov,
Dobry and Sokolsk, twenty-six thousand laborers were supposed to
hack out one thousand five hundred river barges, three hundred
rowing boats and a hundred rafts by spring. Lefort was appointed
admiral of the fleet which was beginning to take shape. Skipper and
Bombardier Peter Alekseev now held the rank of captain. On
November 27 a campaign of land forces was announced, again under
the command of the boyar Alexis Semenovich Shein.

DEATH OF TSAR IVAN

In the midst of this unprecedented surge of activity initiated by the
second tsar, on January 29, 1696 the first tsar, Ivan Alekseevich,
had died, dying as he had lived, unnoticed.[17] Peter's first act as sole
ruler was to travel to Voronezh, notwithstanding an injured leg. By
the time the ice broke on the rivers they had to transfer the galleys
to Voronezh, assemble and launch them. The skipper, bombardier
and captain had to be there on the spot in order to ensure that the
work progressed speedily and efficiently. But there was much to
cause delay and inefficiency. The chief instigator's injured leg
slowed the journey from Moscow to Voronezh. Illness prevented
Admiral Lefort from leaving Moscow and travelling to Voronezh.
Thousands of laborers failed to turn up for work in the places
designated, thousands more fled from the work sites. The soldiers
sent to Voronezh to work on the fleet behaved so badly on the way
that Lefort was obliged to write to the tsar from Moscow: "I beg
of you, be so good as to order the captains to discipline the soldiers
and to see to it that they don't do anything stupid. On the way here
they behaved very badly." In spite of his illness, Lefort hastened
to Voronezh. "The roads are so bad," he wrote to the tsar on March
20, "that they're impassable either by sledge or by cart, and there
are frosts and strong winds, but I'll set off this week. Tomorrow
or the next day, I'll take my medicine and I shan't tarry, whatever
the road conditions are like. I won't stay any longer. I'll prescribe
myself a draught of medicine and the cold frosts won't penetrate
me. Besides, I'll have a doctor with me. I hear from your honor's
letter that God has granted an improvement in your health and I hope

that I shall be better, too, once I'm on my way. Today Prince Boris Alekseevich [Golitsyn] is dining with me and we shall drink a toast to your health. My first overnight stop from Moscow will be Dubrovitsy[18] and we won't forget to toast you there, either. I hear that you haven't any good beer in Voronezh, so I'll bring some for you, and some muscatel, too. Many planks have been sent to you, but you can judge for yourself how dreadful the road is by the fact that they haven't arrived yet. The ropes are ready, too, and have been despatched, but it's very difficult to make them now in this freezing weather. Be so kind as to give my regards to all the captains who are working hard on their galleys. I'll deal with the ones who have been slacking myself."

These men, members of the jolly company, write about all sorts of things in their letters: sickness and feasting, dealing with lazy captains, dispatch of planks and ropes and muscatel wine, all thrown in together. If we are to preserve them in history not as mummies but as living beings we must not imagine them purely as mentors or purely as drinking companions.

Lefort left Moscow and on the road from Elets he wrote to Peter: "The apothecaries have arrived in Efremov, and three are going with me, but the other nine got together for a drinking session and each began to praise his own medicine. After that a quarrel started about medicines and they got as far as drawing their swords. Three were wounded but not very seriously."

Apothecaries stabbed each other and wagoners fled from the road, scattering the goods which they were transporting. Then there was a new and terrible catastrophe. Fire broke out in the locality where the boats were being built, so that "the boat building suffered great damage and the military campaign suffered a setback." The captains in Voronezh were complaining and shouting that there was no coal for the forge. "Our work is at a standstill!" The weather also caused damage and delays. On March 23 Captain Peter wrote to Streshnev in Moscow: "Here, God be praised, all is well and the boat building is proceeding without delays; except after torrential rain there was such a hard frost that the rivers have frozen over again and as a result of the frost there was no work for five days." In another letter to Vinius, dated April 7, 1696, he writes: "Here, God be praised, all is well; only this morning an east wind brought severe cold, snow and storms."

In spite of all the interruptions, God be praised, all was well, and the work was proceeding quickly because, as Peter wrote to Streshnev, "we are earning our bread by the sweat of our brows as God ordered our forefather Adam to do." This bread was eaten in a small cottage consisting of two rooms with verandas and a porch, a bathhouse and a cookhouse.

The fleet which was built consisted of two warships, twenty-three galleys and four fire-ships. At the beginning of April they began to launch the ships. Holy Week was spent in this pursuit. (Easter was April 12). Peter sent holiday greetings to all those left behind in Moscow in a single letter to Vinius, "not from laziness, but because of great lack of time and the holiday." King Romodanovsky reprimanded the captain for including his greetings to him along with all the rest. *Piter* replied: "You were so good as to write of my crime in writing to your royal personage along with the others, and I beg forgiveness, because the likes of us shipbuilders are inexperienced in matters of etiquette." In the meantime, by March the regiments who were to travel on the boats were arriving in Voronezh one after the other. On April 23 the craft with the troops set off. On May 3 the "naval caravan", as the fleet was called, set sail. At the head, in command of four galleys, sailed Captain Peter Alekseev, on the galley *Principium,* which he himself helped build.

THE SECOND AZOV CAMPAIGN (1696)

All the effort which had gone into building the fleet was not in vain. The Russian fleet cut off the Turks' access to the mouth of the Don and Azov was left without assistance. A major Tatar assault on the Russian camp was repelled, followed by almost daily skirmishes, all successful for the Russians except on one occasion when, to use Peter's own words, the Russians neglected to defend themselves in proper battle formation but charged after the enemy in disarray in the manner of their ancestors. As a result several men perished, but they managed to rally their forces. Siege operations started. To his sister Natalia's pleas that he be careful, Peter replied: "I'm following the advice of your letter not to get too close to shells and bullets, but they keep coming after me. Order them not to. So far, though, they come up quite politely. The Turks have brought reinforcements but not attacked so far. I think they are waiting for us to attack."

The bombardment of the town began on June 16 with great success. The besieged residents were unable to remain in their shattered homes and took refuge in dug-outs, but the fortifications remained intact and the besiegers did not know what to do next. The engineers, artillerymen and sappers hired from Austria had still not arrived, so at the request of the troops they set to work in the manner of their ancestors. They began to raise up a great rampart to the same level as the enemy rampart and to excavate a ditch. At last the foreign experts arrived and the citadel shook from the shots aimed by the trained artillerist Grage. Two thousand Little Russian and Don Cossacks, the former led by Acting Hetman Yakov Lizogub, the latter by their ataman Frol Minaev, tried to take it by storm, were driven back from the inner fortifications, but ensconced themselves on the rampart from which the Turks were unable to dislodge them. After this all the troops were ordered to prepare for an assault. But the Turks decided not to wait that long and on July 18 signalled their willingness to surrender, negotiating permission to leave the town fully armed with their wives, children and possessions. The condition was accepted.

"Min Her Kenich," wrote Peter to Romodanovsky, "I beg to inform you that God has blessed your majesty's weaponry. Yesterday, as a result of your royal prayers and good fortune, the men of Azov acknowledged their plight and surrendered." To Vinius he wrote: "Now with St. Paul rejoice ever in the Lord, and again I say, rejoice! Now is our joy complete: by bestowing his grace the Lord God has rewarded our labours of these past two years and the blood that was spilt. Yesterday the men of Azov acknowledged their plight and surrendered. They delivered the traitor Yanushka (Jansen) alive into our hands."

There was great rejoicing in Moscow also. When the news of the surrender of Azov reached the capital on July 31 all leading figures in the government were gathered at the house of the "first minister", Lev Naryshkin. Vinius immediately sent for the patriarch, and his holiness wept for joy and ordered the great bell tolled to summon the people to prayers of thanksgiving, for which a great multitude gathered. Conciliar Secretary Emelian Ukraintsev read out the tsar's letter to the patriarch. "In our previous despatch to your holiness we reported that we were in good health and that our military operations were progressing well. Now we can report that under our command and thanks to the efforts and industrious labors of our boyar Alexis Semenovich Shein the troops of Great and Little Russia piled up an earthen rampart by the enemy's moat from all sides and having covered and leveled the moat from behind that rampart we crossed the moat by the same rampart over to the enemy's rampart defenses, and the ramparts were so close together we could almost touch hands, not to mention weapons, with the enemy; and earth could be hurled over their rampart into the town. And on July 17, a Friday, our Little Russian troops, who were selected for this campaign by drawing lots and were accompanied constantly by that virtuous man and skilful warrior Hetman Yakov Lizogub, together with Ataman Frol Minaev of our Don army and the Don Cossacks, resolved to undermine the enemy's gun emplacement and bravely to enter it. They fought the enemy for a long time and captured the emplacement, waited till nightfall and dragged off four guns. On the 18th, a Saturday, around midday the enemy, ensconced in Azov, saw the daring assault of our troops on the fortress and their dauntless enthusiasm and sensed that they were about to perish. They waved their caps, lowered the standards and sent out two men of quality to negotiate. They begged for their lives to be spared and to be allowed to withdraw with their wives and children, and as a pledge of their resolve and good faith they left two hostages and released the German Yanushka who had turned traitor, deserted our ranks for Azov and converted to Islam the previous year. On the 9th the besieged garrison surrendered the town of Azov and all its contents."

REACTIONS IN MOSCOW AND POLAND

The capture of Azov counts as one of those rare victories which left a vivid impression on the popular imagination. It was our first victory over the dreaded Turks, who not long ago had destroyed Chigirin before the eyes of our troops. For the first time since Tsar Alexis's first Lithuanian campaign, which was followed by such failures and problems,[19] Russians rejoiced at this brilliant feat of Russian arms. They recalled that once [in 1642] Azov had been taken by the Don Cossacks. In Moscow they had wanted very much to hold on to it, but they did not dare, and handed it back to the

Turks.[20] But of course the happiest people of all were those closest
to Peter, the "jolly company," because their enterprise was crowned
with success, and all their efforts in building the fleet and hiring
foreigners amply justified. The new government with its new
methods had proved far superior to the old with its Crimean
campaigns. "Everyone knows," Vinius wrote to Peter, "that this
world-famous town prostrated itself at your feet as a result of your
own efforts and with assistance from the sea."

What impression did the capture of Azov make in Poland, where
Sobieski had departed from the scene?[21] Even before the capture
of Azov the Frenchman Fourni, who had escorted some foreign
officers to Russia and returned by way of Warsaw, had given the
Polish lords a glowing account of the Russian operations at Azov
and the deeds of the young tsar. The senators listened, shook their
heads and said "What a courageous and carefree man this Peter is!
What ever will he do next?" The Ruthenian palatine[22] Matczinski
said: "The Muscovites would do well to recall that it was the late
King John who raised them up and made soldiers of them. If it had
not been for the alliance with him they would still be paying tribute
to the Crimea and stuck at home, but now they have acquired the
skills of warfare." This caused the palatine of Polotsk to remark:
"It would be better, less dangerous for us, if they were still sitting
at home. When they acquire skills and have the scent of blood who
knows what they'll do next? Lord God, don't let it come to that!"

The resident envoy[23] Alexis Nikitin heard the news of the capture
of Azov during mass on August 29, 1696. He told the priest to say
prayers of thanksgiving before the end of the liturgy and when the
singing of the *Long Life* to the great sovereign began, Ivan
Matkowski, a Polish nobleman of Orthodox persuasion, cried out
with all his strength "Long live his majesty the tsar, *vivat*," to which
the whole congregation responded with three cries of *vivat*, and the
envoy gave orders for three salvoes to be fired from two cannon
and as many guns as could be assembled. At the sound of gunfire
a great host of people came running, for whom Nikitin had five
barrels of beer and three of mead rolled out. The people intoned
"Long live his majesty the tsar. The Lord God be praised."

At a solemn gathering of the senate and provincial delegates on
September 1 Nikitin presented the primate with the official royal

account of the capture of Azov and made the following speech.
"Now, illustrious lord senators and all the Polish Commonwealth,
acknowledge your gracious defender and help him boldly in
compliance with the terms of the alliance, for like the veritable Peter
that he is, with the sign of the cross of our Lord he is opening the
doors to Jerusalem, lost but promised to Christians, in which Christ
our Lord triumphed by the cross on his throne. His majesty the tsar
is going straight to Crimean Tatary and will send rescripts to his
allies requesting reinforcements for the continuation of the war in
order to be able to strike without fear at that wild beast which is
lapping up Christian blood and devouring your fatherland. In
compliance with the treaty his majesty the tsar calls upon the
illustrious monarch of Poland to complete that journey which King
John of blessed memory began through Budziak to Constantinople.[24]
The crosses of your crown hetmans should be united here in the
cause of the cross of our Lord. Here should be united the arrows
and swords of the commanders of the duchy of Lithuania in order
to win back your patrimonial lands and to release your brethren from
heathen servitude. You could even add rich Arabia itself to the free
Polish eagle. Now is the time to mow down the enemy outright with
the armorial scythe: it will be harvest time when the cross of the
Lord is in action. Now is the time to march with the cross and
trample down the enemy with armour-shod feet. Now is the time
for the horseshoes of the Polish nobles to trample the infidel who
is cowed and in retreat. Now is the time to extend your territories
in those areas accessible only to Polish horsemen and to add titles
to your charter in accordance with the treaties rather than writing
titles which are not allowed by the treaties."

Three days after this ceremony Nikitin had a visit from the
Austrian ambassador, who told him that the senators were scared
and had resolved that their king no longer should lay claim to the
titles of Kiev and Smolensk to which he had no right. The
ambassador said that the magnates were not very pleased about the
capture of Azov, which was totally unexpected, but that the common
folk approved. Nikitin wrote to Moscow that "On September 11 all
Catholic churches in Warsaw held prayers of thanksgiving for the
capture of Azov, and three salvoes of twelve shots were fired from

cannon just for show, to give the impression that they were rejoicing. And trumpeters, pipers and drummers delivered congratulations from all the hetmans and palatines, played a *vivat* for the great sovereign, but their heart was not in it. I learned from a number of people that they are determined to unite with the Crimea and use the Tatars to defend themselves. They have had messages from the Crimea warning them not to trust Moscow, saying that when Moscow has defeated the Crimea it will not leave Poland in peace. Hetman Ivan Mazepa has received a stream of messages from the Poles."

In September the envoy paid visits to the Lithuanian and crown hetmans and reminded them that the Polish and Lithuanian armies had not been on campaign for two years, thereby letting down the tsar's armies. Crown Hetman Jablonowski replied: "I am making every effort, in public and in private, as I have always done, to persuade all the senators of the necessity of paying the troops' wages and honoring the terms of the treaty with his majesty the tsar. The convocational Sejm has broken up and now we must await the electoral Sejm in the hope that God will grant us a new and good sovereign."[25] "What has passed cannot be brought back," Field Hetman Potocki responded. "It may have been a favorable time for a campaign but disorders here in Poland did not allow us to take advantage of it. The king's health had been failing for some time, then death carried him off. For years now all Sejms have ended in confusion, all broken off, which means the troops have received no pay. The guilty ones will answer to God. Now the army has been raised to rebellion and the convocation Sejm has been broken up. This misfortune has been sent to punish us for our sins; it is God's scourge. The crown hetman tries to justify himself, says he's in no way to blame; but God will visit a plague on both of them, body and soul, the crown hetman and the hetman of Lithuania, and on the queen, too. Unless we can satisfy the army, there's nothing we can do. There will be no action until a new king has been elected." The hetman of Lithuania, Sapieha, responded to Nikitin's complaints in quite a different tone. "The tsar's troops may have set out early, but there was nothing brave in what they did; they took Azov by conditional surrender, not by military assault, and on the sea all they captured were a few gulls."

"The whole world and you know that the tsar's troops did not sleep at Azov," the resident objected, "but fought relentlessly and courageously with the enemy. Even if Azov was taken by conditional surrender, is that any cause for reproach? May God grant that the great sovereign take not only the whole Turkish land but also the realm of Poland and the grand duchy of Lithuania into his permanent possession by conditional surrender, then you Poles always will live in peace and tranquillity, not as you do now, forever quarreling with one another and in disarray." The Poles began to laugh, saying "The Muscovite's long whip will keep anyone quiet!" and one noble said "It's more peaceful where there's fear."

VICTORY CELEBRATIONS IN MOSCOW

Russia's enemies were right to be worried, for the country had a tsar who was not resting on his laurels. Immediately after the capture of Azov he inspected the nearby coastline and decided to build a fortress and a harbor on Taganrog promontory. Azov was strongly fortified and declared a Russian town. The mosques were converted to Orthodox churches. The tsar left Azov on August 15 and wrote to Vinius from Cherkassk: "It is written: worthy is the maker of his own recompense; and so I think it would be appropriate to receive the generalissimo and other gentlemen who have been laboring in the sweat of their brow and to honor them with triumphal gates; a good place might be on the bridge across the Moscow river, or wherever you think best. I write this not to instruct you but to remind your honor of this unprecedented event." Vinius replied that they had "assembled the craftsmen and all the materials and started to build. In the estimation of the master craftsmen Ivan Saltykov and his assistants the job can't be completed before September 18 as it's a considerable task."

They had considerably more time, as the tsar was detained for some time at the Tula iron works. The triumphal gates were built and decorated. Over the pediment between standards and arms sat a double-headed eagle beneath three crowns. On the pediment was written the inscription "If God is for us, who can be against us? An unprecedented event." There was Glory, holding a laurel wreath in one hand and an olive branch in the other, and beneath her the inscription "Worthy is the maker of his own recompense." The pediment supported statues of Hercules and Mars. Beneath Hercules on the pedestal were depicted the pasha of Azov and two fettered Turks, beneath Mars the Tatar murza and two fettered Tartars. Above the pasha was written the verse "Alas, Azov we have lost, that is to our cost." Above the murza "Once on the steppes we did fight, now from Moscow we took flight." Next to Hercules and Mars were pyramids with the inscriptions "In praise of the brave naval warriors" and "In praise of the brave land warriors." On either side of the gates hung pictures on canvas, one depicting a sea battle and Neptune, declaring "Even I offer congratulations on the taking of Azov and am subjugated." The other picture depicted the battle with the Tatars and assaults on Azov .

September 30 saw the triumphal parade of the victors, Admiral Lefort and Generalissimo Shein, with all their regiments. Behind the admiral's gilded carriage, on foot, walked Captain Peter Alekseev. The traitor Jansen also was carried in the parade, wearing a turban underneath a gallows on which could be read the inscription "By the change of four faiths and betrayal of God a villain to Christians and hated by the Turks." The chief organizer of the celebrations, Vinius, also allotted himself a role, that of proclaiming verses to the victors through a megaphone from the top of the triumphal gates. Rewards were distributed according to ancient custom in the form of gold medals, cups, furs, cash supplements to wages and peasant households.

SHIP-BUILDING COMPANIES

On October 30, about a month after these celebrations, the great sovereign had a conference with his boyars at Preobrazhenskoe. The great sovereign presented a written proposal. "The fortress of Azov is in ruins inside and burnt to the foundations, and also lacks any permanent residents, without which it is impossible to maintain it. Therefore instructions are needed as to who should be settled there and in what numbers." It was resolved that there should be three thousand families from the towns of the lower Don, and a four hundred-strong cavalry unit, with Kalmyks.[26] The great sovereign continued: "When the fortress is restored to good order, are we to be satisfied with just this? If so the efforts, bloodshed and casualties of the past two years will surely have been in vain, for it is not possible to curb either Tatar raids or the sultan simply by the capture of this fortress alone, for the infantry cannot intercept the Tatars or make reconnaissance raids from it, and it would be impossible to maintain cavalry in sufficient numbers for the aforesaid tasks. So, since it is impossible to use either cavalry or infantry to fight and restrain the enemy, the enemy, seeing military operations against him suspended, may well be seized by pride even greater than before and declare war. Then not only will we have failed to secure his ruin but also the desired peace. So now, if there is a will, we ask you to work with all your heart for the defense of your fellow believers and for your own immortal memory. Now is the time while Fortune is with us, which never before took us so close to the south. Happy is he who has luck on his side. I think there could be nothing better than fighting by sea, as the route is shorter and many times more convenient than the route overland, but for this we need a fleet or sea caravan consisting of forty or more ships. So we must decide without delay how many vessels there should be and from how many households and trades [they are to be funded], and where to build them." It was resolved: "Ships are to be built, the number to be determined by the number of peasant households belonging to churchmen and other ranks of person, the figures to be registered and reported without delay, and ships to be allocated according to the number of households. Merchants are to be assessed from the customs books based on how much fifth and tenth money[27] was taken from them in the years 1694-1696 and from what businesses."

To take the final decision on the basis of the information collected, on November 4 another session was held, at which foreigners were present, which was a break with tradition.[28] It was resolved that ships were to be built fully equipped with cannon and small arms, to be ready for action by 1698 or sooner, on the following basis: one ship per eight thousand households of peasants belonging to the patriarch, church prelates and monasteries; one ship per ten thousand peasant households from the boyars and other ranks of military servitors; the chief merchants and the senior Moscow merchants and the tax-exempt townsmen of the tax-paying communities and settlements and the towns were to build twelve fully equipped ships instead of paying the tenth money which was collected from them in previous years.

On the same day, on November 4, it was decreed that the three thousand families already assigned to Azov should be joined by a permanent force of three thousand Moscow musketeers and annual contract infantry. As a result of the resolution on ship-building ecclesiastical landowners formed seventeen limited companies and secular landowners eighteen. For the formation of these companies, service and hereditary landowners possessing a hundred or more peasant households were to report to the Chancellery of Crown Appointments in Moscow by December 25, 1696, on pain of confiscation of their service and hereditary estates by the crown. Smaller landowners were to pay a contribution of fifty copecks per peasant household. Everything pertaining to shipbuilding was placed under the jurisdiction of the Vladimir Judicial Chancellery, directed by Lord-in-waiting Protasiev, who was dubbed admiralty secretary in recognition of his new duties. The chancellery circulated the companies with lists of essential equipment for building and fitting out ships, with indications of dimensions and diagrams of ships' components attached. In addition to Russian carpenters, every company was obliged to employ at its own expense foreign shipwrights and carpenters, translators, blacksmiths, a draughtsman, joiner, painter and apothecary with medical supplies. Building materials were to be procured in the forests to the north of Voronezh in the districts of Voronezh, Usman, Belokolodsk, Romanov, Sokolsk, Dobrensk and Kozlov. The government hired foreign specialists in Venice, Holland, Denmark and Sweden and allocated them to the companies. At the same time there was a proposal to link the Volga with the Don by constructing a canal between the rivers Ilovlia and Kamyshinka.

STUDY ABROAD

The more urgent the need for change, the greater the need for foreigners to be hired in great numbers. But how long could this state of affairs continue? Would Russia have to depend upon foreigners forever? It was essential for Russians to be trained, but how was this to be achieved? The foreign specialists were too busy to provide tuition; they had other tasks to perform. Most important, the teachers remained in their own countries and since foreign countries could not send their best people to Russia, it followed that

Russians must be sent abroad to study. This was not a new idea. It was tried in the reign of Boris Godunov, but proved a failure as the men who were sent refused to return home.[29] Things were different now, and they would return. "A new enterprise had begun in Russia: the building of ships, galleys and other craft at crown expense. In order to establish it firmly in Russia forever the sovereign decided to inculcate this art in his people and therefore he sent a great number of noblemen to Holland and other countries to study naval architecture and navigation."[30] Fifty table attendants of the throne room and gentlemen of the bedchamber were sent abroad for this purpose, twenty-eight to Italy, chiefly to Venice, and twenty-two to England and Holland.

IV

THE GRAND EMBASSY
1697-1698

PETER PLANS TO GO ABROAD

The young courtiers were sent abroad to study, but how would they study and who would teach them? Who would decide whether they had been good students and assess their qualifications? Someone had to be educated there in advance of them and find out everything, and who better than the skipper himself, Bombardier Captain Peter Alekseev? As the people set off along a new path the autocratic tsar, endowed with extraordinary strength of will, assumed the lead. The process of learning from foreigners the things they did better than Russians was undertaken with a purpose in mind and in full awareness of what was involved. Already Peter had set this process in motion in Russia: his achievements as skipper, bombardier and captain are direct illustrations. But training could not be completed in Russia. For this it was necessary to go abroad, so Peter would go there, not as tsar but as student, as ship's carpenter, for his mission was different: he was a great man, the leader of a new society, the founder of his country's modern history. The seal on Peter's letters sent from abroad was inscribed "I am a student and I seek teachers." What would Peter study abroad? It had to be shipbuilding, for this was his passion, justified by the fact that reaching the sea was Russia's cherished goal in the sixteenth and seventeenth centuries, bequeathed to Peter by his forebears. Moreover at the time Peter considered that he could wage victorious war against the Turks only by sea. The inner voice which whispered the word "Rome" to the leaders of the German barbarians and inexorably drew them to the capital of the civilized world, the journey of the Russian princess Olga, the wisest of women, to Constantinople,[1] and Peter's journey to the West are analogous phenomena, all expressive of the unquenchable desire for civilization of uncivilized but noble peoples with a historical destiny. In Peter's case, the inner voice was replaced by the loud voice of Lefort, but this changes nothing. Peter would have gone abroad even without Lefort, just as he would have sailed the seas and built a fleet even if he had not discovered the boyar Nikita Romanov's old boat.[2] But Lefort, with his insistence on a tour abroad and a campaign against Azov instead of a journey to the Caspian Sea, and the little boat, which provided the first impulse for shipbuilding, are documented phenomena which we cannot disregard, for throughout history both general movements and urges and individual impulses may be detected, in great and ordinary men alike.

We do not know who devised the itinerary of the tsar's journey abroad.[3] He set off as an ordinary member of the retinue of the grand embassy to visit the emperor of Austria, kings of England and Denmark, the Pope in Rome, the Dutch Estates General, the elector of Brandenburg and the Venetian republic. This arrangement had a dual aim: Peter could preserve his incognito and study, but where necessary conduct negotiations on the alliance against Turkey, discuss conditions for war and peace with the same and speak in person to rulers and their ministers. The purpose of the embassy was described as "the confirmation of ancient friendship and love, and the weakening of the Turkish sultan, the Crimean khan and all their Muslim hordes, the enemies of the Cross of Our Lord." The embassy was to have made Vienna, where the Turkish question was to be discussed, its first port of call. But Nefimov, the tsar's envoy in

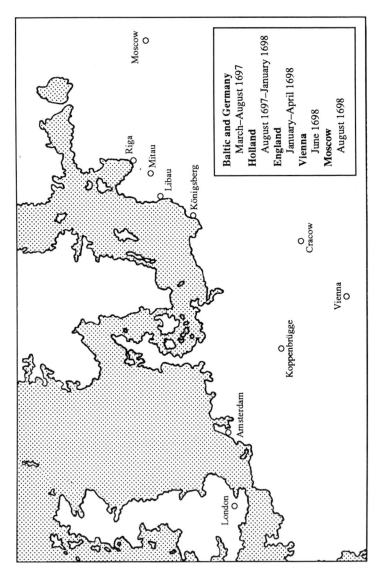

Peter's Grand Embassy to Europe

Baltic and Germany
March–August 1697
Holland
August 1697–January 1698
England
January–April 1698
Vienna
June 1698
Moscow
August 1698

Moscow

Riga
Mitau
Libau
Königsberg

Cracow

Vienna

Koppenbrügge

Amsterdam

London

Vienna, reported that the question was resolved already: he had signed an offensive and defensive treaty against the Turks with the Austrian empire and Venice for three years. This allowed them to change the itinerary to follow a direct route to the Western maritime states to study shipbuilding.

The great and plenipotentiary ambassadors were appointed: General and Admiral, Viceroy of Novgorod, Franz Lefort, General and Military Commissar, Viceroy of Siberia, Fedor Alekseevich Golovin,[4] and Conciliar Secretary Prokofy Bogdanovich Voznitsyn, Viceroy of Belev. They were accompanied by more than twenty nobles and about thirty-five volunteers, including Private Peter Mikhailov of the Preobrazhensky Guards. In the tsar's absence the government remained as it was when he was present, with the same men in their old posts; those who had enjoyed the most influence retained it still. Things were made easier by the fact that even before the grand embassy the tsar was almost permanently absent and people had become accustomed to rule by boyars since 1689. All business was conducted in the name of the tsar just as if Peter had never left Moscow.

DISTURBANCES IN MOSCOW

In February 1697, when the departure of the embassy was imminent, there was a report of a plot against the tsar's life. The clearer Peter's intentions became the louder became the muttering amongst the masses, not just from people who were firmly opposed to Russia's natural and essential progress along a new path but also from men who acknowledged the insolvency of the old ways and the need for reforms but were unable to grasp that these reforms would have to be accomplished precisely by that route which the young tsar was now travelling. They would have preferred Peter to appear suddenly on the Russian throne as a new Solomon in all his wisdom and glory. They wanted the country's governors to be transformed all of a sudden from exploiters who lived off the backs of the people[5] to the strictest and most scrupulous observers of law and order; they wanted their poor country to overflow with milk and honey. These people wanted all problems alleviated and improved at a stroke and considered it possible, but instead what they saw was a demand for prodigious effort, a demand for sacrifices, and so they grumbled.

And certainly some aspects of the young tsar's behavior gave grounds for such grumbling.

They were offended that the tsar avoided the palace, the Kremlin and Moscow, neglected his family duties, spending time amusing himself and consorting with foreigners and taking no interest in affairs of state, with the result that the privy councillors did what they liked. A feud arose between the Naryshkins, the tsar's relatives on his mother's side, and the Lopukhins, on his wife's. Lev Kirillovich Naryshkin gained the upper hand over the Lopukhins, in all probability thanks to Peter's estrangement from his wife. The most eminent of the Lopukhins, the boyar Peter Abramovich, who ran the Chancellery of the Royal Household, was completely disgraced and a rumor began to circulate that the tsar in person tortured his wife's uncle. The Miloslavskys and other disgruntled people exploited this situation, of course, and took malicious delight in spreading similar rumors to indicate how little had been gained by removing the regent.[6]

No one knows the source of the rumor that Tsar Ivan appealed to the whole people with the words "My brother does not live according to the laws of the church, but goes to the Foreign Quarter and consorts with foreigners." In the tavern one of the play soldiers boasted that the sovereign spent all his time with them in the Quarter. A monk who was present at the time retorted: "The sovereign is bringing himself into disrepute, not winning honor."

TRIAL OF THE MONK ABRAHAM

At the end of 1696 or the beginning of 1697 the monk Abraham, who previously served as cellarer in the Trinity-St. Sergius monastery, then as superior of the monastery of St. Andrew in Moscow, submitted to the tsar some notebooks, in which it was claimed that the people were disillusioned by Peter's behavior. "People are grieving and fretting that they had waited in expectation for the great sovereign to grow up and contract a lawful marriage, to leave behind the years of his youth and make everything change for the better. Only the tsar, having grown up and married, is more inclined towards amusement, has abandoned what is good and begun to make everyone grieve and weep." Abraham was tortured to make him reveal the names of those who had been to visit him. The monk revealed that his friends and long-time cronies were the clerk of the Vladimir High Court Nikifor Krenev, the clerk of the office of the Preobrazhensky Chancellery Ignaty Bubnov, crown agent of the Trinity monastery Kuzma Rudnev and Ivashka and Romashka Pososhkov, peasants of the village of Pokrovsk, and that all these men, when they visited him in the St. Andrew monastery, uttered all the words which were written in the pamphlets. Abraham added that when he was steward at the Trinity monastery the boyar Matvey Bogdanovich Miloslavsky had paid a visit and said "Peter Lopukhin was a good man and did much which was useful in the chancellery, and he was tortured for nothing, simply on the word of Lev Naryshkin."

Nikifor Krenev was arrested. He said that he had heard the information written in the pamphlets during the mock battles, from men of various ranks during the battles at Semenovskoe and Kozhukhovo. He had mentioned officials who refused to do anything without bribes to Abraham of his own accord and also heard such things mentioned by ordinary folk. Krenev admitted to expressing the opinion that it would be a good thing if officials were appointed and given a salary which kept them satisfied so that they did not need to take bribes, but he denied saying that the tsar had abandoned the government and left it in the hands of bribe-taking lechers who had no fear of God, or that the sovereign himself knew all about the judges who accepted honors and were installed in the chancelleries in order to make a good living; they also remarked that there were many more secretaries and clerks than there had been.

Rudnev testified that they had remarked that the sovereign did not deign to live in his royal apartments in Moscow but avoided them, and as a result of his absences from Moscow the birth of children from lawful wedlock had ceased, which was most grievous to the common people.[7]

Bubnov testified that they considered the mock battles at Semenovskoe and Kozhukhovo unseemly because many were killed and others were even robbed, and Prince Ivan Dolgoruky had been shot, and people were not happy about the mock battles. The ridiculous words and jokes and matters unpleasing to God spoken of in the pamphlets were based on the prophesy of Vasily Sokovnin and on the comedies at Izmailovo.[8] They said that the numbers of secretaries and clerks were growing and that secretarial posts and clerk's credentials were being obtained by purchase and that priests and artisans were installing their sons in the chancelleries as clerks. They had spoken of the great sovereign's obstinacy, of how he refused to listen to anyone, and of newly promoted people, men of humble origin, and of how the great sovereign had tortured and executed people himself in the trials at Preobrazhenskoe.

The sea voyages also met with disapproval. Abraham thought it improper that during the triumphant entry into Moscow after the capture of Azov the tsar had gone on foot while Shein and Lefort had ridden.

Ivan Pososhkov, the quitrent-paying peasant, said that he had known Abraham for three years.[9] Abraham had summoned him about the minting equipment which he was making as a model to present to the great sovereign. But he denied uttering any of the words which were in the pamphlets. Abraham declared that Pososhkov really had said nothing. Bubnov, Krenev and Rudnev were flogged with the knout and banished to Azov to serve as clerks there. Abraham was banished to the Golutvin monastery.

TRIAL OF TSYKLER AND SOKOVNIN

The monk Abraham had decided to make himself an instrument of popular revenge and popular discontent and tell the tsar the straight truth and condemn his behavior. But there were also people who, for motives of their own, tried to do away with Peter by using others as agents. In 1682, as we saw,[10] one of the most fervent supporters of Sophia was the musketeer colonel Ivan Tsykler, a russified foreigner and a man of fierce and restless ambition. He miscalculated. After Sophia's victory, first Golitsyn then Shaklovity came to prominence, but of Tsykler there was no mention. That is why in 1689 when the struggle between sister and brother flared up again and it became clear which would be the winning side, Tsykler was one of the first to transfer his allegiance to Peter. But again he miscalculated. Peter did not ally himself with people who had taken part in the events of 1682. The young tsar was on informal terms with everyone, went to visit them, but he kept avoiding Tsykler's house. As if this were not enough, Tsykler was assigned to the construction of the new fortress at Taganrog, at a time when assignments in far-flung locations were regarded as honorable exile. Tsykler was full of rage and despair and his thoughts turned to 1682 and the bloody spears of the musketeers. Why should not the same thing be done now? If the musketeers could not be persuaded, the cossacks of Taganrog might be incited to rebel. Two high-born Russian magnates, Alexis Sokovnin and Fedor Pushkin, shared the foreign serviceman Tsykler's aspirations. Sokovnin was a well-known Old Believer, the brother of Feodosia Morozova and Avdotia Urusova, those renowned Old Believer women of Tsar Alexis's reign.[11] One can understand how hard it was for him to witness Peter's innovations, the dispatch of his children to heretical countries and the sovereign's own visit abroad. Then there was trouble closer to home; his son-in-law's father, the boyar Matvey Pushkin, who was appointed military governor in Azov, had invoked the sovereign's anger by objecting to his children's being sent abroad. And so father-in-law and son-in-law came to the conclusion that it would be good to find someone to do away with Peter for them. They knew of Tsykler's discontent and urged him to commit the crime. Sokovnin even tested his ambition by suggesting that he, Tsykler, might himself become tsar after Peter's death. Tsykler incited the musketeers, but they were quick to denounce him.

On February 23, 1697 the boyar Lev Kirillovich Naryshkin sent Larion Elizarev, a sergeant of the Konishchev mounted musketeer regiment, to Preobrazhenskoe where he reported a conversation between himself and Tsykler.

Tsykler: Is all quiet in your regiments?

Elizarev: It's quiet.

Tsykler: Now that the great sovereign is going overseas, who will be our tsar if something happens to him?

Elizarev: There is the tsarevich.

Tsykler: If the time comes God will choose, but there is also the sovereign lady [Sophia] in the New convent.

Elizarev consulted another sergeant from his regiment, Grigory Silin, who testified that Tsykler said that it would be possible to cut the sovereign into five pieces. The sovereign knew that he, Ivan, had a pretty wife and daughter and the sovereign wanted to visit his house and fornicate with his wife and daughter, and he, Ivan, knew what to do with the sovereign.

In his cross-examination and confrontation with witnesses Tsykler remained silent. Under torture he incriminated Sokovnin. "I was in Aleshka Sokovnin's house to buy a horse. Aleshka asked 'What news of the musketeers?' I told him that there was not a sound from them. At that Aleshka retorted 'What are those sons [of bitches] up to? Looks like they're sleeping. Where have they disappeared to? They could kill the sovereign because he rides out alone, goes to fires[12] with just a handful of people and rides near the ambassadors' courtyard on his own. Why do they sleep, why haven't they done anything so far?' I said that their numbers were small and I thought they were afraid of the play regiments. Aleshka replied 'The musketeers are concerned for the tsarevich; that's why they don't want to do it.' I said 'I sense the same concern in them. Think of how you yourself feel, how wretched you feel when you part with your children.' Aleshka said 'I am not alone in being distressed.' On two later occasions Aleshka spoke to me about the murder of the sovereign and about the musketeers; they were being ruined for nothing, and would be ruined hereafter. I said to Aleshka 'Supposing the deed is done, who will rule the tsardom?' Aleshka said 'Shein has few kinsmen, he has one son and is a good man.' I said 'What about Boris Petrovich Sheremetev? The musketeers like him.' Aleshka said 'I think the musketeers will want the tsarevna back, and she will take the tsarevich, and when she comes back she will bring back Prince Vasily Golitsyn and Golitsyn will be a big noise like before.' I said to him 'I don't think the musketeers will bring back the tsarevna.' Aleshka said to me 'If this deed is done to the sovereign, we'll even choose you to rule the tsardom.' I replied 'You reproach the musketeers, but you aren't willing to do the deed yourself because you don't want a stain on your clan's reputation.' Alexis replied 'No one wants a stain like that, but the musketeers can do it because they're doomed anyway. Prince Peter Golitsyn is a sharp and lively man. We expected him to be willing to do the deed. Prince Boris Alekseevich is a drunkard and taught the sovereign to drink.' "

Sokovnin was given ten blows. He confessed and implicated his son-in-law Fedor Pushkin. "After Tsykler's visit my son-in-law Fedka Pushkin came to see me and said 'The sovereign has been the ruin of us all and deserves to be killed, also because he is angry with our father and sent them across the seas.'" Sokovnin also testified that his son Vasily had said "We are being sent overseas to study all sorts of rubbish." After five blows Pushkin confessed and added "On Christmas eve I was at Alexis Sokovnin's house and Alexis told me that the sovereign was intending to attack my father during Yuletide and do him to death and destroy our home; I said that if such a thing were to happen to my father I would go and kill the sovereign."

Tsykler implicated Sergeant Vasily Filippov of the Konishchev Regiment. "Vaska Filippov came to see me and I asked him about the cossacks who had recently arrived, whether he knew any of them and whether they were grateful for the sovereign's favor. Vaska said that he had some acquaintances among the cossacks and had spoken with one by the name of Demka and the cossack had said that they weren't grateful. What did they have to be grateful for? I told Vaska that they had recently received a thousand gold crowns, to which Vaska replied that this meant nothing to them since they hadn't enough to share with the rest of the Host. I asked what might be expected of them and Vaska said that the cossack Demian said 'Give us time; we shall return when the sovereign comes and sort matters out in our own way. We had enough of your interference in the time of Stenka Razin, and now there is no one to interfere with us.' I said to Vaska that this would result in devastation; our serfs and bondsmen would all join them. Vaska Filippov told me that the cossacks were being lured away by the Turkish sultan, who had sent them a letter."

Tsykler admitted to having told Filippov that the sovereign could be intercepted and killed when he was on his way from the ambassadors' residence. He ordered him to inform the musketeers of the plans for the assassination. Tsykler declared: "I planned the sovereign's murder because he called me a rebel and accomplice of Ivan Miloslavsky,[13] yet he never visited my home." He also confessed to threatening that when he went to the Don to build the

Taganrog fortress he would quit the service and ride with the Don Cossacks to Moscow to destroy it and do what Stenka Razin did. Filippov said that he had spoken with a cossack called Peter Lukianov, not with Demian, and Lukianov said "We were given a thousand gold crowns, but how are we supposed to divide that up among the cossack Host? They say, serve and stop moaning, but it's not even a copeck each. When you musketeers are posted away from Moscow on duty, that same day our cossacks will get moving and get on with things in their own way." Tsykler added to this story that as soon as the cossacks were on the move he was intending to join up with them; the sovereign was calling him a rebel anyway. Then the cossack said "The cossacks will write and ask the Turkish sultan to help them destroy Moscow and he will send the Kuban Cossacks to their aid and they will wreak havoc." Tsykler, according to Filippov's testimony, said "There is now much disorder in the realm because the sovereign is going abroad and sending Lefort as ambassador. This embassy will drain the treasury of money, and there is much more disorder besides. So you have reason to rebel." Filippov implicated the musketeer Timoshka Skorniak, to whom Fedor Pushkin had said in Filippov's presence that the sovereign lived an irregular life, in an un-Christian manner and was draining the treasury.[14]

The cossack Petrushka Lukianov at first refused to speak; twenty blows had no effect. Then he admitted that he had been drunk when he spoke and they had no thought of destroying Moscow. If they did not have the sovereign's favor they could hardly steal it. He had heard about the said rebellion from poor cossacks in the upper Don settlements. Then he said that the upper Don Cossack villages were being stirred up by the cossacks Trushka and Iliushka Ivanov the bargeman; these words were spoken to him in a tavern at the time he was escorting the sovereign. Trushka and Iliushka said to him "Our poor cossacks commit robberies because they get paid such a pittance." On the subject of the destruction of Moscow he, Petrushka, spoke with Vaska Filippov. "You will come from one end and we from the other." But they had no intention of starting a rebellion and had not plotted with anyone. They had said everything when they were drunk.

The sergeant Rozhin was also implicated for telling Tsykler "You have done great services, but you should take care of yourself otherwise your line will not be remembered." He advised complaining to the boyars and fellow musketeers about the sovereign and killing him.

Before he was executed Tsykler said that in 1682 after the massacre of the boyars and courtiers by the musketeers he was summoned to see Tsarevna Sophia, who told him that he should order the musketeers to cease their rebellion and he did what she asked and spoke to the musketeers. Before the first Crimean campaign [of 1687] the tsarevna summoned him and told him several times that he and Fedka Shaklovity should assassinate the tsar. And in the ground-floor apartments at Khoroshovo palace the tsarevna summoned him and spoke to him through a window, telling him to arrange with Fedka Shaklovity to assassinate the tsar, but he refused, telling the tsarevna that if the sovereign was gone there would be no one to marry her and that she ought to love him. The tsarevna replied that she was ready to love him but his mother would not allow it. Ivan said that his mother would be happy if even a Tatar loved him. She was angry with him, accusing him of going over to the other side. At the time Princess Anna Lobanova was in the room with her. For that the tsarevna sent Ivan on the Crimean campaign and when he came home from the campaign, she returned to the same topic and promised him Ivan Miloslavsky's estate at Kuznetsovo in the Dmitrov district, which had been allocated to the tsarevich of Georgia, but he refused again and was sent on the second Crimean campaign [1689]; and when he returned she did not speak of it again. Ivan Miloslavsky had been kind to him and he had been married in his house."

Tsykler mentioned his friendship with Ivan Miloslavsky and how Sophia had tried to goad him into committing murder. Peter's eyes grew hazy at the thought of getting at Ivan Miloslavsky, even though he was dead. He wanted to pay back his sister, the daughter of a Miloslavsky....

The great sovereign ordered the execution of Sokovnin, Tsykler, Pushkin, musketeers Filippov and Rozhin and the cossack Lukianov. They began to erect a stone column on Red Square. By March 4 the column was finished and five iron spikes were driven into the stone. On the same day the notorious criminals and traitors were executed at Preobrazhenskoe. And to coincide with the execution the dead boyar Ivan Miloslavsky was exhumed from his grave and taken to Preobrazhenskoe on the back of swine and his coffin was set down by the traitors' execution blocks in such a way that as the heads were cut off the blood dribbled into the coffin onto Miloslavsky. The heads of the traitors were stuck onto the spikes on the column built on Red Square.

PETER DEPARTS FOR THE WEST

Five days later, on March 10, the grand embassy departed Moscow. The first impressions upon crossing the border with Swedish Livonia were unpropitious. The pace was slow, not so much because of the bad spring roads as a shortage of transport and fodder, as there was famine in the land. In Riga the embassy received a polite welcome, but the governor, Erik Dahlberg, considered himself duty-bound not to breach the tsar's strict incognito as the Russians assured him that the news of the tsar's journey was a childish rumor and that the tsar was on his way to Voronezh to build ships. On the other hand, Peter's wish to inspect the fortifications of Riga was bound to arouse the governor's suspicions. This same tsar's father had stood with his troops outside the gates of Riga,[15] and his son was building ships without rest and instead of fighting the Turks was undertaking secret journeys to the West! But it is easy to see how such suspicions and the denial of his request to inspect the fortifications must have annoyed Peter, given how impatient he was to see everything here and now, and how unaccustomed to inactivity and having his desires thwarted. A feeling of hostility lodged deep in his heart. Three days before the embassy departed he crossed the river Dvina to Courland in a small boat.

His frame of mind on departure is best illustrated in this letter to Vinius dated April 8, 1697. "Today we departed hence for Mitau [in Courland]. Here we lived in servile fashion and feasted only with our eyes. The merchants here go about in cloaks and seem very upright, but they haggle with our coachmen over a copeck, they curse and swear, but sell at three times the normal price." In spite of the fact that only their eyes had feasted, Peter had managed to learn something of interest. He wrote to Vinius: "We crossed the town and fortress, where the soldiers stood in five places, less than a thousand men, and we were told that was all there were. The town is well fortified but the fortifications are incomplete. People are very nervous, and they won't allow anyone to enter the fortress and other places even with a guard, and are not very hospitable." As a result of this inhospitable treatment Riga remained in Peter's memory as an "accursed" place.

PETER IN PRUSSIA

Across the Dvina in Courland they received a different welcome. The tsars of Russia were always on good terms with the dukes of Courland. From Mitau Peter went to Libau, where he saw the Baltic Sea for the first time. From Libau Peter set off by sea alone, without the grand ambassadors, to East Prussia, where he was splendidly received in Königsberg by Frederick III, the elector of Brandenburg.[16] Awaiting the arrival of the grand ambassadors, who were travelling overland, Peter wasted no time and began to study artillery. His teacher, Lieutenant Colonel von Sternfeld, gave his honor Mr. Peter Mikhailov the following reference. "In a short space of time, to the amazement of all, he made such good progress and acquired so much knowledge that he may be acknowledged and respected as a meticulous, careful, highly skilled, courageous and fearless master and exponent of the arts of firearms." The ambassadors arrived and were given a sumptuous welcome. The elector wished to take the opportunity to conclude a defensive alliance with Russia, but Peter declined the proposal for fear of making any alterations to Russia's existing relations with other powers before the end of the war with Turkey. A treaty of friendship rather than alliance was signed with Brandenburg, with stipulations on free trade for both sides, promises not to offer refuge to rebels and enemies, and permission on the part of the elector for Russians to cross his territory on their way to study in Germany.

POLISH AFFAIRS

Peter stayed on in Prussia longer than he needed to, being delayed by events in Poland. The interregnum in Poland after the death of Jan Sobieski has been mentioned. There were many candidates for the throne, including the late king's son Jakub, Elector Palatine Karl, Duke Leopold of Lorraine, Margrave Ludwig of Bavaria, Odescalchi the Pope's grandson, French Prince de Conti,[17] Frederick Augustus elector of Saxony[18] and several members of the Piast dynasty, in other words Polish magnates.[19] In the end two candidates emerged in the lead: Conti and Augustus. Russia's attitude to these elections was quite straightforward. It made no difference who occupied the throne of Poland as long as Poland did not leave the Holy League of four powers before the conclusion of a general peace with Turkey. Therefore Russia needed to oppose only one of the candidates, Prince Conti, because France was on friendly terms with Turkey and hostile towards Austria. A Poland ruled by a French king could easily be subordinated to French policies. Indeed, the French envoy had announced to the Polish magnates the sultan's promise to conclude a separate peace with Poland and return Kamieniec if a French prince were elected king. This announcement greatly strengthened the French party, so Peter sent a letter from Königsberg to the gentlemen of the Polish Sejm, saying that until now he had refrained from interfering in the elections, but now he declared that if the French faction gained the upper hand, not only the alliance against the common foe but also the permanent peace would be seriously damaged. The French king, being a friend of the Turkish sultan, aided him in all things to the detriment of the allied Christian rulers. What would happen to the Christian alliance if a French king were to sit upon the throne of Poland? Conti would propose to the Turkish sultan and the Crimean khan that he fight with the Turks and Tatars. "We do not wish to see a king who favors the French and the Turkish side on the Polish throne," Peter concluded. "We want you to elect someone from any nation as long as he is the friend and ally of us and the Holy Roman emperor against the common enemies of the holy cross."

On June 17 the elections were held and produced the double result of one party proclaiming Conti, the other the elector of Saxony. Members of opposing parties crossed swords. Augustus's supporters relied strongly upon the tsar's letter, for ratification of which Peter sent another with the same contents. The Saxon party gained a clear advantage. Vinius, informing Peter of the election of Augustus, wrote "I heartily congratulate you, my lord, on the election of this new king as I know you to be a gentleman with more affection for the German nation than for the French *cockerel*." The tsar sent a letter of congratulation to Augustus and told him to declare to the lords of the Sejm that a Russian army under the command of Prince Romodanovsky had been moved to the Lithuanian border for the protection of the republic against Conti and his supporters. Augustus entered Poland with Saxon troops and swore an oath to the fact that he had converted to Catholicism. On receipt of the letter of congratulation from the tsar he informed the Russian resident Nikitin that he gave his word of honor to act in concert with the tsar against the enemies of the holy cross and that the *affection* which Peter had declared for him would never be erased from his memory. In sending his greetings to the tsar, the king bowed very low indeed.

PETER MEETS TWO ELECTRESSES

Meanwhile, in the wake of the good news from Poland Peter decided to quit Prussia and travel further westwards. Two highly educated women traveled in haste to meet him: Electress Sophia of Hanover and her daughter Sophia Charlotte, electress of Brandenburg.[20] Peter had gone abroad to look at the marvels of civilization and to learn all he could. Now civilized Europe sent two of its own representatives to have a look at Peter, at this marvel sent to them by uncivilized Eastern Europe. The electresses wrote down their impressions of Peter, thus providing us with valuable evidence, for both women observed this amazing creature in frank and clear fashion. They were struck by the duality of his nature; they saw a remarkable man who amazed them with his brilliant talents but at the same time with his shortcomings, which indicated the kind of society he came from and the kind of upbringing he had received. They were struck by the duality and contradictions, but they did not attempt to smooth them out or indulge in cunning sophistries, but remained true to their original impressions and pronounced a most fair judgement on Peter: "This is a man who is very good and very bad at the same time."

When he was a child of eleven people were struck by Peter's unusual good looks and liveliness. Contemporaries thought that he took after his mother's side of the family in his facial features, and especially resembled his uncle Fedor Kirillovich Naryshkin. The good looks and liveliness remained, but his precocious development, the terrible upheavals he had experienced and his intemperance in work and play had undermined Peter's robust nature and left their mark on his handsome features. His head shook and his face was wracked with contortions.[21] His rapid, penetrating gaze created an unpleasant impression on those who were unused to it.[22] Archbishop Theodosius Yanovsky of Novgorod recounts that when he was presented to both tsars, Ivan and Peter, he approached to kiss the hand of the former without any fear, but when he came to kiss Tsar Peter's hand "such a dread overwhelmed me that I almost collapsed, my knees trembled, and from that time on I was convinced that I would meet my death by that very hand."

Peter's meeting with the electresses took place in the duchy of Celle in the small town of Koppenbrügge. At first the tsar refused to visit them and made excuses, but finally agreed on condition that no one else should be present. He entered like a shy child, hid his face in his hands, and responded to all compliments with "I cannot speak." But later, particularly over supper, he became talkative, his shyness disappeared and he allowed the ladies' courtiers to enter the room, offered the men wine from big glasses and danced. The festivities continued until way past midnight. The tsar listened with pleasure to the Italian singers, but explained that he was no great connoisseur of music. When the elder electress asked him whether he enjoyed hunting, he replied that his father had been a keen hunter but that he felt no inclination towards this particular sport, but very much liked shipbuilding and fireworks, at which point he showed them his hands which were rough from hard work. Sophia Charlotte described Peter in the following manner: "I imagined his grimaces to be worse than they actually are; he has no control over some of them. It is evident that he has not been taught how to eat properly, but I like his natural manner and informality." Her mother wrote: "The tsar is tall, has handsome features and a noble bearing. He has a lively wit and his replies are swift and to the point. But despite all the good qualities which nature has bestowed on him, he could do with being somewhat less coarse. This sovereign is very good and very bad at the same time. With regard to manners, he is a true representative of his people. If he had received a better education he would be an accomplished man, for he has many good qualities and a remarkable mind."

PETER IN HOLLAND, ENGLAND AND VIENNA

From Koppenbrügge Peter set off for the Rhine. He left the embassy and with ten attendants made his way down the Rhine and canals to Amsterdam. In the embassy's absence Peter kept himself occupied until it arrived. In the town of Saardam (or Zaandam), famed for its great shipyards, at Rogge's wharf a tall handsome young carpenter from Russia by the name of Peter Mikhailov made his appearance. He lived in the humble abode of a poor blacksmith, visited the families of carpenters who were in Russia and introduced himself as their workmate, a simple carpenter. In his spare time the Russian carpenter visited factories and works. He had to see everything, find out how everything was done. On one occasion at a paper factory he could not resist taking the mould from the worker and scooping some pulp from the vat. An excellent piece of paper was produced. His favorite pastime was sailing in the dinghy which he had bought the day after arriving in Saardam.

Peter's behavior and appearance, which were not those of a simple carpenter, gave him away at once, even though his red friezed jacket and white canvas trousers were no different from those of ordinary workers. People started to say that this was no ordinary carpenter, then suddenly a rumor spread that it was the tsar of Muscovy. One old carpenter went to the barber's and read out a letter he had received from his son in Russia. It told of wondrous things: a huge Russian embassy was on its way to Holland and in it was the tsar himself, who would be coming to Saardam. The shipwright noted the tsar's distinguishing marks, then as though on purpose the door opened and into the barber's shop walked some Russian carpenters, one of whom exactly matched the description— a head which shook, waving his arms about, a wart on the cheek. Naturally the barber was swift to report this amazing event. Soon the rumor was confirmed. Peter had teased some street urchins, who pelted him with sand and pebbles, and the mayor issued a statement forbidding anyone to insult distinguished foreigners who wished to remain unknown. After that the tsar tried in vain to maintain his incognito and to refuse polite invitations and comfortable accommodation by saying "We are not distinguished gentlemen but simple folk and quite happy in our humble cottage." Here was a man who lived in a cottage but spent four hundred and fifty guilders on a sailing boat! Crowds followed Peter wherever he went, driving him into a rage which he had not learnt to control at Preobrazhenskoe with the grooms of the play regiments. Once when he was trying to push his way through an importunate crowd he was particularly annoyed by the stupid face of a certain Marzen and gave him a slap. "Marzen has been knighted," yelled the crowd, and the nickname "Sir" stuck with Marzen forever.

News arrived from Amsterdam of the imminent arrival of the Russian embassy, and Peter set off there after an eight-day stay in Saardam. On August 16, 1697 Lefort and his fellow ambassadors made a triumphal entry into Amsterdam. There was a splendid reception. Peter took part in the festivities which the Estates General laid on for the embassy when they learned that the tsar himself was to be present. Of all the names in Amsterdam the best known to Peter was that of Mayor Nicholas Witsen. Witsen had been to Russia in Tsar Alexis's reign, travelling as far as the Caspian Sea, and was famed as the author of the book *North and South Tartary* and as the publisher of Isbraandt's travels to China.[23] Witsen maintained regular contact with Russia; he dedicated his publications to the tsars, he carried out commissions for the Russian government for ordering of ships in Holland and corresponded with Lefort.

It was to Witsen that Peter applied with a request for the opportunity to study shipbuilding in the Amsterdam docks, and Witsen found him a place in the dock of the East India Company, where the keel of a frigate was laid especially for him. When he heard of this, Peter went to Saardam at night, collected his carpentry tools and returned to Amsterdam next morning in order to get to work at once. The volunteers who arrived with the embassy were also set to work. Peter only responded to shouts of "Shipwright Peter of Saardam!" or "Master Peter!" but if anyone addressed him as "your majesty" or "gracious sovereign" he turned his back on them. Shipbuilding was not Peter's only occupation in Holland. He went to Utrecht with Witsen and Lefort to meet the renowned stadholder of Holland and king of England, William of Orange.[24] Witsen had to take him everywhere and show him everything—the whaling fleet, hospitals, foundlings' homes, factories, workshops. He particularly enjoyed the anatomical cabinet of Professor Ruysch; he met the professor, attended his lectures, visited the hospital with him. He enjoyed himself so much in Professor Ruysch's cabinet that he kissed the excellently preserved cadaver of a baby which smiled as if alive. In Leiden, in the anatomical theater of the famous physiologist Herman Boerhaave, observing the repulsion of his Russian companions for corpses, he made them tear at the muscles of a corpse with their teeth. Of course, Peter had to be very economical with his time. While he was travelling to Leiden by yacht he spent two hours with the naturalist Leuwenhoeck, who personally showed him his best pieces of apparatus and microscopes. This insatiable desire to see and learn everything drove his Dutch hosts to despair. Excuses were to no avail. If there was a shout of "I must see that," he must be taken to see it regardless of difficulties.

Even at night he gave them no rest. Suddenly there would be a loud bang on the side of the carriage "Stop! What's that?" and they would have to light the lamps and show him. This man of genius was a true representative of a people which long was starved of the food of knowledge and now suddenly had it within its grasp. The carpenter also studied engraving; an example which he left behind in Amsterdam depicts a subject in keeping with Peter's situation and his chief preoccupation at that time. It represents the victory of the Christian religion over the Muslim in the form of an angel with a cross and a palm in its hands trampling a crescent and Turkish standards.[25] The subject of the engraving is explained in a letter from Peter to Patriarch Adrian in Moscow. "We are in the Netherlands, in the city of Amsterdam, and thanks to God's grace and your prayers we are alive and in good health and in accordance with God's word spoken to our forefather Adam we are laboring, but not because we are forced but in order to obtain a good sea route so that, having gained complete mastery, on our return we might be the conquerors in Christ's name of our enemies and the liberators of Christians living there, by his grace. This I shall not cease to desire to my last breath."

Besides the patriarch, Peter was in regular correspondence with other government officials, who kept him informed about what was going on in Russia. Fortifications were being erected around Azov: the forts of St. Alexis and St. Peter, the Trinity fort at Taganrog and next to it Fort St. Paul. A harbor was being built at Taganrog. The Tatars were repelled from Azov. On the Dnieper the Turks and Tatars were driven back from the fortresses at Kazykermen and Tavan, which were occupied by the Russians, and King Augustus finally had established himself in Poland. The companies were hard at work building ships; the Swedish king had sent three hundred cannon for the war against the infidel.

Peter corresponded most enthusiastically with Vinius, who was more educated than the others and inexhaustible in his activity. In his letters Vinius constantly demanded the despatch of arms experts, because good iron was available, but no craftsmen. "It pains me greatly that foreigners have sold Swedish iron at a high price, collected the money and gone abroad, when our Siberian ore is much better than the Swedish." No one sympathized more than Peter with Vinius's heartache. He replied: "You write, your honor, of craftsmen. Of those you request, we have found some very good gunsmiths and locksmiths and shall send them forthwith. For the sake of speed we may get them from the same places where Butman hired men for the Olonets works.²⁶ We shall also seek them here, which Mayor Witsen had undertaken to do, but I doubt whether we shall find them soon." News of craftsmen mingled with political news. "The ironworkers that you write of, Witsen can see to it and hire them, and I keep reminding him, but he just procrastinates from day to day, and so far has not given a straight answer. If he can't arrange it I have hopes of getting not only ironworkers but also coppersmiths from the Polish king through his envoy. Peace has been made with the French, and fools here are delighted but wise men are not pleased, because the French have deceived everyone and are waiting for a chance to declare war again."²⁷

In another letter Peter wrote about Witsen again. "I have spoken to Witsen about the ironworkers on many occasions, only he keeps putting off doing anything." In between business matters Vinius reported on the carousing of members of the jolly company left behind in Moscow. "On the royal nameday Prince Fedor Yurievich Romodanovsky held a great and rich feast in the generals' dining hall at Preobrazhenskoe. More than a hundred people sat down at different tables, and he entertained us with such cordiality and kindness and the firing from small arms and artillery was so powerful that the dining room hardly survived intact and one wall bulged out; it went on till four or five o'clock in the morning and it took people three days to recover." Describing another feast Vinius wrote that they "had thrown John Barleycorn and his uncle Bacchus from their great wet silver and glass vials into our stomachs."[28] John was not forgotten in Holland, either. Apologizing for not sending letters to everyone, Peter wrote to Vinius that lack of time and absences were partly to blame for his omission, and also Barleycorn.

Peter stayed in Holland for four and a half months. The frigate for which he had laid the keel was launched. At the East India docks, by devoting himself together with the other volunteers to the study of naval architecture, in a short time the tsar mastered everything a good ship's carpenter needed to know and he built a new ship by using his own labor and expertise and launched it. Then he asked the foreman of the docks, Jan Paul, to teach him naval geometry, which he did in four days. But, as the foreman explained, in Holland knowledge of geometrical science was incomplete. They worked on the basis of a few principles and a long period of practical work, therefore he was unable to show him everything on a drawing. At this Peter became very annoyed that he had come such a long way but not achieved his goal. Then his majesty spent a few days in the company of the merchant Jan Tessing at his home out of town. He sat there most glumly for the aforementioned reasons and when in the course of conversation he was asked why he was so sad he explained. In the company was an Englishman and when he heard this, he said that in England they had mastered the science of naval architecture and other arts completely, and he could learn in a short time. His majesty was immensely encouraged by these words and set off for England with all speed and there in the space of four months he completed his studies.[29]

Peter I
By Sir Godfrey Kneller in London, 1698
Kensington Palace, London

In January 1698 Peter left Holland for England and soon made his way from London to the small town of Deptford where he finished his apprenticeship in the royal dockyard. He hired about sixty foreigners, goldsmiths, and his ambassadors in Holland also hired more than a hundred experts, and Captain Cornelius Cruys, taken into Russian service in Holland, hired many men for the fleet. He was appointed directly to the rank of vice-admiral.

Having spent three months in England[30] Peter returned to Holland. He did not stay but headed south-eastwards for Vienna. The embassy's talks with the Estates General on the question of aid for the tsar's war against the Turks had failed. The Estates excused their refusal to loan the tsar sailors, weapons and ammunition on grounds that their country was exhausted by the war with France, and soon Peter learned that the Estates and the king of England were attempting to bring about peace between Austria and Turkey. This peace was vital to Holland and England in order to release the emperor to fight against France. They were on the brink of a major war over the succession to the Spanish throne, that is, to try to reduce the power of France which was so dangerous for all Europe. But just as beneficial to England and Holland as a declaration of peace between Austria and Turkey would be the continuation of the war between Turkey and Russia, which would keep the Turks occupied and prevent them, at the bidding of France, from deflecting the might of Austria from a war in the common European interest. But these interests were diametrically opposed to the interests of Russia. Peter was doing his utmost to bring the war with Turkey to a successful conclusion and obtain a profitable peace, but how could he hope to wage war and win alone without Austria and Venice? Peter's chief concern now was therefore either to persuade the emperor to continue to fight the Turks or at least to insist that peace talks be conducted jointly and that all allies receive equal satisfaction.

On June 16 the grand embassy made a triumphal entry into Vienna. As usual the tsar went on ahead, arriving with the post-chaises. He was in a hurry to get down to business and in conversation with Chancellor Kinski declared that he was displeased with the emperor's decision to conclude peace on the basis of *uti possidetis* (meaning each ruler retain what he held at the time of the peace negotiations). He declared that it was vital for Russia to protect its borders against the Crimea and to have good defenses. Russia had broken its peace with the Turks for the emperor's sake; all the allies should receive the benefits they desired; they should not listen to the English and Dutch who were concerned only with their own profits; the emperor was rushing to make peace with the Turks to fight the French over the Spanish succession and desert his allies, but as soon as the French war began the sultan would immediately attack the emperor. Troops would leave Hungary for the war in France and the Hungarians would rebel. In addition to keeping all his conquests, the tsar demanded the fortress at Kerch in the Crimea, without which he would gain nothing from the peace as the Tatars would resume their attacks on Russia. Peter omitted to say that with Azov and Taganrog but without Kerch he was locked into the sea of Azov. If the Turks refused to concede Kerch to Russia the allies must continue the war. The emperor replied that the tsar's demands were fair, but to force the Turks to comply the Russians would do best to capture Kerch by force of arms. He promised to uphold the demands of the Russian plenipotentiaries at the congress and not to do anything without the tsar's agreement.

V

THE LAST MUSKETEER REVOLT
1698

THE MUSKETEERS REBEL

There the negotiations had to end. Peter saw all the sights of Vienna, visited the towns of Baden and Pressburg and was preparing to leave for Venice when a letter from Moscow arrived in the mail. Romodanovsky wrote that the musketeers had rebelled and were marching on Moscow. Instead of going to Venice, Peter set off for Moscow.

In 1689, as we saw earlier, very few of the musketeers participated in Sophia's and Shaklovity's schemes. At first the majority distanced themselves from interfering in the quarrel between brother and sister, then they openly took Peter's side, forcing Sophia to accede to his demands and give up Shaklovity. Evidently such behavior should have reconciled the government to the musketeers but it turned out otherwise. Even before 1689 the play regiments were formed, which together with the old-established infantrymen[1] were set against the musketeers. People tended to regard the play regiments as Peter's and the musketeers as Sophia's. This was not the only reason why it proved impossible to reconcile the play regiments and their officers with the musketeers. The play regiments represented new forces coming to life, the musketeers— the outmoded ways of the past. When Peter triumphed over Sophia it was a victory for new ideas and the musketeers were faced with the prospect of ceasing to be musketeers and becoming infantrymen. Such a change posed immense difficulties. They would not agree voluntarily but first would try to see whether their old position could be maintained together with the old ways. Given this situation they had many reasons to be aggrieved. Take the mock military maneuvers, for example. There were two armies: the Russian troops, on whose side the tsar fought, were supplied by the play regiments, the enemy, commanded by the "king of Poland", by the musketeers. They were beaten, a true reflection of their obsolescence in the face of the new army. The sense of humiliation and aggravation was strong. The other side also had good reason to be aggrieved. We have no reason to dismiss the information that some musketeers dug a tunnel under the New convent, coming up under the floor of Sophia's rooms, and would have taken her out through an underground passage had they not been apprehended and executed after a fierce fight with the soldiers guarding the convent. The letter from Vinius to the tsar mentioned earlier is a good example of the attitude of the tsar's confidants to the musketeers and their attitude towards the government. In it he remarked that when the good news of the capture of Azov was received there was rejoicing even in the musketeer districts. The Azov campaigns were very hard on the musketeers. For two years running they had to travel a great distance, leaving behind their families and profitable businesses in Moscow. The tsar was displeased with them and issued reprimands. Who was to blame? Naturally it must be foreigners, most of all Lefort, the man closest to the tsar. The musketeers were exasperated with Lefort. Meanwhile their conditions went from bad to worse. After the capture of Azov they were detained there to guard the town and made to work on building the fortifications. People who were dissatisfied with the tsar and anxious to be rid of him by any means whatsoever turned to the musketeers because they were more dissatisfied than anyone else and doomed to destruction. "Why are they asleep?" said Sokovnin. " They may as well kill the tsar because they have nothing to lose." It is easy to appreciate the feelings of men who had "nothing to lose," and to understand the attitude of Peter and his supporters to men who were dissatisfied and exasperated and whom one's enemies regarded as a potentially reliable and ready weapon. Tsykler appealed to the musketeers and May 15, 1682 came ever more clearly into Peter's mind's eye—the musketeers' spears, the corpses of Matveev and the Naryshkins scarlet with blood.[2] For him everything that was hostile was linked with the musketeers, and the association between enmity and the musketeers could be traced back to the schemes of Ivan Miloslavsky. In his eyes the seed of enmity and the musketeers was planted by

Ivan Miloslavsky. This attitude had found expression in the gruesome spectacle of the execution of Tsykler and his accomplices when their blood flowed into Miloslavsky's coffin, which also expressed Peter's deep bitterness and the way in which the impressions of youth were reviving and taking root at every opportunity.

In Azov the musketeers were tormented with homesickness for Moscow, for the free and easy, peaceful family life in the capital. There was still hope that their tour of duty in Azov soon would end and that they would be transferred to Moscow. But then an order arrived for four regiments—the Chubarov, Kolzakov, Cherny and Gundertmark—to move from Azov to the Lithuanian border to join forces with the troops of Prince Mikhail Grigorievich Romodanovsky, who was awaiting the outcome of the struggle between the parties of France and Saxony in Poland with regiments of noble servitors, dragoons and infantry. The musketeers from Azov arrived in Velikie Luki. Six musketeer regiments were sent to replace them in Azov; the rest were stationed along the southwest frontier. Moscow thus was cleared of musketeers; only infantrymen remained. The most distressed were the four musketeer regiments who had to march from Azov to Velikie Luki instead of returning to Moscow. Many of the musketeers decided that they must get to Moscow at any price. In March more than a hundred and fifty men deserted and turned up in Moscow bearing petitions. When the government asked why they had left their regiments they replied that "their fellow musketeers were quitting service in great numbers because of starvation." They were given until April 3 to leave Moscow, and orders were issued to supply them with a month's rations money from the Chancellery of Musketeers. But in Moscow the fugitives learned some curious things.

Russian people were living in unprecedented times. Indeed, many people asked themselves whether perhaps time itself was coming to an end? The tsar was consorting openly with Germans and went abroad to visit them. No one knew what was happening to him there. The boyars were in power. Everywhere arguments went on about the old and new faiths. Whenever two people met they would start to discuss theological matters, their first question being how many fingers do you use to make the sign of the cross?[3] The musketeer deserters met up with two acquaintances on St. John's square [in the Kremlin], musketeers, like themselves, who were working as freelance public scribes.[4] They struck up a conversation, the first words of which were "So our sovereign has gone away to foreign parts." The sovereign was in foreign parts, and just look what was happening in Moscow in his absence. The scribes told them that the boyars were planning to strangle the tsarevich. The boyar Tikhon Nikitich Streshnev wanted to strangle him and become ruler in Moscow himself. "There's no place for you in Moscow," said the scribes to the musketeers.

It is easy to imagine the musketeers' feelings when they heard those last words. They searched for some way of staying in Moscow, then an invitation came. The former regent, Tsarevna Sophia, was living in captivity in the New convent. Her sisters, the daughters of Miloslavsky, were at liberty in the palace, but things had been difficult for them since 1689.[5] They had ruled together with Sophia. If they needed money, they sent to any government department and took what they wanted. But now things were different. They were out of favor, defenseless. They naturally had a strong desire for things to change; the musketeers might even help them again. They accumulated all pieces of scandal, all rumors unfavorable to the government. Secret messages passed between them and the convent. Here there were discontented female relatives of the musketeers, who were ready to run errands for the discontented tsarevnas. The musketeers who fled to Moscow were bound to turn to the tsarevnas, the only people in the palace likely to take an interest in their fate. They were bound to express the wish to see Sophia restored to power.

Although the tsarevnas were locked up in the palace during the troubles, the musketeers found a way of getting in contact with them. Two of the musketeer deserters, Proskuriatov and Tuma, composed a petition listing the musketeers' grievances and gave it to a musketeer's wife who was going into the palace to give it to one of the tsarevnas. The most active of them was Martha. The musketeers' petition reached her, and her chambermaid gave a letter to the musketeer woman to hand to Tuma. When she gave it to her, Martha told the chambermaid "Look, I trust you. If news of this gets out, you will be tortured and I shall be sent straight to a nunnery."

She told the chambermaid to tell the musketeer's wife that they were being persecuted in the palace. The boyars planned to strangle the tsarevich. The musketeers should come to their aid. Rumors came from the palace: the boyars planned to strangle the tsarevich, but he was swapped and his clothes put on another boy. The tsaritsa found out that it was not the tsarevich. They were looking for the tsarevich in another room and the boyars slapped the tsaritsa on the cheeks. No one knew if the tsar was dead or alive, and orders had been sent on how to deal with the musketeers. On the Arbat, by the fence of the church of St. Nicholas the Miraculous, stood a crowd of musketeers. One of them, Vasily Tuma, read out the letter sent by Tsarevna Sophia from the New convent summoning all four regiments to Moscow where they should station themselves outside the New convent and present her with an appeal to rule as before.

If everyone was to come to Moscow, why should the petitioners leave? On the April 3 deadline a crowd of musketeers went to the house of the head of the Chancellery of Musketeers, Prince Ivan Borisovich Troekurov, and asked the boyar to give them a hearing. Troekurov ordered them to elect four of their best men to talk with him. The delegates appeared and said that they were refusing to return to duty until the spring roads were passable and appealed for an extension to the deadline. They set out their grievances, complaining that they had been reduced to ruin. The boyar interrupted them and ordered them to return to duty at once. The delegates refused to go. Then Troekurov had them arrested and thrown into jail, but on the way they were rescued by their comrades. This news struck fear into the boyars who remembered only too well the 1682 musketeer rebellion. In addition, in 1697 there was talk amongst the infantrymen of the Lefort Regiment of submitting a petition to the tsarevna in the convent to give them bread rations because some soldier recounted that he had been on guard duty in the palace and the lady had come out and said "Why are you half-naked? You get ninety copecks each per month to buy yourselves red tunics." The soldier told her that they did get three copecks per day but it was reduced to two copecks by big deductions.[6]

The boyars' unease was increased by the fact that for some time there had been no news of the tsar from abroad. They had to make ready another armed force, the infantrymen, to fight the musketeers, and Prince Romodanovsky sent for General Gordon to explain the situation. Gordon felt that the prince was exaggerating the danger and told him that there was nothing to worry about; the musketeers were weak and had no leader. Gordon left Romodanovsky to go to Butyrki, where his infantry regiment was stationed, in order to make contingency plans. He was reassured to find all his men present in camp, apart from some who were on guard duty in various locations. The next day the musketeers were still in Moscow but all was calm, apart from two drunks causing a scene in the Chancellery of Musketeers. Meanwhile the boyars were in session in the palace discussing what to do next. They decided to send an infantry detachment to drive the musketeers out of Moscow by force. In the evening a company of the Semenovsky Guards with the help of some townsmen drove the uninvited guests outside the town gates. Only two put up a fight. One was beaten up so badly that he soon died and the other was banished to Siberia together with those who caused the scene in the chancellery earlier.

In a letter dated April 8 Romodanovsky informed Peter of the arrival of the musketeer deserters and of how they had been sent packing by the infantrymen. Peter received the letter when he was still in Amsterdam about to set off for Vienna. "I received your majesty's[7] letter and read it," Peter replied, "for which I thank you and ask you in future not to leave me in suspense. In the same letter you report a rebellion of the musketeers and describe how you used your authority and the services of the infantry to pacify them. We are very glad, but also annoyed and vexed that you did not hold a full investigation, may God be your judge! We have a serious matter on our hands. Why did you take Avtamon (Golovin, commander of the Preobrazhensky Regiment) if that was not the case? If you thought that we had perished because the mail has been delayed, and did not take any action out of fear, thinking there might soon be some news in the mail, let me tell you that, praise be to God, no one has died, we are all alive. I can't think where this womanish fear has come from, thinking that someone is dead just because there was no mail. Also there have been spring floods. You can't expect anything from such cowardice. Please don't be offended. I wrote from sickness of heart." Several days later Peter wrote to Vinius rebuking him for his anxiety over the non-arrival of the mail. "I am very astonished, and give you up to God's judgement, that you of all people should be so anxious about the delay of the mail, when you yourself know what these countries are like. Only someone who hasn't been there can be surprised. I would have hoped that you would use your experience to explain and dissuade them from such ideas, but you yourself are leading them into the trap. Naturally they all think that if someone who has been here is so afraid then it really must be true. I am truly displeased." Vinius hastened to beg forgiveness, and the tsar replied: "The Lord God in his mercy will forgive us all our trespasses. You yourself must understand what this business means to me and why I wrote to you as I did."

It really was a serious business. The musketeers had been driven out of Moscow and brought various items of news and the invitation from the New convent to Toropets, where their regiments now were stationed with Romodanovsky. On the way a musketeer woman caught up with them and handed over a new letter from Sophia. "Now things are bad for you, and they will get worse. Come to Moscow. Why have you stopped? There is no news of the tsar." As if to prove that things could only get worse for the musketeers, orders arrived from Moscow dated May 28. Romodanovsky was to discharge his troops, infantry and cavalry, to their homes and come to Moscow, but the musketeers were to stay put in the towns of Viazma, Belaia, Rzheva Volodimerova and Dorogobuzh until they received further instructions. The hundred and fifty-five musketeers who fled to Moscow were to be banished in perpetuity to the Ukrainian towns of Chernigov, Pereiaslavl and Novobogoroditskoe with their wives and children. The sergeants, corporals and musketeers who had not deserted were to be graciously commended on behalf of the sovereign for their loyal service in not indulging the miscreants and submitting complaints against them.

So the scribes on St. John's Square had told the truth—Moscow was no place for the musketeers. When these orders, sent in the tsar's name, were announced, Colonels Chubarov, Cherny, and Tikhon Gundertmark handed over the deserters from their regiments, about fifty men, to Romodanovsky, and he ordered them be escorted to the fortress and given over to the custody of the military governor of Toropets. But on the road the captains escorting the deserters met with hordes of musketeers, who released their comrades, chased the captains away and threw sticks at them. Romodanovsky wanted to send the Novgorod musketeers to deal with them, but there were too few of them to tackle the mutineers. Then at the request of the colonels Romodanovsky had the original orders read out to each regiment separately at the assembly points, but gave instructions that the Moscow musketeers should not be summoned to military headquarters to hear the orders because of their criminal unreliability and the danger that they would misbehave. In the Chubarov and Kolzakov Regiments the musketeers listened to the document, then the musketeers of the Kolzakov Regiment pleaded for mercy and said that if the criminals turned up they would not support them. The Chubarov musketeers said that there were no criminals amongst them and the men who had been to Moscow had gone because they were starving. Kolzakov brought fifteen criminals from his regiment to the headquarters and from there to Toropets where they were handed over to the military governor. But the musketeers rallied and rescued them from the governor by storm, chased Colonel Kolzakov away and threw sticks at him. He escaped across the river Toropa, over the wooden bridge, leaving his horse behind.

The musketeers of the Cherny and Gundertmark regiments did not go to the assembly points to hear the tsar's orders, but began to break down the fences along the streets near the military headquarters and the house where Romodanovsky was staying, and many of them assembled and stood around in great mobs. Romodanovsky took fright and departed the town with the gentry cavalry regiments for the open country and took up position on the road to Moscow. Chubarov, Gundertmark and Kolzakov joined him. The prince ordered them to ride to their regiments, march them separately out of their camps into the open field and proceed to the destinations allocated. The Chubarov Regiment set off and marched through the companies and regiments of cavalry. Romodanovsky rode up to them, ordered them to halt and tried to persuade them to hand over the Moscow deserters. The musketeers replied that they were not siding with the deserters, but it was not within their power to arrest them and hand them over. To this Romodanovsky replied "There are only a few deserters, but five hundred or more of you!" The musketeers went off to confer. An hour passed and there was no movement. Romodanovsky sent a message urging them not to delay with the handover, but got the same answer. "It's not within our power." After that the regiment set off but the deserters remained behind and turned back towards Toropets. Romodanovsky sent lancers and heavy cavalry to arrest them, which they started to do, but then the Gundertmark Regiment marched off and the criminals mingled with it, making their way across marshy ground and scrubland. The colonel and officers yelled at them not to admit the criminals into their ranks, but the troopers ignored them and tried to fight the cavalrymen who were pursuing the criminals. They shouted "There are no criminals in our regiment! They went to Moscow because they were hard up and starving." The musketeers all set off for the towns to which they had been assigned and Romodanovsky sent them two month's wages in order to remove any pretext for continuation of the trouble.

But the musketeers needed more than wages. They needed Moscow, from where they were barred. In any case, things already had gone too far. The tsar's orders had been disobeyed, the deserters had not been given up. In for a penny, in for a pound. Naturally the deserters, acting out of self-preservation, were bound to do their utmost to urge the rest to rebel. The musketeers marched slowly, reluctantly, covering about five versts per day, then on June 6, on the banks of the Dvina, rebellion broke out. A musketeer called Maslov stood on a wagon in front of the four regiments and read out Sophia's letter of invitation. "I hear that only a small number of men from your regiments came to Moscow. All four should come to Moscow and assemble outside the New convent and appeal to me to come back to Moscow and rule as before, and if the infantrymen who guard the convent try to stop you you should deal with them, kill them and march into Moscow. You must do battle with anyone who tries to stop you, with their bondsmen or with infantry."

A hum of conversation started up in the crowd. "Let's go to Moscow. We'll destroy the Foreign Quarter and kill the Germans, because they have damaged Orthodoxy. Kill the boyars and the musketeers will live in their houses. Send word to the other regiments to go to Moscow because the musketeers are being ruined by the boyars and foreigners and aren't allowed into Moscow. We must get to Moscow even if it kills us, we must reach our goal. Send word to the Don Cossacks. If the tsarevna refuses to take power we can have Prince Vasily Golitsyn until the tsarevich grows up. He was good to the musketeers during the Crimean campaigns and in Moscow. As long as the present sovereign is alive, we shan't see Moscow again. Don't let him into Moscow. Kill him, because he started to believe in Germans and consorted with Germans. All the tsarevnas want the musketeers to come to Moscow. Tsarevna Sophia gave the Toropets Cossacks fifty copecks apiece to go to Moscow." Groups of musketeers gathered. They dismissed the old colonels and captains, replacing them with new ones and set off for Moscow.

But the infantrymen were in Moscow and on the way the musketeers had the idea of going to Butyrki to find out what was going on in the infantry regiments. Musketeer Puzan set off for Butyrki to see some infantrymen in the Salenikov Regiment, whom he knew, and met one of them, but the latter refused to cooperate. "We have strict orders about you. We won't go with you. We have no business with you. You can do what you want." The musketeers had another idea. They would not do battle with the infantrymen, on account of their small numbers (just twenty-two hundred men), but skirt Moscow and ensconce themselves in Serpukhov or Tula and send messages to Belgorod, Azov, Sevsk and other towns inviting the musketeers there to join them without delay, then march to Moscow all together and kill the boyars.

Fear engulfed the inhabitants of Moscow when they learned of the approach of the musketeers. The better-off started to move out to remote villages, taking their property with them. Arguments broke out amongst the boyars about what measures to take. In the end Prince Boris Alekseevich Golitsyn's view prevailed. It was resolved to send Boyar Shein to deal with the musketeers, accompanied by General Gordon and Prince Koltsov-Masalsky. They had about four thousand troops and twenty-five guns. On June 17 the tsar's troops met with the musketeers in the vicinity of the Resurrection monastery near the ford across the Istra river.[8] The musketeers sent Shein a letter in which they complained that in Azov they were subjected to many depredations. They had toiled winter and summer over building the fortifications, then from Azov they were transferred to Prince Romodanovsky's regiment and suffered cold, hunger and want. One hundred and fifty men were housed in one billet, two months' rations money wasn't even enough for two weeks. Men who strayed from their quarters were beaten with sticks. From Toropets Romodanovsky had ordered each regiment to be transferred to other towns, arms, standards and regimental coffers to be confiscated, and ordered the cavalry to surround and attack them. Scared by this, they did not go to the postings to which they were assigned but were going to Moscow, not to raise rebellion but to escape a needless death. They only wanted to be allowed to see their wives and children for a short time then, wherever the occasion arose, then they would be glad to return to duty.

Shein sent Gordon to the musketeers' camp to announce that if they returned to the places assigned them and handed over the men who had deserted to Moscow and also the ringleaders of the recent mutiny, the tsar would pardon them and they would receive their wages at their new postings at local rates. Gordon expended his *rhetoric,* as he himself expressed it,[9] in vain in trying to win over the musketeers. They replied that they would die or go to Moscow, even if for a short time, then they would go wherever the tsar ordered. Their response to Gordon's continued rhetoric was that they would crush his regiment.

The foreigner had failed, so Shein sent the Russian Prince Koltsov-Masalsky to try to talk them over. Corporal Zorin, one of the ringleaders, went to see him with a draft of an unfinished petition, which read: "The regiments of the Moscow musketeers appeal to you in their grief with many tears. They had served the great sovereigns as their fathers and forefathers did before them in the common Christian faith. They promised to preserve the faith to the end of their lives, as it is maintained by the holy apostolic church. In 1682 they suppressed the attempted disorders in their zeal for the faith and on the great sovereign's orders it was forbidden to refer to them as traitors and rebels in respect of that time,[10] and they promised by kissing the cross to serve the cause of piety unswervingly. Then in 1695 they were ordered to serve for a year in towns outside Moscow. The same year at Azov the foreign heretic Franz Lefort plotted to do great harm to the faith; he led the Moscow musketeers under the fortress wall prematurely and stood them in the most dangerous places where many were killed. He plotted to have their entrenchments undermined, thereby causing the deaths of three hundred or more. He also devised a scheme of bribing the rank and file with ten rubles each for the assault on Azov, and promotion for those who served. During the assault the flank on which they fought suffered the most casualties. And they, in their zeal to serve the great sovereign and all Christendom, said that Azov should be taken by using siege towers but he ignored this advice. Reluctant to see Christianity flourish, he detained the last of them outside Azov until October 3.

Then on October 14 he set out from Cherkassk over the steppe with the aim of wiping them out completely. They had to eat carrion and vast numbers perished. In 1696 Azov was taken by siege and they were left there to build the fortifications. They toiled night and day for a whole year under extremely difficult conditions. From Azov they were ordered to Moscow and they marched through Zmiev, Izium, Tsarev Borisov and Moiak, utterly destitute. From these places they were ordered to join the regiment of Prince Commander M.G. Romodanovsky in their winter quarters at Pustaia Rzheva, bypassing Moscow. Doing their duty to the great sovereign they marched night and day to reach the regiment in the appalling conditions of the autumn roads, arriving barely alive.

"When they were stationed at the Polish border in winter, in the forest and the worst terrain, tormented by freezing weather and all manner of depredations, they did their duty, trusting in the great sovereign's favor. An order was issued to all the regiments of the Novgorod district to disperse, and the boyar commander Romodanovsky led them out of Toropets and gave orders that they be killed, but they don't know why. Then they heard that there was panic in Moscow and that the city gates were being closed early, and opened in the second or third hour of the day, and the whole people was being treated impertinently. They had heard that the Germans were going to Moscow, and practising shaving and smoking tobacco to bring about the complete overthrow of the faith."

Zorin demanded that the appeal be read out to all the tsar's troops. Naturally this demand was not met, and Shein could see clearly which way the wind was blowing when the appeal contrasted

Orthodoxy on one hand with the heretic Franz Lefort on the other. Under the modest guise of an appeal was concealed a wicked attack on the tsar, disguised as an attack on his favorite. Shein saw clearly that negotiations and exhortations would simply increase the musketeers' insolence, whereas their defeat was not in doubt. They were a leaderless, ill-organized mob with insufficient artillery. Preparations for battle began. Prayers were said in both camps. The musketeers made confession and vowed to die on each other's behalf and not betray the cause. For the last time a message came telling them to lay down their arms and beg the tsar's forgiveness for their sins. If they did not, cannon fire would begin. The musketeers replied "We are not afraid. We've seen better cannon than those."

Even then Shein proceeded cautiously. Seeing that talks, pleas and verbal threats had failed he tried a more powerful means of persuasion, ordering shells to be fired over the musketeers' heads, but this only made them bolder. They began to unfurl their standards, tossed their caps in the air and made ready for battle. After another salvo, however, the musketeers began to falter, even though there were a few shouts of "Let's make an all-out attack on the main regiment. We'd rather die than be barred from Moscow." After two more salvos only a few remained in the camp, which was quickly captured by the tsar's troops. The battle had lasted no more than an hour. Only two government troops were wounded, one fatally. The musketeers had fifteen killed, thirty-seven injured, mostly fatally. Those who fled from the camp were rounded up. Shein made an inspection "to sort out the criminals from the honest men and determine who had tried to raise rebellion in Moscow. Then the musketeers were subjected to large-scale interrogations and cruel tortures, as a result of which many were executed and hanged by the roadside. The rest were dispersed to prisons and monasteries under armed escort." Confessions were extracted by torture about the events in Toropets and later on the Dvina, but the tsarevna's letter was not mentioned.

PETER RETURNS TO MOSCOW
When he received news of the musketeers' rebellion and their progress towards Moscow from "King" Romodanovsky, Peter replied: "Your honor writes that the seed of Ivan Miloslavsky is

sprouting. I therefore ask you to be firm: nothing else can extinguish the fire. Although we are sorry to abandon this useful mission (the visit to Venice) we shall be with you forthwith." Romodanovsky wrote about the disturbances among the musketeers and Peter imagined the "seed of Miloslavsky" sprouting. The phrase "only firmness can extinguish the fire" showed the extent of the aggravation which convinced Peter that extreme measures were needed to eradicate the evil. Thoughts of striking fear into one's opponents and drowning the opposition in blood usually occur to revolutionaries in the heat of battle, when resistance has hardened their hearts and when they fear for their future and for the future of their enterprise. This ominous reply to Romodanovsky's letter heralded a reign of terror in Moscow.

On the way from Vienna to Russia Peter received word that the revolt had ended with Shein's victory. In the meantime Vinius wrote "Not one escaped; the worst of them have been dispatched to that dark afterlife for a reunion with their brethren who, I imagine, have been put in special places in Hell as even the Devil is afraid that they might raise rebellion in Hell and drive him from his throne."

On August 26 a rumor spread around Moscow that the tsar had arrived back the previous evening. He had been to various places and had visited Mistress Mons.[11] He had not been to the palace, had not seen his wife. He had spent the evening with Lefort, and went to Preobrazhenskoe to spend the night. That evening or night a decision was taken which on the next day was to astound Moscow and strike terror into many people.

Peter had returned to Moscow in a state of great agitation. The seed of Ivan Miloslavsky, the musketeers, had crossed him again. Before his departure there had been Sokovnin, Tsykler and the musketeers; he had only just begun to enjoy himself abroad, indulging in his favorite pastimes, when again the musketeers interrupted his journey. But the musketeers were only skirmishers, only an armed force behind whom stood a mass of people who opposed reform and everything which Peter had declared to be his business, to which he had committed himself irrevocably, without which he could not exist. Peter was well aware of what such people thought of his activity, but he would not renounce it just to please them. On the contrary, he would intensify his efforts and thereby inspire even greater hatred, even greater bitterness. Awareness of this bitterness in others embittered him even more. He was prepared to wage a life and death struggle, he was agitated, he was boiling with rage, he would make the first attack, fling himself at the enemy's standard, tear it down and trample on it. This standard was the beard, it was the long robes of antiquity.

Of course, we should not dwell solely open Peter's personal motives and lose sight of the general course of national affairs. Even before Peter people had turned to the West, had begun to bow to a new authority, and this was bound to be reflected in their clothing and hairstyle. There is no reason to be surprised by a phenomenon which continually repeats itself before our very eyes, when a man strives to express his state of mind, feelings, views and aims first and foremost in his appearance, his clothing and hairstyle. Once the superiority of foreigners and the need to learn from them were acknowledged, then imitation occurred, beginning naturally and necessarily with outward appearances, with clothes and hairdressing, in confirmation of the adage that the mind of a nation is revealed in the cut of its clothing. Russian dress was ugly and inconvenient. On account of it foreigners called us barbarians; uncombed hair made us seem particularly disgusting and absurd, like some kind of primitive forest dwellers. Russians first began to imitate foreigners' appearance in the reign of Boris Godunov, at the time of the first turn towards the West. Some men began to shave off their beards which at once aroused strong reactions from the guardians of antiquity. In Tsar Alexis's reign shaving increased as the move towards the West became stronger. We saw how Avvakum, that fervent guardian of the traditions of our forefathers, refused to bless the son of the boyar Sheremetev because he appeared before him in "depraved fashion," in other words clean-shaven.[12]

The zealots of tradition did their utmost to eradicate "heathen, depraved, vile practices," and it seemed that they attained their goal when the government appeased them by reducing people in rank as a punishment for haircutting. But such zeal harmed only the zealots themselves, who were in no position to hold back the tide of progress and merely succeeded in aggravating their opponents and forcing them to regard the beard and long old-fashioned robes with

РАСКОЛЬНИКЪ ГОВОРИТЪ
СЛУШЇ ЦЫРЮЛЬНИКЪ
Я БОРОДЫ СТРИЇБ НЕ
ХОЧУ ВОТЪ ГЛЕ ДИ Я НА
ТЕБЯ СКОРО КАРАУЛЪ ЗАКРЇЧУ

ЦЫРЮЛЬНЇИКЪ ХО
ЧЕТЪ РАСКОЛЬНИКУ
БОРОДУ СТРИЧЬ ·

The Barber Cuts the Old Believer's Beard
Early eighteenth-century Russian woodcut does
not depict Peter I but refers to his decrees on shaving.

the same hostility as the zealots regarded "depraved fashion." The beard became a standard of the struggle between the two sides, and naturally when the proponents of new ideas won, their first act would be to cast down the enemy's standard. The movement which was to culminate in this victory was unstoppable. In 1681 Tsar Fedor issued an order to all his council and all courtiers and chancellery officials to wear short tunics instead of the previous long robes and caftans. No one dared to show his face in a long robe or caftan not only in the palace but even in the Kremlin. Patriarch Joachim saw with despair that the "heathen, depraved, vile practice" of shaving was gaining strength and again the patriarch raged against it. "This heathen, depraved, vile practice, many times denounced of old, in the time of Tsar Alexis Mikhailovich was completely eradicated, but now again is threatening to destroy the image given to man by God." The patriarch excommunicated men for shaving, even excommunicated those who associated with people who shaved, but his efforts were in vain and only worked to the detriment of the authority of the church and clergy. Joachim's successor, Adrian, issued a strongly-worded missive against shaving, which he called a heretical abomination which made men resemble cats and dogs. The patriarch tried to frighten Russians by asking where they would stand at the day of judgement if they shaved off their beards, "with the just, adorned with their beards, or with the clean-shaven heretics?"

These attacks provide us with a good measure of the strength of the movement against which they were aimed, a good measure of the strength of irritation which they must have aroused in "young, irresponsible" people. We note also that the method used by Peter to attack beards and Russian dress was bequeathed to him by his predecessors, and any other method was unthinkable. Tsar Alexis did battle with shaving by issuing an edict to punish miscreants by demotion in rank. Tsar Fedor issued an edict commanding the wearing of short tunics instead of long robes and caftans. The patriarch for his part punished pagan customs with excommunication. Peter similarly employed force to ban beards and Russian dress. Finally, another circumstance is worth noting. Without doubt Peter's first priority when he arrived in Moscow was to demand a full investigation of the musketeer affair. It is easy to imagine his feelings when he read their petition, which was full of malicious attacks on Franz Lefort (namely on Peter himself) and against Germans who practised shaving. "I am a German who shaves"—was his reaction—"and this is what I am going to do with your beards!"

INTERROGATION AND EXECUTION OF THE MUSKETEERS

On the morning of August 26, 1698 people of all sorts crowded into the wooden palace at Preobrazhenskoe where Peter lived a simple life, receiving the lowborn along with men of high rank. Here, as he conferred with the magnates, he cut off their beards with his own hands, beginning with Shein and Romodanovsky. The only people who were exempted were the most venerable elderly men, for whom the new fashion was inappropriate. Tikhon Nikitich Streshnev and Prince Mikhail Alegukovich Cherkassky were the only ones to keep their beards. Others realized what was happening and began to shave of their own accord. Those who had not yet caught on were given an incentive. On September 1, New Year's Day, a great banquet was held at Shein's. A few appeared wearing beards, but this time it was not the tsar but the royal jester who did the shaving. After that anyone who refused to shave had to pay the famous beard tax.[13]

It had begun. A challenge was flung at those who proclaimed shaving to be an immoral, heretical innovation. Peter gave then no time to recover from this blow but stunned them with a new horror by beginning the bloody interrogation of those musketeers who had dared to take up arms against Germans who practised shaving. From the middle of September they began to summon to Moscow those musketeers who had remained alive after Shein's initial investigation, packing them into surrounding monasteries and villages. They numbered more than one thousand seven hundred. The trials began in Preobrazhenskoe in fourteen torture chambers on September 17, the sad anniversary of Sophia's nameday, when sixteen years earlier the Khovanskys had been executed without trial.[14] Torture was administered with unprecedented cruelty. The admission was obtained that the musketeers had intended to camp by the New convent and invite Sophia to rule. Finally one musketeer, after a third round of torture by fire, confessed that Tuma had brought a letter sent to them by Tsarevna Sophia from Moscow to Velikie Luki. Several other musketeers gave the same testimony. They then got to the musketeer's wife accused of passing on the letter, to women who were living with Sophia in the convent and with her sister Martha. The women were tortured and testified what we already know about the relations between the two sisters and the handing of the letter to the musketeers.

Meanwhile horrible preparations were being made for executions. Gallows were erected along the walls of White Town and Earthwork Quarter, by the gates of the New convent and the four regimental headquarters of the mutinous regiments. The patriarch recalled that in such cases his predecessors had mediated between the tsar and the objects of his wrath, grieved for those who had fallen from favor and calmed tempers. Adrian took an icon of the Virgin and set off for Preobrazhenskoe to see Peter. But the warrior was in a rage and no one and nothing would stop him now. When he saw the patriarch he yelled "What's that icon for? You have no business coming here. Clear off and put the icon back where it belongs. Maybe I do a greater honor to God and his Holy Mother than you do. I am doing my duty and acting in a manner pleasing to God when I defend the people and punish wrongdoers who plot against them."

Peter personally interrogated the two sisters who were implicated in the affair, Martha and Sophia. Martha confessed that she had told Sophia about the arrival of the musketeers and their wish to see her, Sophia, in power; but she denied giving the musketeers a letter. Sophia, when questioned about the letter handed to the musketeers on her behalf, replied that the letter which was reported during the trial was not sent to the musketeer regiments by her. As for the musketeers saying that they were going to come to Moscow to invite her, the tsarevna, to rule as before, no doubt this was prompted not by any letter from her but because they knew that she had ruled from 1682.

On September 30 the first execution took place. Two hundred and one musketeers were taken from Preobrazhenskoe in wagons to the Intercession gates; in each cart sat two men, each holding a lighted candle in his hand. Their wives, mothers and children ran behind the wagons with terrible shrieks. At the Intercession gates in the presence of the tsar himself the sentence was read out: "Under interrogation and torture they all said that they planned to go to

Moscow, and in Moscow to raise rebellion and kill the boyars and destroy the Foreign Quarter, and kill the Germans, and raise up the common people, and that all four regiments knew and plotted. The great sovereign orders that you be put to death for your crime." When the sentence had been read out, the condemned men were distributed to the appointed places of execution. But five, it says in the records, were beheaded at Preobrazhenskoe. Reliable witnesses [Korb] explain this oddity:[15] Peter personally chopped off the heads of these five musketeers. On October 11 there were new executions: one hundred and forty-four men were executed. The next day two hundred and five; the day after that a hundred and forty-one. On October 17 one hundred and nine were executed, on the 18th sixty-three; on the 19th one hundred and six, and two on the 21st. One hundred and ninety-five musketeers were hanged outside the New convent opposite Sophia's cell. Three of them were hanged right outside her windows, holding petitions in their hands, "and in those petitions were written the charges against them."

In Preobrazhenskoe some bloody exercises took place. On October 17 some of the tsar's close associates chopped off the heads of the musketeers. Prince Romodanovsky cut off four; Golitsyn was so unskilled that he increased the agonies of the unfortunate man allocated to him; Peter's favorite "Aleksasha" (Menshikov)[16] bragged that he had beheaded twenty victims; Blumberg, the colonel of the Preobrazhensky Regiment, and Lefort declined to take part on the grounds that such things were not done in their countries. Peter watched the spectacle on horseback and was angry that some of the boyars set about their task with trembling hands. "Many of the criminals and instigators had their arms and legs broken on the wheel; the wheels were driven into the ground on Red Square on stakes, and in punishment for their crimes the musketeers were placed on the wheels and were alive for several days on end and moaned and groaned on the wheels. On the great sovereign's instructions one of them was shot with a rifle, shot by the sergeant of the Preobrazhenskoe Regiment Alexander Menshikov. Of the priests who had served in the musketeer regiments, one was hanged in front of the crown agent's office, and another was beheaded and his head put on a stake and his body placed on the wheel."[17] For five months the corpses remained at the places of execution, for five months the musketeers held out their petitions in front of Sophia's windows.

Besides the inquisition of the musketeers captured outside the Resurrection monastery there was also an investigation into the events at Azov. When news of the rout of the musketeers at Resurrection reached Cherkassk on the Don the cossacks told the military secretary who had come from Voronezh: "Listen here, *play soldier*,[18] it won't be long before we cut you all to pieces, just as you cut up the musketeers. If the sovereign is not back in Moscow by the last day before the fast and there is no news, we won't wait for the sovereign, but we shall refuse to serve the boyars and won't allow them to take over the tsardom. Our ataman Frol Minaev won't restrain us and we shall purge Moscow. We shan't leave Azov, but when the time comes to set out for Moscow and if all our young warriors won't leave the river and our river isn't empty, at least half of us shall set out along the river and we shall capture the towns on the way to Moscow and bring the townsmen with us. The military governors we shall either kill or throw in the river." When news reached Azov of the events at the Resurrection monastery the musketeers began to say: "They have killed our fathers and brothers and kinsmen, so we'll start things in Azov and kill the officers."

Monks spread the rumor that four regiments of musketeers and the infantrymen of the Preobrazhenskoe and Semenovskoe regiments, who had been sent against the musketeers but refused to attack them, had all been killed, and the tsarevich was hiding out at Butyrki. The monks told the musketeers: "You're fools, you sons of...,[19] you can't stand up for yourselves. The Germans will kill you and all the others. The Don Cossacks have been ready for ages." Musketeer Parfen Timofeev said: "When Razin revolted, I joined him. I haven't forgotten the days of my youth!" Another musketeer, Bugaev, said: "The musketeers have no peace anywhere, neither in Moscow nor in Azov. In Moscow they're persecuted by the boyars, who took their wages unlawfully, in Azov by the Germans who beat them while they work and force them to work all hours. In Moscow the boyars, in Azov the Germans, in the ground worms, in the sea devils."

The new inquiry at Azov was not the only one. A priest serving the musketeer regiments reported that in the tavern at Zmiev the musketeers had been airing their grievances and were mustering all the regiments stationed in Ukraine to march on Moscow. The first intended victims of their pikes were named as the boyar Tikhon Streshnev, for decreasing their grain allowance, and Shein, for attacking them at the Resurrection monastery. And when they captured the detachment in Belgorod first of all they were to kill Prince Yakov Fedorovich Dolgoruky if he refused to surrender the detachment. On the march they were saying "Prince Yakov Fedorovich Dolgoruky drove us out into the rain and slush. Then we were supposed to kill the Tatars. Now we shall go to Moscow and kill the boyars."

TSAREVNAS AND TSARITSA EVDOKIA FORCED TO TAKE THE VEIL

On October 11, on the second day of the executions, Peter summoned an assembly of men of all ranks,[20] whom he entrusted with investigating the evil intentions of Tsarevna Sophia and determining what punishment she should suffer. The assembly's decision is unknown. There were strong reasons for suspecting the tsarevna, but the investigation failed to produce any direct proof of her guilt. We saw her reply to her brother "I didn't send any letters, but the musketeers may have wanted me to rule because I was ruler before." It was decided that the best way to destroy the link between the past and the future and to ensure that no one could want her to govern again was to force her to take the veil. Sophia took the veil and the name Susanna and was left to reside in the same New convent under constant supervision by a company of infantrymen. Her sisters were allowed to visit the convent only during Holy Week and for the convent feast of the icon of Our Lady of Smolensk on July 28, and if Susanna fell ill, Peter personally appointed trustworthy persons who could be sent to enquire after her health. He specified: "No choristers are to be admitted to the convent. The nuns sing well enough, only let them stick to religion, not sing in church 'Deliver us from evil' while they are handing out money for murder on the porch."[21]

Sophia was allowed to remain in the convent on the outskirts of Moscow, but the investigation revealed that her sister Martha was much more guilty. She herself admitted that she had informed her sister of the arrival of the musketeers and of their desire to see her as ruler, and Martha's chambermaid confirmed that the tsarevna received the petition from the musketeers and that the letter to Tuma came from her. Martha took the veil with the name Margarita in the Dormition convent in Aleksandrovsk settlement (now the town of Aleksandrov in Vladimir province).[22]

Before he made his sisters Sophia and Martha take the veil Peter had sent his wife Evdokia to a convent.[23] From what we know of the way of life of Peter and his jolly companions, of the lifestyle of Peter the ship's carpenter, skipper and bombardier, leader of a new warrior band, a man who abandoned the palace and the capital for a life incessantly on the move, we may deduce that Peter was not the perfect family man. Peter married, or rather was married off, at the age of seventeen. He was married according to the old custom, to a pretty young woman who at first was pleasing to him. But a young woman raised in the terem[24] had no moral influence on the young warrior who had made his escape to an entirely different world. Evdokia was unable to follow him there and was constantly abandoned for his favorite amusements. Separation led to estrangement as her complaints of desertion began to irritate him. But there was more to come. Peter took to frequenting the Foreign Quarter, where he saw the leading beauty, the charming Anna Mons, daughter of a wine merchant. One can imagine how poorly wretched Evdokia compared in Peter's eyes with the free-and-easy German girl who was at ease in male company, and how sick he became of his wife's appeals to her "little pet, Peter Alekseevich" when he compared these endearments with the civilities of the sophisticated townswoman. But it is also easy to imagine how Evdokia must have felt about her husband's amusements, and how her legitimate complaints must have irritated her husband and how strongly he must have wished to see his wife as little as possible in order not to have to listen to her complaints. He had grown weary of his wife, as he had of her relatives, the Lopukhins. Lev Kirillovich Naryshkin thus was able to dispose of his rivals with ease. Terrible rumors, it will be recalled, circulated around Moscow about the fate of the leading Lopukhin. It was the accursed Germans, especially the accursed Lefort, who were to blame for all this. It was they, together with Pleshcheev, who were credited with supplying Peter with the amusements which were so hateful to the tsaritsa.[25]

The Lopukhins nursed a terrible hatred for Lefort. There is a story that once during a dinner at Lefort's house one of the Lopukhins quarreled with their host, flung himself at him and pulled his hair, as a result of which Peter boxed Lopukhin's ears. When unreliable elements were being cleared out of Moscow before Peter's departure abroad, the tsaritsa's father and two of her brothers were removed also. "On March 23 the great sovereign ordered the following to serve as military governors in the provinces: Boyar Fedor Abraamovich Lopukhin to Totma, Boyar Vasily Abraamovich to Charodna with his nephew Table Attendant Alexis Andreevich, Table Attendant Sergei Abraamovich to Viazma, to depart from Moscow for those towns immediately." After all this Peter naturally had no desire to return from abroad to Moscow and find the despised Evdokia at his son's side. Having married in the traditional manner, Peter decided to dispose of his wife in the traditional Russian manner by persuading the unloved spouse to take the veil and if she refused by forcing her to do so. He wrote to Naryshkin, Streshnev and Evdokia's chaplain from London, asking them to try to persuade her to take the veil of her own free will. Streshnev replied that she was being stubborn and that the chaplain was a man of few words who needed to be further encouraged with a letter.

Nothing had any effect. So when Peter returned to Moscow he decided to compel Evdokia to take the veil. On September 23 she was dispatched to the convent of the Intercession in Suzdal, where she became a nun and took the name Elena in June 1699. The reason for the delay remains unknown, but there is a curious piece of information [in Korb] dating from September 1698 that Peter became angry with the patriarch when he learned that his orders had not been carried out and Evdokia had not yet taken the veil. The patriarch laid all the blame on the archimandrite and four priests who had opposed the veiling as unlawful and who were taken off to Preobrazhenskoe at night. Young Tsarevich Alexis was transferred to the keeping of his aunt, Tsarevna Natalia Alekseevna.[26]

In the ancient Russian Chronicle[27] there is a curious story about how Great Prince Vladimir stopped loving his wife Rogned and how she tried to kill him but failed and was condemned to death by her husband. But when Vladimir came into Rogned's room to kill her, their young son Iziaslav came out to meet him and giving Vladimir a sword said "Do you think that you are here alone?" Vladimir grasped the sense of his son's words and renounced his intention to kill his wife. But usually when husbands and wives quarrel they forget that they are not alone. Likewise Peter, when he sent his wife to a convent, forgot that he was not alone and that the son whom she had borne him remained.

PETER'S TEMPER

The sad events of the summer and autumn of 1698 kept Peter in a state of agitation which on occasion culminated in frenzied outbursts. On September 14 at a party at Lefort's Peter quarreled with Shein and ran off to find out how many colonels and other officers Shein had appointed in exchange for payment. He returned in a terrible rage, whipped out his sword, smashed it down hard on the table and said to Shein "That's how I'll crush your regiment, and you I'll skin alive." The rage increased when Prince Romodanovsky and Zotov tried to defend Shein. Peter rushed at them, struck Zotov over the head and Romodanovsky on the hand, almost cutting his fingers off. Shein would have been killed if Lefort had not restrained Peter, in the course of which he himself received a hefty blow. There was general consternation, but the *young favorite* was able to calm Peter, who carried on feasting and merrymaking till dawn.

MENSHIKOV

This young favorite was Alexander Danilovich Menshikov, sergeant of the Preobrazhensky Regiment, who at the time was better known by his pet name of Aleksasha[28] As regards the origins of the man subsequently known as "illustrious prince" the sources are in full accord. Contemporaries were unanimous in saying that Menshikov came from very humble origins. According to Russian accounts, he was born near Vladimir, the son of a palace stable lad or groom.[29] The importance of the grooms in Peter's mock regiments is well known. It was they who formed the basis of the Preobrazhensky and Semenovsky regiments. This helps to explain how Menshikov's father became a corporal in the Preobrazhensky Regiment. Subsequently the official act, the charter confirming Menshikov's princely status [in 1707], states quite correctly that Alexander

Danilovich's father served in the Guards. But this gives us no
grounds for rejecting the information that the son of the play
regiment groom, who for a long time was known only as Aleksasha,
sold pies, for all these minor servitors and their children also plied
various trades as and when they could. We should not, then, dismiss
the following story by an eye witness.[30] Peter once lost his temper
with Menshikov and told him "Do you realize that I could return
you in a trice to your former condition? Take your pie tray, go round
the barracks and the streets crying out 'Home-baked pies' as you
used to do. Be off with you!" and he pushed him out of the room.
Menshikov appealed to Empress Catherine,[31] who succeeded in
cheering up her husband, but in the meantime Menshikov obtained
a tray of pies and appeared with them before Peter. The tsar burst
out laughing and said "Listen, Alexander, stop wasting your time
in idleness or you'll be worse off than a pie-seller." His anger had
abated completely. Menshikov went to fetch the empress and cried
out "Home-baked pies!" and the tsar laughed and called out to him
"Just you remember, Alexander." "I'll remember, your majesty, I
shan't forget. Home-baked pies!"

Aleksasha, as a result of the favor he enjoyed, by the time in
question was already the leading figure among the tsar's close
associates and when Lefort died [in 1699] he took his place. No one
would be closer to Peter than he was. But at the same time he
inherited a sad legacy from Lefort: the hatred of those people who
opposed Peter and his work. The favorite's appearance was very
striking. He was tall, well-proportioned, lean, with pleasant features
and very lively eyes. He loved to dress splendidly and, something
which surprised foreigners, he was very neat and tidy, which was
then still a rare thing for a Russian. But he did not owe his closeness
to the tsar to outward appearances alone. Observant, objective people
noted in him a great deal of shrewdness, were amazed by the unusual
clarity of his speech which reflected the clarity of his thought. They
admired the dexterity with which he managed to deal with every
job, his gift for picking the right people. That, then, was
Menshikov's good side. Let us now turn to the bad. His was an
uncommonly strong personality, but we have already spoken of the
fearsome nature of strong personalities in a society like Russia in
the time in question. Everything said about Peter also applies to his

"fledglings".[32] They were all forces against which society had established few restraints. In a society of this type, just as in the wide expanses of the steppe where there are no definite man-made paths, anyone can ride off in any direction. One and the same law applies everywhere and always: a force which is not stopped will develop to infinity, a force which is not directed will wander indiscriminately. Menshikov and his fellows wielded great power—for this reason their names have come down in history—but where could they find any checks on their powers except in the power of someone even stronger? But even this power was inadequate. The best proof of this is that this most powerful of men was obliged to resort to boxing his associates' ears and hitting them with a stick in order to keep them in check. But the use of such methods is the best evidence of the weakness of the one who resorts to them, evidence of the weakness of the society in which they are used. Peter the Great, it seems, was a strong man, he was strong by virtue of his unlimited power, but at the same time we know how weak he was, how during his lifetime he failed directly to achieve his most beneficial goals, because in a weak, immature society there can be no firm authority. Authority grows from society and is sound if it is supported by a firm base; nothing can hold firm on crumbling soil or marshland.

Pulled up from below to the heights, Menshikov gave wide scope to his powers. These powers, naturally, showed themselves in the acquisition of honors and riches. In the social conditions which prevailed at the time, given his dizzying rise to power and fast advancement, these powers were unleashed quickly. As we shall see, Menshikov stopped at nothing. Even at the time in question Aleksasha already demonstrated a frightening ambition. Peter did not harbor a blind attachment to his favorite. Once when someone asked the tsar to make Aleksasha a table attendant, Peter replied that Aleksasha would abuse his important position anyway and that it was necessary to reduce his ambition, not increase it.[33] Later Peter did not begrudge any honors to Menshikov when his merits became evident to all.

When he was angry Peter spared neither his old nor his new favorite. Once when Peter caught Menshikov dancing while still wearing his sword he gave him such a blow that blood spurted from his nose. Another time at a feast at Colonel Chambers' he grabbed Lefort, threw him to the ground and trampled on him. A painful thought oppressed Peter and increased his agitation. Comparing what he had seen abroad and what he found in Russia a terrible doubt was imprinted on his soul. Could anything be done? Wouldn't anything that might be achieved by dint of huge efforts still be pathetic and negligible in comparison with what he had seen in the West? The thought of restricting himself to miserable rudiments and not seeing any substantial results from his work was painful to this warrior prince who was brimming over with strength. In particular, it seemed, he despaired of his pet project, shipbuilding, when he recalled what he had seen in Holland and England and what he had left behind in Voronezh.

PETER GOES TO VORONEZH

Two days after the autumn executions of the musketeers, on the evening of October 23, Peter set off for Voronezh, from where he wrote to Vinius: "We have found the fleet and the magazines in a very excellent state, praise God. Only a shadow of doubt clouds our thoughts, fear that we may not be able to harvest this fruit, like the dates which the man has planted them does not live to see. Still, we put our trust in God with St. Paul's words: the husbandman that laboreth must be the first to partake of the fruits."[34] The phrase "a shadow of doubt clouds our thoughts" means that he had been troubled by doubts in Moscow, which the excellent state in which he found the fleet and magazines had failed to dispel. In another letter he wrote: "Great preparations are going on here, with God's help, and we are just waiting for a fine morning in order to dispel the gloom of our doubts. We had begun building a ship which can carry sixty guns." Grave doubts which might have sapped the energy of another man did not force Peter into inactivity. He worked just as indefatigably as he had done before his journey abroad.

In the meantime, there occurred some curious events which were typical of the time. The best of the students of *naval science* whom Peter had sent abroad was Feodosey Skliaev, who kept up a constant correspondence with the tsar. At the time in question he returned from abroad and was supposed to go to Voronezh to meet the tsar. Peter waited impatiently for the arrival of this much-needed man, but there was no Skliaev! At last there came news that he and his companion Vereshchagin were in the clutches of the fearsome king of Pressburg. Peter wrote to Romodanovsky: "Why are you detaining our comrades Skliaev and Lukian (Vereshchagin)? I am very upset. I was especially looking forward to seeing Skliaev, because he is the most skilled at this craft, but you see fit to detain him. May God be your judge. There's no one to help me here. And I imagine you aren't keeping him for affairs of state. For God's sake, release them (if there is a charge against them I'll stand bail) and send them here." Romodanovsky replied: "You wrote claiming that I have detained Lukian Vereshchagin and Skliaev, but I didn't detain them; they only spent a day and night here. Their crime was that they rode through the Pokrovsk quarter when they were drunk and got into a fight with some soldiers of the Preobrazhensky Regiment and beat up two soldiers. An enquiry revealed that both sides were to blame and after I had completed the investigation I had Skliaev flogged for his folly, and also the complainants with whom they had the fight, and at once sent them to Fedor Alekseevich (Golovin). Don't be angry with me for this. It's not my custom to be lenient on stupid behavior, even though it wasn't very serious."

NEW TRIALS AND EXECUTIONS

In the tsar's absence the quarrel between Skliaev and the Preobrazhensky soldiers was not the only problem that Romodanovsky had to sort out. Straight after Peter's departure for Voronezh rumors started to circulate in Moscow of secret gatherings of malcontents. A messenger who was sent at night to carry letters and expensive instruments to the tsar was seized on the Stone bridge [over the Moscow river] and robbed. The letters were found the next day scattered all over the bridge but the instruments and the messenger had disappeared. At the end of 1698 the tsar returned to Moscow and at Christmastide amused himself with one of his favorite pastimes—dressed in mummer's costume, he went carol-singing with a great retinue in eighty sledges.[35] The owners of the houses which the singers visited had to give them money. The very rich Prince Cherkassky was most generous of all, but one merchant gave only twelve rubles to the whole company. Peter lost his temper, collected a hundred peasants from the street and took them to the house of the parsimonious merchant, who now had to give each man a ruble. In January 1699 ten torture chambers resumed their work in Preobrazhenskoe to deal with the remaining musketeers. In February hundreds more were executed and again the tsar himself was in action, aided by Pleshcheev. At the end of February they began to remove the corpses from Moscow. Several thousands were taken beyond the town gates where they lay in heaps for some time until at last they were buried in the earth.

Several days before the executions a banquet was held at Adam Weide's house, but the tsar sat plunged in gloomy thoughts. Lefort tried all his ingenuity to amuse him, but failed. The magnificent house, built for the admiral out of crown funds, was completed and a great celebration was organized to mark the opening or dedication of this temple to Bacchus. The procession of fools moved to the Lefort palace from the house of Colonel Lima, led by the all-jesting patriarch Zotov, decorated with pictures of Bacchus, Cupid and Venus and behind him the whole company, some of them bearing cups brimming with alcoholic beverages, others dishes with smouldering tobacco leaves.

The musketeers who rebelled at Toropets and Azov had been punished. All the remaining Moscow and Azov musketeers were dispersed. It was forbidden to accept them into the infantry, and they and their wives were banned from living in Moscow. But the musketeers were not the only source of trouble; conflict blazed up with renewed strength, bloodshed called for further bloodshed. The king of Pressburg was kept very busy. When they began to bring the musketeers into Moscow for the mass trials a rumor started up amongst the people that they were to be shot at from cannons. There was a wave of sympathy and in Preobrazhenskoe a denunciation was made against Aksinia, the wife of a crown agent and stable lad, who told her serf Gavrila. "You see, he doesn't like the musketeers, he has started to kill them and soon will wipe them all out." Gavrila had replied: "What do you expect from a Muslim? He has turned into a Muslim, he eats meat on Wednesdays and Fridays. If he has started to kill the musketeers he'll wipe out the lot of them, he's become a Jew and now he can't live unless he drinks blood every day." Aksinia added a further insult: "He gave orders for the people of the Kadashev quarter to be flogged with the knout from the Intercession gates to the Yauza gates, and followed after them when they were being beaten." Aksinia and Gavrila were sentenced to death. In the prison at Vologda the musketeer Petrushka Krivoy cried out: "Our fellow musketeers have been executed and the others are being banished to Siberia, but many of our comrades remain all over the country and in Siberia. The one who had them killed, that man's life hangs by a thread. We'll march to Moscow and he'll be impaled on our stakes. We have teeth in Moscow and we'll soon get our hands on the man who tortured and hanged us." In Preobrazhenskoe Krivoy broke down and confessed: "When I left Siberia I was able to meet with my comrades, exiles and fugitives, and with those who were on service in the regiments and with musketeers transferred from the regiments and registered for duty in towns and artisan quarters. I saw some and was in correspondence with others, and we agreed to avenge the wrong done us and the execution of the musketeers by going to Moscow, raising rebellion and killing the tsar and boyars."

As is usually the case, people dissatisfied with the present sought comfort in the future. Dissatisfied with Peter, they turned to Tsarevich Alexis in the hope that he would be different from his father. When a group of musketeers were being held under guard in the monastery of St. Simon, a monastery stable lad Nikita Kuzmin told them: "The musketeers who were in the New monastery of the Saviour and the monastery servants and peasants who transported them to the cannon yard said that not only are the musketeers being ruined, the tsar's family are also crying, and the musketeers' wives said that Tsarevna Tatiana Mikhailovna complained to the tsarevich that the boyar Tikhon Nikitich Streshnev was starving them, the tsarevnas, to death, and if they had not been fed by the convents they long since would have died of starvation, and the tsarevich had told her to give him time and he would deal with them. The musketeers' women were saying that the tsar sent his wife to Suzdal, and she had been driven alone with only a chambermaid and a maidservant past the musketeer settlements in a bad carriage with bad horses. When the chambermaid arrived from Suzdal and the tsarevich realized that his mother was gone, he began to pine and weep, and the tsar told the tsarevich not to cry. After the tsar the tsarevich went out of his apartments onto the balcony, and Lev Naryshkin followed him out and the tsarevich said to him 'Why are you following me? I'm not going anywhere.' Tsarevna Natalia Alekseevna stirred up trouble against the tsaritsa. The tsar told the tsaritsa: 'Pray to God for anyone who condemns me on account of you.' The tsar loves Germans but the tsarevich doesn't love Germans. When a German came to see us and uttered some incomprehensible words the tsarevich set fire to that German's clothes and burned him. The German complained to the tsar, who replied 'Why do you visit him? As long as I am alive, that's where your place is.'" Kuzmin declared that he had heard all this from Vasily Kostiurin, crown agent from the royal grain depot. The executions of the musketeers made an especially strong impression on women, who said: "When he was young the tsar used to kill sheep, but now he has turned against the musketeers. On days when the tsar and Prince Fedor Romodanovsky drink blood they are merry, but on days that they don't drink their fill they don't even feel like eating bread."[36]

As soon as memories of the trial of the musketeers began to fade, protests against the shaving of beards broke out. The clergy with the patriarch at their head now found themselves in an awkward position. They had always proclaimed shaving to be a practice hateful to God and suddenly the tsar was introducing this ungodly practice by his own orders and example. They could either stick to their previous conviction, that is to go against the supreme authority, or keep silent. Naturally they preferred the latter course, thereby bringing upon themselves the censure of zealots of ancestral customs. In July 1699 Archimandrite Josaphat of the monastery of the Sign submitted the following admonition: "I was at the funeral of an artisan in the church of the Holy Conception in the Corner, and at that funeral seeing the corrupt behavior of Ivashka Nagoy and his long-haired companions with whom he went round the market stalls and churches collecting money by deception, I ordered that Ivashka Nagoy and the long-haired Ivashka Kalinin and his elder, Gerasim Bosoy, be arrested and clapped in chains for their corrupt behavior. I had Ivashka Nagoy brought to my cell because he kept silent and refused to speak to anyone when there were many people present, and I reprimanded him for going round the market stalls and to funerals collecting money. And he said that there was no harm in it. 'People give me money on account of my saintliness, and I shall get recompense from God for taking their money and distributing it to the poor. They wouldn't have given it to anyone else. But what I really want to do is go to Preobrazhenskoe to unmask the tsar for shaving beards and consorting with Germans and making the faith German.' I said to him: 'You accursed naked demon of Satan! Have you had a vision and gone off your head? The holy patriarch is our head and bears the image of God and he has heard of no corrupt behavior from the sovereign.' Nagoy replied: 'What sort of patriarch is he? He lives to earn a crust, just to eat and sleep, he hangs on to his robes and white headdress as long as he doesn't denounce anyone. All you officials are bought men.'"

At Preobrazhenskoe Nagoy confessed that his name was not Ivan but Paramon. Under torture he revealed that he had heard about the tsar when they were reading the prologue in church and had spoken about the patriarch in all innocence; the devil had made him do it. When he was subjected to trial by fire he repeated what he had said before. He was sentenced to flogging with the knout and exile to hard labor in Azov.

In the reign of Tsar Michael, as we saw, tobacco was banned, but at the beginning of Alexis's reign tobacco was in use and sold from the treasury. But tobacco met with strong protests wherever it was introduced, and Russia was no exception. Defenders of ancestral traditions again armed themselves against the damned weed and forced the government to introduce severe sanctions against its use. Before his visit abroad Peter already had allowed the sale of tobacco. Martyn Orlenok, a member of the senior merchants' guild, was appointed to collect the duties. Then, when he was in England the tsar granted the exclusive rights of trading in tobacco with Russia to the marquis of Carmarthen for £20,000 (forty-eight thousand rubles), the full sum to be paid in advance. This approval of the use of tobacco naturally strengthened the displeasure of the defenders of ancestral traditions. "What sort of sovereign is it who releases accursed tobacco into the world?" they asked. "Priests today are wolves and cursers of God's church, and an antidote against tobacco, because the priests and men of other ranks drink tobacco and take the antidote."[37] The struggle and antagonism from both sides intensified, as did expressions of dissatisfaction with the tsar and his actions and the flood of denunciations and interrogations at Preobrazhenskoe. Then people appeared who tried to take advantage of the situation by making false denunciations. Some monks got drunk and rode around Moscow at night shouting to passers-by "Let us pass or we'll kill you." It so happened that the tsar also ran into them, but took no notice, saying that they were drunk. But a little later a denunciation was made to the effect that the monks intended to kill the sovereign. This denunciation also came from monks. It became impossible for a strict abbot to discipline a monk who was living immorally. Immediately someone would denounce the abbot for treasonable words or plots. False denouncers were punished severely, but this had little effect.

The affair of Avdotia Nelidova provides an excellent example of the resourcefulness of those who were determined to save their own skins by dragging others to Preobrazhenskoe.

In May 1698 the table attendant Peter Volynsky appealed for the trial and punishment of his wife's serving woman Avdotia Nelidova, who was charged with putting the evil eye on people. In the torture chamber Avdotia produced evidence of treason against the sovereign. Before the Azov campaign, around Holy Week and later, Volynsky's [future] wife Avdotia Fedorovna, when she was still a widow after the death of Prince Ivan Nikitich Zasekin, was visited by Zhukova,[38] a serving maid from the palace, and with her the chorister Vasily Ivanov. Tsarevna Sophia had sent Anna from the New convent to ask the widow Avdotia whether she had been to Preobrazhenskoe as the tsarevna had told her, and Avdotia said to Anna "I went to Preobrazhenskoe and I picked up some earth from the tsar's footprint and gave the earth to Fiona Semenova, the serf of Fedor Petrovich Saltykov, for her to make a potion in her home with which to poison the sovereign."[39] About three days later Zhukova again visited Avdotia and asked what she had done with the poisoned potion. She replied that she had gone to the Maria grove with this potion but didn't have time to pour it from the jug into the sovereign's print. Avdotia showed the mixture to Nelidova. It was as red as blood, and she admitted that if she had succeed in pouring it into the print the sovereign would have been dead within three hours. She, the widow Avdotia, visited the home of Secretary Lukin and when she returned home she said to Nelidova "I did not know that the tsar would be at Lukin's. Had I known I would have taken the potion with me." Nelidova asked her "Why are you contemplating such a wicked deed against the great sovereign?" and when the brothers of Voeikova and her own brother Vasily Golovlenkov visited the widow, Nelidova told all three of them of the boyarina's schemes, after which Golovlenkov did not visit his sister for about thirty weeks. The boyarina was angry with Nelidova and banished her to her estate at Riazhsk with orders that she be drowned in the river.

The peasant woman Fiona was taken to Preobrazhenskoe, where she announced that she was able to cure various illnesses with potions, but she did this in all innocence without any incantations. She often had been to Princess Avdotia Zasekina's house and cured her of a fever, but she had not made a poisoned potion for her. "I am a good woman," said Fiona. "I have no truck with wicked deeds, but Dunia Nelidova is a known criminal. She made two women and two girls from Princess Zasekina's household hysterical by putting the evil eye on them, and on her pupil who had learned to sew better than her. She tried to put a curse on her mistress, too, and was charged and banished to a distant estate."

Nelidova repeated her previous testimony, adding that Zasekina's servants, who had orders to put her in the water, took pity on her and told her to run away. She had run away, been captured and put on trial for the evil eye. All those implicated by Nelidova testified that she had slandered them. Avdotia Volynskaia simply declared that Zhukova visited her so often because she was a relative. But under torture Nelidova repeated her testimony and added that Fiona had made another potion for Golovlenkov to make Tsarevna Martha Alekseevna fall in love with him. Fiona did not confess when tortured. Finally during the second round Nelidova confessed that she had slandered all of them.

The time in question was not without its cases of pretenders. There was a man travelling round Pskov district and calling himself

Captain Peter Alekseev of the Preobrazhensky Regiment and robbing the gullible.

ROBBERY

Preobrazhenskoe had more and more cases, but in addition to trying these political crimes the king of Pressburg also was involved continuously in trying cases of robbery. Let it not be forgotten that we are dealing here with a young society, in which the government was waging war against robbers, who gave peaceful citizens no rest. In such societies men who eradicate robbers are regarded as heroes and in this respect the activities of Prince Fedor Yurievich Romodanovsky were beyond reproach. He was proud of his bloody activities. When Peter was in Holland the well-known James Bruce,[40] a member of the jolly company, came to see him from Moscow all covered with burn marks and said that Romodanovsky had burnt him at a banquet when he was under the influence of John Barleycorn. The tsar wrote to Romodanovsky: "Beast! When are you going to stop burning people? People wounded by you have come to see me. Stop consorting with Barleycorn. Keep your ugly mug away from him." Romodanovsky replied: "In your letter you allege that I am consorting with John Barleycorn, but that's not true, lord. Some typical Moscow drunkard has been to see you and spoken when he was befuddled. I don't have time to associate with Barleycorn—*we are always up to our elbows in blood*. You may have the leisure to renew your acquaintance with Barleycorn, but we don't have the time. As for James Bruce's claim that I burned him, it was his fault because he was drunk, not mine." Peter responded: "You write that Bruce did this because he was drunk. Maybe that's true, but in whose house and in whose presence? You may be up to your elbows in blood, but I imagine that makes you drink even more out of fear. But we cannot because we are studying all the time."

Robberies occurred on a grand scale in Moscow. The following examples are taken from two letters to the tsar from Romodanovsky. "Of those thieves who robbed the Almaznikovs and Bagin in the New Foreign Quarter, seven have been caught. They confessed to the robberies, and a lot of clothing and silver plate and other goods have been recovered from various places, and the people who were burgled recognized many of their possessions. But the other robbers, whom their fellows have implicated, can't be caught, they are holed up somewhere in Moscow. They are Vaska Zverev, a house serf, Yakushka Kalachnikov, Vaska Tsviakun, Sidorka Alekseev, Levka Levugin; and of the thieves described above Vagan, known as Ivashka, servant of Prince Peter Golitsyn, accused two of the slaves of Prince Grigory Dolgoruky of taking part in the robberies, and these men are now on military service with Prince Grigory in your regiment. The thieves who confessed and implicated their fellows came from the tradesmen of the artisan quarter, butchers, carters and boyars' bondslaves." The second letter reads "Eight of the same gang of thieves have been caught: Afonka, Popugay, Aleshka Zakhodov, Kuska Zaika, Mitka Pichiuga, Petrushka Kadnikov, a junior boyar from Galich, Petrushka Selezen with two of his brothers. Two of those robbers, Zakhodov and Kadnikov, confessed that with the previous robbers Kalachnikov and Levugin and Mitka Pichiuga they attacked a foreign serviceman called Opaev outside the Tver gates and beat him savagely and cut him to pieces."

These letters make clear that now, as before, most robberies were committed by household servants. On June 29, 1699, at evensong, servants of Prince Nikita Repnin and others attacked the sentries at the Resurrection gates, beat up them and their officer and swore at them. Robberies were on the increase as a result of the ease of finding a hideaway. At the beginning of 1699 captured robbers declared that they persuaded men to go out for robberies in groups of twenty, thirty and forty men armed with bows, arquebuses, spears and pole-axes. Their hideaways and camps for dividing the spoils were in various districts of the townsmen's settlements outside the Tver gates.

But there was another type of robber who did not need to hole up in the townsmen's settlements outside the Tver gates. Afanasy Zubov and his men were brought to the torture chamber and interrogated by torture on the basis of eyewitness reports on a charge of murdering townsmen in Alatyr, who were killed by Zubov's servants. Under torture he said that he sent his men out on robberies and went himself, only he had not ordered them to kill, and he also confessed to other robberies. At this time Prince Ivan Sheidiakov was also executed at Boloto [in Moscow] for robbery and murder. Tarbeev brought a charge against Vasily Tolstoy and Semyon

Karandeev, accusing them of stopping by the side of the road and stabbing him. Yury Dokhturov, Vasily Dolgy, Semyon Karandeev and Tarbeev were at the church of the Passion of Our Lady, got into a fight and cut each other with knives. The table attendants Vasily Zheliabuzhsky and his son Semyon complained to the great sovereign against Andrei Apraksin whom they accused of beating and injuring them. They said that Andrei beat them up after picking a fight at the Kalmyk horse fair near Fili. Andrei confessed his crime to the sovereign, saying that he was drunk and didn't know what he was doing when he beat Zheliabuzhsky. The tsar resolved that Zheliabuzhsky and his son could claim from Andrei money to the sum of twice their service salary. In addition, the tsar was going to sentence him to merciless flogging by the knout for giving false testimony and for misconduct. But at the request of Tsaritsa Martha Matveevna, whose maiden name was Apraksina, and also on the mediation of General Lefort, to whom Apraksin gave three thousand rubles for his intervention, the tsar rescinded the punishment, but Andrei's servants were flogged with the knout. As a result of the Zheliabuzhsky case, a procedure was established whereby all cases were ordered to be tried by inquisition, but accusatorial trials and confrontations with witnesses were abandoned from then on.[41]

The difficulty of resolving the cases of such gentlemen is illustrated by the following letter from Romodanovsky to the tsar. "You wrote, my lord, regarding the case of Khilkov against the boyar Kondraty Fomich Naryshkin that he should be handed over on the basis of the previous signed petition, and I won't object, only from now on I can't deal with cases according to your wishes or I shall be continually in dispute and conflict. In the present case, you ordered me to deal with it, even though I reported many times that it was impossible for me to take the case on account of Khilkov being a relative, which would lead to complaints against me. But you, my lord, then ordered me to take the case, saying that I might be related to Khilkov but Lev Kirillovich was your relative, too, so I did as you wished and took the case. And I'll do as you wish again, but it's impossible for me to take on any more cases. I write to you truly, my lord, not on account of my relationship by marriage to Khilkov but because I felt it was my duty."

Society also required the government to track down a particular variety of villain—witches. In 1696 as a result of the complaints of all the peasants of one of the communities of Yarensk district the criminal Vaska Alekseev was interrogated and tortured on a charge of sorcery and confessed that he put the evil eye on ten people by chanting spells and named them all by name. He had renounced the Lord Christ and his life-giving cross and believed in the Devil. He learned sorcery from his uncle Napalkov and his other uncle Parfenev also practised sorcery. Another one, Mishka Alekseev, confessed that he put the evil eye on four people and made them have hiccups. He learned his sorcery from Sergushka Shelepanov. Sergushka was arrested, interrogated and confessed that they rejected the Orthodox Christian faith, had renounced the Lord Christ and the live-giving cross of the Lord, believed in Satan and cursed the cross of the Lord, but they wore a cross as though they were Christians so that people didn't suspect, and he had caused the death of Akulinka Ignashkina by putting the evil eye on her. Under torture Sergushka and Misha said that people put under a curse never accused innocent people of causing their hiccups but always accused the one who had put the curse; they could not put the blame on each other.

ABUSE BY GOVERNORS

As we have observed, the property of peaceful citizens suffered at the hands of both robbers and military governors. Cases of abuse by governors did not decrease during the time in question, which prompted the reformer to take decisive measures. First of all it was considered undesirable to keep governors in one town for more than two years; after that they were allowed to remain in their former post only at the request of the local people. Some governors began to find ways of extracting such a request from the townsmen. At the end of 1695 a complaint arrived from Stary Oskol that a few of the local tradesmen had drawn up a fake document allegedly written by all the town inhabitants requesting that Matvey Afrosimov, the governor of Stary Oskol, remain in office for a third year. In fact, the other inhabitants of Stary Oskol and its district knew nothing of this petition. At the inquiry the junior boyar Sukin said that the governor had summoned him to his residence and he was forced to sign the document by threats that the governor would beat him to death. The clerk of the town hall declared that he had signed on behalf of citizen Sorokin in his absence because the governor threatened him with ruin and beating, and so on. In Mtsensk Governor Tutolmin personally beat the postal agent Peter Smirnov with a cane then stripped him and beat him with sticks because the agent refused to supply the clerk of the Crown Appointments office with transport without an official authorization and had no reason to do so. As a result of the beating, the agent died. Yury Saltykov reported that he lodged a complaint against dragoons, cavalrymen, musketeers and townsmen in Viazma on account of their having marched and ridden over his Viazma estate in the village of Borodina in broad daylight and destroyed it. The governor of Viazma was ordered to send the men who had done the marching and riding to Mozhaisk for investigation. Four townsmen were taken to Mozhaisk and under interrogation they confessed everything and implicated twelve of their comrades whom the governor of Viazma arrested. But then he took huge bribes from them and released them from the town hall.

In 1697 an investigation was carried out on the basis of complaints by the inhabitants of Kungur against their governor Stepan Sukhotin. In front of the investigator Gavrila Dubasov the district elder of Kungur in 1695, Pankraty Nikitin, a peasant from the village of Ilinskoe, was questioned and in the interrogation swore on the holy immaculate gospel of our Lord that he would tell the whole truth. In 1695 he, Pankrashka, and the townsmen and peasants of the district had not written a petition for Stepan Sukhotin to remain their governor in Kungur for a third year and had not authorized anyone to sign such a petition, but the clerk Maksim Bogomolov signed his, Pankrashka's, name on such a petition in his absence and without his permission. When he was governor in Kungur Stepan Sukhotin and his son Nikita inflicted insults, impositions and ruin on the people of Kungur and the peasants of the district and took huge sums of money from them for nothing. Stepan had gone to the Kungur district to register the district peasants and on that occasion he took two hundred and twenty rubles of communal money from the district office, and on top of that took six copecks from each person. After that he took another eighty rubles of commune money from him, Pankrashka, in return for the people of Kungur not having to brew beer for him, Stepan. He also attacked Pankrashka and made him hand over a ruble, and in Kungur rural district at the Kungur picket gates he detained peasants who were travelling from Kungur to Solikamsk and the Chusov settlements with grain for sale and refused to let them pass unless they took his seals. The cost of the pass and the seals for transport in winter was eight dengas per load, and in summer he charged three copecks for eight bushels for a pass for river transport.

On the same day the current district elder Nikita Posokhin was questioned and testified that when Stepan Sukhotin was in Kungur he detained the townsmen in the town hall and in prison for no crime, beat them with sticks and the knout and took money (a long list followed), and assaulted and ruined other Kungur peasants. As a result of the ruin suffered under his governorship Kungur peasants had fled to Siberian towns (a list of those who had fled followed). Also Stepan beat Yakushka Zaganov, a Kungur artisan, with a cane in the town hall for no reason and Yakushka died as a result of the beating. He also beat the district elder Fedka Gladky in the governor's residence for no reason. Krasilnikov, a clerk from the town hall, was tortured and ordered to make allegations that the people of Kungur were planning to kill the governor. The townsmen said that in 1692 Afonka, a musketeer from Kungur, was sent to Siberia to look for fugitives, and Nikita, Governor Sukhotin's son, had forced Afonka's wife, Ustiuzhka, to live with him and had a child of the male sex by her. Stepan Sukhotin then forced Afonka's wife and his son Mishka, aged nine years, to come and live in his house and gave her in marriage to his servant Fedka. When Afonka returned from Siberia Stepan Sukhotin did not admit him into Kungur but sent two musketeers to arrest him and detained him in the town hall and during that time used violence to force him to hand over three horses, two rifles, a sheath with a bow and arrows, two powder kegs, two Bashkir saddles, and five rubles, and also tormented him into writing a letter saying he would not appeal to Sukhotin for the return of his wife and binding his son over to Kalashnikov under a contract of life indenture in repayment of alleged debts. The peasants said that Sukhotin sent out townsmen, clerks and musketeers in spring when it was still bitterly cold to visit towns, villages and hamlets of Kungur county and seal up the huts and bath houses, and then charged each household two altyns, eight copecks and a grivna and as a result of this outrage during that bitterly cold weather women who had given birth and ailing babies met untimely deaths.[42]

Persecuting Old Believers gave governors opportunities for self-enrichment. In 1697 Pastukhov, a townsman from Romanov, admitted the following: "Last year a number of complaints were made against me in respect of deeds of purchase, but Governor Ivan Grinkov did not bring me to justice or subject me to trial for default,[43] but concealed me, because I was feeding his dogs and bears, and he summoned me and urged me to tell him from which of the towns inhabitants of Romanov he could get the biggest bribes. This year he called me to the town hall and interrogated me thoroughly and ordered me to make allegations of religious dissidence against myself and towns inhabitants of Romanov (a list of men's and women's names follows), saying that they were being rebaptized and remarried. The governor promised me a third of what he got from the schismatics. I denounced them, and on the basis of my false testimony the governor had those who were accused of being schismatics brought to the town hall. He asked them to give him fifty rubles, but the townsmen told him refer their case to Moscow, at which Grinkov released them on bail, but he kept me in his office for a long time and plied me with beer and vodka until I was drunk. When the clerk Karelin arrived in Romanov with a warrant Grinkov transferred me and citizen of Romanov Trusov from the office to his own home and kept us in his chambers under lock and key for a long time, posted guards, locked us in a trunk and filled it with clothes. We told him that we were suffocating in the trunk and he sent a man who drilled some holes in the trunk so we could lie there without suffocating.

"When as a result of the complaint of the district head and his associates an investigator was sent to investigate us we asked for a trial, but Grinkov did not hand us over. 'You're going to disappear,' he said. He sent a man to the estate of his brother Fedor telling him to come with some men. When his brother arrived with lots of men, he sent us with his brother by night to Moscow and we arrived in Moscow by night at the house of his brother Nikifor Grinkov. Nikifor gave us money and ordered us to testify as his brother specified in order that our stories tallied and his brother was not ruined. When I was brought back to Romanov Ivan Grinkov sent me money and told me to speak about the schism under questioning and to implicate whoever he told me to, and to offer up my own skin and theirs in a judicial confrontation" (namely to demand torture for himself and the defendants).

The elders of the Moscow tax-exempt settlements usually were elected by the inhabitants of the settlements. The following record of an election of an elder in the Burghers' Quarter has come down to us. "By order of the great sovereigns the elder of the Burghers' Quarter Yury Samoilov and the burghers (a list of names follows) of higher, middling and lower status in this year of 7204[44] elected as their elder Filipp Olferiev, a good man and wealthy; and in the capacity of elder of the great sovereigns he is to deal with and take care of all community matters and consult with laymen on all things concerning the sovereigns' business and community affairs, and he is to collect the same revenues as last year."

But at this time we also encounter the following curious incident. An elder appealed to the tsars to allow him to remain in post for a further period because he had earned profits for the treasury and there were no complaints against him from citizens. The request was granted. He was to "act as elder, collect money revenues and grain supplies in full measure and to administer justice among the peasants fairly and without officious hindrances, so that citizens had no cause to make complaints against him."

THE CHAMBER OF MAGISTRATES

Bearing in mind his major and expensive undertakings and large military expenditure, and wishing to increase crown revenues as quickly as possible while fully aware that they could be increased only by raising the prosperity of taxpayers, Peter no longer could afford to leave traders and entrepreneurs in the grip of rapacious local administrators. How could they be freed? There was a ready-made model. In addition to what he had seen in the West, in Little Russia, which was incorporated into the body of the realm some time before, there existed since time immemorial a system of urban self-government under Magdeburg Law.[45] Peter resolved to introduce a similar system for Russian towns.

On January 30, 1699 the decree on the establishment of the Chamber of Magistrates[46] was published. "The great sovereign has become aware that the chief merchants and leading merchants' guilds, and all the townsmen and traders and entrepreneurs in many of their lawsuits in the chancelleries suffer great losses and ruin in their trade and other enterprises at the hands of chancellery officials and men of other ranks; and others have abandoned their trades and enterprises because of this, and this has caused shortfalls in the great sovereign's tax revenues, and great losses in duties and other collections. Out of pity for them the great sovereign has decreed that all their cases of law, petitions and trade and the collection of crown revenues shall be administered by the magistrates, and they shall elect well-to-do and just men from their own ranks to be magistrates, whomsoever and as many as they shall choose, one of whom is to be chief magistrate and to sit as president on a monthly term." For other towns with the exception of Moscow it was decreed: "Let the following decree be proclaimed in all the towns to townsmen and merchants of all ranks and to the entrepreneurs and rural dwellers of the great sovereign's communities, villages and hamlets: as a result of the many abuses, taxes, requisitions and bribes suffered at the hands of governors and chancellery officials, it is resolved that the same governors and chancellery officials no longer shall be in charge of all their business in the towns and all cases of secular lawsuits and petitions and the collection of revenues shall be administered by their elected secular representatives in the local offices." All these elected representatives were to come under the authority of the Moscow Chamber of Magistrates (or Town Hall), which reported directly to the sovereign. All sums collected in the towns came here, and from here money was disbursed for expenditure, but only on the personal instruction of the tsar. In return for their liberation from the governors and chancellery officials the traders and entrepreneurs had to pay double the previous levy of taxes.

The establishment of the Chamber of Magistrates was the start of a series of reforms which were intended to stimulate social forces and accustom citizens to taking communal action, to protect their

common interests by pooling their efforts and to wean them away
from a life based on the individual set apart, according to which
the weakest surrendered himself unarmed into the custody of the
strongest. But these were early days and one can easily imagine how
clumsily society at first coped with the changes and what strange
habits the men of the community brought to their new activities.
The men of the community were freed from the governors and
chancellery officials, but in the absence of practice in communal
activity, in repelling the force of the strong by pooling the resources
of the weak, they immediately brought forth from their own ranks
men of violence after the model of governors and chancellery
officials. In Venev, for example, the district elder and his assistants
dismissed their elected customs and tavern magistrates from revenue
collection because they failed to give them any money. They chose
others who gave them a hundred and twenty rubles. In order to
discourage similar incidents in future Peter ordered those who had
taken the money as well as those who had given it to be laid on the
block, then raised from the block and flogged mercilessly with the
knout and banished to the galleys in Azov with their wives and
children and to proclaim in all the towns, villages and communities
that henceforth anyone who offended would be sentenced to death
without mercy.

ALEXIS KURBATOV
But here as elsewhere cruel punishments and threats had little effect
on their own. The reformer considered it vital before the new
enterprise was firmly established to appoint a trusted and capable
man to run it and to guide the inexperienced and protect them from
the strong. The tutor of the young enterprise was Alexis
Aleksandrovich Kurbatov, the first of the "profit-makers" and "chief
inspector of the Magistrates Office."

Kurbatov was the majordomo or steward of the well-known
westernizer Boris Petrovich Sheremetev. He had traveled abroad
with his master, a journey which had a strong effect on the
development of a Russian richly endowed with talents. In the
Chancellery of Posts a letter with the inscription: "Deliver to the
great sovereign without unsealing" was picked up. In this letter the
sovereign found not some accusation about a wicked plot or

treasonable utterances but a project for stamped or "eagle marked" paper.[47] Stamped paper was quickly introduced as a valuable source of revenue, and the inventor, who turned out to be Kurbatov, was given the post of secretary, rewarded with a house and villages and appointed as a *profit-maker,* in which capacity he sought ways of making profit for the state and gained the opportunity to inform the tsar of his opinion on all matters not anonymously but in open letters. Later we shall learn more about his work, especially in the capacity of chief inspector of the Magistrates Office.

DECREE ON TRADING COMPANIES

Russian merchants had long acknowledged that they could not compete with foreign merchants because the latter traded jointly. Ordin-Nashchokin had proposed that less wealthy Russian traders should unite with the rich ones in order to free themselves from dependence upon foreign merchants. Now Peter prescribed that "Merchants of all ranks in the towns of the Muscovite realm are to trade in companies in the manner of merchants of other countries. Goods are to be dispatched to the towns of Archangel, Astrakhan, and also through Novgorod, by companies, and all merchants are to establish a procedure by common consent amongst themselves about how best to disseminate their trade, so that the great sovereign's revenue collections are augmented. Provincial centers should be established, in Great Novgorod, Pskov, Astrakhan and other towns to which smaller towns and rural districts should be attached, and in those towns the local magistrates shall supervise the magistrates of the attached towns, also supervise the collections of the customs and tavern magistrates."

There were no changes in the peasants' way of life. As previously this vast country remained thinly populated, as previously this meant that the workers were attached to the land and as previously tried to flee their feudal dependency, so the pursuit of fugitives was one of the most vital activities of the government and private individuals. Several peasant families fled from the Zvenigorod district from the lands of the St. Savva monastery. Four years later they were captured (in 1696) and told interesting accounts of their flight. They went to Dankov and took up residence as peasants of a local clerk called Yakovlev. A year later the clerk decided to eject them from his lands because they had no warrant of manumission. He gave them a ruble and told them to go away. "Somewhere have a warrant made out in your owner's name and that will exculpate me." The peasants set off where their feet took them and in Tula district they found a benefactor, some deacon, who wrote them a deed of manumission, signed the names of the archimandrite and cellarer, all official, and took sixty copecks for his pains. The peasants at once returned to Dankov and gave the clerk the warrant. "That's your warrant, " he said. "Now it's all legal and I shan't have to pay monetary compensation[48] for you." The clerk began to exploit the peasants' labor quite happily and married off the daughter of one of them to a junior boyar, taking from the groom twenty stooks of rye.

IMPROVEMENTS IN SIBERIA

Siberia, where governors and strong men of various kinds enjoyed considerable license well away from the government's supervision, was an object of special attention because disturbances there had a bad effect on the treasury, which accrued such a large income from Siberian goods. In April 1695 an exception was made for Siberia, except for Tobolsk. Siberians were not to be required to change their governors every two years "because such frequent changes are starting to cause large payment arrears and loss of income because the governors, having forgotten their oath and despising strict orders, import liquor and other goods into Siberia and also distill liquor there and make a huge profit for themselves. In the taverns little of the sovereign's liquor is listed for sale, perhaps twelve or ten buckets per year, and sometimes as little as one bucket, and some years not even one bucket was sold." When they traveled to Siberia governors were allowed to bring a certain quantity of liquor and other goods duty-free. Every two years the governors traveled to the Siberian towns, every two years they took all these supplies with them, took government water transport and courier tax, demanded transport from the post stations and towns and usually caused offense, burdens and ruination to all sorts of people in the process. Therefore, the less frequently governors traveled, the better. In the edict it also said that governors were sending out servitors to collect fur tribute and extorting huge bribes and loans from them.

They chose the best sables for themselves, leaving the poor quality ones for the treasury and in a short time they amassed huge fortunes and subjected the servitors and tribute-paying natives to great insults, burdens and thefts and did not allow them to go to Moscow to lodge complaints. For this reason many servitors were attacked in their winter quarters and others turned traitor in response to the governors' persecution and went away to China, and the Mongol renegades, taking revenge for insults suffered, were robbing and assaulting many servitors and tax-paying natives."

At the end of the same year another edict was issued to the Siberian Chancellery. "Previous governors committed robberies, tortured and executed many people, and the tribute collectors took away wives and children from the tribute-payers and natives by force, and the complaints of these natives were not given justice and restitution by the governors. In the future governors are not to torture or execute any Russians or tribute-paying natives for any matters not subject to torture under the terms of the Law Code [of 1649] without prior consultation with the sovereign. To collect the tribute send well-to-do men, *chosen by civilians*. If the governors steal from or deplete the crown treasury or execute anyone, they themselves will be executed and all their hereditary estates and homes and service estates and property will be confiscated by the great sovereign without restitution."

Having exhausted all measures to curb the malpractices in which officials in Siberia indulged, in October 1697 the tsar issued an edict forbidding servitors and men of all ranks, their wives and children in Siberia to wear expensive clothing, "which it is not appropriate to their rank to wear; for it is well known that servitors who have such excessively expensive clothing make it not from their rightful earnings, but get those riches from robbing the great sovereign's treasury or by robbing of the natives; and if a man by some honest enterprise should make a living over and above his necessary expenses, he should use those earnings to buy himself decent weapons and armor and necessary clothing so that he is always ready to serve us and to fight the enemy, or to build himself a solid stone residence in which his belongings can be safe in the event of a fire."

The junior boyars of the metropolitan of Siberia sent by him as agents to administer church business behaved no better, if not worse, than the servitors sent by the governors. This was evident from the tsar's edict to Governor Glebov in 1697. "The agents are inflicting great ruin, insult and burdens upon the people of the rural districts and towns by their unjust assaults. By their blows they are forcing maidens and widows into making false accusations of sexual assault against well-to-do men of the towns and rural districts, then they take huge bribes from these men on the basis of the false accusations; they strip other maidens naked and crush their breasts till they draw blood and subject them to all manner of abuse. Any maids and widows who do not confess even under such torment are sold to the sort of men to whom no one would give his daughter in marriage, and the scoundrels take the money."

The establishment of magistrates, as is evident from an order issued in 1699, could not be applied to Siberia. "There will be no magistrates in the towns of Siberia, but revenues will be collected as before in the Russian and Siberian towns by keepers of customs houses and taverns and by honest sworn officials who are supervised by governors with utmost care. There will be no magistrates because in some of the Siberian towns there are no townsmen,[49] and where they do exist, they are often poor specimens, poverty-stricken exiles, therefore there are no candidates to be magistrates. Even in those towns in which there are merchants there is no one who can be entrusted with the collection of fur tribute or with other revenue collection, because they are badly off."

Just as Peter spared neither punishment nor threat for unconscientious governors, he would also stop at nothing in order to reward a good one. The following curious royal edict was sent in 1698 to Ivan Nikolaev, governor of Irkutsk. "On our orders your brother, our table attendant Samoil Nikolaev, was sent to Siberia to be governor of Nerchinsk, and in Nerchinsk he served us with great loyalty, and in the course of doing his duty zealously and justly in comparison with former Nerchinsk governors he made a good profit for our treasury. And the local inhabitants, tradesmen of the Russian and Siberian towns, can bear witness to his Christian piety, and he never had any complaint made against him by anybody, and by his good fruits in our distant country he has been most useful and profitable to us, the great sovereign. This year your brother Samoil's servant reported to the Siberian Chancellery that last year your brother Samoil Nikolaev died in Nerchinsk, leaving two children, the table attendants Ivan and Mikhail. And we, the great sovereign, have rewarded your nephew Ivan Samoilovich Nikolaev, notwithstanding his tender years, for his father's loyal service and appointed him governor in Nerchinsk in his father's place. In view of his youth the junior boyar Luka Kochmarov is to act as clerk for signing papers, as your brother testified that he is a good and zealous man."

Even in European Russia at the time in question monasteries did not present a very edifying picture. All the more reason, then, to be cautious about their disruptive influence in unruly Siberia. In 1698 Peter forbade exiled and itinerant monks in the Yenisey region to rebuild monasteries, and forbade people to give them land without authorization,"as there is already in Siberia a sufficient number of male and female convents where Orthodox Christians of all sorts take vows and save their souls."

In the reigns of former great sovereigns, as we have noticed, many decrees were issued to try to curb abuses by governors and others in Siberia. These decrees had little effect, but now a new spirit was emanating from the living, and the dead letter of the law was given fresh life. Vinius, who was entrusted with running the Siberian Chancellery, deemed it possible in 1698 to bring Peter some good tidings from Siberia. "On the subject of behavior in Siberia," Peter replied, "you tell me that the governors are doing better than previously, for which praise be to God." It would be wrong to imagine that Vinius was simply boasting, because shortly afterwards he informed the sovereign of a new misfortune for unhappy Siberia caused by the tobacco franchise holder Orlenok. Wrote Peter to Romodanovsky, "Vinius has written to me complaining that Orlenok and his assistants have committed acts of violence and murder in Siberia. Be so good as to apply your ingenuity to investigating this business to prevent a rebellious outbreak in those wild regions." This attentiveness and the speed of the orders issued by strong men best explain why the governors in Siberia were doing better than previously.

RUSSIA'S FRONTIERS

The government also needed to pay unremitting attention to the cossacks on the frontiers of European Russia on the Don and Dnieper. We saw earlier that cossack schismatics had left the Don to join the shevkal[50] and were carrying out hostilities against their own country. In the autumn of 1696 twenty-seven of them suddenly felt homesick and at night stealthily deserted the shevkal and made for the Terek, whence the governor sent them to Astrakhan. Among them were six men with their wives and children, two monks and two nuns. The sovereign gave orders for the following speech to be read to them: "Neglectful of God, you betrayed the great sovereign, left the Don to join the shevkal, went to sea to engage in piracy, and assaulted, robbed and killed all sorts of people on the Terek. Such robbery and treason deserves to be punished by death, but the great sovereign has ordered that your crimes be pardoned and that you be released with your wives and children to live on the Don as before."

But the main damage was being caused not by those who fled from the Don but by those who fled to it. In 1690 table attendants, crown agents, Moscow servitors, palace attendants, landowners of Riazan, Shatsk, Riazhsk and provincial servitors, men of Riazan, Meshcher, Riazhsk, lancers, cavalrymen, and junior boyars, murzas, Tatars and infantrymen of the select regiments submitted a signed petition. "Our slaves and peasants keep escaping to the Don, the Khoper and the Medveditsa with their wives and children, many villages and hamlets are deserted, and in our absence, when we are performing our duties and on campaign, our homes, possessions, horses and other belongings are pillaged, and our remaining slaves and peasants are lured away, our wives and children are locked up in huts and chambers, our children are stabbed and beaten to death and put into the water and abused. We have been utterly ruined by this exodus, but still we have to do our crown service and we are paying postal dues and sales taxes and musketeer grain tax on behalf of these fugitive house slaves and peasants and carrying out fortification repairs." That same year Alexis Mosolov complained that when he was on the Crimean campaign his fugitive slaves arrived from the Don, cut his six-year-old son to pieces, threw the body into the water and utterly devastated his estate.

As a result of these complaints atamans were questioned. They replied: "Fugitives from the crown lands and landlords' serfs and town inhabitants from the Ukrainian towns are arriving on the Don, Khoper and Medveditsa with their wives and children and live just as they wish, but the governors and chancellery officials are letting them leave the Ukrainian towns in exchange for bribes. If they did not let them leave, they wouldn't be able to get here, not only with their wives and children but even on their own." Royal rescripts were sent to the Ukrainian governors and chancellery officials with strict orders not to allow fugitives to pass beyond the boundary and to erect barriers. A rescript was sent to the Don forbidding the cossacks to take in fugitives on the river. The old settlers were ordered to drive them away and send them back to their places of residence. Orders were given to capture Mosolov's thieving and murdering peasants and banish them to Korotoiak.

But the cossacks' unwillingness to give up fugitives is illustrated by the following incident. At the end of 1697 the Kalmyk chieftain Munkotemir reported to the governor of Tsaritsyn that twenty-five bands of his warriors had run off to the township of Panshin on the Don. The governor sent a message ordering the ataman of Panshin to give up the fugitives on the basis of the tsar's earlier order according to which harboring Kalmyks was forbidden on pain of death in order to prevent disputes and quarrels with the local chieftains. The cossacks replied to the governor's envoy, saying "We refuse to surrender the Kalmyk immigrants, we cannot surrender them and we shall continue to accept them in future. We received a letter from the Host's headquarters in Cherkassk telling us to accept such runaways in order to protect them from their pursuers and other people and not to allow them to be insulted. The tsar's order was sent to the governor in Tsaritsyn, not to us. We don't have any such order and we aren't subject to the governor of Tsaritsyn. If the Kalmyks come and try to get back their runaways by force of arms, we won't give them up but will fight to protect them."

The amount of work and duties was increasing, but many people did not want to work harder and serve longer, and so there was an increase in incidences of flight to the Don. Throughout the years 1695, 1696, 1697, 1698 and 1699 the governors and chancellery officials of the Belgorod and Sevsk regimental districts kept reporting that regimental and garrison soldiers, servitors and officials of all ranks, their children, relatives, dependents and peasants were refusing to do their crown service and pay their taxes, to work on building sea-faring ships and river craft, to work in the forests or do duty as pilots, oarsmen and ferrymen, and were fleeing to the Don Cossack settlements. In 1699 about three hundred and thirty households fled from Voronezh district alone. Another rescript was sent to the Don, specifying that fugitives were not be be given sanctuary, and the cossacks were to arrest earlier migrants and take them back to their former places of residence in their own, cossack, transport, because "you took in those fugitives without our authorization."

But the tsar went even further than asking the cossacks to violate one of their fundamental principles by demanding that they refuse to accept new fugitives and send back old ones. He also forced the cossacks themselves to work for the common cause. Peter had taken Azov, thereby securing the river Don for Russia. But it was vital to maintain frequent and unimpeded communications with Azov and to keep the troops there supplied with provisions of various kinds, so Peter sent the servitor Shatnev to inspect the river Don from Korotoiak down to Azov and to clear the waterway with the help of inhabitants of the cossack settlements on the Don in order to avoid delays to shipping on the river. There were various types of delay. In 1698, for example, pilots and oarsmen travelling by boat to Azov on the rivers Voronezh and Don with grain supplies abandoned their vessels in the cossack settlements and ran off. The cossacks and other inhabitants carried off the grain to their homes.

Naturally the sovereign, especially a sovereign like Peter, could not take a lenient view of such incidents, and grievances on the great river increased. We shall see what happens when the aggrieved find a leader.

There were also alarming reports from the Dnieper. In August 1696 the governor of Kiev, Prince Boriatinsky, sent Suslov, a resident of Starodub, with two lancers to Secretary Nikitin, the Russian resident in Poland, to get news. Suslov brought Nikitin his own news. "The Poles have the firm intention of taking back Ukraine and they are in constant communication with Hetman Mazepa. This spring, for instance, an envoy from the king visited the hetman in the company of some Greeks, pretending to be a merchant. The officers in the Little Russian Host are now all Poles. Obidovsky, Mazepa's nephew, hasn't a single cossack servant. The cossacks have serious complaints against the hetman, colonels and company commanders, who they say are trying to ruin the old cossacks by taking away all their liberties and making them into their subjects, and confiscating all their lands for themselves. A village which once produced a hundred and fifty cossacks for service now sends only five or six. The hetman keeps about him and favors only volunteer regiments of light cavalry and infantry, trusting in their loyalty. There's not one native-born cossack in these regiments, they're all Poles. Last summer the cossacks of the Kiev Regiment in Zaporozhie almost killed their colonel Mokeevsky because of the burdens he placed on them. In the present campaign the hetman kept his regiments apart, anticipating a revolt from the cossacks. If all the regiments had been in one place the cossacks had the real intention of killing all the officers. The cossacks say that if they still had their old liberties they could have captured the Crimea on their own. If the present hetman and the Polish bosses are not replaced it won't be a question of capturing the Crimea but of being enslaved by the Crimea and Poland. Abbot Innocent of the monastery of St. Cyril in Kiev is in secret communication with Bishop Shumliansky,[51] and goes to Baturin nearly every week. Naletov and Fateev, two clerks from the government office in Kiev, visit the abbot the whole time, and the abbot sends them supplies, barrels of beer and wine." Suslov ended his report with the statement that he dare not talk about anything else unless he could report orally to the great sovereign himself.

When Nikitin made this known to the great sovereign, Suslov and the two clerks from Kiev were brought to Moscow to be questioned. Suslov announced that Popara, a nobleman from Lvov, told him that the Poles very much regretted losing Ukraine and that if there was some minor disturbance in Moscow they would march into Ukraine and reunite it with their own lands as before. Buinovsky, another noble, said the same. For example, the Poles took East Prussia; although it was part of Sweden for many years, still it was restored to Poland. "It's very bad that the officers in Ukraine are Poles," Popara said. "If they were Russians Ukraine would be more reliable."

He had heard complaints against the hetman and the officers in the Kiev Regiment and from Paley's cossacks.[52] The news which Suslov promised to report only to the tsar in person was that it was possible to collect many more retail duties in Kiev than were normally collected. Suslov had heard about the cossacks' plans to kill the cossack commanding officers from Popara and some of Paley's cossacks who had come over from the Pereiaslavl side. He had heard about Shumliansky's relations with the abbot of the St. Cyril monastery in Lvov. The clerks declared that they had visited the abbot very rarely, and then only on the governor's business. At the same time it was learnt that Abbot Innocent had died. The tsar had a copy of Suslov's testimony delivered to Mazepa and the clerks were released to return to Kiev with a strict warning not to visit foreigners in future and not to tell tales. Meanwhile Mazepa received a letter to the effect that the great sovereign did not deign to believe all these rumors and did not doubt him because he, the hetman, his officers and all the Host did their duty loyally, not sparing their health and lives. Then, at the hetman's request, they sent Suslov himself to Baturin giving Mazepa permission to torture him.

In October 1696 Mazepa wrote to the tsar with the news that Semyon Paley was receiving frequent communications from Sapieha, hetman of Lithuania, which had not happened before. Sapieha had told Paley to beware of Mazepa and not to visit him in Baturin. "I sent one of my men to Khvastov in secret," Mazepa wrote the tsar. "The envoy was to find out about the situation there, whether Paley was summoning any troops for duty of any kind. I specifically ordered the colonel and company commander of Kiev to keep their men secretly in Khvastov to keep permanent watch on Paley, as I am surprised to see that he does not deal with me as openly as he used to, doesn't send me the letters he receives from the crown and Lithuanian hetmans, and I detect in this some change of attitude and subterfuge. I dare to recommend to you, great sovereign, that the boyar who is governor in Kiev should not admit Paley into Kiev with too many of his men. He is used to going there often; he has his own house in the lower part of the city which I, in an attempt to attract him to your royal service, bought for him from the monks of the Caves monastery[53] with four hundred gold

crowns from my own pocket." Mazepa learned also that the new
king of Poland had sent Paley four thousand ducats to recruit
cossacks. On hearing this the hetman sent out rescripts to all the
regiments forbidding anyone to go over to the Polish side.
A month later Mazepa wrote that he had ordered the colonel of
Kiev, Mokeevsky, to send some sensible men to Khvastov to observe
what was going on there. On his return from Khvastov one of these
observers reported to the colonel that Paley's troops, infantrymen,
who arrived from the vicinity of Kamieniec-Podolski, were saying
"It's bad that Paley is serving both sides at once. Now there is a
new king in Poland, with plenty of money, he ought to serve just
him loyally, and all of us might get a rich reward from him and
Paley. If Paley wavers between two sides he will meet the same end
as others have met at his hands." Decent men were saying "As
believers in the Eastern Orthodox faith, it's best that we support the
Orthodox Christian monarch." But such men were few. Paley
himself was drunk every day and when he drank sometimes he
would mention the tsar's name and other times drink to the health
of the Polish king.
    At the beginning of 1699 Mazepa reported that in contravention
of the articles of the peace treaty forbidding colonization of the
deserted towns across the Dnieper, the previous year a settlement
was established in Moshny where the inhabitants persuaded and
enticed people to cross over from the left bank. The burden of
feeding the troops was forcing many people to flee across the
Dnieper with the result that in addition to Moshny settlement other
settlements had been founded at Drabovets, Korsun and Boguslav.
It was difficult to keep track of fugitives because of the impossibility
of posting guards all along the Dnieper. Apart from this the
inhabitants of the river bank of the east side could not survive
without the timber on the western side, but when they crossed over
to get firewood the settlers over there robbed them, stole their
horses, carts and axes, and stripped them of their clothes. Mazepa
asked the sovereign for permission to demolish Moshny settlement
and to send the settlers back seeing that the settlement was inhabited
in contravention of the treaty.
    In the Siberian borderlands all was quiet on the Chinese side.
Russians traded profitably with Peking and in 1698 Vinius wrote

to Peter abroad that a Russian church had been built in Peking and many Chinese were baptized. "This is very good news indeed," Peter replied, "Only for God's sake, act cautiously and not hastily so as not to anger the Chinese leaders, or the Jesuits, who have had their nest there for a long time. For this reason we need to have priests there who are not so much learned as intelligent and obliging, lest this holy business come to grief as a result of arrogance, as happened in Epania." Vinius therefore ordered questioning of the tradesmen in Nerchinsk who had come from China in order to find out as much as possible about the newly-built chapel on Chinese territory. For example, where was it located, amongst houses or on its own, a long distance away from Chinese residences? Did the Chinese visit the church or attend the services? Did they speak well of it, or did they mock and insult it? To which church were they most favorably inclined, to the Greek faith or the Jesuit church, and what priests and junior clergy did the church have, and how did they live, how many were there, and how many Russian people? How was the church decorated, did it have enough service books, and where were dead Christians buried, next to the chapel, or somewhere in the grounds? Were rites carried out openly or secretly for safety, and had any Chinese been baptized?

THE PETER ARTEMIEV AFFAIR

While Peter and Vinius were worrying about the Orthodox church in Peking and its relations with the Jesuit church, in Moscow remnants of Jesuit influence were discovered. In 1697 the priest of the church of Saints Peter and Paul (and Saints Adrian and Natalia) in the Burghers' Quarter submitted a denunciation of his deacon Peter Artemiev to Patriarch Adrian. After the reading of the gospels Artemiev allegedly delivered a homily praising Poles and Lithuanians for their faith. He read the "Our Father" at a pulpit in the Roman manner on half bended knees and offered up other Roman prayers. Instead of the life-giving cross he wore a small pouch, and in it kept a small image of the Latinist Anthony of Padua, who was a heretic. He spoke of the Holy Spirit proceeding from the Father and the Son,[54] confessed and took communion from Jesuits, and took a very tearful farewell with the Jesuits who were expelled from Moscow. He called the consecrated assembly a *fence,* which he boasted of jumping over, and called the patriarchs *losers,* because they had lost the true Orthodox faith.[55] He abused the boyars and judges and dishonored them on account of their torture of Old Believers. He called the boyars and judges who supervised the rack in the Constantine torture chamber "dumb" teachers, who enlighten with fire instead of the Gospels and teach with the knout instead of the Acts of the Apostles.

Peter Artemiev was the son of a priest from Suzdal. Since his youth he had shown himself to be a nervous man, of painful susceptibility and disturbed imagination. These qualities must have been intensified by depravity, as he himself confessed. This young man entered the school run by the Greek teachers the Likhuds[56] and in 1688 went to Venice with Ioanniky, the elder of them. Abroad he was taken over by the Jesuits and converted to Catholicism. The ease with which the conversion was accomplished is evident from Artemiev's own account. When he asked the Latins in what way their Roman church was better than the Greek, they replied that there was no difference, the Roman and Greek churches were the same, the only difference being that in the Roman church people were very learned. The young man was reassured that they were the same and he sought out very learned men and books written by very learned men. The exultation, passion and mysticism of certain Catholic writers were very much to Artemiev's liking.

On his return to Russia Artemiev was consecrated deacon in the church of Saints Peter and Paul where his sermons and behavior attracted attention. Patriarch Adrian, a sick man, for some time failed to investigate the priest's denunciation, but in the meantime the deacon acquired followers, which was not difficult in that unsettled time. "And many succumbed to his charms." Amongst others Artemiev was very welcome in the homes of the builders of the church of the Dormition on the Pokrovka, Guriev and Sverchkov, who also were visited by Latin priests. Guriev and Sverchkov tried to persuade the patriarch to have Artemiev's father transferred from Suzdal to Moscow to their own church of the Dormition. The patriarch at first refused to listen, judging the father by the son. "Is he the father of that deacon Peter?" he asked. "The one who supports Calvinists, Lutherans and Papists? If I had not been so ill, he would have been sent packing long since. But he won't escape me, I'll have a special assembly called [to try] him. If the father is the same sort of man as the son, both will have to be burnt." Then Adrian relented and said: "I had been thinking for some time about sending for the father to deal with the deacon. They say that his father is a good man."

The good man must have been driven to despair by the *missive* he received from his son at that time. "Father! Dear Father!," wrote Peter, "I climbed into the sore of Christ's abyss in heaven, and now I am climbing, climbing into his Crucifix, painted by you; I crawl into the wound on his ribs with my heart, nail my hands to his hands, and taking away his lips, put my lips there and talk to him like St. Bernard; I do not wish to live without wounds, Lord, when I see you all covered in wounds. Leave a small corner near you on the cross for me, Lord, and I shall be crucified with you! I heard from you that for this reason I was called Peter,[57] and I shall be a communicant of Peter's warmth, in truth he did not sin. I am a close confidant of Peter, for which reason I publicly preached from the dais in the church of his patron saint."

When he arrived in Moscow the father nearly gave his son a box round the ears "for that missive." Meantime the priest of Saints Peter and Paul submitted another denunciation. The patriarch sent Peter to the New monastery of the Savior, but people urged Adrian to finish the business. "Now this problem may be on a small scale," they wrote, "but the evil of Latinism can infiltrate from the loss of just a single son and cast many into the western abyss. When this mild case of Latinism spreads and multiplies, the whole body of Orthodoxy could decay, then what will happen?" In June 1698 the patriarch summoned a council which condemned Peter to be tonsured and banished to the Vaga monastery in the parish of Archbishop Afanasius of Kholmogory. But the exhortations of the latter had no influence on the prisoner and Afanasius reported to the patriarch, "Babylon cannot be cured completely, what's more we ourselves were very nearly caught in his traps."

In Peter Artemiev's testimonies we find some interesting information about the behavior of his famous teachers, the Likhud brothers. "My teacher Ioanniky, the senior, after he arrived from Italy, went many times to visit the Roman priests at the Austrian residence in the [Foreign] Quarter and boasted that he was of their faith, but said that he had to keep it secret out of fear, which they believed. But I took my teacher's book *The Sword*, which is against the Romans and showed it to the Austrians. They then went to see the teacher, showed it to him and exposed his hypocrisy, but he replied that the book had been written by his brother Sofrony without his participation when he, Ioanniky, had been in Italy, which may be true, because Ioanniky is much more inclined to tell the truth than his brother Sofrony, and much more ardent in his belief in God."

VI

BEGINNING OF THE GREAT NORTHERN WAR
1699-1703

THE NEW CALENDAR

On December 20, 1699 the people of Moscow learned of another innovation. From now on years were to be numbered not from the creation of the world, as previously, but from the birth of Christ. The new year would start not on September 1 but on January 1. "The great sovereign is aware that not only many European Christian nations but also Slav peoples who are in accord with our Eastern Orthodox church, such as the Wallachians, Moldavians, Serbs, Dalmatians and Bulgarians, as well as the great sovereign's own subjects the Cherkass and all the Greeks, from whom our faith was taken, all are in agreement about numbering their years starting eight days after the birth of Christ." As a token of this goodly undertaking and to mark the new century, after saying prayers in church everyone was to wish one another a happy new year. Well-to-do homeowners were to set up decorations made of trees and branches of pine, fir and juniper in front of their gates and to keep these decorations up until January 7. It was also specified that during the firework display and gun salute on Red Square three shots were to be fired from small cannon or firearms, and rockets were to be let off in the homes of courtiers, military servitors and tradesmen, and bonfires and tar barrel beacons were to be lit every night from January 1 to 7.[1]

REASONS FOR THE GREAT NORTHERN WAR

That is how the year 1700 began in Moscow, a year famous in the history of Europe for the beginning of two major and influential wars: the War of the Spanish Succession in the West and the Great Northern War in the East.[2] As a result of the first France fell into decline for almost a century; the second resulted in the loss of Sweden's former status and the emergence of a new power, Russia, among the countries of Europe.

Peter, as we observed earlier, was very displeased with his allies' attempts to end the war with Turkey. This would mean that he either would have to bear the whole weight of the war upon his own shoulders or to conclude a peace which would leave him only half-way towards his goal. This helps to explain why the idea should have taken root in Peter's mind that if he failed on the Black Sea he should consolidate his position on the Baltic, which would be much more advantageous, closer to both the real Russia and the real Europe. But if it was impossible to continue the Turkish war without allies it was even more impossible to wage war unaided against Sweden. It followed that a new war was possible only if a new coalition could be formed.

Such a coalition did prove possible. At the time of its domination of the northeast Sweden had succeeded in alienating nearly all its neighbors. Denmark, Poland and Russia were robbed by Sweden under its warlike kings Gustavus Adolphus and Karl Gustavus.[3] The activities of Gustavus Adolfus resulted in Sweden's becoming protector of northern Protestant Germany, but Sweden then betrayed this obligation by making an unnatural alliance with France against Germany, thereby losing its influence there to Brandenburg, which was obliged to embark upon a struggle with Sweden both for its own and for common German interests. Throughout Peter's visit to Prussia the elector of Brandenburg strongly urged him to join an alliance against Sweden, but naturally the tsar was unable to agree as long as he had the war with Turkey round his neck. Now the circumstances had changed and Peter, driven back from the Black Sea by the allies' peace with the Ottomans, was now free to seek allies for a war against Sweden with the aim of consolidating Russia's position on the Baltic Sea.

King Augustus II of Poland
contemporary engraving

PETER BEFRIENDS AUGUSTUS OF POLAND
On his way home from abroad in response to news of the musketeer
revolt, Peter met Augustus II, the new king of Poland,[4] in the little
town of Rawa in Galicia. In the course of their conversation there
was mention of mutual aid. "King Augustus said that many Poles
were opposed to him and asked that he not be abandoned if they
tried to act against him. To which Peter replied that he was ready

to help, but he did not anticipate that there would be any trouble from the Poles as there were no precedents. But he asked Augustus that for his part he should help to avenge the insult which Governor Dahlberg did him in Riga where he had barely escaped with his life.[5] The king promised to do so." This fleeting conversation was a long way from constituting an alliance. "They bound themselves to each other with firm avowals of friendship, without any obligation in writing, and parted."

During his three-day stay in Rawa Peter was captivated completely by Augustus in the way that a young man inexperienced in the ways of the world is enchanted by the social graces of a dandy, even though the dandy might be infinitely inferior to the savage youth in respect of intellect and moral fiber. Peter loved to make merry and Augustus knew how to make him merry, and a firm friendship was formed between the two neighbors, a friendship which lasted until the time when Peter, who grew in stature as a result of misfortune, drew far apart from Augustus, whom misfortune merely dragged down. When he returned to Moscow Peter strutted around in Augustus's tunic and sword and was lost for words to extol the virtues of his immoral friend. But as much as he liked the king, equally he disliked the unruly and wretched kingdom of Poland. Soon after his return, during a banquet at Lefort's, Peter said: "In Vienna I started to grow fat on the greasy food, but poverty-stricken Poland soon took off all the fat again." The Polish resident intervened to defend his fatherland. "I am amazed," he said, "that your majesty should have had such an experience. I was born and bred in Poland, but I am fat enough." The tsar replied: "You got fat here in Moscow, not in Poland."

VOZNITSYN AT KARLOWITZ CONGRESS

Whatever Peter's thoughts about a new alliance and a new war, the first priority was to end the old war as advantageously as possible. Conciliar Secretary Prokopy Voznitsyn, now dubbed crown councillor, was appointed Russian plenipotentiary ambassador at the congress which was to bring the Turkish war to an end. The plenipotentiary was instructed to make the cession of Kerch[6] his first priority. If the Turks refused he was to confine himself to the generally accepted basis of demanding the cession of what was already captured. The congress opened in Karlowitz in October 1698. The Turks had been most scared by the Germans and the victories of the imperial generals and therefore were eager to make peace with the emperor of Austria as quickly as possible. The ambassadors of England and Holland had the same aim, because they needed the emperor's troops to fight France in the forthcoming War of the Spanish Succession. It is therefore not surprising that the Turkish plenipotentiaries first of all reached an agreement with the Austrians. Voznitsyn attempted to hinder it by hinting to the Porte's dragoman Alexander Mavrocordato that Turkey merely needed to delay making peace a little until the inevitable outbreak of the war over the Spanish succession, whereupon the Turks could fight successfully against an Austria which had been deflected to the west. This ploy was too unsubtle. Why should the Russian plenipotentiary act in the interests of Turkey? War in the west might actually be delayed as a result of the Turkish war continuing. Turkey was in no position to resist and hastened to take advantage of the forthcoming war in the west to end its own burdensome war. In Constantinople they feared imperial weaponry, but also feared the link which existed between the Russian tsar and his co-religionist Ottoman subjects. Members of the peace lobby in Constantinople pointed to this link as the main reason for concluding a hasty peace. Indeed, Wallachia and Moscow were already in communication through the intermediary of Hetman Mazepa. Finding himself caught between the devil and the deep blue sea, between the demands of the Turks and the no less hateful Catholic Germans, the hospodar of Wallachia sought salvation from the Orthodox tsar; he asked to be accepted as his subject and for troops to be sent to Bessarabia. "With tears we beseech you to save us from the Papists and Jesuits who rage against the Orthodox more than against the Turks and the Jews. The secular war may end at some point, but the Jesuit war never will."

Mavrocordato, who usually assured the Russian ambassadors that he did his best to oblige the great sovereign on account of their common faith, accepted gifts from Voznitsyn but did not oppose the conclusion of peace between Turkey and Austria. The mediators each accepted a fur coat from Voznitsyn and also did not oppose the peace. Having satisfied the emperor, the Turkish plenipotentiaries wanted to reward themselves at the expense of the other belligerents and had no intention of giving in to the latter's demands. "The Turks' difficulty in reaching an agreement with us drags on, and it's not easy for us to come to terms with them," wrote Voznitsyn to the tsar. "God knows on what terms we shall manage to make peace and they won't accept a short truce. The allies' ambassadors have daily meetings with them; and the Austrians and Venetians claim that they have sorted out their affairs and that the Poles also will be satisfied. Now they are waiting for me, and if I stick to my present position they intend to abandon me. If we have to return Azov and the Dnieper towns to the Turks and the purse to the khan (in other words keep on sending the annual purse or tribute), that cannot be called a peace. If we go as far as the Danube, not only are there thousands but masses of people who share our nationality, our language and our faith, and none of them wants this peace."

Voznitsyn had no opportunity to make peace, so he proposed a truce. The Turks refused and began to make threats. Then Voznitsyn changed his tack: instead of reproofs and gifts he tried firmness, declaring that he was not afraid of war. It worked: the Turks concluded a two-year truce. "I only managed to get an armistice, or laying down of arms for a limited period," Voznitysn wrote. "Even that was difficult to achieve, given that you, sire, have not had any satisfaction from the Turkish peace settlement, whereas they (the allies) are all satisfied and have abandoned you. At first I tried to persuade them to join the armistice, advising them to do that and not make peace for the time being. But the Germans refused orally and the Poles in writing. I am not surprised by the Germans, as they are bound by a short alliance, but I am surprised that the Poles dared to act thus and managed to conclude their business in only two sessions, and even more surprised at the terms they accepted. They have abandoned their eternal alliance with you, thereby breaching the eternal peace, making peace for a trifle. The Turks promised to return Kamieniec to them uninhabited. The Germans led them on and deceived them because for them peace is vital, a matter of life and death. They made peace without any inconvenience to themselves and with no concessions and stopped the Turks' throat with their other allies. I imagined that the Germans had a close friendship with the Venetians, but in fact they have a secret antipathy towards them. The Germans won't hear of the Venetians gaining strength. In truth, sire, the Germans know how to conduct their business and they made this peace with a firm hand and at a time which suited them. I report all this in humility and beg your royal kindness. Have mercy on your sinful and wretched orphan: I did the best I could."

UKRAINTSEV IN CONSTANTINOPLE

It was vital to take advantage of the truce either to conclude a stable peace or to prepare to fight a successful war, which now must be waged one to one. With the first aim in view Conciliar Secretary Emilian Ukraintsev, now also dubbed councillor,[7] was appointed envoy to Constantinople with Secretary Ivan Cheredeev as his assistant. But to help Ukraintsev to conclude a profitable peace and to show the Turks the danger of going to war with Russia, Peter sent his envoy by sea on a Russian warship. It was necessary also to show the Turks and the Crimeans the whole Russian fleet and at the same time to reconnoiter for future use the route to Kerch, on which Peter had designs. The first admiral of the Russian fleet, Lefort, was no more: he died in March 1699. He was replaced by General-Admiral Fedor Alekseevich Golovin, whom we have encountered already in relation to the Treaty of Nerchinsk.[8] Golovin was also put in charge of foreign affairs and became the first knight of the Order of St. Andrew the First-Called, established on March 10, 1699. Thus Golovin achieved pre-eminence amongst the men in power and the role of first minister, as foreigners called him. This was the role formerly filled by Lev Kirillovich Naryshkin.

In April 1699 extraordinary envoys Ukraintsev and Cheredeev set off for Constantinople. They did not travel empty-handed. They were carrying furs worth five thousand rubles, one and a half puds of tea, ten puds of whalebone to distribute in the course of the sovereign's business. They travelled to Voronezh, where they had an audience with the tsar, then from Voronezh by boat to Azov, sailing past the towns of Kostensk, Uryv, Korotoiak and Divye Gory. Below Korotoiak on both sides of the Don they passed thirteen estates where there were no permanent settlements, villages or hamlets, but only the tents of entrepreneurs who went there temporarily to fish and trap, teams of forty men, who occupied the land for quit-rent, renting it from the bishop of Voronezh and from monasteries. From these estates they sailed down past fifty cossack settlements where, when they drew level with a settlement, the station atamans and cossacks rode out to meet them and fired shots from cannon and firearms as a mark of respect. When they drew level with the main town of Cherkassk the envoys gave orders for the infantrymen who were escorting them to fire a shot from their guns, and the shot was answered by cannon from all over the town. The envoys disembarked from their ships and went to the cathedral, then to visit Ataman Frol Minaev.[9] The ataman returned their visit in a barge. From Cherkassk they sailed to Azov and from Azov to Taganrog, where two versts from the town the forty-gun warship *Fortress* and its captain the Dutchman Peter von Pamburg were waiting for them. From Taganrog to Kerch the envoys crossed the Sea of Azov in a royal convoy of sea-going ships and galleys, commanded and headed by the privy boyar Fedor Golovin, knight of the glorious order of the apostle Andrew and general-admiral of the military-naval convoy. The commander of the ship *Apostle Peter* was the tsar himself. In the convoy, as well as the *Fortress* there were nine ships, ten galleys, a yacht, two galliots, and three brigantines. Ataman Frol Minaev and fifty select cossacks accompanied the convoy in four sea-going longboats.

When the convoy reached Kerch the local pasha, visibly shaken, asked what was the purpose of such a big convoy and an escort sent from Constantinople insisted that the envoys travel there overland, through the Crimea and Budziak. "It is the great sovereign's command," Ukraintsev replied, "that we travel by sea on his royal majesty's ship. We have no orders to travel overland, and rightly so, because that route is a long one. Evidently you, escort, want to take us through the Crimea for some cunning scheme; only we refuse to go through the Crimea as we have no business with the Crimean khan and nothing to discuss with him." The escort tried to scare the envoys. "Obviously you don't know the Black Sea and what it's like after August 15. It didn't get the name Black for nothing. Men's hearts turn black on it when they are in danger." "We trust in the will of God, but we won't travel overland," replied Ukraintsev, and with that the discussion ended.

August 28 the envoys put to sea and reached Constantinople in
safety. To see a Russian ship enter the harbor at Constantinople in
triumph to the sound of gun salutes and stand at anchor opposite
the Seraglio was a marvel without precedent. The envoy's first task
was to send Captain Pamburg to greet the French, English and Dutch
ambassadors. The French and Dutch gave Pamburg a cordial
reception and thanked him for his good wishes, but the Englishman
refused to admit him, sent a servant to the entrance hall and told
him to say that he had no reason to meet Pamburg and had only just
sat down at table to dine. People began to arrive to look at the
strange spectacle. Frenchmen came from the ambassador's suite,
then the grand vizier arrived and for a long time rode around the
ship, expressing admiration and wonder that the ship had got from
Kerch to Constantinople so quickly. Finally, the sultan himself
arrived.

PEACE WITH THE TURKS

Negotiations did not start until November. The envoys proposed the
following conditions: (1) Permanent peace or a lengthy truce under
which each side would retain what they possessed at the time of
negotiations, in other words Russia would retain all its conquests.
(2) The Tatars were not to encroach on Russian territory. (3) When
Azov, Kazykermen and other fortresses were under Russian rule,
unruly elements on both sides would be pacified. The great
sovereign did not wish to retain these fortresses for his own glory
but solely in order to pacify unruly elements on both sides. (4) If
during the peace the cossacks were to wage war on Turkish and
Crimean territory, they were free to kill them as wrongdoers; when
they returned from campaign they would be sentenced to death on
the tsar's orders; the Turkish and Crimean sides would act
reciprocally. (5) The great sovereign had ordered that the tribute
which formerly was paid to the Crimean khan and his officers be
stopped on account of their many wrongs and not be paid in future.
(6) All prisoners were to be freed at an agreed place of exchange.
(7) Free trade on both sides. (8) The Zaporozhians were to be
allowed to trap and fish freely up to the mouth of the Dnieper. (9)
Border disputes were to be settled by envoys. (10) Russians were

to be allowed freely to worship in the holy places. (11) The holy places were to be returned to the Greeks. (12) Orthodox Christians on Turkish territory were to practice their religion freely.

The foreign minister, the *reis-effendi*, replied that the first clause was the most difficult and unexpected, as all the other sovereigns at the Karlowitz congress had returned some part of their conquests to the sultan. Only the Russian tsar was refusing to give anything back. The foreign minister demanded the return of Kazykermen and other forts along the Dnieper in order to deter the Crimean khan and Tatars from lawlessness and to force them to put their horses to pasture. The envoys replied that these forts would not restrain the unruly Tatars; on the contrary, they could be a refuge for robbers. Before the capture of Kazykermen some beys had lived in the town, launched one rustling raid after another, and took huge gifts from the Tatars in the process.

The talks dragged on. After three months there was still no progress whatsoever. On February 24, 1700, at the eleventh session the envoys announced to the foreign minister a medium or compromise. The sovereign would allow Kazykermen and other small forts to be razed to the ground and cede the empty land to the sultan to remove these places as objects of hostility and war. On March 2 at the twelfth session the foreign minister replied that the sultan did not regard such a small concession as an act of friendship or as a concession at all; the settlements must be ceded to the sultan in their entirety. They were built by the present sultan's father to constrain the Zaporozhian Cossacks, who went out onto the Black Sea and destroyed the Turkish coastal towns. The envoys replied that at that time the cossacks were under Polish rule, living in lawless and disobedient fashion and went to sea at their own whim, but now the cossack hetmans and the cossacks were all obedient subjects of the tsar. Ukraintsev reported that they were getting no help from the the ambassadors of Austria, Venice, English and Holland, who were all "hypocrites and calumniators." The patriarch of Jerusalem sent word to the envoys that that it was not worth starting a war for the sake of Kazykermen and that they should not postpone making peace for such a trifle. The khan sent several messages to the sultan urging him not to concede

Kazykermen to the Russians. If he did it could be dangerous for the Tatars for the Muscovites and cossacks could get from there to Perekop in one night. The Serb Savva Raguzinsky let Ukraintsev know that "the ambassadors who are in Constantinople are all opposed to our peace, so you should not believe anything that they say. They all intend that the Muscovites be involved in war with the Turks for a long time to come." The patriarch of Jerusalem confirmed that "of course, the Romans, Lutherans and Calvinists do not wish there to be peace between the great sovereign and the sultan. They are the natural enemies of Orthodox Christians."

At the next session, after lengthy arguments and bargaining from the Turkish side, the foreign minister finally declared that the sultan agreed to the razing of the Dnieper settlements and the conclusion of a thirty-year truce. Then new difficulties arose: the Turks were refusing to include the new settlements built by Peter at Taganrog, Pavlovsk and Miius in the treaty. "During negotiations they behave in a most cunning manner, fabricating and dragging things out; all this procrastination and cunning behavior causes me constant grief and tears," Ukraintsev reported. "I have not seen the Austrian, English and Venetian ambassadors all this time because the Porte refuses to admit them. I am in contact through their couriers, but I am getting no help from them, not only no help but also no information, and no warnings, but they receive a lot of information in Galata[10] because they live there in perfect liberty, conversing with each other and with the Turks all the time, but they don't report any of it to me. Only when I send a messenger with greetings do they send one to me in return, but they don't call on me themselves to discuss anything at all. And they won't intervene to ask the Porte to meet with me, saying that if they were to ask this of the Porte and the Porte were to refuse them, they would have incurred only shame and humiliation. The English and Dutch ambassadors are firm supporters of the Turkish side in all matters and are better inclined towards them than to you, the great sovereign. English and Dutch trade with Turkey long has been very great and very rich, and they are envious and hate the fact that you have started to build sea-going ships and to navigate in the region of Azov and at Archangel. They anticipate great damage to their own trade at sea."

In April, after four sessions the following wording was agreed: the settlements on the Dnieper were all to be destroyed and the places on which they stood to belong to the Turkish side, empty, and all lands along the Dnieper from the Zaporozhian Camp to Ochakov were to be empty of inhabitants also. Only at the halfway point between Ochakov and Kazykermen were people to be allowed to live to provide transport for travellers and merchants across the Dnieper, and this settlement was to have an encirclement of a small ditch and stockades, and adequate dwellings, but the encirclement must not resemble a fort or have any defenses inside. Azov with all its old and new suburbs and the lands and waters lying between those suburbs were all to be in the possession of his majesty the tsar, and the land from Perekop and from the edge of the Perekop Sea to the first new Azov suburb (Miius) was to remain uninhabited. On the Kuban side of Azov the Turks ceded land within ten hours' travelling time. "We were unable to get more than than out of them," wrote Ukraintsev.

There followed a clause about the Tatars. The Turks declared that the tsar ought to continue to give the khan gifts from his royal kindness and not out of compulsion. Peace could not be concluded without this tribute because the sultan could not put the khan in such a dishonorable position. With respect to the clauses about the return of the holy places in Jerusalem to the Greeks, the Turks declared that this had nothing to do with affairs of state. The sultan was free to decide all matters in his own realm and one sovereign had no business to instruct another in such matters, but if the tsar were to request this of the sultan later, the sultan probably would grant the tsar's request. On May 28 after many conversations and disputes the Turks conceded the point about the khan's tribute and the Russian envoys postponed negotiation of the article about the holy places till a later date. The business was reaching its conclusion when suddenly in June the Turks again began to speak of the need to raze the new Azov suburbs of Taganrog, Pavlovsk and Miius. The envoys refused point-blank and announced that they would allow only another month for talks. After that they received a letter from the patriarch of Jerusalem. "I think that these crafty men are doing this to test you or to gain some advantage, but I don't think that they will refuse to make peace. This is what I expect and I don't think I am mistaken." Sure enough, on June 28 the Turks sent word that they were dropping their demands for the razing of the new Azov *churches*![11] On July 3 articles were exchanged and several days later the Serb Savva Vladislavich Raguzinsky visited Ukraintsev and told him that the Polish ambassador Leszczynski was begging the Turks on behalf of the senate and the Polish Commonwealth not to make peace with the Russian tsar but to form an alliance with the Poles and help them to regain Kiev and all of Little Russian Ukraine. Leszczynski complained that his king was a great friend of the Russian tsar and that the Poles would refuse to obey him and depose him from his throne. But the Turks ignored everything, Leszczynski said.

TRIPLE ALLIANCE AGAINST SWEDEN

While Ukraintsev was in Constantinople attempting to end the war in the south, in Moscow lengthy negotiations were taking place to start a new war which would encompass northeastern Europe. Sweden, as we noticed earlier, had succeeded in making enemies of all its neighbors. It was not difficult to draw them into an alliance against the common foe. All that was required was an energetic man who would act on the strongest of personal motives in favor of an alliance which reconciled the interests of all the powers. The man who emerged was a Swedish subject, alienated by the the Swedish government's efforts to strengthen its inner resources in order to maintain its preeminence in northeastern Europe and to decrease the threat from hostile neighbors. Sweden's resources in no way matched the status which Sweden had acquired accidentally during the reign of Gustavus Adolphus, and therefore there arose a natural desire to increase them by whatever means possible. One aspect of Swedish history stands out distinctly: the constant and stubborn struggle waged by the kings against the strong aristocracy, in the course of which the kings relied on other classes of the population. King Charles XI, a clever and thrifty despot, was able to run things in such a way that the council gave him unlimited power and the right to decide the fate of the overthrown aristocracy.[12] Charles XI made good use of his victory and by means of the famous *reduktion* the aristocracy was robbed, deprived of all lands which at one time

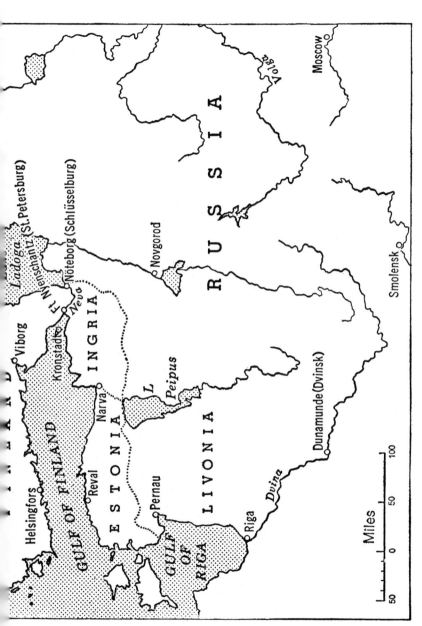

Russia on the Baltic

belonged to the crown and then by various ways entered into private ownership. The *reduktion* commission also turned up in Livonia. Here the local squires were deprived not only of the lands granted them by the Swedish kings but also of all lands which at one time during the independent existence of Livonia belonged to the head of the Livonian Order, masters and higher clergy. Not content with the fact that only a thousand of their five thousand estates remained to the Livonian gentry, Charles XI demanded that they produce indubitable proof of their rights of ownership to the land which remained in their hands.

PATKUL

This misfortune pushed forward Captain Johann Reinhold von Patkul, a man of very strong character, from the ranks of the landowners. Patkul was gifted, energetic and unscrupulous, impassioned to the point of frenzy, vindictive and cruel, and in Livonia and Stockholm his voice was louder and more effective than anyone else's in condemning insults and deprivations. He stirred up the landowners, urged them to join forces to repel the misfortune and wrote petitions to the king on their behalf. One can easily imagine what irritation this "restless man" caused in Stockholm at the king's court and in Riga to the governor general Count Jacob Hastfer, who was an ardent executor of the king's will in Livonia. Patkul was summoned to Stockholm and charged with high treason. Realizing that things were likely to end badly for him, he escaped to Courland, but was condemned to death in Stockholm in his absence. From Courland Patkul crossed to Brandenburg, then to Switzerland. He visited France and Italy, where he studied at his leisure. But Patkul's restless nature did not allow him to spend long in these peaceful pursuits. He did not wish to remain a fugitive. Somehow or other he must return to Livonia but this was impossible as long as Livonia remained a province of Sweden. Therefore it must be torn from Sweden. One should speak of Patkul's patriotism with the greatest of caution. Patkul acted exclusively in the interests of his class which were closely bound up with his own personal interests. He had no thought of restoring Livonian independence. He had to wrest it from the Swedes then hand it to one of the neighboring powers. Patkul lighted upon Poland. As a member of the Livonian nobility he was attracted by the system of the Polish gentry republic, under which it was impossible to imagine anything like the Swedish *reduktion*. As a German he was attracted by the fact that the present king of Poland was one of the German electors. Patkul appeared at the court of Augustus II and at the end of 1698 and beginning of 1699 submitted several memoranda one after the other in which he indicated how and with whom it would be best to conclude an alliance for a successful attack upon Sweden and the conquest of Livonia. Patkul pointed out that it was essential and possible to conclude an alliance with Denmark, Russia and Brandenburg. When it came to dividing the booty, he was most frightened of Russia. "We must beware," wrote Patkul, "lest this powerful ally snatch from under our noses the roast which we are putting on the spit. We need to convince him on the evidence of history and geography that he should confine himself to Ingermanland and Karelia. You must make an agreement with the tsar that he go no farther than Narva and Lake Peipus. If he seizes Narva it will be easy for him to occupy Estonia and Livonia. You must also make the tsar agree that in the event of conquering Ingermanland and Karelia the Muscovites will not give vent to their customary cruelty and will refrain from beating, burning and looting. You must stipulate that the tsar supply money and troops, especially infantry which is capable of operating in trenches under enemy fire." Patkul advised Augustus to act in utmost secrecy, "so that your left hand does not know what your right hand is doing." He advised him to beware of the Poles, who would oppose the conquest of Livonia as a means of strengthening royal power. The Sejm would make a fuss and once war was decided upon the Swedes would find out and take steps. What was needed was a surprise attack on Sweden and the capture of Riga.

Patkul's advice was taken. Showering Sweden with avowals of friendship, Augustus conducted negotiations for an alliance with King Christian V of Denmark,[13] who readily agreed to act against Sweden on the basis of his enmity with the duke of Holstein-Gottorp, Frederick III, the friend and brother-in-law of the young king of Sweden Charles XII. In Poland the first man in the state after the king, the cardinal-primate Radzejewski, was bought off for a hundred thousand reichsthalers. He promised to persuade the

Sejm to grant permission to leave Saxon troops, who would move
to attack Riga, in Courland on the pretext of building the harbor at
Polangen. Radzejewski was shown the treaty which the king had
concluded with Patkul as the plenipotentiary of the Livonian
nobility. By the terms of this treaty Livonia was to be joined to
Poland in perpetuity with the right to send deputies to the Sejm, and
would have its own army, its own internal administration, laws and
institutions. But in secret clauses the nobles pledged to recognize
the supreme power of Augustus and his successors even in the event
of them no longer being kings of Poland, and to send all revenues
direct to them.

General Carlowitz was sent to Moscow to persuade the tsar to
declare war on Sweden. Patkul accompanied him under an assumed
name. They arrived in Moscow in September 1699 and encountered
the Swedish ambassadors, who had come on behalf of the recently
enthroned young King Charles XII to confirm the Treaty of Kardis.[14]
To gain access to the sea Peter was ready to ally with Poland and
Denmark to fight the Swedes, but he could not embark upon a new
war until peace was concluded with the Turks. Carlowitz reminded
Peter of his proposal, made to Augustus in Rawa, of fighting the
Swedes with him. Now the time was right for the tsar to establish
himself on the Baltic Sea, trade with all the nations of the world
and receive profits the like of which had never been had by any
potentate. He could seize the monopoly of trade between east and
west, not to mention the fact that he would obtain the means to enter
into close relations with all the most important states of the Christian
world, gain an influence in European affairs, establish a fearsome
fleet on the Baltic Sea, and form a third power there, to deprive
France of the notion of worldwide monarchy and thereby win greater
glory than by conquering the Turks and Tatars. His majesty would
have the chance to make himself indispensable to England and
Holland when in the event of a war with France over Spain or over
something else he sent his troops and fleet to their aid. In this way
the Muscovite nation would learn the art of warfare at someone
else's expense and successfully wage war with the Turks and Tatars
without the need of help from foreign officers. In order to achieve
all this his majesty the king of Poland, from a true and just heart,
was offering the services not only of his German army but also his

own lofty personage. He pledged to make such a strong diversion on the Swedish side that his majesty the tsar would have no need to fear an attack from that quarter, for his majesty the king would occupy the greater part of the Swedish forces by attacking that spot where the Swedes concentrated their best troops. To this end the king made two proposals: (1) that in the interests of such a great undertaking his majesty the tsar free his hands as soon as possible to eliminate distractions from any other quarter. (2) That all negotiations and relations be kept in the utmost secrecy. All this, which was outlined in general terms, could be explained in much greater detail and his majesty the tsar could rest assured that the king was ruled in this matter by motives of pure love and loyal friendship.

The secret was kept. No one guessed the subject of Golovin's discussion with Carlowitz. Only the Danish envoy Heinz, by virtue of common interests, and the translator Peter Shafirov were admitted to the conference. To prevent Stockholm from hearing about it the Swedish ambassadors were received by the tsar in the customary manner and dismissed with the assurance that the great sovereign would observe the peace treaties. Only the tsar declined to ratify the treaties by kissing the cross on the grounds that they were old and the tsar had sworn the oath on them to the late King Charles XI. There was only one unpleasantness: the ambassadors brought back to Sweden a demand from the Russian side for satisfaction over the insult caused to the grand embassy in Riga, of which the tsar himself had been a member.

In the meantime, on November 11, 1699 in Preobrazhenskoe a secret treaty for an offensive alliance against Sweden was signed. Augustus pledged to open hostilities by sending his troops into Livonia, and promised also to persuade the Polish Commonwealth to break with Sweden. The tsar pledged to move his troops into Ingria and Karelia straight after peace was signed with Turkey, not later than April 1700, but earlier in case of necessity, and to send the king auxiliary forces under the guise of mercenaries. If it proved impossible to conclude peace with Turkey and Augustus did not wish to wage war with Sweden alone, the tsar undertook to do all within his power to reconcile him with Charles XII.

Augustus honored his pledge. At the beginning of 1700 Saxon troops made a surprise attack on Livonia, but did nothing apart from capturing Dünamünde. Riga did not surrender. Golovin reported to Peter in Voronezh that "In all the letters coming from the Swedish border people are writing that Riga is on full alert against the Polish forces and especially the Saxons. Alas, as a result of irresponsible and reckless indulgence in the distractions of Venus, they lost valuable time in frivolity which could have been put to good use." The other ally, the king of Denmark, was more successful in the first instance: he forced the duke of Schleswig-Holstein to flee to Sweden. The third ally, the tsar of Russia, did not move, awaiting news from the south, from Constantinople. No reassuring news came, and so in view of the impossibility of breaking off with Sweden, instead of sending troops into Ingria Peter sent a grand embassy to Stockholm, headed by the privy boyar Prince Yakov Dolgoruky and the lord-in-waiting Prince Fedor Shakhovskoy and sent word of their departure to the residence [in Sweden] of the privy table attendant Prince Andrei Khilkov. All possible means were used to reassure Kniperkron, the Swedish resident envoy in Moscow. The resident reported to Stockholm that when his daughter burst into tears at the news that Russia had broken off relations with Sweden, Peter himself comforted her, saying that he would not start an unjust war or break a peace just ratified. According to Kniperkron, the tsar told him that if the king of Poland seized Riga he, the tsar, would take it away from him.

Meanwhile Augustus himself turned up in Livonia and captured Kokenhusen. But small numbers of troops and lack of siege equipment prevented him from doing anything in Riga. He sent Baron Langen to Moscow to demand from Peter the aid which was promised and the promised attack on Ingria. But Peter remembered very well the other, chief condition—not to declare war on Sweden until the war with Turkey was over. To all Langen's assurances he replied: "If I receive news of peace today I shall move my troops against the Swedes tomorrow." He kept his word. On August 8 Peter received a message from Ukraintsev that peace was signed, on August 9 he gave orders for the troops to be moved up to the Swedish border, and Augustus was notified the same day. "Dearest brother, sovereign and neighbor! Until this time we were obliged to delay the start of this business not from doubt but because we were restrained by difficult circumstances. Now, with God's help, having obtained a thirty-year truce with the Porte (thank God, with satisfaction) we have set things in motion by sending orders yesterday to the governor of Novgorod to declare war as soon as possible, invade the enemy's territory and occupy convenient positions. I have also ordered other troops to march immediately and at the end of this month we shall be there with them, and we trust in God's help that your majesty will see nothing but benefit in this."

But his majesty the king of Poland saw things differently, as did his majesty the king of Denmark earlier. We mentioned that the latter succeeded in invading Holstein and forcing the duke to move to Sweden to his relative and friend Charles XII, with whom we must now become better acquainted.

CHARLES XII

Charles was born in 1682, which made him exactly ten years younger than Peter.[15] His strong character began to make itself felt when he was still a child, and from the very outset was revealed in a single-minded fashion. The conquering hero of the future was reflected in his daring and reckless quest for danger, whereas from early childhood the Russian Peter displayed a brilliant versatility and a brilliant receptiveness to everything around him, offering a glimpse of the reformer but not of the soldier or conqueror. The young Charles's Herculean strength, like that of the young Peter, sometimes had very unpleasant consequences for those about him. The king's pastimes acquired a particularly unpleasant character when in the spring of 1698 Duke Frederick III of Holstein-Gottorp arrived in Stockholm to marry Charles's elder sister [Hedwig Sophia]. Frederick and Charles became inseparable companions and there was no end to their escapades. Sometimes they would organize hare-baiting in the Diet chamber, other times by day they went into Stockholm to celebrate, the duke and his retinue in just their shirts with sabers drawn, shouting and larking about; by night they went out to roam around town and break windows. They amused themselves by pulling off people's wigs and hats or knocking dishes

King Charles XII of Sweden
Engraving circa 1710

out of the hands of pages who were serving food; they smashed furniture and threw it out of the windows. On one occasion they broke up all the pews in church and forced the congregation to pray standing up. Several days in a row the friends entertained themselves by cutting off the heads of sheep and calves brought to the palace for their sport. The floor and walls of the royal apartments were awash with blood. During these games sixteen-year-old Charles could not be occupied with anything of importance. Courtiers who dared to try were pushed out of the door. The people complained, saying that the duke of Holstein was deliberately corrupting the king in order to kill him and occupy the Swedish throne himself, in the absence of a male heir. But society rallied its forces. One after another representations were made to the king about his behavior from various quarters. One Sunday three preachers in three different churches delivered a sermon on a single text: "Woe to the country which has a young king!" Charles was highly irritated by all this, which apparently had no effect, but only apparently. The young warrior calmed down and when the duke left Sweden, Charles appeared to be an entirely different person, serious and involved. Now he could not be persuaded to take a break even for a moment. Then all of a sudden he again would devote himself enthusiastically to pleasures, balls, masquerades and theater. His strength was bubbling up but finding no outlet.

Meanwhile Duke Frederick, in the hope of receiving help from Sweden, began to goad Denmark into a quarrel, building fortresses and bringing in Swedish detachments, whereas Denmark, on the basis of the old feudal relations, denied his right to do so. Danish troops invaded Schleswig and levelled the fortifications at Tenning; but as soon as they went away the duke rebuilt the fortifications. Hostility grew and Denmark was glad of the opportunity to consolidate its power in Holstein. The Danes were not afraid of Sweden, as they had entered secret relations with Augustus II and Russia. Frederick was driven out by Danish troops, then arrived in Sweden and announced to Charles XII that he was placing himself and his country under his protection. "I shall be your protector," replied Charles, "even if it costs me my crown." Swedish troops received the order to move out of Pomerania into Holstein. The majority of the members of the Swedish state council opposed the war, but in vain. England and Holland tried to prevent it, also in vain. A spark had been tossed into the powder keg. The ruling passion of the young king had flared up and would not be quenched. "The king dreams only of war," wrote a French envoy,"he has been told too many tales of the exploits and campaigns of his ancestors. His heart and mind are filled with it, and he regards himself as invincible at the head of his Swedes." Soon another spark fell. There came news that Augustus II had invaded Livonia. The king received the news when he was out hunting. Without the slightest emotion, with a smile on his face he turned to the French envoy and said "Soon we shall make King Augustus go back to where he came from." Returning to Stockholm, he announced that he would never start an unjust war, but would end a just one by the complete overthrow of the enemy. "First I'll put an end to one," he said,"then I'll speak with the other."

On the evening of April 13, 1700 Charles said goodbye to his grandmother [Queen Hedwig Eleonora] and two sisters before setting off for the holiday palace at Kungser. That night the king left Stockholm, but he did not go to Kungser. Never again would he return to Stockholm, never again would he see his grandmother and sisters.

THE PEACE OF TRAVENDAL (1700)

Fifteen thousand Swedish troops under the command of their king quite unexpectedly crossed the Sound and appeared at the gates of Copenhagen, which had no means of defense. Fearing the destruction of his capital, King Frederick IV[16] hastened to conclude a peace treaty with Charles, confirming the complete independence of Holstein and undertaking to pay Duke Frederick two hundred and sixty thousand thalers. The treaty was signed in Travendal on August 8, the very same day that Peter received news of the peace treaty with the Turks, which allowed the movement of Russian troops to the Swedish borders.

As we recall, Patkul was afraid that Peter would take Narva. Peter indeed intended to begin the war by conquering the two important fortresses at Narva and Nöteborg (Oreshek) in order to use these two bases to continue the war and occupy the whole territory lying between them, a territory with no other significant defenses, unin-habited territory which he could fortify at his leisure. At the same time, Narva was more important than Nöteborg, being closer to Riga where Augustus was supposed to operate. On March 2, 1700, in response to news of the failure of the Saxons in Livonia sent by Golovin from Voronezh, Peter wrote: "A great pity, but there's no help for it! It occurred to me that Brandt[17] told me that in Rugodiv (Narva) there are ships' cannon for sale and I told him to buy some. Send Kormchin (a table attendant who had studied engineering abroad) to see those cannon, to try them out and buy some, but also tell him to have a good look at the town and the surrounding country. Also, if it is possible for him to find some business there, to go to Oreshek, if not, to somewhere in the vicinity. That place is essential: on the channel from Lake Ladoga to the sea (look at a map), and vital as a base for auxiliaries. He's not a stupid chap and can keep a secret. It's essential that Kniperkron should not find out, because he knows that he (Kormchin) is educated."

"On the 18th we announced the peace with the Turks with a splendid firework display, on the 19th we declared war against the Swedes," Peter wrote to Fedor Apraksin, who was in charge of the fleet at Voronezh. War was declared because of the "many wrongs" committed by the Swedish king and especially because at the time of the sovereign's journey through Riga the citizens of Riga caused him much unpleasantness and annoyance. The troops marched towards Narva. Augustus's envoy, Langen, was in despair that he and the Danish envoy had failed to deter Peter from his campaign against Narva. He comforted himself with the thought that in time this town would not evade them. Patkul was ecstatic at the news that Peter finally had declared war against Sweden but his ecstasy was cooled at once by the alarming thought of where the tsar would move his troops. Supposing it was to Narva? Patkul was even more anxious insofar as he had met Peter and seen what a dangerous ally Augustus had got for himself.

In a state of anxiety Patkul wrote to Langen: "The question is this: where has the tsar aimed his weapons? You are well aware of what efforts we made to deflect him from Narva. We were guided by important considerations, the chief of which was that it would not be in our interests to allow the tsar into the heart of Livonia by letting him take Narva. In Narva he will gain a base from which to seize Revel, Dorpat and Pernau before they hear about it in Warsaw, then he will conquer Riga and the whole of Livonia. You cannot help feeling afraid when dealing with such a ruler when you recall his forces and his progress, which you have grasped very well, as I see from your report to the king. Finally, common sense demands that we take all possible steps to ensure that Livonia does not fall under the arbitrary rule of this powerful friend and ally of the king. On one hand, you must not forget that we are weak and it is essential for us to have the tsar's help and friendship if we are to achieve anything, and that we shall deal Sweden a considerable blow if it loses Narva so early on. This is why we must not argue too much with the tsar for fear of annoying him, and I think it would be wrong to quarrel with him over Narva. But we must be very skilful in the way that we give the tsar memoranda from which to make copies for the royal chancellery, thereby preserving the right which the king has by dint of the last treaty, so that it will be possible to act subsequently when there is no longer any reason to treat the tsar cautiously, as we are obliged to do now. Observe the behavior of the Danish envoy carefully to see whether he is encouraging the tsar to take Narva and keep it for himself. Persuade the tsar to make the Polish Commonwealth declare war against Sweden, too. Find out from the tsar whether he might concede something from the Kiev area to the Poles. Suggest to him that the acquisition of Ingria and Karelia and his establishment on the coast of the Baltic would compensate him a hundredfold for such a concession."

Patkul wrote this letter to Langen on September 9, but the Russian forces had launched their campaign against Narva on August 22. Our old friend Peter Mikhailov, captain of the bombardiers' regiment, marched as far as Tver with the Preobrazhensky Guards. Here he received word from the king of Poland that Charles XII soon would reach Livonia with eighteen thousand men and disembark at Pernau. Peter was bewildered, as evidenced by the following letter to Golovin. "I can't stop wondering. Is this the truth or a lie? If it's true, it means that the king of Denmark has been overpowered. We leave here and march to Novgorod tomorrow, in haste. I have sent a message to Bruce to stop if he has not gone over the border. Please take care of things there and give instructions to the others. We shall set off and do as God directs."

THE RUSSIANS BESIEGE NARVA

In Novgorod Peter decided to continue the march towards Narva. There were no rumors about Charles XII's arrival but there was news that Narva was poorly fortified and guarded by only a few troops. On September 23 Peter halted outside Narva and quickly began preparing for a siege together with the Saxon engineer General Hallart, whom King Augustus had sent. Difficulties immediately arose. In Hallart's opinion many fewer military supplies had been laid in than were needed. There was another problem, too. Because of the poor state of the roads in the fall and a shortage of transport they had made slow progress and valuable time was being lost. A force of only thirty-five to forty thousand men had gathered outside Narva, exhausted by the difficult march and shortages of food, and the guns turned out to be useless. Finally on October 20 all the Russian batteries opened fire on the town. They were hoping that the town would not hold out for long given its poor facilities when suddenly news arrived that Charles XII had landed at Pernau with, it was said, a large army. After a council of war the Russians fortified their camp. The bombardment of the town continued until at last a shortage of shells, bombs and powder forced them to hold their fire. They had to wait until more supplies arrived.

The first siege of Narva, like the first siege of Azov, was marked by treachery. One of the foreign servicemen, Hummert, who enjoyed the tsar's special favor, went over to Narva, having left his wife and children in Moscow. Later Peter gave orders for a dummy to be hanged in front of Hummert's Moscow home. But from Narva Hummert re-established contact and gave advice about how best to wage the war, how to operate against Narva and explained the reasons for the failure of the first siege. "Unless the troops are properly coordinated and trained, it is impossible to bring war to a successful conclusion, because this leads more to one's own ruin than to the enemy's loss. Your majesty has immeasurable power, but it needs to be used correctly, just as you have men as good an any in the world, but you need to improve them with proper order and instruction." The siege, in Hummert's words, had not succeeded because "we had spies and scouts and had a good knowledge about everything but no one wanted to get down to business, they wandered around like cats around hot porridge but no one wanted to get his fingers burned. First of all you had to build entrenchments for keeping your wine flagons and grain sacks, although there was nothing to fear and you left till last what should have been done first. At first our people were very eager to attack, but what's the use when the dogs are good but the hunters are useless, or vice-versa? If the hunters are good but the dogs are useless there will be a poor catch!" Hummert's letters survive but there are no replies, only the information that Hummert was hanged by the Swedes.

On November 17 the boyar Boris Petrovich Sheremetev, who had been sent to Wesenberg to keep an eye on the Swedish army, fell back to Narva at the news of the enemy's approach. The same night Peter left the camp. It is understandable that this should have given rise to accusations and justifications. But of what could Peter be accused? Of cowardice? Both before and after Peter proved that he was not a coward in the face of the enemy. But reckless daring and the wish to subject himself to senseless danger were quite alien to Peter's character, which distinguished him from Charles XII. Peter could leave the camp at the news of the approach of the enemy convinced that to stay was dangerous and pointless and that his presence could be more useful elsewhere. Here was a man who was quite incapable of false shame. Peter led his troops to the gates of Narva as he led them to Azov, counting on the fact that two allies would be occupying the enemy. He had no experienced generals, the war had not yet had time to educate them. In a campaign aimed at capturing a fortress it was possible to do without them. Peter had an experienced engineer, Hallart, with whom he intended to organize everything himself, but circumstances changed. The Swedish king was coming to the rescue of Narva with a fine and, as rumor had it, large army, encouraged by its brilliant success in the Danish campaign. In the art of warfare, as in all other arts, Peter regarded himself and his fellow-countrymen as novices who had just begun to study. And now these novices had to match themselves against the masters. In all likelihood Peter would have retreated hastily from Charles at Narva if he had been left with just Admiral Golovin, whom he called field marshal in order to preserve a semblance of unity. But when he was in Novgorod he was visited by Duke Charles-Eugène Ducroy, a highly recommended general from the emperor of Austria's service. At the news of Charles's approach Peter suggested that the duke take command of the Russian forces. The latter refused for a long time, but finally accepted the proposal. The troops were in the reliable hands of an expert. For the tsar and the former field marshal to stay longer merely would damage the unity of command and distract the attention of subordinates. Peter left with Golovin for Novgorod, "in order to spur the remaining regiments who were still under way to make haste to Narva, and in particular to make a rendezvous with the king of Poland."

CHARLES DEFEATS THE RUSSIANS

Charles marched quickly towards Narva on the heels of Sheremetev and on the morning of November 19 appeared in front of the Russian camp with about eighty-five hundred troops. Apart from the skill, experience and daring of the Swedish side the main reason for Charles's success was that the Russian troops were stretched thinly over a huge distance in their camp and it was easy to break through their unclosed ranks. In addition, a strong gale blew right into the faces of the cold, hungry Russian soldiers, and they could make out nothing more than twenty paces away. Finally, their poor physical condition was exacerbated by a decline in morale caused by the awareness of their lack of skill and inexperience in the face of an enemy who was feared for these qualities. To this was added suspicion of whether their foreign commanders would fight wholeheartedly against their fellows. This is why, when the Swedes broke in to the camp a cry went up from the ranks of terrified Russian soldiers, "The Germans have betrayed us!" These fearful cries sapped their final strength and they all turned and fled. Sheremetev's cavalry fled by swimming across the Narova, as a result of which a thousand men drowned.

The flight of Sheremetev freed Charles of his greatest fear because more than anything he had feared a cavalry attack from the rear. The infantry rushed across the bridge, the bridge collapsed and many men drowned in the Narova. Discipline evaporated. Embittered with fear, the Russians began to fling themselves on the

foreigners and beat them. When he saw what was happening Ducroy
yelled "Let the devil himself fight with soldiers like these!" and took
flight along with the rest of the foreigners and surrendered to the
Swedes. In the midst of this universal confusion and flight two
regiments did not collapse or flee—the Preobrazhensky and
Semenovsky Guards. Enclosing themselves with turnpikes and gun
carriages they fought off the Swedes until nightfall. Meantime the
king's horse got stuck in a bog and he clambered out with difficulty
and mounted another. When that one was killed, the king mounted
a third and said with a laugh "It looks like the enemy wants to train
me in horseback-riding." When it was quite dark, the king ordered
a cease-fire and he lay down in his wet clothes on a cloak by the
watchman's fire.

The Swedes were still far from being assured of victory. The
desperate action of the Preobrazhensky and Semenovsky Guards
scared them. As well as them, a detachment under the command of
General Weide stood firm. There was little order amongst the
Swedes. Two of their detachments, having wrongly identified each
other, fought each other and many were killed. At night the soldiers
made for the tents abandoned by the Russians, found a quantity of
wine and got so drunk that they were in no fit state to guard the
prisoners. If the Russians had taken advantage of this the outcome
of the battle of Narva could have been quite different. But the
Russian generals, Prince Yakov Dolgoruky, Prince Alexander of
Georgia, Avtamon Golovin and Ivan Buturlin, out of touch with
Weide, ignorant of what was going on and fearing that the battle
would end badly for them, next day entered negotiations with the
king and agreed to withdraw after surrendering their artillery to the
Swedes. When Weide received word of this capitulation he followed
the other generals' example. "I shall allow the Russian soldiers to
keep their weapons on account of the bravery with which they
defended themselves," said Charles. The Swedes were only too
pleased to speed the Russians on their way across the river. They
set to work at night and long before dawn succeeded in raising a
bridge, across which the Russians went, but the generals were taken
prisoner on the grounds that the Russians had broken the treaty by
taking their treasury with them whereas there was nothing about the
treasury in the treaty.

On November 21 Charles entered liberated Narva in triumph. Seventy-one distinguished Russian prisoners also were sent into the town, amongst them ten generals.

VICTORS AND VANQUISHED

A dazzling victory was won, but how would the victor take advantage of it? He had two routes, two enemies, to choose from, and opinions were divided. Piper, Wrede, Vellinck, Stenbock and others advised accepting King Augustus's peace proposals and putting all their efforts into pursuing the fleeing, terrified Russians. They could station themselves in their winter quarters, feed the army at the Russians' expense and fan the dissatisfaction with the tsar among the musketeers, Tsarevna Sophia's supporters and among the common people, who were displeased with the introduction of foreign customs. The Russian realm would be in turmoil and Sweden could gain advantages, as once it had done during the time of the pretenders.[18] Sweden could make its possessions on that side of the border more secure and force the Russian government to divert its attention exclusively to the Black Sea. At first Charles favored this plan. In his bedroom hung a map on which was marked the route to Moscow. He forbade his soldiers to cross the Russian border in search of forage. Otherwise, he said, the Swedish army will find no sustenance there. But soon the plan was abandoned. On Charles's part the chief motive was hatred of Augustus and scorn for the Russians. These enemies, he thought, will always be easy to topple, just a few troops are needed to restrain them for a while. People were quick to take up Charles's proposition because war in Russia, a cold, poor country which promised little in the way of booty, held little appeal for the Swedish soldiers and officers. Charles left Narva for the strong fortress at Lais (fifty versts from Dorpat), in order to await reinforcements from Sweden, with which he intended to march against Augustus in the spring.

Meanwhile word of the battle of Narva spread throughout Europe, arousing amazement about the eighteen-year-old victor. Poets tuned their lyres and medals were struck in Charles's honor, one of which depicted the victor of Narva with the legend "The reality is greater than the expectation" *(superant superata fidem)*. On another Charles casts down three enemies with the legend "Justice triumphs at last!"

As well as medals in honor of Charles there was a medal struck to mock Peter with blasphemous analogies from the story of the apostle Peter. On one side of the medal Tsar Peter was depicted warming himself by the fire of his cannon from which bombs were flying towards Narva, with the legend "Peter stood and warmed himself." On the reverse were depicted the Russians fleeing from Narva with Peter at their head. The royal crown tumbles from his head, his sword is abandoned, he wipes away the tears with a kerchief and the legend reads "He went out and wept bitterly."[19]

But he who laughs last laughs longest. People close to Charles immediately noted the harmful effect which his extraordinary success had upon him. From then on he was consumed by a powerful passion for war. War for war's sake became his life's goal. The notion of his invincibility and infallibility combined with that of a mission from on high. Belief in his own invincibility was linked, it is true, with scorn for the enemy which had been vanquished. "There is no pleasure," he said, "in fighting the Russians because they don't fight back like others but run away. If the Narova had been covered in ice, we would scarcely have managed to kill one man. The best sight was when the Russians ran onto the bridge and the bridge collapsed under them, like Pharaoh being swallowed up by the Red Sea. All over the heads of men and horses, arms and legs bobbed up out of the water. Our soldiers shot them like wild ducks." Kronstedt, the later famous artillery commander, wrote to Sweden after the battle of Narva that "Our king trusts so firmly in God's help that he is not afraid to launch an attack on sixty thousand men with a force of four thousand." "The king now thinks of nothing but war," General Stenbock related. "He no longer listens to other people's advice; he takes the view that guidance about what he must do comes directly from God." The colonel of the king's guard Posse commented, "In spite of the cold and hunger the king still refuses to let us go to winter quarters. I think that if he has only eight hundred men left he will invade Russia with them, without a thought about how the soldiers will be fed. He is not in the least affected if one of our men is killed."

Let us turn from the victor to the vanquished. Peter did not throw down his arms or weep as his enemies represented it on medals. After Narva he was just as great as he was after the first unsuccessful campaign against Azov. He displayed the same amazing activity, allowing no obstacles to stand in his way. Prince Anikita Repnin[20] received instructions to restore order to the regiments which had left Narva "in confusion." In Novgorod, Pskov and the Caves monastery (near Pskov) fortification work was in full swing. "Trenches were dug and churches demolished, palisades with embrasures were erected and turf laid down on both sides of the palisades; they also made gun emplacements and laid turf around them. The work was carried out by dragoons and infantrymen and men of various ranks, and priests and church folk of every rank, men and women. The towers were piled up with earth, and they laid turf on top. They raised mounds. The wooden tops of the towers and the wooden roof of the fort were all demolished, and at that time there were no services in the parish churches except for the cathedral." Woe betide anyone who refused to work or thought of making a profit from the common cause. Peter arrived at the Caves monastery and ordered the first gun emplacement to be laid by the holy gates in his presence and appointed Lieutenant Colonel Shenshin to supervise the work. When he arrived at the site and failed to find Shenshin there, he ordered him to be lashed in front of the emplacement without mercy and sent to Smolensk as a trooper. In Moscow Leonty Kokoshkin was hanged in front of the Chancellery of Crown Appointments for taking five rubles when he was overseeing the arrival of transport in Tver. Elisey Poskochin was hanged in Novgorod for taking money for wagons.

Twenty-three thousand men survived the defeat at Narva. Prince Boris Alekseevich Golitsyn was entrusted with forming new regiments, and ten dragoon regiments were formed, each of a thousand men. In spring they were sent to Pskov. Infantry was formed from volunteers. People came forward, but they had to create new artillery because the old was surrendered to the Swedes at Narva. Peter gave orders for "part of the bells from churches and monasteries from distinguished towns throughout the land to be collected to make cannon and mortars."

ANDREI VINIUS

The manufacture of arms was entrusted to Vinius, "supervisor of the artillery."[21] The lively, indefatigable and experienced old man was perfectly capable of carrying out this important and difficult task, but he was no exception when it came to self-interest. When he made Vinius supervisor of artillery, Peter considered it essential to relieve him of the job of organizing the postal service. Vinius asked whether he was angry with him for some reason. "I have received your letters in which you write about the readiness of the artillery," Peter replied, "and that you are working on it, and that is very good and vital work, because time is like death. You ask in your letter whether I took the post from you because I was angry for some reason, but is your conscience perhaps pricking you? I have been speaking of this for some time and you knew about it and told other people and publicized it. The reason it was taken from you is that in your hands it was of no use to the country but only to you, for however many times I told you about the mail in other countries, my words fell on deaf ears. Therefore I have entrusted it to someone else, but if it proves just as futile there, it can be taken away from that person, too."

Vinius carried out his new commission with distinction, but complained about the craftsmen and the magistrates. "The work is being badly impeded by the drunkenness of the workmen; it's impossible to cure them of their vice, either by kindness or blows. I beg you to issue an order to the magistrates that they carry out the orders from the Artillery Chancellery more conscientiously; they are holding up the work" Peter replied: "We were much encouraged by your honor's letter, from which we see that thanks to God's help and your hard work the artillery is almost ready. Tell the magistrates that if the mountings aren't ready as a result of their delays, they will pay not only with money but with their lives." To what extent Vinius exaggerated the difficulties in order to show off his own efforts in a good light is unclear; in any event, he wrote that there were only two good craftsmen, one a German and the other a Russian. Of the remaining Russians one was good but a drunkard, the other two were always on the bottle and were not afraid of any punishment. Be that as it may, in November 1701 Vinius boasted that nowhere had such fine artillery been made in such a short time and by such craftsmen. In less than a year more than three hundred guns were produced, which were without a fault, and ten thousand rubles were saved in comparison with previous contracts. Two hundred and fifty boys were sent to school, to make good engineers, artillerists and craftsmen.

SHEREMETEV'S CAMPAIGN

After Narva Peter refused to confine himself to defensive measures alone. An offensive was vital, firstly to revive the flagging spirits of his men, then to prove to friends and enemies alike that the defeat at Narva had not exhausted them, that spirit and strength remained. The extent to which his men's spirits failed and the measures required to spur them into action may be seen from Peter's letter to Boris Sheremetev two weeks after Narva, on December 5, 1700. "No! One must not lose everything in misfortune, therefore I command you to continue with what has been started, in command of the Novgorod and Cherkass cavalry with whom we told you before (only then there were too few men) to guard the places close by (for the time being) and further distant, the better to inflict damage on the enemy. There can be no excuses: there are sufficient men, and the rivers and bogs are frozen over, so the enemy cannot catch you. I write again: don't make excuses. If there is sickness, it started with the deserters, whose comrade, Major L..., was condemned to death."[22]

Sheremetev sent a detachment to the castle at Marienburg but Colonel Schlippenbach fought off the Russians, reinforced the castle and in January 1701 entered Russian territory with three companies of cavalry and three of infantry. Fifteen versts from the Caves monastery there was a battle between the Russians and the Swedes in which the Russians killed sixty Swedes and took fifteen prisoners. Schlippenbach retreated. For some time this was the limit to hostilities from both sides. The Russians were not resolved to pursue the Swedes deep inside their own territories, and Schlippenbach had too few men for any major engagements. The people living on the frontiers were the only ones to suffer badly. The cossacks took about four thousand prisoners from Livonia back to Little Russia.

PETER AND AUGUSTUS MEET IN BIRZE

In the meantime Peter needed to ratify his alliance with Augustus, in order to prevent him from making a separate peace with Charles and to attempt to bring Poland into the war against the Swedes. Peter considered a private meeting with Augustus and private talks with the Polish magnates to be the best way of achieving this. The meeting of the sovereigns took place in February 1701 in the township of Birze (in Dünaburg district). The sovereigns made merry at lengthy dinners and dealt with important business. Once after a feast Augustus overslept and missed mass, but Peter appeared in church and in his usual manner scrutinized the Catholic service closely and asked what various rites signified. One of the Polish senators remarked that it was within his power to unite the Greek church with the Catholic. "The Lord indeed gave the tsars dominion over the peoples," the tsar replied, "but over the conscience of men Christ alone has dominion, and the unification of the churches can be accomplished only by God's will."

Peter's visit was to arrange not the unification of the churches but the unification of Poland and its king and the Russians against the Swedes. He explained to Shchuka, the Lithuanian vice-chancellor, that Poland now should take advantage of the unification of the Russian and Saxon troops to join its troops with theirs and take Livonia from the Swedes. Shchuka replied that Poland was exhausted by the wars which recently ended, and it was much more profitable to make use of the peace than to seek new acquisitions. They might be induced to go to war, but for that they would need to be promised more substantial gains. "What do you mean by that?" asked Peter. "Everything is in your majesty's hands," replied the vice-chancellor. Peter insisted that Shchuka explain what he meant, to which the latter replied: "In its last treaty [of 1686] with Russia, Poland was deprived of its old borders. Would your majesty not be willing to return at least half of what was conceded, for example Kiev and its vicinity?" The tsar declared that this was impossible and Poland would have to make do with Livonia. Talks were continued by Golovin who had arrived with the tsar. He stated that the surrender of Kiev was impossible without the agreement of the boyar council and the cossack hetman, for it would lead to disturbances inside Russia. "If it is difficult for Russia it will be even more difficult to persuade the Polish Commonwealth to go to war," Shchuka replied. "At least return to us the townships over the Dnieper: Terekhtemirov, Staiki, Tripolie and some other villages from the Starodub regimental district and do not forbid the settlement of Chigirin and other places around." "None of those places can be conceded without consultation with the hetman, because his majesty the tsar will take nothing from Ukraine by force," said Golovin. With that the talks with Shchuka ended, but a new treaty was signed with Augustus. The allies undertook to continue the war with all their forces and not to end it except by mutual agreement. The tsar promised to send the king between fifteen and twenty thousand well-armed infantrymen, to use as he saw fit, with a pledge to supply funds for establishing provision stores, to lay in ten thousand pounds of powder at Vitebsk and to pay a hundred thousand rubles every year for the next three years. The king would deploy his troops in Livonia and Estonia to deflect the common foe and provide security for Russia, and to give the tsar the opportunity for successful operations in Izhora and Karelia. The tsar would leave Livonia and Estonia in the hands of the king and the Commonwealth without any claims on them. As the outcome of the war was uncertain and since as a result of the war for the Spanish succession the king's German possessions [in Saxony] might be subjected to great danger, the allies agreed to accept the mediation of the French, English, Brandenburg and Holland and to listen to the mediators' peace proposals which, however, must not be to the detriment of the current and former treaties in any way. Word of the new treaty was sent to the king of Denmark. In a secret clause the tsar undertook to send the king twenty thousand rubles "as a reward and favor to those Polish senators who are capable of seeking to bring the Commonwealth into the alliances which have been made."

According to the reports of those who saw Peter in Birze, he made a very sound assessment of his own and foreign naval power, saying that he would have as many as eighty ships, each with sixty to eighty guns, including one built from his own designs called *Divine Foresight*. On this ship was depicted St. Peter and beneath him a boat, in which children are putting to sea (the tsar wished to convey the fact that Russian navigation was still in its infancy). The whole device was composed by the tsar. The tsar was very knowledgeable about geography, sketching and drawing, and studied these topics diligently.

THE RUSSIAN ARMY AND THE SAXON GENERAL

At the beginning of March Peter returned to Moscow and right after his arrival an adjutant general arrived from Augustus to collect the money. They took it from the chancelleries and from the Chamber of Magistrates,[23] but there was not enough. A thousand gold crowns were taken from the Trinity monastery; Lieutenant Menshikov of the Preobrazhensky Guards gave four hundred and twenty gold crowns, the rich chief merchant Filatiev gave ten thousand rubles. Another pledge was also honored. Prince Repnin led twenty thousand infantrymen to join forces with Augustus's Saxon troops, who were under the command of General Field Marshal Steinau. On June 21 Repnin reached Kokenhusen and his men earned Steinau's admiration. "For the most part they are good men," wrote the general. "No more than fifty have had to be rejected: they are armed with good Maastricht and Liège rifles; some of the regiments have swords instead of bayonets. They march so well that I don't have a single complaint against them. They work hard and quickly and carry out all orders unquestioningly. I find it especially commendable that in the whole army there is not one woman and not one dog. In the military council the Muscovite general complained loudly and asked that the wives of the Saxon grenadiers be prevented from going into the Russian camp in the morning and evening and selling vodka, because this leads his men into bad habits of drunkenness and other vices. General Repnin is a man of about forty; he doesn't understand much about war, but he is eager to learn and very deferential. The colonels are all Germans, old, incapable people, and the other officers are inexperienced."

DEFEAT ON THE DVINA

But the highly experienced teachers showed themselves up in front of their curious pupils. Charles XII attacked the Saxons at Riga just as suddenly as he had the Russians at Narva. In July he made a successful crossing of the Dvina in sight of the enemy forces and after a two-hour battle utterly routed Steinau. The Saxons lost all their artillery, all their supplies and two thousand men, whereas in the Swedish ranks only five hundred men were killed. There were only four thousand Russians with Steinau; the rest were with Repnin eight miles from Riga. Patkul attributed this failure to the fact that the Saxons had adopted a defensive position instead of going on the offensive. "I insisted that the king and the tsar meet in person in order to make plans for the next campaign," wrote Patkul to the Swedish resident in Copenhagen. "I explained to each of them that it was vital to make preparations for the campaign earlier, to join both their armies to make a surprise attack on the enemy before he had time to receive reinforcements from Sweden and Pomerania. This was what they decided on at Birze. In response to my proposals, the tsar gave us all that was necessary, in short he acted like an honorable sovereign. But no sooner had we arrived in Warsaw than people began to try to talk the king into a defensive war. I did all I could to oppose this plan, a worse one than which it was difficult to imagine. The enemy himself could not find a better one because we gave him time to stop the unification of the allies' forces."

It should be noted that in his desire primarily to present his advice as infallible, Patkul confuses the issue. Of course, the allies should have united their armies as soon as possible after Narva and made a joint attack on Charles's negligible forces, but this was not done. On the question of military operations it was decided in Birze that the king's army with Russian auxiliaries should not lay siege to Riga until August. The tsar would send Kalmyks into Finland, and the main Russian army would operate from the direction of the Caves monastery or Narva, without any attempts to lay sieges or engage in major battles. If Riga was taken, the king would help the tsar to seize Narva. It would be wrong to lay all the blame on those of Augustus's advisers in Warsaw who proposed a defensive war. First one should note the circumstance that Repnin's corps joined up with Steinau only on June 26 precisely because in Birze August was set as the date for launching the siege of Riga and the tsar sent orders from Birze to Moscow to halt the troops who were leaving on campaign. So it was the arrangements made in Birze, not the change of plan decided in Warsaw, which wasted time and gave Charles the opportunity to receive reinforcements from Sweden and Pomerania. Charles was able to attack the Saxons, who were not reinforced with Repnin's whole force because Steinau sent only four Russian regiments to Riga, making the remaining Russians work on the entrenchments on the Dvina, delighted that the Russians worked so hard and so well and that Repnin was deferential. We deemed it necessary to go into these explanations in order to show how cautiously Patkul's statements have to be treated.

Be that as it may, Charles had won a second brilliant victory, this time not over the Russians, who were famed for their lack of experience in military matters, but over the Saxons. Again the victor was faced with a choice—should he pursue Augustus or turn his attention to the Russians? Again, at first he had in mind the latter course and ordered Schlippenbach to move from Dorpat towards Pskov and await his arrival. But soon Charles changed his mind, and one should not be too hard on the nineteen-year-old king for the persistence with which he now began to try to topple Augustus from the Polish throne. Perpetually to be rushing from one place to another, beating the Russians then attacking the Saxons, beating the Saxons then turning back to attack the Russians, was most inconvenient. The main question was: which were the more dangerous, the Saxons or the Russians? Against more dangerous enemies Charles also would have had to fight with the main army himself. Charles was quite right to regard the Saxons as more dangerous than the Russians. It is true that Charles was advised to make peace with Augustus and direct all his forces against Peter. But Charles felt the deepest contempt and mistrust for Augustus and refused adamantly to rely on his word in the event of a peace treaty being signed, considering himself justified to be worried that as soon as he struck deep into Russia, Augustus again would start hostilities against Sweden. From this stemmed his desire first to overthrow Augustus, then to acquire the new Polish king as an ally and operate against Russia in safety.

Let us assume that Charles was more annoyed with Augustus than with Augustus' allies. The king of Denmark, after all, was justified in being hostile to Sweden as a result of his enmity with the duke of Holstein. The tsar of Russia was seeking to reach the sea and regain ancient Russian possessions snatched by the Swedes in somewhat dishonest fashion during the Time of Troubles. But the elector of Saxony, who had no such motives, was the chief initiator of the alliance against Sweden, he had been the first to act on Patkul's suggestion. Let us assume that Charles was carried away by his annoyance with Augustus, but at the same time it is impossible to deny that even without that annoyance he had good reason to seek Augustus's overthrow from the Polish throne first. In a letter to the king of France Charles spoke of Augustus thus: "His behavior is so shameful and vile that he deserves God's vengeance and the contempt of all right-thinking people." In Charles's letter to the Swedish state council we find expressions of the same conviction that it was wrong to enter into relations with a man like Augustus. "If King Augustus," wrote Charles, "once allowed himself to commit such a deception, we can have no faith in his word; to enter into relations with a man who dishonored himself would be to do damage to one's own honor."

And so Augustus was a valuable ally for Peter not by dint of the strength of his arms but because he aroused the hatred and mistrust of the Swedish king. He deflected that fearsome enemy from Russia's borders and gave the tsar time to revive his troops and teach them how to beat the Swedes.

SHEREMETEV'S VICTORY AT ERESTFER

Russian successes began in the far north, where in June 1701 six Swedish ships under English and Dutch flags tried to steal up on Archangel, but they were repulsed and two ships which ran aground were kept by the Russians as booty. Peter was very pleased. "Wonderful!" he wrote to Apraksin and offered congratulations for the "unexpected piece of good fortune" that the "mischievous Swedes" had been repelled.

At the end of 1701 Sheremetev undertook an offensive against Schlippenbach in Livonia and, taking advantage of his superior numbers, beat the Swedes at Erestfer homestead on December 29. Three thousand Swedes fell in battle, three hundred and fifty were taken prisoner, and the Russians lost about a thousand men. Peter was overjoyed by this first victory against the Swedes. Menshikov galloped off to present the victor with an order of St. Andrew, a diamond-studded portrait of the tsar and a warrant for his promotion to general-field marshal. In Moscow there were great celebrations and prayers of thanksgiving. For a whole day bells pealed and a hundred cannon roared, and on the towers and walls of the Kremlin standards captured from the Swedes were unfurled. Narva was avenged.

After the victory Sheremetev set off to lay waste to Swedish territory. He lay waste all of Yuriev (Dorpat) district, but the weariness of the horses and deep snows forced the field marshal to abandon his campaign of devastation. Sheremetev considered himself very fortunate that the enemy made no use of the deep snow to attack on skis from the forests. A hundred and forty prisoners were taken for interrogation whilst the Cherkassians (Ukrainian cossacks) took Finnish natives for themselves. Sheremetev reported that he had not ordered the Finns to be confiscated from the Cherkass because he wanted to make the latter "keener."

GRIEVANCES OF THE LITTLE RUSSIAN ARMY

On March 3 Mazepa (a knight of St. Andrew since February 8, 1700) related to the tsar that "When they returned from doing your royal duty on the Livonian borders, the colonels with the commanding officers and men began to criticize me and complain about me among themselves, behind my back, firstly, because of the hardships they had to endure and the losses to their farms as a result of the long campaign; secondly, because many of their comrades were beaten and abused when they were collecting fodder, and deprived of their weapons and horses, and in spite of their complaints they were given no restitution in the villages where they were robbed and killed. They are complaining particularly that when they were discharged in Pskov their field guns were confiscated. The men who are returning from war are inciting the ones who stayed in Little Russia to rebel, all complaining against me with one voice, claiming that I don't defend their rights and liberties and that I don't appeal to you, great sovereign, on their behalf now that such new things are being done to them. As I don't know why the cannon were taken away I cannot give them an answer and silence their complaints. I humbly beseech you to send an order of explanation and exhortation on the question of the cannon. When I receive it, I shall at once send circulars around all the regiments to silence the complaints. In particular I shall write to the Zaporozhians amongst whom the town cossacks have spread the same gossip and scandal, and where it has never been difficult to incite quarrels and unnecessary words even when there are no grounds."

Mazepa spoke in more detail to Table Attendant Lutavinov, who was sent to visit him. He said when the cossacks were stationed at Pskov they had gone to buy horse fodder for tokens, but the local inhabitants refused to sell to them for tokens. As the cossacks had no other money, they had ridden around the district and taken horse fodder, but then their horses and weapons were taken away and about forty men were thrown into the water and others beaten to death. They appealed for restitution to the boyar Boris Petrovich Sheremetev, but he had done nothing. The cossacks said that the hetman had been to Moscow and received a knighthood, but he did not report to the great sovereign or appeal to him about them and their hardships, although they were utterly ruined in the course of these duties. They were saying in secret amongst themselves: if the hetman refused to petition the sovereign about the offenses they had suffered they would go to serve the king of Poland or Sweden. "I myself am afraid of them," said Mazepa, "because all reliable infantrymen have been sent to Pskov and there are now very few reliable men in my service, and only three hundred Moscow musketeers. I ask you to send me more musketeers and to form a regiment of a thousand for my protection. The great sovereign should order me to join his service: I need to select a good force of thirty or at least twenty thousand men and march through Lithuania, because that route is the shortest and well supplied with food."

TROUBLES IN ZAPOROZHIE

Not long after that the hetman notified the tsar that in January he had dispatched the Zaporozhian Cossacks to serve in Pskov and that the Zaporozhians, who knew neither fear nor shame, had marched in such a disorderly and lazy fashion that they only just reached the Smolensk border by Shrovetide, and it was impossible to recount how many misdemeanors, robberies and offenses they committed during their march against the people of Little and Great Russia; the enemy himself scarcely could have behaved worse. For this reason, Mazepa added, they should be stationed in a place where they would serve better.

Peter immediately gave orders for the Cherkass cannon to be returned and for an inquiry into how they had been ill-treated. Sheremetev replied that the Cherkass themselves decided not to take the guns because they had nothing on which to transport them. When they were in Pskov and in other towns during the campaign they laid waste Russian villages and hamlets, beaten, drowned and robbed people. Mazepa was given to understand that this sort of behavior by men under his command had been graciously overlooked only as a favor to him. But from now on he should give them strict orders that they were not to cause damage to their own people instead of to the enemy.

Mazepa had written about the disorderly conduct of the Zaporozhians on active service, but there was also no peace from the ones who remained in the Camp. At the beginning of 1701 the Zaporozhians sent Mazepa a complaint that saltpeter workers who extracted saltpeter along the river Samara had promised to pay them a hundred crowns per cauldron but had not kept their promise. In his report to the tsar about this complaint the hetman wrote that as well as taking a hundred crowns per cauldron the Zaporozhians were ill-treating the saltpeter workers in various ways, taking money, drink and food from the saltpeter camps all the time, which is why saltpeter was so expensive. The Zaporozhians insisted that they owned the river Samara from its mouth to its source and the forests which grew along its banks, and the distant forest gullies and the pits where the saltpeter was extracted. They threatened to destroy the saltpeter camps and drive out the workers and refused to allow anyone the use of the Samara forests not only for saltpeter mining but for any purpose whatsoever, just as they did not allow cattle grazing there. The Samara was the only suitable location for the extraction of saltpeter.

In April a new report arrived from the hetman. The Zaporozhians had assembled about three thousand men, made ready four cannon and appointed colonels with the intention of aiding the Crimean khan by attacking the Nogay horde. The hetman sent them a reprimand. How dare they treat openly with the Crimean khan and attack the Nogay horde? The commander replied: "It was difficult for us to get a message to Moscow and wait for the tsar's instructions or inform your excellency, because the khan summoned us all of a sudden when he was already in the field. He promised us his horses and to give us all the booty. The deed was not done because of the changeable winter weather; some of our men were ready to respond to the khan's call, but not the whole camp responded and some refused to attack Orthodox people. We have had freedom here since time immemorial. If someone wants to go somewhere he goes and gets booty wherever it suits him. It is impossible to stop the cossacks from pursuing their own gains. We also wish to report that now the host of the lower Dnieper is being restricted more and more by the people of the towns. There is nowhere for the cossacks to catch game and fish, and it's impossible to live on the allowance from the tsar for a whole year, therefore our men were forced against their will to aid the khan against the Nogay horde. It seems to us that you have no reason to be angry with us; on the contrary, you should be glad that the Muslims call upon our services when they quarrel with each other. We are making every effort to ensure that they summon not only the cossacks of the Zaporozhian Camp but also the registered town cossacks to bring about their own downfall."

The hetman volunteered to march to the Livonian campaign through Lithuania. His wish was granted and he received his marching orders. But at the same time Mazepa complained that the cossacks and peasants were in a very bad mood on account of the arduous campaigns and were saying amongst themselves that soon they would be utterly ruined and the Muscovites would finish them off with these frequent and difficult campaigns. They had only one thought—to escape from the Dnieper. To prevent some mishap suddenly befalling him, the hetman begged the sovereign to order a thousand musketeers to be assigned to him, five hundred of whom would attend the hetman and five hundred be based in Putivl in turns. Their wives and children should be allowed to join them in Putivl because now the musketeers had been living in Baturin for seven years without their wives and in their despair were committing outrages that it was shameful to speak of. But it was unsuitable for them to live in Baturin with their wives because they committed serious offenses and endless thefts on the people of Baturin.

That was not the end of it. In July 1701 Mazepa sent Golovin news of Tatar intrigues. The khan's vizier had summoned the hetman's messenger and asked him "Where is your tsar? Building ships in Voronezh and laboring in vain. Why does your tsar ignore the khan and the Crimean land? Why does he refuse to give us the tribute as he used to? If he is relying on his strength, the khan is strong, too. When we mount our horses, there will be twenty thousand sabre-bearing men with him. If he is relying on the Kalmyks, that is a vain hope. They are no better than gypsies. They'll take the tsar's cash, but they will never fight us properly. Tell the hetman that if he doubts my words he should call a council and announce what I have said to the commanding officers and the rank and file. He will see that they all will rise in revolt out of friendship for us. Only let him assure every one that he is at liberty to say anything. We know very well what is going on in Ukraine, we know that the cossacks are all destitute. If they join with us in brotherhood as before, in a few years they will all be as rich as they were in Khmelnitsky's time. I speak on behalf of the khan and the whole Crimean land. We feel sorry that you, as military men, will soon be ruined for staying with the Muscovite people."

After reports like these, it is understandable why Mazepa received orders to return to Baturin. The hetman was offended or at least gave the impression that he was offended, and on July 20, 1701, he wrote to Golovin: "His illustrious majesty the tsar's royal personal edict ordering me to return to Baturin and send the acting hetman in my place with a few dozen troops reached me on Lithuanian territory, about twelve miles from Mogilev. God, who tests the hearts and bellies of men, knows best the regret and humiliation I felt in front of the inhabitants there when I turned back. I am worried not so much on account of the effort expended on such a long and arduous journey, as for the fact that I was thwarted in my intention of travelling that military highway with fervent eagerness and at no little cost to myself, so that I might prove to his majesty before the eyes of the whole world, not in words or on paper but in action, that I am his loyal subject." Mazepa sent the four colonels of Mirgorod, Pereiaslavl, Poltava and Lubensk and the acting colonel of Nezhin with seventeen thousand troops to Pskov and appointed the colonel of Mirgorod (Daniel Apostol) as acting hetman.

After the battle of Erestfer [in December 1701] this acting hetman sent Mazepa a complaint. "The general halted at Erestfer homestead and stationed the Russian troops around him at a short distance along all the roads and the paths and gave all the troops permission for volunteers to form raiding parties to lay waste and burn. Our Little Russian troops, who were the most eager for booty, went almost as far as Yuriev in Livonia and brought back much loot to their camps. But the Russian troops, probably on express orders, confiscated the booty from the cossacks along all the roads and beat the men savagely, causing humiliation and insult to our poor army. Now we hear that the commander himself (Sheremetev) is strutting about in our feathers and profiting from our booty, but he condemns and curses our enthusiastic and loyal service to the monarch. When we were in the Pskov district we heard folk saying that we performed no brave deeds or duties, but we put up with it in view of the ill-will of the commander to all our land. When they hear from us what unendurable ill-feeling there is towards us over there, it's unlikely that anyone from our Ukraine will agree to go there on the tsar's service, even under duress and compulsion." But it turned out that the Russian troops had not taken too much booty from the cossacks, because Apostol brought back four standards, five cannon and as many as twenty captured officers to Little Russia, while the rank and file cossacks brought Finnish prisoners, horses and a large number of other items. The standards, cannon and officers were taken from them but they were allowed to keep the rest of the loot.

Meanwhile the Zaporozhians continued to cause trouble. In October 1701 they destroyed the saltpeter works along both banks of the Samara; they refused to allow the lands along the river to be surveyed; finally, they robbed some Greek merchants on their way from Turkey to Russia. The sultan sent a demand to Baturin that the goods stolen from his subjects be returned to them at once, and it was vital not to upset the sultan at this dangerous time for fear of war with Turkey being added to the war with Sweden.

Golovin asked Mazepa's advice about what to do with the Zaporozhians. "Your excellency," Mazepa replied, "you have the brain for dealing with the great monarch's affairs, you can decide easily what punishment is suitable for the Zaporozhians without my advice. I would have ground their noses in it long ago and made them desist from their mad behavior, and I would have punished them for their latest crime if I had not been afraid of reducing them to despair and alienating them from the sovereign. It has often happened in the past that dissatisfaction with this side has led them to appoint someone as acting hetman and go off to neighboring countries in search of a protector, which they might easily do now."

Golovin wrote to Mazepa and told him to invite the best Zaporozhians to visit him in Baturin and send them to Moscow. "There is an old saying," Mazepa replied, "a peasant is as black as a crow and as crafty as the devil. I have already spoken to the Zaporozhians who were going to Moscow to collect their allowance. I questioned them about the robbery of the Greeks and made clear that this affair could not be resolved until they gave up the instigators. But they have only one reply—there were no instigators, we all did it, the whole Zaporozhian Host consented to it. They have a secretary called Zelenetsky, a criminal and a long-standing traitor, who was formerly adviser to Petrik,[24] and went off with him to the Crimea and brought the Tatars and Zaporozhians to attack Ukraine. He was defeated at Tsarichenko and escaped to Zaporozhie where he is living to this day, having left his father, mother and wife in Poltava. He is said to enjoy great standing amongst the Zaporozhians. At the cossack assembly he keeps silent, but in the barracks in secret he does what he likes. If God is willing we could get our hands on him and the Zaporozhian secrets would be revealed, for it is inconceivable that the Zaporozhians would act so boldly without the assurance of help from either the khan or the Poles."

Golovin was angry that instead of giving advice about how to punish the Zaporozhians Mazepa got off with offering a compliment. Mazepa replied: "As God is my witness, I acted thus only in order to avoid arousing the suspicion that I was motivated by personal malice towards the Zaporozhians rather than acting for the common good and doing my duty, because my first report about the robbery of the Zaporozhians going to serve in Pskov was utterly disregarded, and now they have returned and are barking with their dog's lips, claiming that 'the hetman wanted to have us escorted to Siberia or Archangel into eternal servitude, he persuaded the sovereign to refuse to give us any cloth or even five rubles apiece for our labors.' The words of these curs do not frighten me, but it's hard to tolerate the scoundrels." Mazepa expressed dissatisfaction that the

Zaporozhians were not punished as suggested in his report. In the same letter in reply to Golovin's question as to whether punishing the Zaporozhians might not be harmful to Ukraine, he wrote: "God preserve us from some new piece of mischief from the Zaporozhians. There's no doubt that many of the town cossacks would join them."

When the Zaporozhians Gerasim Krysa and his comrades arrived in Moscow to collect their allowance they were placed under guard and interrogated about whether they, Krysa and his comrades, had taken part when the Greeks and the saltpeter workers were robbed. "The robbery of the Greeks was carried out with the general consent of the whole Zaporozhian Host," responded Krysa. "At the time when their goods were plundered, we were there in the Camp and divided up the goods. We robbed them because they passed by our Camp, abused us and belittled the Zaporozhian Host, whereas previously Greeks and other merchants never passed us by, they hired us as escorts. Therefore these Greeks according to our custom were subject to arrest, and we robbed them. We don't know how the saltpeter workers were ruined. We heard about that incident when we were on the march. Only the Zaporozhian Host is not to blame in this case, either, because the saltpeter traders stole our goods."

That was at the end of 1701. At the beginning of 1702 an order from the tsar was sent to the cossack commander that they were to return in full everything which was stolen from the Greeks. If they did not, Krysa and his comrades would be executed and the dispatch of the allowance and supplies would be halted. When this document arrived in Zaporozhie and was read out in the assembly, the cossacks yelled at the field ataman Peter Sorochinsky: "You started this! It was you who told us to divide up the goods stolen from the Greeks among the barracks, but we wanted them to be stored in the Host coffers for the time being. Now you can take the consequences!" Sorochinsky laid down his command and Konstantin Gordeenko was made commander in his place. As Mazepa put it, the Zaporozhians were crestfallen and began to come to their senses when the bad news arrived from Crimea that the khan refused to give them aid against Russia, referring to the peace treaties with the tsar. There was nothing to be done—the Zaporozhians wrote a petition to the great sovereign admitting that they divided up some red calico and other inexpensive items which they could not get back, but valuables such as pearls and so forth already had been returned to the Greeks. "Be merciful to us, your slaves, great sovereign, let your royal anger abate and release our emissaries."

They were also in communication with the hetman of the Zaporozhian Cossack army over the question of Polish demands and a Polish alliance. On his return from Birze, Golovin informed Mazepa of his conversation with Shchuka and asked his opinion. Mazepa replied: "It would be possible to cede the three townships of Terekhtemirov, Staiki and Tripolie across the Dnieper without causing any damage to his majesty the tsar, but they should be ceded on the condition that the permanent peace be ratified properly and printed in the [Polish] constitution. But Chigirin, Kanev, Cherkasy, Krylov and other places must on no account be ceded. If they are, then on the right side of the Dnieper only Kiev will remain in his majesty's possession and it will not be safe, because people will go over to settle in the Chigirin area from this side of the Dnieper. In one summer a large number of people could go across; the Zaporozhian Cossacks will be drawn to that side. Nothing must be ceded to the Polish side from the Starodub regimental district because the Starodub district is divided off from the Poles by the river Sozh, and my authority as hetman does not extend beyond that river and it is not suitable for Poles to settle here across the river. No good can be expected from the Poles. To this day they have not ratified the treaty of permanent peace [of 1686] or printed it in the constitution, on the grounds that the peace was concluded by the king, not by the Commonwealth. Many holy churches have been converted to the Union.[25] In the past year the main Russian cathedral church in Lvov was taken from the believers and given to the Uniates. The king summoned the Russian troops to Narva then surrendered them to the Swedes and retreated from Riga. You've got to be careful when dealing with the Poles. The chroniclers write: as night follows day, a Pole cannot be brother to a Ruthenian, and until now they have acted true to form."

But soon matters took such a turn that there was no further need to discuss making concessions to the Poles.

AUGUSTUS URGES SACK OF LIVONIA

In August 1701 Prince Grigory Dolgoruky, who was visiting King Augustus, reported to Peter: "His majesty the king tells me that he has received news that the king of Sweden is marching on Poland with his armies. He had no worries about this. When the Swedes invade Poland with a large army they may embitter the Poles against them, but given the present long distance of the Swedish troops from the Muscovite borders your majesty's troops should invade Livonia to prevent any aid being given to the Swedish troops. They should carry out maximum plunder and destruction to deprive the Swedish troops of supplies in Livonia and force them to go back home across the sea for the winter."

The advice was taken. Plunder and devastation accompanied Sheremetev's advance into Livonia. After the victory at Erestfer the field marshal wanted to rest but Peter refused to allow himself or anyone else to rest, particularly at a time when it was vital not to relax the pressure for a moment. At the beginning of January 1702 Sheremetev asked leave to return to Moscow. "My wife is living in someone else's house. I need to find her a home where she can lay her head." This excuse sounded odd. Sheremetev corrected himself and wrote that he needed to be in Moscow to report on vital matters. "It's up to you," Peter replied, "but if you arrive on Good Friday or Easter Saturday, you'll have to go back on Easter Sunday."

Not only did Peter allow Sheremetev no rest, he also allowed none to Supervisor of Artillery Vinius, who was even older than Sheremetev. On February 21 Vinius wrote to the tsar that "When I recently arrived in Moscow, Privy Councillor Tikhon Nikitich Streshnev conveyed your instructions to me, your slave, informing me that you were good enough to require me to translate a statute of military laws. Last year, sire, I was on your service in the army with the hetman. When I got to Glukhov, at the beginning of the month of July, I lay sick for several weeks, and on the days when I felt better I worked on the Dutch dictionary, but I did not work on the military statute because I thought someone else was doing it. Now when I came to Moscow I found Swedes billeted in all the rooms of my house and they still haven't been removed. At first there were more than two hundred of them and they wouldn't let me into the house, so for about three weeks I had to live in someone else's house. For this reason, sire, my work has been held up and I have suffered considerable damage from the billeting. Now I have begun work on the military statute and I shall work as best I can. But I am finding it very hard to write with my right hand, I can barely sign my name, but I am hoping to finish the Dutch articles this Lent, and the rest later. Don't be angry with me, most gracious sovereign, your most humble servant. Really I have become decrepit, I can hardly walk, I'll soon be seventy. The spirit is willing, God knows, but my strength gets less every day."

In the spring the decrepit, enfeebled old man set off for Novgorod and Pskov on artillery business. He returned to Moscow and prepared to leave again, this time for Siberia! He had to inspect mines and factories there. Wrote Vinius from Tobolsk, "I set out from Moscow on my journey on July 28, crossed the borders of Kazan over remote and difficult terrain and reached the iron works in Siberia, which Prince Mikhail Yakovlevich Cherkassky built on the Kamenka river, and I found such a large number of iron mines in other places that I can't imagine that they will be exhausted before the end of the world. The forests are more likely to run out than the mines."

At the end of May Peter began to urge Sheremetev to march from Pskov into Livonia. "We have information," he wrote,"that the enemy is preparing transport from Pomerania to Livonia for ten thousand men, but the king himself has set off for Warsaw. Now is the hour to make a preemptive strike (asking the Lord to give us strength), while the transport is not yet ready."

Sheremetev moved off with an army of thirty thousand to attack Schlippenbach who had eight thousand. On July 18 the armies met at Hummelshof and the Swedes suffered a terrible defeat, with losses of about five and a half thousand dead, three hundred taken prisoner and the whole of their artillery captured. Russian losses were about four hundred dead and the same number wounded. When Peter heard about the victory, he wrote to Sheremetev telling him to lay waste Livonia "to deprive the enemy of a refuge and make it impossible for them to give aid to their towns." The order was carried out. Sheremetev took two substantial towns (Wolmar and Marienburg)

and six small ones and caused dreadful devastation to the whole
territory.

"I beg to inform you," he wrote to Peter, "that Almighty God
and the Blessed Mother of God have granted your wish. There is
no more of the enemy's territory to lay waste. All has been laid
waste and devastated without trace. The raiding parties have
returned from within twenty-five versts of Riga and went right to
the Polish border. Only Pernau and Kolyvan (Revel) remain intact,
and the coast between them and the coast from Kolyvan to Riga,
and Riga itself. Otherwise, everything is totally devastated and laid
waste. I shall send units of Kalmyks and cossacks in various
directions to confuse the enemy. I do have one problem: where am
I to put the prisoners of war? The prisons are full, and they are
mainly officers. I'm worried because they (the prisoners) are angry.
You know what they have got up to already, not sparing themselves.
What if they do some mischief, such as setting fire to the powder
magazines? What if they start to die as a result of hardships? The
money for food is running out, and one regiment is too little to
escort them to Moscow. Give me instructions on what to do with
them. I have selected a hundred families of the best people from
the Finns, those who know how to use an ax and other crafts, more
than four hundred souls in all, for sending to Azov. When it is less
hot I shall have them driven to Moscow and handed over to Tikhon
Streshnev, who can deal with them as he sees fit. On August 31 I
am leaving for Pskov as it's impossible to stay here any longer. We
are in dire straits for we have run out of food and horses, and we
are greatly burdened with prisoners and livestock, have nothing on
which to transport the guns and nowhere to obtain new wagons, and
there aren't any in Pskov."

APRAKSIN'S OPERATIONS IN INGRIA

"Boris Petrovich had a good time in Livonia," wrote Peter to Fedor
Apraksin. At the same time Lord-in-Waiting Peter Apraksin was
having an equally good time in Ingria, travelling along the Neva
river to Tosna and the Izherian land, laying waste and devastating
everything and driving back a detachment of Swedes from Tosna
to Kantsy (Nyenschanz, Neva fortress).[26] Colonel Tyrtov was sent
by Apraksin on boats into Lake Ladoga, where he had several fights

with the Swedes and forced them to withdraw to the vicinity of Oreshek (Nöteborg). But the tsar was unhappy that Apraksin had not followed orders and had devastated an area which Peter regarded as Russian and in which he wished to establish a foothold as close as possible to his cherished goal, the sea. Apraksin explained that he had burnt settlements along the banks of the Neva with the aim of hampering the enemy's transport of food supplies. Peter himself spent all summer of 1702 in Archangel, for in spring he received news that the Swedes were planning to make a second attempt to reach the town. In anticipation of the enemy's arrival Peter occupied himself with building ships. The summer passed and the Swedes did not appear, and in September Peter turned up on Lake Ladoga to take personal command of the conquest of Ingria and of the coast. "If your honor has nothing else important to do in Livonia, then please join me here without delay," Peter wrote to Sheremetev. "The time is very propitious and we must not miss this opportunity. Without you we won't be able to do everything we have to." Five days later he wrote another letter to the same. "Please come and join us on Ladoga without delay. Your presence is vital and it cannot be otherwise. With regard to other matters, such as the supplementary forces and the artillerymen, do as you think fit, but let's not waste this God-given opportunity."

When Sheremetev arrived, Peter led the troops to Nöteborg, once known as Oreshek in the lands of Novgorod, on the Neva channel. This was a small fortress enclosed by high stone walls. The Swedish garrison there consisted of no more than four hundred and fifty men, but had about a hundred and fifty guns; the besieging force had about ten thousand men. After putting up a desperate resistance, on October 11 the commandant was forced to surrender the town. Nöteborg was renamed Schlüsselburg (Key Town). Peter was overjoyed to have gained this key to the sea, all the more since the operation was extraordinarily difficult. Delighted letters were sent to members of the tsar's company. To Apraksin he wrote: "I inform your honor that with the help of God, the bringer of victory, this fortress has surrendered after a fierce and extraordinarily difficult and bloody assault (which began at four in the morning and ended at four in the afternoon), on the condition that Commandant Schlippenbach and his whole garrison be released. I have to tell your honor that this was accomplished beyond all human expectation and can only be ascribed to God's honor and miracle-working."

Peter also informed the supervisor of artillery in Siberia. "It's true that this nut was very hard but, praise God, we have succeeded in cracking it.[27] Our artillery did its job splendidly." Vinius replied in his usual high-flown language. "Sovereign, as I journeyed in these distant Siberian lands, travelling on your illustrious sovereign's behalf to out-of-the-way places over wastes under the dismal clouds of many troubles and cares about the orderly state of the newly-built iron works and worrying about how to eradicate the mischief done by the cannon masters sent from Moscow, suddenly like a ray of sunshine your letter from Nöteborg illuminated me with great joy, when I heard that the all-powerful Lord has deigned to grant you that hard nut as the true heir and has granted victorious strength to our new artillery and powder which were besprinkled with tears."

FOUNDING OF ST. PETERSBURG

In April of the following year, 1703, Russian troops marched from Schlüsselburg along the right bank of the Neva under the command of Field Marshal Sheremetev. They marched through forests great and small, and at last caught sight of a small earthwork fort occupying no more than a couple of acres of land at the mouth of the Okhta river on the Neva. This was Kantsy, or Nyenschanz, which guarded the mouth of the Neva. Opposite the fort, over the Okhta, was a settlement of about four hundred wooden huts. The Russian troops were joined by Bombardier Captain Peter Mikhailov, who travelled with a convoy of sixty boats to inspect the Neva mouth. On the evening of April 30 the bombardment began and on May 1 Kantsy surrendered and was renamed Slottborg [Castle Town]. But the next day in the evening the sentries reported that enemy ships were seen on the sea. On May 5 two Swedish ships, a schooner and a large boat approached the mouth of the Neva. Bombardier Captain Peter Mikhailov and Lieutenant Menshikov with both Guards regiments in thirty rowing boats stole up to the enemy ships, surrounded them and captured them, in spite of the fact that the Swedes had cannon and the Russians did not. There were about eighty men on the two ships. "But as the enemy yelled for mercy too late," wrote Peter to Apraksin, "it was very hard to restrain the soldiers who burst on board and stabbed nearly all of them; only thirteen remained alive. I dare to write that there were only eight boats. I congratulate your honor on this *unprecedented victory*."

Peter and company were overjoyed, like children when they first succeed at something or earn their first reward. "Two enemy ships taken! An unprecedented victory!" For this victory Bombardier Captain Peter Mikhailov and Lieutenant Menshikov were made knights of the Order of St. Andrew. In Voronezh they celebrated by doing battle with John Barleycorn, and John won the day.

Peter stood by the sea. Congratulating him on the capture of Nyenschanz or Slottborg, Vinius wrote that with this fort "a wide gateway to innumerable profits has opened up for you."

In the ninth century the great road from the Varangians to the Greeks began at the mouth of the Neva and it is with this route in the middle of that century that Russia began.[28] For eight and a half centuries Russia continued to venture east. It reached the eastern ocean, but in the end began to pine for the western sea where Russia was born, and returned to it in search of the means for its regeneration.

On May 16, 1703, on one of the small islands of the Neva estuary the sound of axes rang out as they built a wooden fort. This fort was *Pitersburkh*, the capital of the Russian empire.[29]

APPENDIX

MUSCOVITE RANKS IN THE SEVENTEENTH CENTURY

Below are listed, in descending order of precedence, the ranks (chiny) of the Muscovite upper and middle service class. All servitors in A, B and C held noble status, which entitled them to own land and serfs. No specific duties were linked to these ranks, although office evidently once was related to function, table attendant, for example. Frequently promotion to a given grade depended on clan status and an individual's seniority within his own clan, although there were examples of promotion of outsiders and on merit.

Servitors in grades A and B were mostly Moscow-based and performed a variety of military, civil and diplomatic duties as required, ranging from the highest military commands and chancellery offices filled mainly by boyars, of whom there were sixty three in 1693, to fairly menial ceremonial duties by the palace attendants, about 2,000 of the younger members of noble clans.

Holders of C grades, resident in the provinces, provided the backbone of junior command and troopers in the army. In the 1690s all these grades coexisted with the ranks of the "new model" infantry (general, major, lieutenant, etc.), a variety of foreign terms such as "admiral" and "generalissimus", and civilian ranks such as "councillor", all of which were direct designations of office.

The older ranks died out with their holders and in 1722 were superseded once and for all by Peter's Table of Ranks.

A. The Boyar Council

1 Boyar (boiarin)	3 Conciliar noble (dumnyi dvorianin)
2 Lord-in-waiting (okolnichii)	4 Conciliar secretary (dumnyi diak)

B. Moscow Nobles (non-boyar grades)

1 Table attendant (stolnik)	3 Moscow noble (dvorianin moskovskii)
2 Royal attendant (striapchii)	4 Palace attendant (zhilets)

The addition of the words "privy" or "close" (blizhnii) and "chamber" (komnatny) to some of the above grades—blizhnii boiarin, komnatnyi stolnik—denoted regular attendance on the tsar or other members of the royal family in person. Young men from noble clans also did duty as chamberlain (spalnik), gentleman of the bedchamber (postelnichii), carver (kravchii) and other functions.

C. **Provincial Nobles**
 1 Provincial servitor (dvorianin gorodovoi)
 2 Junior boyar (syn boiarskii; deti boiarskie (pl.))

Below A, B and C came the lower (sluzhilye liudi po priboru) non-noble service classes: clerks (podiachie), musketeers (streltsy), infantrymen (soldaty), dragoons (draguny), cavalrymen (reitary), artillerymen (pushkari), postal drivers (iamshchiki), free homesteaders (odnodvortsy) and others.

The English terms listed are the ones used in the Academic International Press edition of Soloviev's *History*. Scholars have yet to reach a consensus on standard usage. On this and related matters, see Richard Hellie, *Enserfment and Military Change in Muscovy* (Chicago, 1971) and R.O. Crummey, *Aristocrats and Servitors. The Boyar Elite in Russia, 1613-1689* (Princeton, 1983).

NOTES

Additional information on personalities and topics found in the text and notes is available in Joseph L. Wieczynski, ed., *The Modern Encyclopedia of Russian and Soviet History* (MERSH); Harry B. Weber, ed., *The Modern Encyclopedia of Russian and Soviet Literatures* (MERSL); Paul D. Steeves, ed., *The Modern Encyclopedia of Religions in Russia and the Soviet Union* (MERRSU); and David R. Jones, ed., *The Military-Naval Encyclopedia of Russia and the Soviet Union* (MNERSU).

For a comprehensive account of the period immediately preceding the era covered in this volume, see S.M. Soloviev, *History of Russia from Earliest Times*, Volume 25, *Rebellion and Reform, Fedor and Sophia, 1682-1689,* edited, translated and with an Introduction by Lindsey A.J. Hughes (Academic International Press, 1989) (Soloviev, Vol. 25), and Lindsey Hughes, *Sophia Regent of Russia, 1657-1704* (New Haven, 1990) (Hughes, *Sophia*).

CHAPTER I

1. According to legend, Romulus and his twin brother Remus, sons of the god Mars and Rhea the Vestal Virgin, were rescued by a shepherd after their wicked uncle tried to murder them, and raised by a wolf. Romulus is said to have founded Rome in 735 B.C. For analogies with Peter's early upbringing amid danger and hostility, see Soloviev, Vol. 25. Peter, of course, went on to found St. Petersburg, the new city of St. Peter and successor to Moscow, the "Third Rome."

2. Peter was born on May 30, 1672 and died on January 28, 1725. There are many studies of his life in English, but few of the reliable ones deal in much detail with the period covered by the present volume, 1689 to 1703. See in particular, M.S. Anderson, *Peter the Great* (London, 1978); J. Cracraft, ed., *Peter the Great Transforms Russia* (Lexington, 1991); B.H. Sumner, *Peter the Great and the Emergence of Russia* (London, 1951). R.K. Massie, *Peter the Great. His Life and World* (London, 1981) is a lengthy popular study.

3. See Soloviev, Vol. 25, p. 1.

4. Henry VIII, reigned 1509-1547, rejected papal supremacy in order to obtain a divorce from his first wife, and in 1534 assumed control of the Church of England.

5. In this passage, and subsequently, Soloviev refers to the *bogatyri*, strong men or epic warrior adventurers of early Russian legend, who

performed amazing feats of strength, rather in the manner of Hercules (a possible translation of the term). The song is probably one of the many *bylina*, early Russian epic tales in which the *bogatyri* figured.

6. Empress Catherine II, the Great, reigned 1762-1796. Her reign was remarkable for territorial conquests in Poland and on the Black Sea and for reform in the spirit of Enlightened Absolutism. She regarded herself as Peter I's "spiritual daughter." For extensive treatment of Catherine and her era see the relevant volumes in Soloviev's *History*.

7. Michael (Mikhail) Lomonosov (1711-1765) rose from peasant origins to become a scientist, inventor, poet, historian and grammarian. He founded Moscow University in 1755.

8. The Old Believers (starovery), also known as dissenters, schism-atics (raskolniki), and Old Ritualists (staroobriadtsy), were anathematized by the Russian Orthodox Church in 1666-1667 as a result of their rejection of the reforms of Patriarch Nikon, who sought to bring Russian Orthodox texts and rites back into line with the Greek. The Old Believers, led by Archpriest Avvakum, regarded the reforms as an arbitrary and foreign-influenced violation of cherished traditions, associating them with the coming of Antichrist and acceptance of heresy. In the 1680s both church and government persecuted the dissidents energetically, as Soloviev describes in Volume 25, but the movement continued to spread. See M. Cherniavsky, "The Old Believers and the New Religion," *Slavic Review* 25 (1966), pp. 1-39.

9. In pre-Petrine Russia the women of the aristocracy were hidden away from the male gaze in special chambers known as the terem. Royal women were especially closely guarded, going out heavily veiled in draped carriages and attending church in a curtained area. See N. Shields Kollmann, "On the Seclusion of Elite Muscovite Women," *Russian History*, 10 (1983), pp. 170-187. Tsarevna Sophia (see Note 10 below) defied these conventions when she became regent, participating in public ceremonies and receiving foreign ambassadors. Under Peter remaining restraints were swept away and all royal and noble women were required to appear in public in Western dress, although older customs survived in the provinces.

10. Tsarevna Sophia Alekseevna (1657-1704) was the fourth daughter (tsarevna, or tsar's daughter) of Tsar Alexis and his first wife, Maria Miloslavskaia. In May 1682 she came to the fore after her brother Tsar Fedor (see Note 12 below) died childless and a dispute arose about the rival claims to the throne of her handicapped brother Ivan and her nine-year-old half-brother Peter. At the end of May, following a rebellion by the musketeers, she became regent and Ivan and Peter co-tsars. Her rise to power and regency form the subject of Chapters II and III of Soloviev Vol. 25. There, as here, Soloviev often refers to Sophia as a female *bogatyr* (see Note 5 above) or warrior maiden, of which "Amazon" is an approximate

translation. For a modern biography of Sophia, see Lindsey Hughes, *Sophia Regent of Russia 1657-1704* (New Haven, 1990).

11. Tsar Alexis (Aleksei) Mikhailovich (born 1629, reigned 1645-1676) was the second Romanov tsar. On his reign, which saw serfdom confirmed in Russian law and the beginnings of significant Westernization, see P. Longworth, *Alexis, Tsar of All the Russias* (London, 1984) and J.T. Fuhrmann, *Tsar Alexis. His Reign and His Russia* (Academic International Press, 1978).

12. Tsar Fedor Alekseevich (born 1661, reigned 1676-1682) was the son of Tsar Alexis and his first wife Maria Miloslavskaia, therefore Peter's half-brother. His short reign saw war with Turkey and military and cultural reforms. Fedor himself was well educated and, although sickly, was not the helpless invalid sometimes portrayed in traditional histories. His reign forms the subject of Chapter I of Soloviev, Vol. 25. See also L. Hughes, MERSH, Vol. 11, pp. 77-79.

13. Natalia Naryshkina (1651-1694) was Tsar Alexis's second wife. They were married on January 22, 1671. Peter was their first child.

14. Artamon Sergeevich Matveev (1625-1682) was Tsaritsa Natalia's guardian and "benefactor." After a long service career, in 1670 he became a boyar and from 1671-1676 directed the Chancellery of Foreign Affairs and was close to the tsar. After Alexis's death the Miloslavskys, relatives of the tsar's first wife, had Matveev and members of Natalia Naryshkina's family banished. See Soloviev, Vol. 25, pp. 10-16. On Matveev, L. Hughes, MERSH, Vol. 12, pp. 142-44.

15. Nikita Moiseevich Zotov (1644-1717) continued to enjoy Peter's favor. On his role as "archbishop of Pressburg and patriarch of all the Yauza and Kokui" in Peter's All-Drunken Synod, see below, Chapter II, note 9. Later he served as privy councillor and president of the Privy Chancellery. See L. Hughes, MERSH, Vol. 36, pp. 128-130.

16. The musketeer rebellion of 1682 resulted in an amendment to the decision made on April 27 whereby Peter succeeded as Tsar Fedor's sole heir. Instead, the dual monarchy of Tsars Ivan and Peter under the regency of Tsarevna Sophia was created. The bloodiest events occurred on May 15-17 when Artamon Matveev (see Note 14 above) and other officials were hacked to pieces in front of Peter's eyes, the musketeers invaded the royal apartments and Peter's uncle Ivan Naryshkin was dragged off and tortured to death. See Soloviev, Vol. 25, Chapter II, and Hughes, *Sophia*, Chapter III. On the musketeers, see below, Note 39.

17. Simeon Polotsky (1628/29-1680), poet, theologian and publisher, was born Samuel Piotrowski Sitnianowisz in the Polish-ruled town of Polotsk (in present-day Belarus). Educated at the Kiev Mohyla Academy and possibly at the Jesuit college in Wilno, in 1656 he took monastic vows and in 1660 visited Moscow, when he read verses to the royal family. In

1663-1664 he settled permanently in Moscow and became tutor to Alexis's children, notably Alexis, Fedor and Sophia, instructing them in grammar, poetics, Polish and Latin. He also served as court poet, founded a school for government clerks, and towards the end of his life ran a small publishing operation. With his Polish "Latinist" background, he was regarded with suspicion by the Moscow church authorities, especially the patriarch. See L. Hughes, MERSH, Vol. 29, pp. 8-11.

18. Russia's two leading regiments of guards, the Preobrazhensky and the Semenovsky, had their origins in Peter's boyhood military games at the palace of Preobrazhenskoe and nearby village of Semenovskoe where Peter and his mother spent much of the period 1682-1689. Here he formed "mock" or "play" regiments—*poteshnye*—amongst the first recruits to which were stableboys and grooms—*poteshnye koniukhi*—who were trained by foreign officers. See D.L. Schlafly, "'Playmate Regiments' of Peter the Great," MERSH, Vol. 28, pp. 119-122.

19. Vladimir (Volodymyr) I (born about 956, prince of Kiev, 980-1015) is best known for his acceptance of Christianity from Byzantium and baptism of his people about 988. According to the Russian Primary Chronicle, in the "Tale of Bygone Years," from which the reference to drink is quoted, the pagan Vladimir first "tested" other faiths, including Islam, Judaism and Catholicism, but rejected them on various grounds in favor of Eastern Orthodoxy. The term "Rus" refers to the territory and Eastern Slavic peoples of the 9th-13th-century Kievan state over which Vladimir ruled, which incorporated much of what is now western Russia, Ukraine and Belarus. The notion of "all Rus" continues to excite controversy.

20. By the seventeenth century the office of royal carver (kravchii) was merely honorary. For a table of Muscovite ranks, see below pp. 275-276.

21. Boris Alekseevich Golitsyn (1654-1714) had acted as Peter's attendant or tutor (diadka). In 1687 he became director of the Chancellery of Kazan. Prince Vasily Vasilievich Golitsyn (1643-1714) was one of the outstanding seventeenth-century Russian statesmen. He was unusually well educated by Russian standards, with a taste for Western books and culture. Already prominent in Fedor's reign when he carried through the abolition of the Code of Precedence (see Note 64 below), in 1682 he rose to greater prominence as the regent Sophia's favorite. As director of the Chancellery of Foreign Affairs he negotiated the 1686 treaty of "permanent peace" with Poland, and led two unsuccessful campaigns against the Crimea. On his downfall, see below, pp. 33-35. His career during the regency is charted in Soloviev, Vol. 25. See also L.A.J. Hughes, *Russia and the West. The Life of a Seventeenth-century Westernizer, Prince V.V. Golitsyn, 1643-1714* (Newtonville, 1984).

22. Andrei Artamonovich Matveev (1666-1728) was the son of Artamon Sergeevich (see Note 14 above) and bitterly hostile to Tsarevna Sophia and

her circle on account of his father's murder in 1682. Under Peter, Matveev served as envoy to Holland, France, England (where an escapade resulted in the Act on Diplomatic Immunity) and Austria, and later as senator. His account of the 1682 rebellion, written towards the end of his life, was influential in blackening Sophia's reputation.

23. The source is the Frenchman Foy de la Neuville, who was in Russia in August-December 1689 as an agent of the king of Poland. His account of his journey, first published in French in 1698, appeared in English in 1699 under the title *An Account of Muscovy, as it was in the year 1689*. On Neuville's relations with Matveev, Golitsyn and others, see L. Hughes, "Russia in 1689," in L. Hughes, ed., *New Perspectives on Muscovite History* (London, 1993), pp. 177-187.

24. All given names in Russia have several diminutive forms (Boris— Boria, Boriska), which in the modern language are used by friends and family. In the period in question they often were used to express deference and subservience, be it a noble addressing the tsar or a peasant his master, and by superiors addressing or referring to inferiors. On patronymics as indicators of status, see Chapter II, Note 1.

25. Elizabeth (born 1709, empress of Russia 1740-1761) was the daughter of Peter I and his second wife Catherine. Peter Fedorovich, born 1728, was the son of Elizabeth's sister Anna, duchess of Holstein. In 1742 the childless Elizabeth brought Peter to Russia as her nominated heir. After her death in December 1761 he reigned for six months as Peter III before being overthrown by his wife, who ruled as Catherine II. The source of this story is Jacob Stählin (1709-1785), a German member of the Russian Academy of Sciences who collected and published dozens of "authentic anecdotes" from witnesses.

26. Peter's account is taken from his own preface to the *Maritime Regulation* of 1716, which gave his version of the pre-history of the Russian navy.

27. Prince Yakov Fedorovich Dolgoruky (1639-1720), who took Peter's side in 1682, was a veteran of military, court and diplomatic service. In 1700-1711 he was a prisoner of the Swedes. In 1712 he became a senator. On his unsuccessful embassy to France in 1687, see Soloviev, Vol. 25, pp. 203-205. Also G.E. Munro, MERSH, Vol. 9, pp. 204-207.

28. Franz Timmerman (? -1702) was a merchant who came to Moscow in the 1660s. See L. Hughes, MERSH, Vol. 39, pp. 61-63.

29. Carsten Brandt (? -1693) came to Russia in the 1660s to help build the ship "Eagle", which was destroyed by Stenka Razin. See Chapter III, p. 115. The little boat or dinghy (botik) became known as the "grandfather of the Russian navy." In the *Maritime Regulation* Peter dated its discovery to 1688. In 1722 the boat solemnly was transferred to St. Petersburg and in 1723 paraded before the fleet at Kronstadt. It is still preserved in the St. Petersburg Naval Museum.

30. Tsar Michael (Mikhail) Fedorovich (reigned 1613-1645) was the first Romanov tsar. The reference to " purging and pacification" is to the aftermath of the Time of Troubles (1598-1613) when the extinction of the Riurik line in 1598 and the election of Tsar Boris Godunov (1598-1605) gave rise to a series of pretenders to the Russian throne amidst civil disorders and foreign invasion, which ended with Michael's election.

31. The great Trinity-St. Sergius monastery, 45 miles northeast of Moscow in the present town of Sergiev Posad (formerly Zagorsk), was founded in 1345 by the most important Russian saint, Sergius of Radonezh. It was, and remains, a major place of pilgrimage. The tsars customarily visited the monastery for the feast of St. Sergius on September 25.

32. Evdokia Fedorovna Lopukhina (1669-1731) and Peter were married in Moscow on January 7, 1689. Evdokia and her family were said to be upholders of traditional Muscovite values, although in fact very little is known about Evdokia at this stage of her life. In 1699 (see Chapter V, pp. 184) she was banished to the convent of the Intercession in Suzdal and forced to take the veil as Elena. In 1718 she was transferred to the convent of the Dormition in Ladoga, but after the death of Catherine I, her successor as Peter's wife, in 1727, and the accession of her grandson Peter II, she was able to return to Moscow and play some part in politics. She is buried in the New convent.

33. Ivan Alekseevich (born 1666, reigned 1682-1696 as Ivan V) was the last son of Tsar Alexis's marriage to Maria Miloslavskaia. His disabilities included partial sight, limited mobility and a speech defect. Most Russian sources drew a discreet veil over his incapacity. In 1684 he was married to Praskovia Saltykova, a marriage which produced five daughters, one of whom reigned as Empress Anna (1730-1740). See Hughes, *Sophia*, pp. 91-95.

34. See L. Hughes, "Sophia, 'Autocrat of All the Russias,'" *Canadian Slavonic Papers*, 28 (1986), pp. 265-286. The translation of the term *samoderzhitsa* (the female equivalent of *samoderzhets*) as "autocrat" is subject to debate.

35. The tsarevnas were Anna and Tatiana, daughters of Tsar Michael, and Evdokia, Martha, Ekaterina, Maria and Feodosia, daughters of Alexis. Peter also had a younger sister Natalia (born 1673).

36. Lev Kirilliovich Naryshkin (1664-1705) was a younger brother of Tsaritsa Natalia. In 1690-1702 he headed the Chancellery of Foreign Affairs.

37. Fedor Leontievich Shaklovity (?-1689) was a man of humble origins whose career as a clerk began in the 1670s in Tsar Alexis's Privy Chancellery and continued in the important Chancellery of Crown Appointments (Razriad). He emerged as a supporter of Sophia in 1682, and later that year became head of the Chancellery of Musketeers. From then on he remained one of Sophia's closest advisers and, rumor would have

it, a rival of Vasily Golitsyn for her affections. See L.A.J. Hughes, MERSH, Vol. 34, pp. 146-148.

38. See above, Note 18.

39. The corps of musketeers (streltsy) was formed in the middle of the sixteenth century as the first regular infantry troops in Muscovy. By the late seventeenth century they numbered about twenty thousand. The musketeers lived in special garrisons, received wages, provisions and land from the government, and in peacetime engaged in small-scale trade and handicrafts. As well as waging war, they did guard, escort and fire-fighting duties. An elite corps of mounted troops provided a royal bodyguard. They were administered by a government department, the Chancellery of Musketeers (streletskii prikaz). As Soloviev recounts in Vol. 25, by the late seventeenth century the musketeers were beset by problems: their grievances included ill-treatment and exploitation by their officers, poor wages and terms of service, often on long and arduous campaigns. Many had turned to the Old Belief. In May 1682 the injustice apparently done to the "true tsar" Ivan, who was bypassed in favor of his younger half-brother, combined with resentment against unpopular officers to spark rebellion, which was to the advantage of Sophia's party. Unrest continued after the injustice to Ivan apparently was righted, when Prince Ivan Khovansky incited the musketeers to further rebellion. See L. Hughes, "Strel'tsy," MERSH, Vol. 37, pp. 205-210 and next note.

40. Prince Ivan Andreevich Khovansky (?-1682) began his career as a military commander in the reign of Tsar Michael. Under Tsar Alexis during the Russo-Polish war of 1654-67 he suffered several notable defeats and earned the nickname of the Braggart (Tararui). In 1682 he emerged from comparative obscurity (until 1680 he was much away from Moscow as a provincial governor) to take over the Chancellery of Musketeers in the wake of the May rebellion and fomented further revolt in the cause of the Old Believers. Sophia succeeded in isolating and then executing him and his son in September 1682. The troubles of that year are sometimes referred to, inaccurately, as the *Khovanshchina*. They form the subject of Chapter II of Soloviev, Vol. 25.

41. Before her marriage to Tsar Alexis, Natalia spent some time in Smolensk when her father Kirill Poluektovich served as a captain of the musketeers. Sandals woven from bast (bark strips, also used to make containers) were worn by peasants and poorer town inhabitants. Nonetheless, the Naryshkins belonged to the military servitor or service gentry class, from which the seventeenth-century Romanovs customarily selected their brides.

42. Silvester Medvedev (1641-1691) came to Moscow in 1665 and entered Simeon Polotsky's school for government clerks (see Note 17 above). Subsequently he took monastic vows and became Polotsky's

disciple and from 1680 his successor as court poet and publisher. Like his teacher, he clashed with the conservative Patriarch Joachim (see Note 54 below), and in the 1680s headed a "Latinist" group of churchmen who tended towards Catholic interpretations of such matters as transubstantiation. He was a supporter of Sophia, to whom he composed eulogistic verses. See L. Hughes, MERSH, Vol. 21, pp. 181-182.

43. The reference is to the words spoken by the priest during the communion service. Arguments had raged over elements of ritual, such as order of service, since the beginning of the schism in the 1650s, among laymen as well as churchmen. Even the most insignificant changes could be regarded as heresy.

44. On July 5, 1682 a "debate" between Orthodox prelates and Old Believer leaders on matters of the Old and New beliefs, initiated by Prince Ivan Khovansky with some of the musketeers' support, took place in the Kremlin. On this occasion the patriarch won the day, with Sophia's backing. The schismatics lost face and their leaders were arrested and executed. See Soloviev, Vol. 25, pp. 128-134.

45. From the beginning of her regency Sophia disregarded the tradition of female seclusion and regularly was seen in public at state and church ceremonies. (See Note 34 above). July 8 was the feast of the wonder-working icon of Our Lady of Kazan, associated with the capture of the Tatar stronghold of Kazan in 1552, and hence of relevance to Vasily Golitsyn's "victory" (as Sophia termed it) against the Crimean Tatars in the summer of 1689.

46. One of Soloviev's chief sources for the events of August-September 1689 is the diary of the Scottish mercenary General Patrick Gordon (1635-1699), who entered Russian service in 1661. He was to remain in Russia, with brief visits to Scotland, for the rest of his life and in the 1690s was one of Peter's closest companions. Only parts of the original diary, which is in the Military Historical Archive in Moscow, have been published. See *Passages from the Diary of General Patrick Gordon of Auchleuchries in the Years 1635-1699* (London, 1859). Soloviev consulted a German-published translation. On Gordon, see P. Dukes, "How the Eighteenth Century began in Russia and the West," *Russia and the West in the Eighteenth Century* (Newtonville, 1983), pp. 2-19.

47. In 1686 Golitsyn signed a treaty of "permanent peace" with Poland by which Russia pledged to contribute to the war effort of the Holy League against the Turks in return for the permanent cession of Kiev and its district, which was assigned only temporarily to Russia by the 1667 Treaty of Andrusovo. The new treaty involved Russia in two inconclusive campaigns in the south against the Crimean Tatars, the first in 1687, the second in 1689. In 1689 food and water shortages forced Golitsyn to sign a truce and retreat, but Russian success in a few skirmishes allowed Sophia to proclaim

a Russian victory, to which Peter and his circle objected. See Soloviev, Vol. 25, pp. 197-202.

48. The New convent (Novodevichy monastyr) was founded by Tsar Vasily III in 1524 just a few miles to the south of the Kremlin on the Moscow river. Many of the nuns came from royal and noble families. The cathedral of Our Lady of Smolensk dates from the convent's foundation, but most of its churches and dwellings were commissioned by Sophia in the 1680s in Moscow Baroque style. See Hughes, *Sophia*, pp. 152-154.

49. Probably Fedor Fedorovich Pleshcheev, who later was a member of Peter's "jolly company." He accompanied Peter as a volunteer apprentice ship-builder on the grand embassy (see Chapter IV below).

50. Gavrila Ivanovich Golovkin (1660-1730) was a chamberlain in Peter's youth and later the tsar's companion on most of his trips abroad. He subsequently became chancellor, from 1706 heading the Chancellery (from 1718 College) of Foreign Affairs.

51. Ivan Eliseevich Tsykler later turned against Peter, as Soloviev describes in Chapter IV, pp. 142-148.

52. Ivan Borisovich Troekurov (?-1703) was a leading boyar who headed several government departments in the 1670s-1680s, including the Chancellery of Crown Appointments (1682-1689), and subsequently took over the Chancellery of Musketeers.

53. Peter Ivanovich Prozorovsky (1633-1713?) subsequently became director of the Chancelleries of the Royal Treasury and the Exchequer.

54. Joachim (secular name Ivan Savelov) took monastic vows in 1655 and rose to prominence under Patriarch Nikon. He became patriarch in 1674. By all accounts a semi-literate and narrow-minded conservative, he evidently found it hard to reconcile himself to a female ruler. In addition, he strongly opposed the admission of Jesuits to Moscow under the terms of the agreement with the Holy League, condemned the employment of foreign officers in the Russian army and resented the influence of the "Latinizer" Medvedev on the government.

55. The identity of this particular Buturlin is not specified. It was probably Ivan Ivanovich Buturlin the Elder (1661-1738) who served Peter as chamberlain and personal attendant and was a founder member of the Preobrazhensky Guards. He was captured by the Swedes at the battle of Narva in 1700, returning to Russia only in 1710 when he resumed a successful military career and ended the war as a general. After Peter's death he was disgraced and demoted for opposition to Alexander Menshikov.

56. In the Old Russian calendar New Year's Day was celebrated on September 1 and years were numbered according to the Orthodox computation from the notional creation of the world. Thus September 1, 1689 was the beginning of the year 7198. Both these practices were ended

by Peter, who decreed that January 1, 1700 be celebrated in Russia as the beginning of the new century. He did not adopt the New Style (Gregorian) calendar, which was then in use in most of Catholic Europe. In the seventeenth century it was ten days ahead of the Old Style (Julian) calendar then used in the Orthodox world and most Protestant countries, including England.

57. Patrick Gordon. See Note 46 above.

58. The 1686 treaty with Poland. See Note 47 above.

59. The Moscow Foreign Quarter, *nemetskaia sloboda*, or literally "German Quarter" after the Muscovite practice of referring indiscriminately to Northern Europeans as "Germans," was founded in 1652 on the Yauza river as the residence of foreign military personnel, craftsmen and merchants serving in Moscow. The original intention was to separate "heretics" from Russians, but by Peter's time barriers were breaking down. It was to the Quarter that Peter was to turn for his first foreign friends and advisers and his first foreign mistress. See S. Baron, "The Origins of 17th-century Moscow's Nemeckaja sloboda," *California Slavic Studies*, 5 (1970), pp. 1-18.

60. One of Golitsyn's titles was guardian or protector (oberegatel) of the royal seal.

61. See Note 59 above.

62. See Note 16 above.

63. All these men served with Golitsyn in the Crimea. Leonty Nepliuev was active in the Ukraine in the 1680s (see Soloviev, Vol. 25). Emelian Ukraintsev (1641-1708), a diplomatic specialist, spent most of his career in the Chancellery of Foreign Affairs, acting as its director from 1689-1699. In 1700 he helped negotiate the peace with Turkey. See below, Chapter VI, pp. 226-228, and L. Hughes, MERSH, Vol. 40, pp. 174-177.

64. The Code of Precedence or "place system" (mestnichestvo), which originated in the sixteenth century, regulated military ranks, to a lesser extent civil and court appointments, and on occasions social rankings, such as seating at banquets, on the basis of the previous service record of the candidate and members of his clan, the candidate's place within his own clan's hierarchy and the standing of his clan in relation to others. It was considered a serious slight to family honor to accept a ranking below someone who was inferior according to the complex computations of the Code, and anyone thus slighted was obliged to submit an appeal. See entry by Hugh Graham in MERSH, Vol. 22, pp. 8-13, and N. Shields Kollmann, "Ritual and Social Drama at the Muscovite Court," *Slavic Review*, 45(1986), pp. 486-502. The Code was abolished in January 1682 with the approval of Tsar Fedor. For Soloviev's account, see Vol. 25, pp. 83-89

65. Pustozersk (which roughly translated means "barren lake") was situated on the estuary of the Pechora river where it enters the White Sea opposite Novaia Zemlia. Founded in 1499, its remoteness and the harshness

of its climate made it an ideal place for a penal colony. Earlier famous
detainees included Archpriest Avvakum and A.S. Matveev.

66. It seems that the family may never have reached Pustozersk. In
Pinega, in Archangel province, by the 1700s they were able to live fairly
comfortably, even entertaining visiting friends and relatives, but Peter never
again called on the talented man's services. Golitsyn died and was buried
in Pinega in 1714. See L. Hughes, *Russia and the West*, pp. 79-84. After
his death his wife and son Alexis (who had "lost his wits") were released
from exile.

67. In Russian, *Leshii Medved*. "Leshy", the adjective from the Russian
les (forest), is a translation of Silvester (Latin "silvestris": belonging to
woods). *Medved* is the Russian for "bear."

68. On the controversy over transubstantiation and Medvedev's treatise
Manna, which allegedly gave a Catholic interpretation, see Vol. 25, pp.
227-231.

69. Ivan Stepanovich Mazepa (1639?-1709) is one of the best-known
figures in Ukrainian history. He was educated in Germany, Italy and France,
returning to Ukraine in 1663 to serve under Right Bank Hetman
Doroshenko. In 1674 he transferred his allegiance to Hetman Ivan
Samoilovich. On the struggle between the hetmans of Right and Left Bank
Ukraine, see Soloviev, Vol. 25, passim. When Samoilovich was deposed
following accusations of treason during the first Crimean campaign in 1687,
Mazepa succeeded him, apparently not without the help of a "gift" to Prince
Vasily Golitsyn. As is clear from what follows later in this volume, Mazepa
was a difficult and controversial character, who continued to waver between
Poland, Russia and even Turkey. In 1708 he rebelled by joining Charles
XII against Russia, but was forced to flee to Moldavia after Peter's victory
at Poltava in 1709. See entry by J. Cracraft in MERSH, Vol. 21, pp. 150-
154 and T. Mackiv, *English Reports on Mazepa, 1687-1709* (New York,
1983).

70. This chronicle, "A Short Account of the Years 1682, 1683 and
1684, and What Occurred in the Realm During Them" remains one of the
chief sources for the early part of Sophia's regency. There is no translation.

71. Holy fools or "fools in Christ" (iurodivye) were a common
phenomenon in Muscovite Russia and later. Simple-minded pilgrims, they
were credited with the gift of prophesy and it was deemed a duty to feed
them. One of the best known in the West—the Simpleton—appears in
Mussorgsky's opera Boris Godunov.

72. Several portraits of Sophia were painted and engraved, the best
known made in Amsterdam about 1689 with allegorical figures representing
magnanimity, generosity, piety, prudence, chastity, justice and faith. They
sometimes are called "coronation" portraits as they depict Sophia in royal
regalia. See Hughes, *Sophia* , pp.139-145.

73. This letter, dated between September 8-12, was not in Peter's hand. It was almost certainly dictated by Peter's advisers.

74. The monastery of St. Cyril (Kirillo-Beloozerskii monastyr) was founded in 1397 on the shore of Lake Sivensky in Novgorod province. By the seventeenth century it was one of the richest and most powerful of Russian monasteries, a place of pilgrimage and detention.

75. The rich and influential Solovetsk monastery was founded on one of the islands of the Solovki group on the White Sea in 1430. It was a center of Old Believer resistance but was returned to the church after a long siege in 1676.

76. The Kazan Chancellery administered the lands and affairs of Kazan region. In fact, Golitsyn had been its director since 1687.

77. Tikhon Streshnev (1644-1719) was related to Peter by marriage through the tsar's paternal grandmother, Evdokia Lukianovna Streshneva, wife of Tsar Michael. Peter usually addressed him as "father" and he was one of the few boyars allowed to keep his beard when Peter made shaving compulsory in 1698 (see below, p. 178). He remained influential until his death, becoming one of the first senators in 1711.

78. See Note 30 above. Dmitry the Pretender, or False Dmitry I, ruled 1605-1606. He claimed to be Dmitry the son of Ivan IV who was killed under somewhat dubious circumstances in 1591. Dmitry was viewed by many as a tool of both the Poles and the Pope. On his brief reign, see Soloviev, Vol. 14, edited and translated by G.E. Orchard. Prince Andrei Vasilievich Golitsyn was murdered by the Poles.

79. Clan solidarity amongst the boyar class meant that insults must be contested and that those found guilty of disrespect pay an appropriate fine. Compare appeal procedures in the former Code of Precedence (see Note 64 above), which dealt with "insulting" appointments.

80. Franz Jacob (Frants Yakovlevich) Lefort (1659-1699), a native of Geneva, came to Moscow in 1676. In 1678 he entered the tsar's service, fighting in the Ukraine and the Crimean campaigns of 1687 and 1689 when he was close to Prince Vasily Golitsyn and therefore unlikely to have been a member of Peter's circle. He came to prominence in the 1690s, when he was Peter's inseparable companion. He was promoted to full general in 1693, admiral in 1695, chief ambassador of the grand embassy in 1697. He died of a fever in March 1699.

81. Soloviev's source is the British engineer John Perry, who worked in Russia on a canal project. See his *The State of Russia under the Present Czar* (London, 1716, reprinted London, 1967).

82. Kokui was a crude name for the Foreign Quarter. The patriarch of Kokui, one of the names for the mock ecclesiastical office held by Zotov (see note 15 above) until his death in 1717, was a leading member of Peter's All-Drunken Synod. On the latter, see below, Chapter II, Note 9.

CHAPTER II

1. Fedor Yurievich Romodanovsky (1640-1717) served as attendant in Peter's household. In the 1680s he became head of the Preobrazhensky Chancellery, which oversaw Peter's play troops and developed its own department to investigate political crimes. He became mock tsar or "Prince-Caesar" and was addressed by Peter as "your majesty." See G. Munro, MERSH, Vol. 31, pp. 153-156.

2. Peter regularly adopted a "commoner's" name and identity, in this case taking the surname Alekseev derived from his patronymic Alekseevich, "son of Alexis." On the grand embassy of 1697-1698 (see below) he traveled incognito as Peter Mikhailov. In both cases the absence of patronymic (father's name) was an indication of allegedly non-noble origins.

3. See R.H. Warner, "The Kozuchovo Campaign of 1697," *Jahrbücher für Geschichte Osteuropas*, Vol. 13(1965), pp. 487-496. The Simonov monastery is to the southeast of Moscow near the Moscow river.

4. Fedor Matveevich Apraksin (1661-1728), later count and admiral of the Russian navy, was the brother of Tsaritsa Martha Matveevna (second wife of the late Tsar Fedor). He was one of Peter closest friends and drinking companions.

5. F.Yu. Romodanovsky, F.F. Pleshcheev, T.N. Streshnev, F.M. Apraksin, G.I. Golovkin, N.I. Repnin, I.I. Buturlin, A.A. Matveev, F.A. Golovin appear elsewhere in this volume and are footnoted accordingly. See index. Soloviev does not specify which Trubetskoy he had in mind; both Ivan Yurievich (?-1750) and Yury Yurievich (1668-1739) served as chamberlains to Peter in the 1670s. The former served in the Preobrazhensky Guards and later reached the rank of general-fieldmarshal. The Kurakin mentioned is probably Prince Boris Ivanovich (1676-1727), who was in Peter's entourage in his boyhood and later had a successful diplomatic career. His *History of Tsar Peter Alekseevich and his Close Associates*, written in the 1720s but not published in Russian until 1890 (there is no English translation), is an important source for the 1680s-1690s. The author was highly critical of many of the tsar's "associates."

6. The four examples given were all "Russified" foreigners. Soloviev gives further details of the career of Andrei Vinius (1641-1717), who figures prominently in the present volume, below. See also J. Wieczynski, MERSH, Vol. 42, pp. 108-110. Adam Adamovich Weide (1667-1720) began his military career in Peter's play regiments. He was a prisoner of the Swedes in 1700-1710. Andrei Yurievich Krevet or Crevet (Andrew Craft) was a translator in the Chancellery of Foreign Affairs with whom Peter often corresponded. James Bruce (Yakov Vilimovich Brius) (1670-1735) was of Scottish origin. He became senator, director of the Departments of Mines and Manufacture (1717), translator and printer as well as pursuing a military career.

7. Peter Pavlovich Shafirov (1669-1739), a converted Jew, rose to power later in Peter's reign. See G. Munro, MERSH, Vol. 34, pp. 122-126.

8. The Russian Barleycorn, the personification of inebriation, is Ivan (Ivashka) Khmelnitsky (from "hops"), the "nephew" of Bacchus (Dionysus), Greek god of wine and intoxicating herbs.

9. The ancient custom of "slavlenie," roughly the equivalent of English carol-singing, in which the performers were rewarded and entertained by those they visited. Like many Russian customs, it combined pagan and Christian elements. On the All-Drunken, All-Jesting Synod, see R. Zguta, "Peter I's 'Most Drunken Synod of Fools and Jesters'," *Jahrbücher für Geschichte Osteuropas*, 21 (1973), pp. 18-21.

10. See Chapter I, Note 41.

11. Peter's son Alexis, by his first wife Evdokia, was born in February 1690. On his later career and tragic end in 1718, see R.Crummey, MERSH, Vol. 1, pp. 120-123.

12. Wife of the so-called prince of Macedonia, a Greek in the service of the tsar.

13. Tsar Alexis's Code of Laws (Sobornoe Ulozhenie) of 1649, consisting of 967 articles, remained the basic Russian statute until the 1830s. Its clauses included the final confirmation of serfdom. See R. Hellie, trans. and ed. *The Russian Law Code (Ulozhenie) of 1649*, 2 vols. (Irvine, Col., 1984-1985).

14. Solvychegodsk, in Archangel province, was a center of salt-mining, the domain of the Stroganov family of merchants and entrepreneurs, who later were made counts.

15. Archbishop Lazar Baranovich of Chernigov (ca. 1620-1693) was the author of many literary and theological works, and from 1650 to 1657 rector of the Kiev Academy. He and other educated members of the Ukrainian clergy were regarded with suspicion by the Moscow Orthodox hierarchy on account of their "Latin" (i.e. Catholic) tendencies.

16. As a result of the 1686 treaty of permanent peace with Poland and rapprochement with Poland's ally Austria, Golitsyn gave permission for Jesuit fathers to come to Moscow to officiate for the small community of foreign Catholics, who long were denied resident pastors.

17. One of these priests, the Bohemian Father Georgius David, left an account of his time in Moscow, and of the expulsion of himself and his companion Father Tobias Tichavsky in 1689. See *Status Modernus Magnae Russiae seu Moskoviae* , ed. A.V. Florovskij (The Hague, 1965).

18. Russian has specific terms for non-Orthodox places of Christian worship: "kostel" for a Catholic church, "kirka" for a Protestant one. "Tserkov" is reserved for Orthodox churches, as at the end of Joachim's tirade.

19. Adrian (1627-1700) was archimandrite of the important monastery of the Miracles in the Kremlin. He was to be the last of the patriarchs until the restoration of the office in the twentieth century.

20. Soloviev uses the term "shevkal" both to denote the man's title (chieftain, shah) and capitalized as his name: Shevkal. His territory was in present-day Daghestan, on the west coast of the Caspian Sea.

21. During the church reforms of the 1650s Russian Orthodox Christians were ordered to make the sign of the cross with three fingers rather than two. This symbolic change was one of the Old Believers' greatest grievances. See Chapter I, Note 8.

22. The four-pointed crucifix was regarded by Old Believers as Latin and heretical. The Orthodox cross, which has head and foot-rests, was eight-pointed.

23. Alexis was metropolitan of Moscow in 1354-1378 and a powerful political figure. His feast is on 12 February (Old style).

24. The Likhud brothers, Ioanniky (1643-1717) and Sofrony (1652-1730), came to Moscow in 1685, and were the founders of the Slavic-Greek Latin Academy, founded in Moscow in 1687. On the Academy, see Soloviev, Vol. 25, pp. 229-231.

25. The Moscow Typography or Printing Press, which until the beginning of the eighteenth century published almost exclusively religious literature, had a small school attached to it.

26. This is a continuation of Soloviev's analysis of Ukrainian affairs in Vol. 25. By the "Russian territories under Polish rule" Soloviev has in mind Right Bank Ukraine, west of the Dnieper (although it should be noted that the Russian Left Bank hetman referred to himself as hetman "of both banks of the Dnieper") and Belarus (Belorussia or White Russia) in the grand duchy of Lithuania. For a modern analysis of this period, see O. Subtelny, *Ukraine: A History* (Toronto, 1988).

27. On the Crimean campaign of 1689, see Soloviev, Vol. 25, pp. 197-202.

28. See Note 69 above.

29. Raicha seems to have been a notorious trouble-maker. On previous escapades, see Soloviev, Vol. 25, pp. 33-34.

30. Prince Yury was the son of Metropolitan Gedeon of Kiev, the former Prince Gedeon Sviatopolk-Chetvertinsky (?-1690), who was consecrated in 1685.

31. Ivan Samoilovich (? -1690), the son of a priest (hence the nickname Popovich, from "pop" [priest]) became Left Bank hetman in 1672 and was deposed in 1687. See Soloviev, Vol. 25, pp. 184-193; L. Hughes, MERSH, Vol. 33, pp. 76-79.

32. Jan (John) III Sobieski (1629-1696) ascended the elective throne of Poland in 1674. His most famous exploit was the relief of besieged Vienna in 1683. On his reign, and the Polish background in general, see

N. Davies, *God's Playground. A History of Poland*, Vol. I, (Oxford, 1981), pp. 472-491.

33. Zaporozhie or the Zaporozhian Camp (Sech, Sich), the stronghold of the Zaporozhian Cossacks and their chief or ataman, was situated on islands above the Dnieper rapids near the present-day town of the same name. Under the 1667 Russo-Polish Treaty of Andrusovo the Camp came under the protectorship of Moscow, but the Zaporozhians clung fiercely to their freedoms, which included exploitation rights along the river, and continued to offer allegiance and fighting power as it suited them. To confuse matters, the title Zaporozhian Host (voisko) is used to refer to the whole cossack army of Ukraine. See next note.

34. The town-registered cossacks formed the regular units of the main Ukrainian cossack army (host), whose commander was the hetman of the Ukraine (at that time Mazepa), who in turn received his orders from Moscow. The "free" cossacks of Zaporozhie deliberately kept apart from these less independent brethren.

35. The crown hetman was the commander of the Polish king's army.

36. The reference is to former Hetman Samoilovich (see Note 31) who was banished to Siberia in 1687.

37. The efimok (Polish: joachymik) was the Russian name for the foreign silver coin, the Joachimsthaler, from which Russians minted silver coin by overstriking. The native silver minted coinage was introduced by Peter I at the beginning of the eighteenth century.

38. John (Jan II Kazimierz) Casimir, king of Poland, 1648-1668.

39. On Orthodox Bishop Shumliansky's earlier exploits, see Soloviev, Vol. 25, pp. 150 ff. Lvov (Lwów, Lemburg) was in Polish Ukraine.

40. See Chapter I, Note 56.

41. Podolia, Galicia and Volhynia were in Poland, but in the 1670s parts came temporarily under Turkish rule.

42. The Uniate or Greek Catholic church was created by the Brest union of 1596. Most Orthodox believers in Polish territories accepted the Pope and Catholic dogma whilst retaining the Orthodox rites and icons, although some held out (see Note 64 below) and others (like Shumliansky) wavered in their allegiance according to the political tide.

43. The rank of table attendant (stolnik) was the highest of the non-boyar ranks of the Muscovite nobility. (See chart on pp. 275-276) Originally bearers of the title served at the tsar's table, but by the period in question they performed mainly military duties. They were based in or near Moscow.

44. Semyon Paley (Palij) (1640s-1710), whose real name was Hurko, went to Zaporozhie in the 1670s and crossed to the Right Bank in 1685.

45. See Note 42 above.

46. Sables, and other small animal furs, were counted in units of forty (sorok) pelts.

47. That is, the Russo-Turkish Treaty of Bakhchisarai of 1681. See Soloviev, Vol. 25, p. 60.

48. France traditionally acted as the protector of Turkey against its arch-enemy, the Habsburgs.

49. In other words, Kochubey had transferred his allegiance from the Right Bank (Polish) cossack hetman, Peter Doroshenko (Hetman, 1665-1676), to the Left Bank (Russian) Hetman, Samoilovich.

50. The reference is to the cossack hetman Bogdan Khmelnitsky (1595-1657), who transferred Ukraine to Muscovite rule in 1654, but previously had agreements with the Tatars, although it might equally be to his son Yury, who gained the backing of the Turks as Ukrainian hetman after the surrender of Doroshenko to Moscow in 1676, but failed to secure his position and eventually was executed by the Turks in 1685.

51. Bogdan Khmelnitsky. See previous note.

52. The complaints here express concern about growing "class" conflict between the cossack landlords and the ordinary cossacks and peasants whom they were enserfing. Previously notions of equality had reigned in the Ukraine.

53. The question marks are Soloviev's.

54. A reference to the campaigns against Turkey in 1677-1678 when the Russians evacuated Chigirin on the Dnieper.

55. Both Demian Mnogogreshny (?-ca.1696), hetman from 1662-1672, and Ivan Samoilovich ("Popovich" because he was the son of a priest) were exiled to Siberia.

56. Stefan Czarniecki (1599-1665), field hetman of Poland, was a commander during the Russo-Polish war of 1654-1667.

57. Literally, Stone Weir.

58. Boris Petrovich Sheremetev (1652-1719), later field marshal and count, was one of Peter I's outstanding commanders, winning many victories in the Baltic during the Great Northern War. He had travelled abroad, to Poland and Austria as a diplomat in the 1680s and on a private visit to Europe in 1697, hence his reputation as a "Westernizer".

59. See above, Note 52.

60. Ivan Serko (?-1680) was commander (ataman) of the Zaporozhian Camp from 1663-1680, during which time he made many changes of allegiance.

61. Tsar Alexis was at first reluctant to accept Khmelnitsky's allegiance and referred the matter to an Assembly of the Land. See above, Note 50.

62. That is, to become a Uniate.

63. This is a reference to the Polish *liberum veto*, whereby any individual qualified to attend the Sejm (parliament) could challenge any decision, halt proceedings and veto action by declaring "I deny" or "I won't allow it."

64. The Orthodox brethren or fraternities were formed in response to the 1596 Union of Brest (see Note 42 above). Their activities included the founding of schools and support to Orthodox monasteries, churches and clergy.

65. The powerful Sapieha clan more or less ruled Lithuania from the 1680s onwards, and were continually at odds with the Polish king.

66. Artamon Matveev. See Chapter I, Note 14.

67. Before he became king in 1674 Sobieski was field hetman from 1666 and from 1668 grand crown hetman or commander-in-chief of the Polish army. He was born near Lvov.

68. A reference to visits by French Jesuits in 1689? See Soloviev, Vol. 25, p. 205.

69. A reference to the restoration of Smolensk by Poland to Muscovy in 1632.

70. The articles of the 1654 Treaty of Pereiaslavl between Bogdan Khmelnitsky and the Muscovite tsar, by which the latter became ruler of Ukraine.

CHAPTER III

1. The Don Cossack Stepan (Stenka) Razin led a major rebellion against the authorities in 1670-1671. Before declaring war on Moscow and the landowners, he earned notoriety for his daring raids on merchants along the lower Volga and on the Caspian Sea. The ship, the *Eagle* (Orel), was destroyed in 1669.

2. Russia's allies in the Holy League, which it joined in 1686, were Poland, Austria and Venice.

3. On Mazepa and Zaporozhie, see Chapter I, Note 69 and Chapter II, Note 33.

4. Dositheus, patriarch of Jerusalem 1669-1707, was one of the leading Orthodox churchmen of his era. As a subject of the Muslim sultan he was in a delicate political position, which is why his intervention was unexpected.

5. Vasily Golitsyn's campaigns against the Crimea in 1687 and 1689 failed to conquer or constrain the Tatars, who subsequently were able to aid the Turks. See Chapter I, Note 47.

6. Nicholas (Nikolay) Spafarius-Milescu (1636?-1708) was a native of Moldavia who settled permanently in Russia in 1671. He worked in the Chancellery of Foreign Affairs as interpreter and envoy, and in the latter years of his career advised Peter I on eastern affairs. See C.M. Foust, MERSH, Vol. 37, pp. 20-24.

7. See Chapter I, p. 46.

8. Letter to F.M. Apraksin, April 16, 1695.

9. The cavalry of noble military servitors *(dvorianskaia konnitsa)* was a levy of irregular troops mounted and equipped for military service on a given campaign. It was "old" insofar as it was in the process of being replaced by regular units of foreign-trained infantry, the "new model" forces described in the next line. See J. Keep, *Soldiers of the Tsar* (Oxford, 1985); R. Hellie, "The Petrine Army. Continuity, Change and Impact," *Canadian-American Slavic Studies*, VIII (1974), pp. 237-254.

10. The term "courtiers" *(tsaredvortsy)* in this instance refers to non-boyar servitors (from table attendant down) resident in Moscow. See Appendix, pp. 275-276).

11. Peter was a deacon in the All-Jesting, All-Drunken Synod. On this, see Chapter II, note 9.

12. Min Her Kenich [Dutch: *Mijn Heer Koning*, My lord the king] is one of many examples of Peter's use of foreign forms of address, in Latin script and usually misspelt, in his letters to friends and associates. He often signed his own name "Piter," as in the letter to Vinius referred to next. On Romodanovsky, see Chapter II, Note 1.

13. Soloviev consulted these and others of Peter's letters in the State Archive. Volume I of the monumental *Letters and Papers of Peter I* (materials to 1701) was published in St. Petersburg in 1887. At present the publication has reached Volume 13 and the year 1713 (published 1993). There is no consolidated edition of Peter's letters in English, although individual documents have been translated.

14. See Chapter I, Note 8.

15. St. Sergius Town (Novosergievsky gorod) was named after St. Sergius of Radonezh. See Chapter I, Note 31.

16. On Patriarch Joachim (died 1690) see Chapter I, Note 54.

17. On Tsar Ivan V Alekseevich (born 1666), see Chapter I, Note 33. At the onset of their joint rule in 1682, Ivan, the elder, was designated "first" tsar.

18. Boris Golitsyn's estate near Moscow.

19. The Lithuanian campaign of 1654-1656 opened the Thirteen Years War against Poland, which was provoked by Moscow's annexation of Ukraine. Tsar Alexis captured Smolensk and most of the major towns of Belarus, but subsequently the latter had to be returned to Poland. The Turks destroyed Chigirin in 1678.

20. For further details, see Volume 17 of this series.

21. King John III Sobieski (see Chapter II, Note 32) died on April 17 (New Style) 1696.

22. In the Polish context Ruthenia *(Rus)* and Ruthenian *(ruski)* were used in reference to parts of the Belorussian and Ukrainian-speaking lands of the Commonwealth. A palatine *(wojewoda)* was a regional official appointed by the king.

23. As yet Russia did not maintain permanent accredited ambassadors and embassies abroad, but several cities, including Warsaw, had a more or less permanent Russian resident envoy *(rezident)*.

24. This may be a reference to Sobieski's first victory over the Turks in 1673 and lifting of the siege of Vienna in 1683.

25. The throne of Poland was elective. After the death of a king a convocational Sejm prepared for the election of his successor. The electoral Sejm met to confirm the new king's contract. In fact, the matter was not decided until summer 1697, after Sobieski's son Jakub was forced to withdraw his candidacy and Frederick of Saxony grabbed the throne from the prince of Conti and became Augustus II. See below, p. 220.

26. Native tribesmen, who provided auxiliary fighting forces.

27. Fifth and tenth money was a levy of one fifth and one tenth of the income of townsmen and merchants to contribute to the cost of military campaigns.

28. This piece of information comes from the diary of Patrick Gordon. See Chapter I, Note 46.

29. Tsar Boris Godunov reigned 1598-1605. One of the young men ended up as an Anglican vicar in Huntingdon, England. See Volumes 14 -16 of this series.

30. An extract from the *Maritime Regulation* (1716).

CHAPTER IV

1. Saint Olga (ca. 890-969), widow of Prince Igor of Kiev and grandmother of Vladimir I, was baptized into the Orthodox faith in Constantinople in about 957. See Volume 1 of this series.

2. See Chapter I, pp. 12-13.

3. On the grand embassy *(velikoe posolstvo)* see P. Petschauer, MERSH, Vol. 13, pp. 96-98.

4. Like many of Peter's associates F.A. Golovin (1650-1706) started his career as a personal attendant in the palace. He negotiated the Treaty of Nerchinsk with China in 1689 (see Soloviev, Vol. 25, pp. 207 ff.) and in the crucial period from 1699 until his death directed the Chancellery of Foreign Affairs.

5. The word Soloviev uses is *kormlenshchik,* the term for a provincial official acting under the old system of supporting or "feeding" himself from the region under his control, often with extortion and bribery.

6. The Miloslavskys were the maternal relatives of Maria Miloslavskaia, mother of the regent Sophia Alekseevna who, of course, lost all their remaining influence when Sophia was ousted in 1689.

7. Tsaritsa Evdokia gave birth to sons Alexis in 1690 and Alexander in 1691. The latter died in 1692. Some books list a third son, Paul, but his birth and death (allegedly in 1693) are not mentioned in official records.

8. This may refer to the amateur theater organized by Tsaritsa Praskovia Fedorovna in her residence at Izmailovo. Vasily Sokovnin was the son of Alexis Sokovnin, who was involved in the Tsykler plot.

9. Ivan Tikhonovich Pososhkov (1652-1726) is best known for his *Book on Scarcity and Wealth* (1724), a memorandum intended for Peter I, which earned him the retrospective title of "the Russian Adam Smith." His family were settled on crown estates, where they paid quit-rent *(obrok)* and worked as craftsmen. See L. Hughes, MERSH, Vol. 29, pp. 100-106.

10. See Soloviev, Vol. 25, p. 101, 107.

11. Feodosia Prokopievna Morozova (1639?-1675) was married to G.I. Morozov, brother of Tsar Alexis's favorite B.I. Morozov. In the 1650s-1660s she came under the influence of the Old Believer leader Archpriest Avvakum, whom she sheltered along with other religious dissidents. In 1671 she was imprisoned but refused to accept the revised service books and rituals. She died of starvation in the Panfutiev monastery in Borovsk. Urusova was her sister. See G.E. Orchard, MERSH, Vol. 23, pp. 80-82.

12. Firefighting was one of Peter's hobbies, a penchant shared by his grandson Peter III.

13. Ivan Mikhailovich Miloslavsky (?-1685), a kinsman of Tsar Alexis's first wife, was one of Tsarevna Sophia's chief supporters and regarded by some (including Peter) as the chief instigator of the massacre of the Naryshkins in 1682.

14. This detail underlines the fact that failure to report "seditious utterances" heard in the presence of a third party was itself a crime.

15. In August 1656 during the Thirteen Years War against Poland Tsar Alexis laid siege to Riga, but did not take the city.

16. Frederick III was elector of Brandenburg from 1688-1701. From 1701-1713 he reigned as Frederick I of Prussia.

17. François-Louis de Bourbon (1664-1709), Prince de Conti, was a candidate for the throne as a boy in 1673.

18. Frederick Augustus Wettin (1670-1733), elector of Saxony since 1694, later known as Augustus the Strong, was famed both for his military successes, his strength and his sexual exploits: he allegedly fathered over three hundred children. See Norman Davies, *God's Playground. A History of Poland* (Oxford, 1981), pp. 492 ff.

19. The first Polish dynasty, who ruled in Poland from the tenth to the fourteenth centuries. There were many descendants.

20. Sophia of Hanover (1630-1714), daughter of Frederick V, elector of the Palatinate, and Elizabeth Stuart, married Ernst-Augustus of Brunswick-Lüneburg (elector of Hanover from 1692) in 1658. As a granddaughter of James I, in 1701 she was proclaimed heir to the English throne. Her elder son, Georg Ludwig, reigned in England as George I (1714-1727). Sophia's daughter Sophia-Charlotte (1668-1705) in 1684 married Prince Frederick of Brandenburg, subsequently king of Prussia (see Note

16 above). She had lived in Paris and was well-versed in philosophy and art. She should not be confused with her ill-fated sister-in-law Sophia-Dorothea (born 1666), who married the future George I, was divorced by him in 1694 and imprisoned in Ahlden until her death in 1726.

21. A certain carpenter in Saardam pointed out this shaking of the head as a distinguishing feature by which his fellow-countrymen could recognize the Russian carpenter as the tsar. J. Scheltema, *Anecdotes historiques sur Pierre le Grand et sur ses voyages en Hollande et à Zaandam dans les années 1697 et 1717* [Historical Anecdotes Concerning Peter the Great and His Travels to Holland and to Zaandam in the Year 1697 and 1717] (Lausanne, 1842). [Soloviev's note]

22. "Tsar Peter is very tall and quite well proportioned, with a handsome face. His eyes are big but so wild that he is pitiful to look at. His head shakes continually, although he is only twenty years of age." Foy de la Neuville, *Relation curieuse et nouvelle de Moscovie* [Curious and New Account Concerning Muscovy] (The Hague, 1699), p. 188. [Soloviev's note] On Neuville, see Chapter I, Note 23.

23. Nicholas Witsen (1641-1717) first visited Russia with a Dutch embassy in 1662-1667 and wrote an account of a trip to Patriarch Nikon's New Jerusalem monastery. His book *Noord en oost Tartary* was published in 1705.

24. William (1650-1702) became William III of England in 1689. He was the son of William II of Orange and Mary, daughter of Charles I of England, and married Mary, daughter of James II of England, who was his co-ruler in England until her death in 1696.

25. Reproduced in M. Alekseeva, *Graviura Petrovskovo vremeni* [Engravings of the Petrine Era] (Leningrad, 1990), p. 21. Peter studied with the engraver Adrian Schoenbeck, who later worked in Russia.

26. The Olonets iron works and ore-workings were in the vicinity of Lake Ladoga in Karelia. They were expanded further after the founding of St. Petersburg in 1703. "Butman" is the Dane Heinrich Butenant.

27. The Peace of Ryswick between Louis XIV and William III (September 1697), by which Louis renounced French conquests made against the coalition of Augsburg and recognized William as king of England.

28. See Chapter II, Note 8.

29. From Peter's own Foreword to the *Maritime Regulation*. See Chapter I, Note 26.

30. Although Peter's stay in England was just as influential as his time in Holland and produced some rich anecdotal literature, Soloviev omits it, perhaps because of the difficulties of obtaining English sources. For accounts of Peter's visit, see L. Loewenson, "Some Details of Peter the Great's Stay in England in 1698," *Slavonic and East European Review*, 40 (1962), pp. 431-443.

CHAPTER V

1. The first foreign-led "new model" infantry regiments were formed in the 1630s. See above, Chapter III, Note 9.

2. For an account of these events, see Soloviev, Vol. 25, pp. 110-113.

3. On the two- and three-fingered sign of the cross, see Chapter II, Note 21.

4. Freelance public scribes *(ploshchadnye podiachie)* plied their trade in public places such as town squares, drawing up contracts and writing letters for a largely illiterate population.

5. Sophia's sisters were Evdokia (1650-1712), Martha (1652-1707), Catherine (Ekaterina) (1658-1718), Maria (1660-1723) and Feodosia (1662-1713). All unmarried, they lived lives of comparative obscurity after 1698, except for Maria, who went to Germany in 1716 and was implicated in the Tsarevich Alexis affair in 1718.

6. In the original conversation the sums were actually stated in altyns (three copecks) and dengas (half a copeck), the normal mode of reckoning before the copeck became the standard unit later in Peter's reign.

7. Romodanovsky, it will be recalled, was Peter's mock or substitute tsar, "prince-caesar," and Peter addressed him accordingly, even when, as in this case, issuing a dressing-down.

8. The monastery of the Resurrection at New Jerusalem, about sixty kilometers to the northwest of Moscow.

9. Patrick Gordon's diary is one of the main sources for this section of the *History*. Soloviev also uses depositions from the interrogation of the musketeers and other persons implicated in the rebellion.

10. See Soloviev, Vol. 25, p.146

11. Anna Mons (?-1714), the daughter of a German wine trader in the Foreign Quarter, had been Peter's mistress since the early 1690s. The affair ended in 1703 after the discovery of her liaison with a German diplomat. She married the Prussian envoy Keyserling, and was widowed in 1711.

12. Archpriest Avvakum (1620-1682), leader of the Old Believers (see Chapter I, Note 8) was anathematized for "schism, sedition and false teaching" by the church council of 1666 and burnt at the stake in 1682. For the incident referred to here, see Soloviev, Vol. 24.

13. The beard tax was not officially introduced until 1705, when tokens had to be purchased to prove payment. Only priests and peasants were allowed to keep their beards without paying a fine and even peasants had to pay if they came into town on business.

14. See Soloviev, Vol. 25, pp.139-142.

15. Much of the information about the executions comes from the Austrian envoy Johann Georg Korb (1672-1741). His book (published in Latin in Vienna in 1700, and translated into English as *Diary of an Austrian*

Secretary of Legation at the Court of Czar Peter the Great, 2 vols. (London, 1863) was denounced and banned by Peter for giving a biased and excessively bloody view. This should be borne in mind when considering Korb's evidence. For further details on Korb, see G.E. Orchard, MERSH, Vol. 17, pp. 174-175.

16. On Menshikov, see below, Note 28.

17. Evidence of the government official Ivan Zheliabuzhsky (1639-?1709), whose memoir, covering the period 1682-1709, is one of the few Russian eye-witness sources for the period. See G.E. Orchard, MERSH, Vol. 46, pp. 37-38.

18. On Peter's "play" soldiers, see Chapter I, Note 18.

19. Soloviev supplies only the initial "b". The reference is probably to sons of whores *(bludnye deti).*

20. Korb's is the only evidence for this "assembly."

21. Sophia remained in the New convent (see Chapter I, Note 48) until her death in July 1704. Her tomb is in the main cathedral of Our Lady of Smolensk. On the last years of her life, see Hughes, *Sophia,* Chapter 10.

22. According to some sources, Martha had an affair with the church deacon Ivan Gavrilovich, who was also implicated in the musketeer affair. [Soloviev's note]

23. See Chapter I, Note 32.

24. See Chapter I, Note 9.

25. Alexander Gordon, *The History of Peter the Great, Emperor of Russia* (Aberdeen, 1755). Gordon, a relative of Patrick Gordon, served in Russia during Peter's reign.

26. Peter's sister Natalia (1673-1716) was a pioneer of the Russian theater, organizing a private company in Moscow which later transferred to St. Petersburg.

27. *The Russian Primary Chronicle* or *Tale of Bygone Years.* For an English text see S. Cross, transl. and ed., *The Russian Primary Chronicle* (Cambridge, Mass., 1953). On Vladimir, see Chapter I, Note 19.

28. Scholars have still not entirely solved the puzzle of the origins of Peter's favorite, Alexander Danilovich Menshikov (1673-1729), although recent Russian research suggests that his father served in the Semenovsky Guards. In the 1690s Alexander served Peter as an orderly and non-commissioned officer in the Preobrazhensky Guards, accompanying him on the grand embassy. Later he acquired more titles than anyone except the tsar, including prince of Russia and prince of the Holy Roman Empire, amassed a vast fortune, sat in the Senate and directed the College of Foreign Affairs, and ended his life in exile after Peter's death. Oddly, there is no extended scholarly study of Menshikov's career in English. See K. Papmehl, MERSH, Vol. 21, pp. 202-207.

29. According to the Soviet editor, the source used by Soloviev for this information has been lost.

30. The source for this and many other anecdotes from Peter's reign is Andrei Konstantinovich Nartov (1683-1756), Peter's instructor in turning (one of the tsar's many hobbies), who completed his training abroad. As Peter liked to have his lathes near at hand, even on campaign, Nartov spent much time in his company.

31. Peter's second wife, crowned empress consort in 1724 and ruled 1725-1727 as Empress Catherine I. Catherine was of Lithuanian/Livonian peasant stock and her original name was probably Martha. She adopted the name Catherine, in Russian, Ekaterina Alekseevna, when she converted to Orthodoxy. She became a member of Menshikov's household a year or so after the capture of Dorpat (Tartu) by the Russians in 1702. Peter probably met her there in early 1704, had several children by her, and married her in 1712. Soloviev tells her story in Vol. 33 of this series.

32. The popular reference to Peter's helpers and protégés as "fledglings" (ptentsy) of Peter's nest is derived from a line in Pushkin's poem *Poltava*, about Peter's famous victory of 1709.

33. Menshikov received his first commission, as ensign, only in 1700. Until then he officially held non-commissioned rank.

34. 2 Timothy 2: 6.

35. See above, Chapter II, Note 9.

36. All these testimonies are taken from the records of the infamous Preobrazhensky Chancellery, the inquisitorial wing of the regimental offices at Preobrazhenskoe, headed by Romodanovsky to investigate cases of treason and sedition.

37. The speaker seems to confuse *antidor* the word actually used, which denotes the consecrated bread distributed to the congregation after mass, and *antidot*.

38. Anna Zhukova was the maid of Tsarevna Martha.

39. This form of black magic, using substances (in this case earth) which bore traces of the intended victim, was supposed to have the desired effect, the subject's death or disfigurement, without direct contact with the victim. There was an attempt to put a similar curse on Prince Vasily Golitsyn. See Soloviev, Vol. 25, p.197.

40. Chapter II, Note 6.

41. In the accusatorial system (sud) there was no crown prosecutor. Charges were brought and evidence collected by the plaintiff(s) against the defendant(s), the latter being interrogated in a confrontation (ochnaia stavka) with witnesses. Torture customarily was administered to both defendant and plaintiff. In the inquisitorial process (rozysk), as in criminal law, the crown brought the charges and there was a crown prosecutor. It appears that both systems co-existed well into the eighteenth century, even though Peter favored the rozysk method. See R. Wortman, "Peter the Great and Court Procedure," *Canadian-American Slavic Studies,* Vol. 8 (1974), pp. 303-10.

42. Women usually gave birth in the bathhouse.

43. Trial for default (pravezh) entailed repeatedly beating the debtor until the outstanding sum was paid to the creditors.

44. 1695 by the Orthodox reckoning from the notional date of the Creation. The Soviet text has 7104 in error.

45. The magistrate or jurat system of city administration of the German town of Magdeburg was adopted in many parts of Germany, Poland and Bohemia.

46. *Burmistrskaia palata.* In 1700 the institution's name was changed to *Ratusha* or Town Hall, as in Dutch, German, Swedish. See C. Peterson, *Peter the Great's Administrative and Judicial Reforms* (Stockholm, 1979).

47. The stamp on the paper was in the form of the Russian crest, the double-headed eagle, in different sizes according to the value of the transaction for which the paper was required.

48. *Pozhilye dengi*—a fine for harboring runaway serfs.

49. The term used is *posadskie,* namely members of the registered tax-paying artisan community. Merely dwelling in a town did not bestow registered status; in other words the Siberian towns were not entirely devoid of population, but had few citizens of any substance.

50. See Chapter I, pp. 57-58.

51. The Orthodox bishop of Lvov.

52. On Paley, see Chapter I, pp. 75-76.

53. The term used is *mezhigor,* probably signifying the monks living in the catacombs "in the midst of the hills" over which the Kiev Caves monastery was built.

54. The Orthodox rejected the *filioque* (and Son) of the Catholic creed, asserting that the Holy Spirit proceeded only from the Father.

55. In the original both these references involve play on words which sound similar, first, between Russian *sobor* (assembly, cathedral) and *zabor* (fence), and second, between *patriarkh* and the verb to lose, *poteriat'*.

56. On the Likhuds, see Chapter II, Note 24.

57. According to tradition, the apostle Peter was crucified in Rome. The rest of the sentence seems to refer to Peter's "sin" in denying Christ at the Crucifixion while warming himself at a fire.

CHAPTER VI

1. On the Muscovite New Year and calendar, see Chapter I, Note 56. This reform was denounced by traditionalists, who claimed that Peter had "stolen" eight years from God (the new century, 7200, was celebrated in September 1692) and argued that the world could not have been created in the barren month of January.

2. War of the Spanish Succession (1701-1714), which began after the death of the childless Charles II of Spain in 1700, started as a Bourbon-Habsburg conflict between supporters of Philip of Anjou, grandson of Louis XIV, and Charles, son of Leopold I of Austria. Subsequently, many other countries were involved. The Treaty of Utrecht (1713) partitioned the Spanish empire. The early phase of the Great Northern War has been comparatively neglected in English scholarship. See L. Lewitter, "Russia, Poland and the Baltic, 1697-1721," *Historical Journal*, XI (1968), pp. 3-34 and R. Hatton (Note 15 below).

3. Gustavus II Adolphus reigned 1611-1632; Karl X Gustavus reigned 1654-1660. On their exploits, see David Kirby, *Northern Europe in the Early Modern Period. The Baltic World 1492-1772* (London, 1990).

4. See Chapter III, Note 18.

5. On the alleged "insult" to Peter in Riga in 1697, which served as a pretext for the war, see Chapter IV, p. 148. See also P.P. Shafirov, *A Discourse Concerning the Just Causes of the War Between Sweden and Russia, 1700-1721*, ed. W.E. Butler (Dobbs Ferry, N.Y., 1973), an official justification of Russia's position by Peter's associate.

6. Kerch was of strategic importance because it stood at the outlet from the Sea of Azov into the Black Sea.

7. The old Muscovite titles of offices were paralleled and eventually replaced by new designations, as in this case *dumnyi diak* (literally, clerk or secretary of the boyar council or duma) eventually was superseded by various forms of *sovetnik* (councillor). See Appendix, pp. 275-276.

8. See Soloviev, Vol. 25, pp. 207-214.

9. Minaev was ataman or commander of the Don Cossacks, and Cherkassk on the Don was their capital.

10. A suburb of Constantinople.

11. The Russian *kostel* (Polish *kosciol*), the term used by the Turks, refers to a Catholic church, hence, presumably the exclamation mark, as the new churches in Azov were Orthodox churches (tserkvi). See Chapter II, Note 18.

12. Charles (Karl) XI reigned 1660-1697. He died of cancer at the age of 42. On the *reduktion,* resumption of crown lands, referred to below, see Kirby, *Northern Europe* , pp. 224-225, 254-256.

13. Reigned 1670-1699.

14. The Treaty of Kardis was signed between Russia and Sweden in 1661 and formed the basis, with periodic ratifications, of Russo-Swedish relations until the outbreak of the Northern War. See Volume 20 of this series.

15. The standard English biography of Charles (Karl) is R.H. Hatton, *Charles XII of Sweden* (London, 1968).

16. Reigned 1699-1730.

17. Christopher Brandt, a Dutch merchant who acted as Peter's agent and informant abroad.

18. On the Time of Troubles and pretenders, see Chapter I, notes 29 and 78, as well as Volumes 14-16 of this series. Swedish troops invaded Russian territory, including Novgorod, in 1611, and there were Swedish candidates for the vacant throne of Russia.

19. References are to the Gospel accounts (Matthew, Mark and Luke) of St. Peter's denial of Christ after the Crucifixion.

20. Prince Nikita (Anikita) Ivanovich Repnin (1668-1726) had been Peter's chamberlain and served in the play regiments. He was to fight in all the major battles of the Great Northern War.

21. See Chapter I, p. 50.

22. L. may be Prince Yakov Lobanov-Rostovsky. [Soloviev's note]. In 1688 Lobanov-Rostovsky was flogged for highway robbery. See Soloviev, Vol. 25, p. 220.

23. See Chapter IV, pp. 203-206.

24. See Chapter II, pp. 77-82.

25. On the Uniate church, see Chapter II, note 42.

26. A fort and entrenchments (shantsy) at the mouth of the river Neva near the site of the future St. Petersburg.

27. The name Oreshek is based on the Russian for "nut" (orekh), as is Nöteborg on the Swedish (nöt).

28. The trade route from the Baltic, home of the Varangians, or Norsemen, who came to rule in Rus in the ninth century, to the Black Sea and Byzantium ran through the river systems from the Neva to the Dnieper. See Volume 1 of this series.

29. On the founding of St. Petersburg (from 1924-1991, Leningrad) and its early economic, social and architectural history, see J. Bater, *St. Petersburg. Industrialization and Change* (London, 1976) and J. Cracraft, *The Petrine Revolution in Russian Architecture* (Chicago, 1988).

INDEX

Abraham (Avraamy), monk, 140-142.
Academy of Sciences, 281.
Adrian, patriarch of Moscow, xx, 53, 55-56, 155, 177, 179, 217-219, 291, 298.
Adrianople, 116-117.
Afanasius, archbishop of Kholmogory, 48, 219.
Afanasy, deacon, 37.
Afonka, musketeer, 201.
Afrosimov, Matvey,199.
Agrakhan river, 57, 121.
Aitemirov, clerk, 59, 76-77.
Akhtyrka, 87.
Akkerman (Belgorod), 75.
Aksakov, Constantine, xv.
Aksinia, 190-191.
Alatyr, 197.
Aleksandrovsk, 183.
Aleksasha, see Menshikov.
Alekseev, Mikhail, 199.
Alekseev, Peter. See Peter Alekseevich, tsar.
Alekseev, Sidorka, 197.
Alekseev, Vasily, peasant, 199.
Alekseevsk, 31.
Alexander II, emperor, xiii, xx.
Alexander the Great, 4.
Alexander, Prince of Georgia, 248.
Alexis (Aleksei) Mikhailovich, tsar, 8, 10, 13-14, 18, 27, 50, 100, 115, 117, 123, 128, 143, 154, 175, 177, 193, 278-280, 282-283, 289-291, 293, 295, 297.
Alexis Petrovich, tsarevich, 51, 55, 184, 191, 299.
Alibek, 57-58.
Almaznikov, 196.
Amsterdam, xv, 153-155, 166, 287.
Andrusovo, Treaty of (1667), 284, 292.
Anna Mikhailovna, tsarevna, 22, 40, 191
Anna, empress of Russia, 282.
Anthony of Padua, 217.
Antichrist, 278.

Apostol, Daniel, colonel, 93, 264-265.
Apostolenko, Grigory, colonel, 68.
Apostolets, colonel, 75.
Apraksin, Andrei Matveevich, 198.
Apraksin, Fedor Matveevich, 48, 50, 120, 243, 259, 271, 273, 289, 295.
Apraksin, Peter Matveevich, 271-272.
Apraksina, Martha Matveevna, tsaritsa, 198, 289.
Arabia, Arabs, 117, 130.
Arbat, 165.
Archangel, 47-49, 115, 120, 123, 206, 230, 259, 266, 272, 287, 290.
Aristotle, 62.
Armenians, 102.
Artemev, Terenty, 60.
Artemiev, Peter, deacon, 217-219.
Asia, 115.
Astrakhan, 57-59, 115, 206, 211.
Augsburg, coalition of, 298.
Augustus II, king of Poland (Frederick Augustus Wettin, of Saxony), xvii, 150-151, 156, 222-223, 235-238, 241-243, 245-249, 253, 255-256, 258-259, 269, 296-297.
Austria, xvii, 101-102, 119-120, 123, 127, 137, 150, 159, 224, 229-230, 247, 281, 290, 293-294, 303.
Avvakum, Archpriest, 175, 278, 287, 297, 299.
Azov, xiii, xiv, xvii, 44-45, 115-116, 135, 137, 142-143, 156, 160, 162-163, 170-172, 181, 190, 193-194, 205, 213, 225-228, 230-232, 245, 251, 303; first Azov campaign (1695), 119-123; second Azov campaign (1696), 126-133.

Babylon, 219.
Bacchus, 49-50, 157, 190, 290.
Baden, 161.
Bagin, 196.
Bakhchisarai, Treaty of (1681), 32, 293.

THE EDITOR AND TRANSLATOR

Lindsey Hughes was born in England in 1949. She began to learn Russian in 1965, when the subject was introduced into her high school as an experiment, and went on to study Russian language and literature for her bachelor's degree, graduating with First Class honors from the University of Sussex in 1971. As an undergraduate she spent eleven months in Moscow working for Progress Publishers and writing a dissertation on seventeenth-century churches, which later grew into her doctorate on Moscow Baroque architecture, received from the University of Cambridge in 1976. While studying at Cambridge she visited the USSR on a six-month British Council scholarship to the Moscow Architectural Institute. Since then she has returned to Russia regularly, sometimes several times a year. In 1974 she began lecturing at Queen's University, Belfast, moving in 1977 to the University of Reading. Since 1987 she has been a member of the faculty of the School of Slavonic and East European Studies, University of London, where she is currently Reader in Russian History, teaching courses on all periods of Russian history from Riurik to the present and offering special papers on the history of Russian art and Early and Early Modern Russia. She is the author of a biography of Prince Vasily Golitsyn (Newtonville, 1984), *Sophia, Regent of Russia* (New Haven, 1990), editor of *New Perspectives on Muscovite History* (London, 1993), joint editor of *The Russian Chronicles* (London, 1990) and has published forty or more articles and several dozen contributions to *The Modern Encyclopedia of Russian, Soviet & Eurasian History*. Her translation of Volume 25 of Soloviev's *History of Russia* was published in 1989. She lives in London with Jim and two cats, Sophia and Catherine, and currently is working on a study of Russia in the reign of Peter I.

FROM ACADEMIC INTERNATIONAL PRESS*

*Request catalogs **OP—out of print